D0152463

The Curriculum
Process in Physical Education

The Curriculum Process in Physical Education

Ann E. Jewett
University of Georgia

Linda L. Bain
University of Houston

wcb
Wm. C. Brown Publishers
Dubuque, Iowa

Book Team

Edward G. Jaffe	*Senior Editor*
Lynne M. Meyers	*Associate Editor*
Colleen A. Yonda	*Production Editor*
Mark J. Schilling	*Designer*
Faye M. Schilling	*Photo Research Editor*
Mavis M. Oeth	*Permissions Editor*
Aileene Lockhart	*Consulting Editor*

wcb group

Wm. C. Brown	*Chairman of the Board*
Mark C. Falb	*President and Chief Executive Officer*

wcb

Wm. C. Brown Publishers, College Division

Lawrence E. Cremer	*President*
James L. Romig	*Vice-President, Product Development*
David A. Corona	*Vice-President, Production and Design*
E. F. Jogerst	*Vice-President, Cost Analyst*
Bob McLaughlin	*National Sales Manager*
Marcia H. Stout	*Marketing Manager*
Craig S. Marty	*Director of Marketing Research*
Eugenia M. Collins	*Production Editorial Manager*
Marilyn A. Phelps	*Manager of Design*
Mary M. Heller	*Photo Research Manager*

Photos courtesy of Gene Turner, University of Georgia

Library of Congress Catalog Card Number: 84-070982

ISBN 0-697-00132-6

Printed in the United States of America
10   9   8   7   6   5   4   3   2

Reviewers

Barbara Swerkes	*California State University, Northridge*
Gretchen A. Brockmeyer	*Springfield College*
Candace J. Norton	*Georgia Dept. of Education*
Elizabeth S. Bressan	*University of Oregon*
Joanne M. Lunt	*Winthrop College*
Judith E. Rink	*University of South Carolina*

Contents

Preface

Educators have been planning school physical activity programs in North America for almost a century. Only very recently, however, have physical educators given serious attention to the need for establishing a sound theoretical basis for the practical activity of designing a curriculum. The authors of this text view curriculum development as both a theoretical and practical activity. We believe that the designing of a curriculum, or a physical education program, is a practical activity that is based upon a set of beliefs about the role of education in society. Thus, any competent curriculum planner must be engaged in theorizing at some level. On the other hand, curriculum theory can contribute very little to the improvement of schooling if it is not continuously examined for relevance to physical education practice. We believe that this book is the first to analyze the curriculum development process in physical education as a practical activity based upon a particular set of beliefs and theoretical propositions. This has required our attention to both theoretical and practical considerations, and to the whole range of curriculum activity—from theorizing to design to the implementation of programs in school settings.

The state of the art in physical education curriculum does not permit presentation of several comprehensive, sophisticated, competing theories of physical education. The physical education literature offers many models for physical education programs, but little guidance to the serious student of curriculum in critically examining them. In this volume the authors have attempted to present a classification of value perspectives, to review the major curriculum models that have been proposed, and to provide examples and illustrations of application of these models in a wide range of educational settings. We believe that this book is the first physical education curriculum text that endorses no single model, but attempts to encourage the reader to critically examine the most important of those available.

Our title emphasizes a *process-oriented approach.* The process of curriculum development requires a series of decisions or judgments and the ability to explain and justify those decisions. This text is designed to help you clarify your own beliefs, to guide you in learning to design your own physical education program, and to enhance your ability to make sound professional judgments about your physical education curriculum. Our examples do not emphasize the finished product since our goal is to help teachers learn the skills of curriculum planning and the process by which curriculum materials are developed.

This is a book in which the curriculum process in physical education is examined carefully. It is not a book on instruction or evaluation, however. There are many fine books dealing with physical education instruction, and, although some of these have been referred to as curriculum books, their focus is on either the activities of teachers as they interact with students or on the implementation of a curriculum plan. We encourage you to consult these other sources when you are ready to study instructional strategies, techniques, and related teacher behaviors. This text is concerned with instruction only to clarify how it is affected by curriculum decisions.

Similarly, this is not a book on evaluation in physical education. This, too, is a field in which the authors acknowledge several outstanding textbook resources that are currently available. The domains of curriculum, instruction, and evaluation are inherently interrelated. We believe that the physical education profession is presently more in need of a textbook resource for *understanding the curriculum development process* than of better guidelines for instruction or evaluation. This textbook represents our combined efforts to make such a resource available.

There are three major sections in this book. Part 1 provides a theoretical base and examines the different value perspectives and alternative curriculum models found in the physical education literature. The theoretical approaches are clarified with practical examples. Students are encouraged to study and critique the models and their corresponding examples to clarify their own beliefs about physical education.

Part 2 leads students through the process of curriculum design, much as it is experienced by teachers with curriculum planning responsibility. The process includes identifying goals, selecting and sequencing learning activities, and developing curriculum materials. Relationships between program design, instructional methods, and program evaluation procedures are discussed. Numerous examples of curriculum materials are included both in the text and in the appendices. The emphasis in this section is upon developing the student's ability to make professional judgments related to program development.

The final section of the book, Part 3, deals with practical and theoretical issues related to curriculum development in physical education. The topics discussed have been selected to stimulate the interest of students in developing a carefully considered position on each of a variety of practical and theoretical physical education curriculum issues.

The format of the book has been designed to emphasize the process approach and the direct involvement of students in shaping their own learning experiences. Each chapter begins with an outline to clarify the content, and a scenario (or comparable device) to stimulate problem solving, imagination, and creative thinking. Students are encouraged to think of curriculum development not only as a process, but also as an activity with a future orientation. Readers are urged to raise critical questions, to attempt to generate alternative solutions to today's problems, and to consider the potential of the physical education curriculum for supporting desired directions for our future.

Practical examples of curriculum materials to illustrate the total range of different approaches and exercises for students are included throughout this text. Each chapter concludes with a brief summary of the key ideas presented within it and is supplemented with recommended readings to assist individuals seeking more depth on the topics discussed. Finally, a single alphabetical bibliography has been compiled for the convenience of the reader.

The authors wish to express their appreciation to the authors and publishers who granted permission for use of materials. We wish to acknowledge our debt to our students and colleagues at the University of Wisconsin, the University of Georgia, and the University of Houston for the things we have learned together that are reflected in this textbook. We gratefully acknowledge the assistance of the particular professional colleagues who assisted in the development of the material on curriculum models for chapter 3. We are thankful to Elizabeth Bressan, Catherine Ennis, Wilma Harrington, Leslie Lambert, and Candace Norton for their excellent responses to our invitation to write position papers for chapter 10. We are particularly appreciative of the outstanding typing and editorial services of Donna Sanders. Each of these persons has contributed toward making this textbook a more effective resource for students of physical education curriculum.

The co-authors accept joint responsibility for the total content of the text. We recognize that our own curriculum interests and philosophies differ in some important respects, but we have tried to minimize our personal biases and present the major alternatives with equal objectivity.

Study of the curriculum process in physical education has not yet attracted a large number of scholars. We believe that a new climate is developing that will support the need for study and research in this area. The advancement of both theory and practice in this field will depend upon professionals who are at an early stage in their careers. We hope that some of you will want to join us in this arena, which is largely uncharted and sometimes frustrating, but more often challenging, exciting, and rewarding.

The Curriculum
Process in Physical Education

Part 1

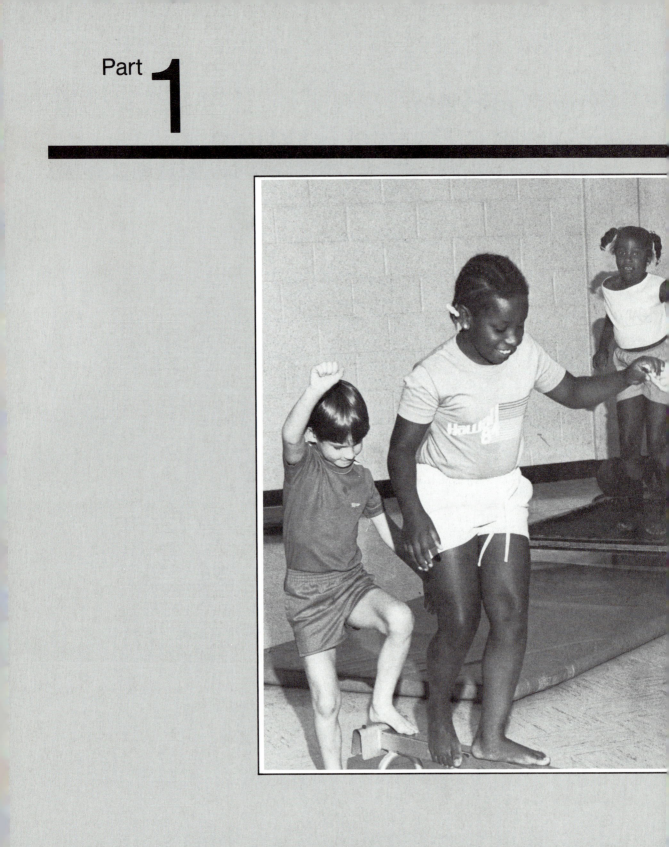

Curriculum Theory

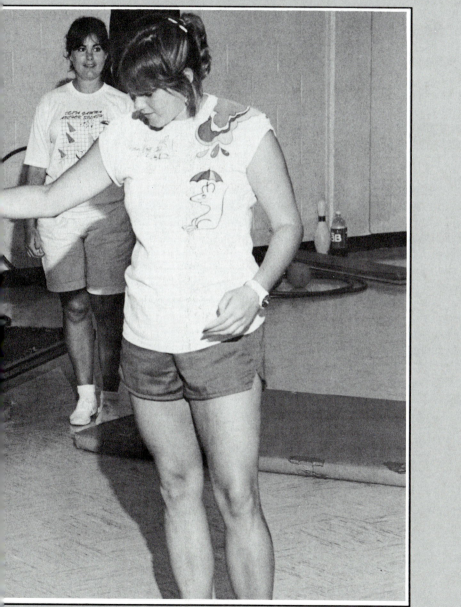

Part 1

In Part I we explore the significant concepts of curriculum theory that are relevant to physical education to clarify your own beliefs about the field. You are setting the stage for developing your ability to design your own curriculum.

Chapter 1 begins with a scenario intended to open up your thinking and to illustrate that the physical education curriculum need not always be what you have experienced. We try to cut through the mass of curriculum jargon to clarify the basic terminology of curriculum development. Specifically, we attempt to delineate the theorizing process as it moves from theory to conceptual framework to curriculum model.

Chapter 2 is introduced with a series of metaphors. The metaphors are intended to further extend your horizons and to challenge you to think about the physical education curriculum from many different perspectives. We hope you will find the metaphor a useful tool for analyzing different value positions and their impacts on various aspects of the curriculum. Five different value orientations for physical education curriculum development are presented in chapter 2: disciplinary mastery, social reconstruction, learning process, self-actualization, and ecological validity. They are discussed in historical perspective and are examined in terms of the three dimensions corresponding to the major curriculum elements: the individual learner, the society in which he or she participates, and the subject matter (cultural heritage) to be transmitted and extended.

In chapter 3 we move toward translating theory into physical education curriculum models. The scene is set through a description of physical education curriculum design from preschool through post-secondary education. The major focus of this chapter is upon the delineation of seven different physical education curriculum models, selected partly because they can be studied in more depth in other published materials. They are examined here in terms of their basic beliefs, the conceptual frameworks they identify, and the designs proposed for implementing each. We emphasize that the seven models can be identified as generic models and illustrate each with at least one specific design for implementation. Do not assume that any of the illustrations are "pure" examples of the generic model, nor that the generic model must necessarily be implemented in accordance with the particular illustrations or specific model provided. You will want to study each of these models carefully, consider our observations about them, and possibly consult the original source for a more thorough understanding. When you have finished your study of Part 1, you should have a pretty clear concept of your own philosophy of physical education and you should be ready to learn how to put some of this theory into practice.

Introduction to Curriculum Theory

1

Outline

Futurists in any professional field or scholarly area are interested in helping humankind to create a better world. One of the techniques used most frequently in the attempt to extend creative thought is the writing of alternative scenarios. A standard scenario is based on extrapolation of current trends. A scenario writer selects a position concerning which of the myriad of possible future good and bad events is most likely to occur, projects a critical decision, and describes its probable consequences.

As a student of the curriculum process in physical education, you are asked to consider how the critical choices of today's curriculum decision-makers may influence the nature of our future world. A single scenario, to encourage you to open up your thinking, opens this chapter. As you read it, you may be uncomfortable with some aspects of this projected future of physical education. If so, ask yourself which curriculum decisions led to these consequences, and what alternative choices may presently be available. Later, when you have completed your consideration of the alternatives presented throughout this text, you may wish to write your own scenario for a curriculum for 2035 A.D.

Scenario: The Movement for Life Curriculum, 2035 A.D.

From Ennis, Catherine D., "A Future Scenario for Physical Education" in *Journal of Physical Education, Recreation and Dance,* Vol. 55, No. 6 (1984). © 1984 American Association of Health, Physical Education, Recreation and Dance, Reston, VA. Reprinted by permission.

Earth, by the year 2035, had established global movement programs in response to worldwide interest in human longevity. Thousands of computer programs were being successfully utilized for fitness instruction and refinement of motor performance skills. Quality of life centers were available to enhance the satisfaction individuals might receive from longer lives. Significant, global, multinational agreements had been finalized by 2001, following a major breakthrough in genetics research. The motivating factor for this global, multinational unification occurred in 1997 with the development of an effective and acceptable longevity drug. This single discovery had the greatest impact on the world since the production of the silicon chip. Independent nations were eager to accept multinational unification in order to gain access to the longevity drug. The adoption of a world language and currency by the year 2003 paved the way for worldwide cooperation in economics, agriculture, and education.

By 2017, the longevity drug had been improved to extend the life span of an adult by approximately fifty additional years beyond the one hundred year average recorded at the turn of the century. Of all the disciplines touched by the discovery, physical education had the greatest impact on the "longevity society." By 2010, the drug was known to be effective only for those individuals who were in good health at age thirty-five. Good health was measured by circulorespiratory efficiency as well as a disease-free body. Studies had consistently shown that circulorespiratory efficiency must be achieved as the individual's physiological capacities develop during adolescence and must also be maintained throughout life. Furthermore, for the drug to have an enduring effect, it must be coupled with the benefits of exercise throughout life.

In response to this need for fitness, movement specialists developed the "Movement for Life" curriculum, which was financially sponsored and globally disseminated by the multinational council. These programs were so effective that the term "Movement for Life" became permanently associated with the fitness program and the entire movement concept. By 2025, the Movement for Life curriculum had dual emphases. First, the curriculum emphasized the development of circulorespiratory efficiency and skilled movement from childhood throughout life to ensure initial eligibility and prolonged positive effects from the longevity drug. Second, the Movement for Life program emphasized the enhancement of the quality of life itself. These programs were offered concurrently throughout the world in order to reach every segment of the population.

Curriculum Theory

The extensive utilization of computers in education in the 1990s paved the way for Movement for Life programs in the school systems. The development of microbeam technology allowed the computer, not only to provide an individual movement learning package for each student, but also to provide the potential for playback of performance with auditory corrective feedback. The advent of computer refinement analysis in the 2030s provided immediate feedback as the individual performs. Computer packages were available for individuals, as well as groups, for a variety of purposes, activities, and performance levels.

The primary role of the movement specialist by 2035 was essentially that of computer program designer. Furthermore, the quantity of information available required designers to become highly specialized. Programs available included the following: approaches to fulfilling the different movement purposes; motor performance at different movement process levels; achievement of specific physical activity skills, knowledges, and strategies relevant to selected popular games; and analysis of particular dance forms and techniques. It was also possible to combine two or more programs to gain a better understanding of a movement topic. For example, the object projection program could be simultaneously combined with the perceiving program and the pitching skill program to assist the student in comprehending the overarm throwing motion.

Computer-monitored individual movement packages and computer refinement analyses provided the most successful individualized instruction of the era. Students found it easy to be motivated and self-directed concerning movement skills and physical fitness when there was a computer package specifically designed for their purposes, interests, and skill levels. Each school had a part-time movement specialist to assist and to add a personal touch when needed, but most students found the computer instruction very effective in providing programs to develop the skill and fitness needed to become eligible for the longevity drugs.

Maintenance programs for individuals who had qualified for the drugs were offered through continuing movement education centers, sponsored by community groups, private clubs, school systems, or spas. Businesses and industries also recognized the importance of Movement for Life programs by providing computers and released time for their employees. Individuals experienced the joys and rewards of movement early in life and found little difficulty structuring movement time into their lives. Computer-monitored individual movement packages and computer refinement analyses were the technological core of the global movement program. Although there were additional programs that emphasized special facilities, such as circular swimming pools, artificial turf golf courses, and simulated snow ski slopes, the computerized instructional programs provided the foundation for the Movement for Life concept.

The second emphasis within the curriculum was on the quality of life. The computer learning packages provided the technology for individuals to pursue movement activities that they considered enjoyable, interesting, and valuable. However, there were still several categories of individuals who required additional opportunities to find movement satisfaction in life. Some individuals, who were successful with the computer learning packages initially, later lost interest and required redirection. Also, approximately 8 percent of the population were unable to develop fitness levels high enough to qualify for the longevity drug. Still others chose not to take the drug. In the decade of the 2020s, the leading Movement for Life designers received large multinational grants to develop centers to increase the quality of life for those groups needing additional assistance in achieving movement satisfaction.

The goal of the quality of life movement centers was to identify the needs and interests of the above categories of persons and to direct those individuals toward programs and opportunities that might enhance their joy and overall movement satisfaction. The centers provided the individual with counseling, movement aptitude testing, and unusual physical activities. Many individuals seeking redirection were placed in high risk activities where computer-monitored individual movement packages were originally unavailable. However, in 2030, portable wrist computers were developed with the capabilities of instruction and feedback in such activities as rock climbing and parachuting. Data from quality centers collected between 2030 and 2035 indicates that the number of individuals needing redirection had diminished by 65 percent since the development of portable wrist computers for high risk activities.

The second and third categories continued to present a major concern for the quality of life centers. These individuals appeared to have little extrinsic motivation for movement and frequently chose to lead basically sedentary lives, relying on computers and robots to perform their daily chores. Although the quality of life centers attempted to provide enticing movement alternatives to these people, only a few were converted. Some individuals who refused to take the longevity drug sought movement experiences in natural wilderness environments and some of these individuals reported a higher degree of satisfaction with life than any group involved in planned Movement for Life programs.

Quality of life centers experienced only limited success. The majority of the population was satisfied with the quality of movement experiences provided by the computer learning packages. The population that could have received the greatest benefits from the centers either chose specifically not to participate or functioned successfully without further guidance.

Movement for Life specialists, in 2035, considered that the large majority of the population in the multinational cooperative world community was meeting the basic goals of Movement for Life curricula. They were reasonably well-satisfied with the technological base and the delivery systems in use. Efforts to increase the viability of the quality of life centers continued. Researchers and innovators sought to integrate new approaches to quality movement experiences into multidimensional patterns for improving the overall quality of life. Particular attention was focused on the development of individual movement creativity, on investigations of the nature of personal meaning as sought by unique, moving human beings, and on the potential of movement interactions as a channel for strengthening global communication and cooperation. (Ennis 1984)

Why Curriculum Theory in Physical Education?

How do changes in physical education curricula come about? What will cause the movement studies curriculum of 2035 to be different from the current physical education curriculum? What might make the 2035 curriculum differ in these particular ways rather than in other specifics that could be described in alternative scenarios?

To a large extent, curriculum planning is the result of public policy. National priorities for extending technological achievements, for expanding equality of opportunity, and for strengthening environmental protection have resulted in significant changes in school curricula in recent decades. Regional economic, social, and political concerns have modified teacher certification regulations and the neighborhood school concept, and have led to the introduction of new types of field experience, bilingual instruction, and alternative schools. Local school boards have implemented public policy decisions by introducing competency testing, by making heavy financial commitments to programs in music, athletics, or special education, or by prohibiting or requiring instruction in particular subject matter. Public policymaking, at all levels, affects school curricula in important ways. Similarly, curriculum planning at the local level tends to reinforce public policy and to determine long-range policymaking beyond the local school district.

Curriculum planning is an important public concern. It is also a major professional responsibility. Most of the decisions reflected in local curriculum guides, in textbook selections, and in annual and daily decisions concerning specific content and instructional procedures are based on professional judgments. Curriculum planning is, necessarily, a blend of professional judgment and public policymaking.

How is a public policy commitment or a particular professional judgment implemented in the educational experience of those participating in local school programs? Curriculum theory provides the basis for ensuring that any curriculum serves its public effectively. The role of curriculum theory is to provide guidelines for sound decisions and to provide planners with a description of available alternatives. Curriculum theory provides a systematic basis for decision-making in selecting, structuring, and sequencing content. Theory provides, not only guidelines for planning decisions, but also an appropriate basis for ongoing evaluation. How well are we doing in maintaining the desired value orientation and in effecting the intended outcomes? Curriculum theory can also help to identify gaps in our knowledge, thus establishing research priorities. Furthermore, curriculum theory is an essential basis for providing the rationale and justification for particular decisions made by curriculum specialists. It is crucial in establishing and maintaining communication with our public.

What is a Curriculum Theory?

What is theory in any realm of scholarship? There is general agreement that a *theory* is a set of related statements explaining some series of events. *Theory building* is a process of defining, classifying, and describing phenomena. Many curriculum scholars have concluded that, according to this definition, we have not yet produced a curriculum theory. Vallance (1982) suggests that this may be because the curriculum in its practical form is never sufficiently regular for explanation by coherent and regularized principles. Because education is both a science and an art, it is exceedingly difficult "to develop rules and principles which apply equally to both aspects."

It is difficult to argue that many curriculum theories have been produced that present a coherent group of general propositions used as principles of explanation for a class of phenomena. Consequently, the term *theorizing* is being used with increasing frequency in the curriculum field. Theorizing is the activity preliminary to the production of a theory. It is defined as the process by which theories, conceptual frameworks, and models are developed. Huenecke (1982) has provided an excellent distinction in the use of the two terms.

> A presentation about curriculum theorizing assumes that all involved share common meanings for such terms as "curriculum" and "theory." Strangely enough, this assumption may be foolhardy. In this discussion, theorizing is defined as the activity preliminary to theory completion, it is mainly a deductive approach to viewing phenomena and their potential relationships. Theorizing may in part be based on the outcomes of research, but it differs from research in that research is taken to be largely inductive, examining specific circumstances and conditions with an aim toward generalizing to broader contexts. Theory attempts to identify and describe, explain and predict; it may also prescribe or suggest desirable elements, relationships, or outcomes. Theorizing strives to enlarge vision, to present new possibilities, and to bring deeper understanding.

The purpose of theorizing is to achieve insights into the workings of the curriculum. It is the attempt to "survey, analyze, synthesize, and test the knowledge available about curriculum problems" (Vallance 1982, 9). Theorizing is an appropriate activity for practitioners at all levels. The most practical of physical educators should be frequently engaged in trying to understand what the curriculum includes and how it operates. This text is concerned with physical education curriculum theory, curriculum theorizing, and the practical uses of curriculum theory.

What is Curriculum?

Definitions of curriculum have varied greatly during the past half century of its development as a field of study. Broadly defined, the school curriculum includes all experiences conducted under school auspices, from formal classroom instruction to interscholastic athletics. More specifically, the curriculum is defined as the planned sequence of formal instructional experiences presented by the teachers to whom the responsibility is assigned. The authors take a somewhat middle-of-the-road position, supporting Macdonald's (1977,11) definition of curriculum as a purposefully selected cultural environment. Curriculum is the study of "what should constitute a world of learning and how to go about making this world."

Scholars also differ on the use of the term *curriculum* as it relates to *instruction*. Curriculum is frequently used as a broad generic term, including instruction. When a distinction between the two is drawn, curriculum is defined as an educative agency's plan for facilitating learning; instruction is defined as the delivery system or the aggregate of educative transactions that constitutes the teaching-learning process for implementing the plan. The major focus of curriculum is on ends, on the "why" and "what" questions; instruction tends to emphasize means, or the "how" questions. Curriculum theory describes alternatives for making decisions about scope, structure, and sequence of content. Instructional theory details the range of potential teacher behaviors and teacher-learner interactions. The physical education curriculum is that portion of the planned educational environment that relates to human movement knowledges, understandings, and skills.

Basic Assumptions

A curriculum theory is based on assumptions about society, human beings, and education. Each curriculum theory must accept a particular set of assumptions concerning the goals of the society, the role of the individual within the broader society, and the kind of future world desired. Curriculum theories vary in their basic assumptions about the nature of an individual human being, the ultimate perfectibility of a person, and the potential for self-direction. Basic assumptions underlying a given curriculum theory also relate to concepts about the role of the school in society, who determines educational objectives, and how the process of education can best be facilitated.

From Theory to Conceptual Framework

A physical education curriculum theory is concerned with the planning of educational programs dealing with human movement phenomena. To operationalize a curriculum theory requires the development of a conceptual framework or the selection of one already available. Physical educators may use a conceptual framework designed specifically for physical education, or they may use a more general conceptual framework and develop a physical education curriculum directly from a general curriculum theory.

A conceptual framework for a curriculum is a "structure which attempts to systematically describe the curriculum by identifying and operationally defining the elements and the

ways in which they are or may be related to each other"
(Jewett and Mullan 1977,1). The process of developing a
conceptual framework involves four steps. First, it is essential
to identify the major components of the theory to be organized
as dimensions of the conceptual framework. The author of a
conceptual framework for physical education curricular
decision-making starts with a set of related statements that
have been selected and systematically organized to formulate
a physical education curriculum theory. The second step is to
create a conceptual scheme for clarifying relationships among
the key concepts. Third, each key concept must be carefully
defined. The final stage is an ongoing process of refining and
revising major components, key concepts, and relationships
among the elements of the conceptual framework.

A conceptual framework is essential as a basis for sound
curriculum design and decisions. The goal is the creation of
enriched movement learning experiences, resulting in quality
physical education curricula.

From Framework to Curriculum Model

A conceptual framework for curriculum development is
based on an identifiable theory. Through use of a conceptual
framework, it is possible to translate theoretical
generalizations and propositions into proposed curriculum
models, each of which offers the curriculum planner a
particular pattern for consideration in designing a local
curriculum. A curriculum model is a design for developing
curricula for particular educational settings. A curriculum
model should be developed within a particular conceptual
framework and be consistent with the curriculum theory upon
which the conceptual framework is based.

More than one model can be developed from a given
conceptual framework. Use of a particular conceptual
framework does require acceptance of the basic assumptions
underlying that framework and a philosophy consistent with
the theoretical base; yet models may vary in terms of target
populations, organizational structures for educational
institutions, or environmental resources or limitations. Most
importantly, since models are created by individual curriculum
planners, they may exhibit all the variability of the creative
thinking of their different designers.

A curriculum model permits numerous variations when
implemented in particular settings. An individual model will
require modification to fit different climates or socioeconomic
circumstances. It will require variation, even within a school

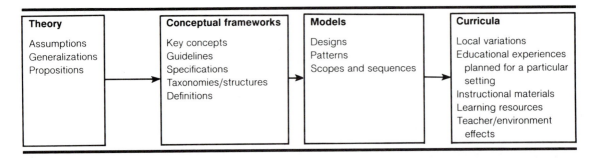

Theory	Conceptual frameworks	Models	Curricula

Assumptions
Generalizations
Propositions
	Key concepts
	Guidelines
	Specifications
	Taxonomies/structures
	Definitions
		Designs
		Patterns
		Scopes and sequences
			Local variations
			Educational experiences
			  planned for a particular
			  setting
			Instructional materials
			Learning resources
			Teacher/environment
			  effects

Figure 1.1
From curriculum theory to
curriculum practice

district, to be used with elementary school, middle school, or secondary school learners. Adjustments will be required if the learners are predominantly from specific ethnic backgrounds, or if a number of handicapped children are included in the groups. The model selected by the 2035 A.D. Movement for Life curriculum designer would provide different programs for persons at various levels of fitness in their efforts to qualify for the longevity drug. Numerous variations in the computer skill instructional packages would be required to accommodate individuals with different purposes, interests, and performance ability levels. The quality of life centers would need to provide access to and guidance in totally individualized education experiences for a highly diversified clientele.

Why Study Curriculum Theories?

Of the many reasons to study curriculum theories, probably the most important, is to clarify your own educational philosophy. Each of us has a value orientation that guides our educational decisions. However, many curriculum planners and educators have not carefully examined these personal viewpoints. An effective way of clarifying your own beliefs is to compare your philosophical position with several alternatives, thus sharpening your perception and understanding of the specifics of an educational philosophy and increasing the consistency of your personal theoretical base.

Study of curriculum theories also has the potential for the development of new perspectives. Curricular understanding has usually evolved from personal experience. Because each individual's experience is limited, we may frequently be unaware of other attractive alternatives until we seek new perspectives through the study of various theories.

The study of curriculum theories is also an approach to honing practical skills in curriculum development. Curriculum

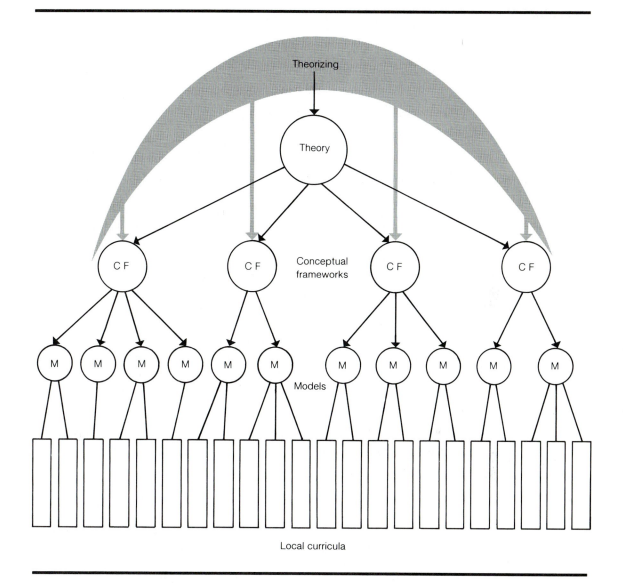

Theorizing

Theory

C F   C F   Conceptual frameworks   C F   C F

M M M M M M M M M M M

Models

Local curricula

development is a process in which most teachers will be involved throughout their careers. "Cookbook" approaches, which copy someone else's program, are generally ineffective because each school and program is unique. Creating your own program, and ensuring that the program will be an educational vehicle in which to take pride, requires a broad understanding of curriculum development possible only with in-depth study of curriculum theories.

Figure 1.2
Process of curriculum development

Summary

Curriculum planning is the result of public policy and is a major responsibility of the professional educator. Curriculum theory provides the basis for ensuring that any curriculum serves its public effectively. The role of curriculum theory is to provide planners with guidelines for sound decisions and descriptions of possible alternatives.

Theorizing is the activity preliminary to the production of a theory. It is the process by which theories, conceptual frameworks, and models are developed. Theorizing is an appropriate activity for practitioners at all levels.

Each curriculum theory is based on a particular set of assumptions about society, human beings, and education. A curriculum theory is operationalized through the selection or development of a conceptual framework. A curriculum model is a design for developing curricula for particular educational settings; the model must be developed within a selected conceptual framework and be consistent with the theory upon which the framework is based.

Physical educators study curriculum theories in order to clarify personal educational philosophies, to develop new perspectives, and to increase practical skills of curriculum development. The quality of the Movement for Life curriculum of 2035, or of any educational program at any time in the near or long-range future, depends upon the theoretical understandings and the creative implementation abilities of today's professionals who will be responsible for future curricular decision-making.

References

Ennis, C. D. 1984. A future scenario for physical education. *Journal of Physical Education, Recreation and Dance* (September):4–5.

Huenecke, D. 1982. What is curriculum theorizing? What are its implications for practice? *Educational Leadership* 39(4) (January):290–94.

Jewett, A. E., and M. R. Mullan. 1977. *Curriculum design: Purposes and processes in physical education teaching-learning.* Washington, D.C.: AAHPER.

Macdonald, J. B. 1977. Values bases and issues for curriculum. In *Curriculum theory,* ed. Alex Molnar and John A. Zahorik, 10–21. Washington, D.C.: Association for Supervision and Curriculum Development.

Vallance, E. 1982. The practical uses of curriculum theory. *Theory Into Practice* 21(1) (Winter):4–10.

Recommended Readings

Beauchamp, G. A. 1975. *Curriculum theory.* Wilmette, IL: Kagg Press.

Berman, L. M., and J. A. Roderick. 1977. *Curriculum: Teaching the what, how and why of living.* Columbus, OH: Charles E. Merrill.

Haag, H. 1978. *Sport pedagogy: Content and methodology.* Baltimore, MD: University Park Press.

Jewett, A. E. 1980. Status of physical education curriculum theory. *Quest* 32 (2):163–73.

McCutcheon, G., ed. 1982. *Theory into practice* 21(1) (Winter).

Ulrich, C., and J. E. Nixon, eds. 1972. *Tones of theory.* Washington, DC: AAHPER.

Curriculum Theories

2

Outline

This chapter is introduced by a series of metaphors written by students of physical education curriculum theory. They were selected to illustrate the use of metaphor as a way of organizing thinking. Kliebard (1982,15), the leading exponent of curriculum theory metaphor, points out that "curriculum metaphors provide a language or explanation which permits us to 'see' things that otherwise might not be visible to the naked eye." Thinking of the curriculum as if it were something else frees us to consider ideas and to search for insights beyond everyday reality. As a vehicle for thought, a curriculum metaphor can open up new questions and stimulate us to seek additional alternatives.

It may be appropriate to begin a systematic analysis by generating and examining curriculum metaphors. A metaphor can serve as a lens through which the object or focus of study is perceived. Vague concepts can be held up to scrutiny and modified for more accurate thinking and increasingly precise communication. You may wish to critique each of the following metaphors, and also to analyze Kliebard's 1972 metaphors of production, growth, and travel, before you attempt to write a curriculum metaphor reflecting your own philosophy of physical education.

Curriculum Metaphors

Metaphor of the Orchestra
Margie Garnto

The curriculum is an orchestra, and each student is a separate musician in the orchestra. Each student must have a foundation on an instrument, for which a certain amount of drill work and practice is necessary. Once basic musical skills are established, freedom is acquired to explore new directions in playing. Each musician realizes that, in order for the orchestra to play its best, each of them must play his or her best. The conductor cannot play the music but can guide the musicians through the piece. The conductor's purpose is to guide the whole and yet give opportunity for individual musicians to display their style. As a keen observer and listener, the conductor is always striving to improve each member and the orchestra as a whole.

Metaphor of Sailing
Jeff Davis

The curriculum is an ocean and the students are the sailboats, which are controlled by a very spirited but gentle wind. Their destination and route over the water have been determined prior to departure. The most expert yachtsmen have studied long-range weather forecasts, tested water soundings, and designated a new course likely to provide enjoyable scenery and a safe journey. The sailboats are all shapes and sizes; therefore the wind will have to vary according to each boat. If the wind blows too hard, it will cause waves too large for the smaller boats to travel. However, if the wind does not blow hard enough, the boats will not move and the destination will be unattainable. The route the boats will take over the water must offer each boat an equal opportunity for docking. It cannot discriminate against the boat's size, color, or fair market value. Each boat must receive sufficient stimuli to reach the projected harbor.

Metaphor of Space Exploration
Harry Cypher

The curriculum is the galaxy of stars within the universe. The students are space explorers sent to learn how to investigate the galaxy for the benefit and improvement of society. Before their explorations can truly begin, the novice explorers are given basic training under the guidance of a Master Explorer. During this training the Master Explorer teaches the novice explorers the tools and skills they will need to efficiently and effectively investigate the stars they will visit on their journeys through the galaxy.

As training ends, the novice explorers decide on flight plans for their first journey into the galaxy. The Master Explorer may give advice and guidance, but does not try to influence the flight plans. These novice explorers are as varied as the stars they will visit, and must plot for themselves, based on their interests and particular talents.

As they venture into the galaxy, they will study charts, graphs, and accounts of previous explorations. From these, the novice explorers will gain a basic understanding of the star that will aid the search for personal meanings and discoveries. In times of doubt and confusion, the novice explorers will always be able to return to the support station to seek advice, assistance, and guidance from the Master Explorer. Renewed and refreshed, the young explorers will be able to return to the galaxy and use the exploratory processes learned to investigate new stars waiting on the horizon.

The curriculum is the camera's numerous available accessories that make possible the development of beautiful prints. The student is the photographer. The types and models of cameras are as unending as the wide variety of films carefully tucked inside. The photographer selects a camera and, handling it with care, looks through the viewfinder to appraise and choose appropriate angles. The photographer with a wide-angle lens may choose oceans and mountains that cover vast lots of land. The close-up phenomena of a bee gathering pollen from a red rose requires the zoom lens camera. Since a movie camera would not be best suited to film still life scenery, the photographer wisely chooses the still camera for areas that are not cluttered with a variety of movements. The specific camera selected by each photographer determines the possible settings, lenses, type of film, and overall makeup. The result is a unique print. The goal of each photographer is to create a personal image of the scenery at hand.

Metaphor of Photography
June Baker

The curriculum is a Ringling Brothers Circus, full of surprises and excitement. The students are the performers. In addition to working diligently at improving their chosen acts, the performers must also help to erect the "big top." Under the guidance of the skilled ringmaster, every performer is free to develop his or her act to its fullest potential. Under the big top of curriculum there are many varied acts, but the experienced ringmaster blends these acts into a harmonious show, knowing that, once the lights come on, the performers will become part of "The Greatest Show on Earth"—life.

Metaphor of the Circus
Curt Fludd

Metaphor is a useful tool for scholars to communicate curriculum concepts and for students to analyze various aspects and value positions. The study of curriculum metaphors can stimulate the search for personal answers to key questions. A useful curriculum metaphor highlights the relationships among knowledge, learner, teacher,and society. It suggests possible answers to such questions as:

1. What is the relationship of the school to the society whose needs it serves?
2. What is the major purpose of the curriculum?
3. What is the role of subject matter knowledge?
4. What is the role of the student?
5. What is the role of the teacher?
6. What are the rights and responsibilities of the individual in contrast to the rights and needs of the larger group?

A successful metaphor uses one image consistently, makes the philosophy of the author come to life, and adds an additional dimension to interpersonal communication, while it describes all the key elements or aspects of the curriculum.

Curriculum metaphors are particularly useful in examining contrasting value orientations. After reading the following section on value orientations in curriculum development, the reader may wish to review the previous metaphors and attempt to determine how effectively they illustrate the particular value orientations described.

Value Orientations in Curriculum Development

A number of serious scholars have engaged in classifying philosophical orientations for the development of curriculum theory (Eisner and Vallance 1974; Macdonald 1975; McNeil 1977; Orlosky and Smith 1978; Giroux, Penna and Pinar 1981; Huenecke 1982). The classifications available permit descriptions of curriculum orientations in terms of major emphasis, focus, and implications for practice, as well as value positions. The authors consider value orientation the most significant characteristic for classifying and differentiating among curriculum theories.

Educators have come full circle from the traditional position of attempting to develop value-free curriculum models. For over fifty years we sought objectivity in the scientific approach to curriculum development. But this approach was never value-free; its particular value position was simply implicit. Today we must recognize the importance of making values explicit in curriculum work. Five different value orientations, identified in the study of curriculum theory, have been selected for consideration by the student of physical education curriculum development: disciplinary mastery, social reconstruction, learning process, self-actualization, and ecological validity. In the following section, each of these value orientations is described and viewed in historical perspective as it has influenced physical education curricular practice. In chapter 5, attention is given to the statement of physical education program goals in terms of curriculum value orientations.

Disciplinary Mastery

The most traditional orientation to curriculum development places top priority on mastery of the subject matter, acquisition of the important knowledge, or the integrity and primacy of the academic discipline. The role of the school is viewed as the transmittal of the cultural heritage from one generation to the next. Educators are concerned with guiding young people in acquiring the tools they need to participate in their cultural heritage and in attaining access to the best wisdom of the ages. Those who place high value on disciplinary mastery assert that mastery of the most important subject matter is the key to the best in schooling.

The concern for disciplinary mastery was expressed from the mid-1950s into the 1970s in the "structure of knowledge" orientation to curriculum development. During that era educators in all fields worked at analyses of the key concepts in their particular subject areas, and proposed curriculum patterns organized in terms of these knowledge structures. Many curriculum projects were subsidized, particularly in mathematics and the biological and physical sciences, with a primary value orientation toward mastery of the key concepts of a particular subject matter discipline.

The recent focus on "back to the basics" is another reflection of the disciplinary mastery orientation. Those who choose to evaluate schools in terms of demonstrated student competence in reading, writing, and mathematics skills are asserting the need for mastery of basic fundamentals as the first step in achieving competence in those disciplines selected as most worthwhile.

Disciplinary or subject matter mastery is still the predominant value orientation in physical education curriculum development. In selecting curriculum content, we have consistently emphasized the importance of basic movement skills, both in elementary school movement education and in secondary school sports education. Elementary school children are expected to master basic disciplinary or motor performance tasks, variously designated as locomotor and non-locomotor movements, fundamental throwing, kicking, and striking patterns; series of perceptual-motor skills; body, space, and effort relationships; or gymnastics, dance, and games progressions. In most secondary school programs throughout the United States and Canada, the content is still determined on the basis of those movement forms that constitute our popular sports, physical recreation, and athletics activities. Mastery of the discipline is sought through a quest for achieving performance skill in basketball, football, baseball, track and field, and gymnastics. Physical educators plan to maximize the acquisition of skill through explanation, demonstration, practice drills, and simulated game play. Mastery of movement fundamentals and sports skills has clearly been the primary value reflected in most statements of physical education curriculum goals.

Social Reconstruction

Since the 1950s social reconstruction has been a popular term with educators who attribute high value to social reform. In this view, cultural change is more important than cultural transmission. The school has a responsibility to the future and educators should accept a role in making school curricula the vehicle for creating a better society.

From a social reconstruction perspective, societal needs take precedence over individual needs. If the nation needs more engineers, nuclear physicists, or genetics scientists, curricula are modified to strengthen education in the appropriate subject matter areas. Vocational programs are provided to develop occupational skills for jobs created by new technology. When decision-makers aim to raise the level of appreciation and participation in the fine arts, government subsidies are made available to support educational programs in music, graphic arts, drama, and dance. Curricula based on a social reconstruction value orientation are planned to include instruction and practice in the skills of participation in a democracy, in leadership skills, and in group cooperation and problem solving. Special programs are developed in problem areas such as race relations, gender identification, family living, and drug use and abuse.

Curricula designed with this orientation tend to reflect an assumption that the school should be a bridge between what is and what might be. Educational innovation is directed toward progress from the real to the ideal. Students are encouraged to think of themselves as future change agents who can learn to contribute toward a society that more nearly approaches their desires than the world in which their parents matured.

The social reconstructionists tend to view the school as society in microcosm. The physical educators among them are inclined to express allegiance to the concept that "sport is life in microcosm" and to select curriculum goals relating to the development of interpersonal sensitivity, awareness of others, and the development of social group skills.

Learning Process

Another identifiable value orientation in curriculum development is the learning process approach. From this perspective, how we learn becomes as important as what we learn. The processes by which knowledge is generated in each broad subject field are an important curriculum concern. A major point in the rationale is that the knowledge explosion has made it impossible for the school curriculum to cover all important product knowledge; consequently, learning the process skills for continuing learning has taken on increased importance.

The emphasis on high technology in recent decades has highlighted the need for curriculum focus on learning process in order to develop individual abilities to cope with rapid change. The communications revolution is changing the school and its curriculum just as it is changing everything else in our lives. Education must be concerned with developing process skills that can be applied to learning whatever becomes important to the individual to learn.

Problem solving skills continue to be important. Higher level conceptual abilities are increasingly needed. New skills are needed for computer learning, which can now be applied in all fields. The process focus ranges all the way from the technology of packaging and presenting materials to students to a kind of technology of the mind. This curriculum orientation also encompasses concerns for the aesthetic processes, as well as for the scientific processes, and for learning processes specifically relevant to the diverse subject fields appropriate in today's curriculum.

Self-Actualization

Since the early 1960s, professional preparation programs for teachers have stressed the concept of self-actualization as a key value in curriculum development. "Perceiving, behaving, becoming" is still a widely accepted ideal (ASCD 1962). The function of the curriculum is viewed as a process of self-discovery, synthesis, and personal integration. "It is child-centered, autonomy and growth oriented, and education is seen as an enabling process that would provide the means to personal liberation and development" (Eisner and Vallance 1974,9).

Curricula directed toward self-actualization assign a high priority to the achievement of individual autonomy and self-direction. Each person is responsible for identifying his or her own goals, for developing personal uniqueness, and for guiding individual learning. This perspective overlaps the preceding one in that process skills for individual development and personal learning are of major importance.

The self-actualization orientation encourages individual excellence. "Be all you can be" is a predominant theme. Curricular experiences are designed to challenge the individual to extend self, to cross boundaries, to exceed previous limitations, and to gain new perceptions of self.

Ecological Validity

A fifth value orientation identifies the primary goal of education as ecological validity. This perspective is based on the assumption that each human personality is unique. It incorporates the concept of "celebration of self" or self-actualization, identified as the fourth value orientation. But it goes beyond that to a view of the holistic person integrated within a particular environment. The individual is seen as an integral component of the ecosphere, responding to the environment, and at the same time determining, to some degree, the nature of his or her universe. According to this view of curriculum, the individual is a functioning element in the total biosphere. The ecology of the natural environment is to be respected and preserved. Humankind is understood in its biological relationships with the physical environment and its potential impact on other forms of life.

The world is viewed with a new appreciation of global interdependence. The school is responsible for the development of individuals who function effectively as citizens of a single world and whose commitment to human futures goes beyond personal competence, local achievement, and national pride. The curriculum is directed toward a sociological ecosystem, as well as a biological ecosphere.

This perspective has a future-orientation. Individual education is designed to assist in creating the future. The curriculum is concerned with learning to ask and examine critical questions. Students develop skills for writing alternative scenarios for desired human futures. The curriculum establishes ecological validity by viewing the individual as an integral part of the total environment in his or her particular place and time; it takes the perspective that we can create, to some extent, the nature of the world in which all of us will live.

This perspective overlaps that of the social reconstructionist in that planned social change is a necessary strategy. Its challenge is multidimensional, however. Precedence is accorded neither to societal needs nor to individual needs. Value orientation is toward the development of a unique human person whose individual validity can be established only in a globally interdependent society. Its ideal is a future human condition, dependent upon the incorporation of both biological and sociological balances within a total ecosystem.

Historical Perspective on Value Orientation in Physical Education Curricula

The first school programs in physical education in the United States were gymnastics programs. At the turn of the century, the potential values of the German system over the Swedish system were being hotly debated. This emphasis on imported systems of gymnastics was consistent with the subject-oriented curriculum that comprised the total school program. The value orientation of the period was clearly disciplinary mastery.

In 1918 the famous Seven Cardinal Principles of Education were published. They had a great impact on the development of school curricula. The writings of John Dewey and the rise of the Progressive Education movement helped to shift the focus of school curricula to concerns of individual development. These concerns in education, along with the rise of the playground movement, and the growth of both public and private youth-serving agencies, were reflected in the 1920s and 1930s in curricula that were much more child-centered.

The manifestations of these values in physical education were seen in programs offering a wider variety of activities and in the burgeoning of sports and recreational activities as the core of most curricula. The powerful heritage of British sports lent support to the rapid growth of interscholastic and intercollegiate athletic programs and to the domination of physical education curricula by the popular competitive sports.

The philosophy of the progressive educators had its value base in the concept of self-actualization, but very few physical education curricula that demonstrated a commitment to self-actualization of the participants were actually developed. The shift in emphasis toward sports and recreational activities represented a change in perceptions of the nature of the subject field more than a change in value orientation. Physical education programs were still designed to achieve subject matter mastery, but the subject matter was viewed as sports activities rather than gymnastics and exercises. To be sure, the disciplinary mastery emphasis was tempered somewhat by a social reconstruction orientation demonstrated in the statements of goals related to character building, reminiscent of the British tradition. The implicit assumption was that building the character of individual participants would lead to a better society.

Curricula during the 1940s took a dramatic turn toward greater emphasis on societal needs. World War II demanded a group commitment toward achieving victory. Social reconstruction dominated as the value orientation in curriculum development. There was general agreement on the need for teamwork and leadership skills, on essential human survival skills, and on the importance of opportunity for participative experience in a lifestyle appropriate to citizenship in a democracy. Utilitarianism was a positive criterion in the selection of curriculum content. Vocational education curricula, life adjustment programs, and courses such as driver education, flourished. Physical education programs emphasized fitness activities, often simulating military physical training programs with such techniques as circuit training, obstacle courses, grass drills, and climbing ropes and cargo nets. School children were taught drownproofing and wilderness survival skills. Team sports were stressed, although lifetime sports activities became increasingly popular after the Allied victory. The social reconstruction orientation was highly relevant for persons whose primary goal was a military victory to be followed by building a better world in the context of cooperating in the establishment of the United Nations.

The 1950s are viewed as a period of major curriculum reform. This was a period of heavy emphasis upon disciplinary mastery. Many curriculum projects were subsidized by Federal funds. The majority of the early projects were concerned with mathematics and the physical and biological sciences. There was a strong commitment toward improving public education in order to surpass the Russians.

The learning process value orientation was also evident in the search for more effective instructional strategies for achieving subject matter mastery. The "new math" provided an entirely new conceptual scheme for organizing mathematics instruction. The Biological Sciences Curriculum Studies project offered three different approaches to learning biology, each with it own set of curriculum materials.

Physical educators of the period were caught up in this enthusiasm for disciplinary mastery. We became very conscious of the need to delineate and clarify our own body of knowledge. The new subdisciplines of kinesiology and exercise physiology held top priority in doctoral programs, in funding, in staffing, and in establishing research laboratories.

In retrospect, this curriculum reform of the 1950s was a reform in the suburbs. It was oriented toward the secondary schools and toward the college preparatory curriculum. The reform movement developed some new dimensions during the 1960s. Curriculum projects increasingly focused on elementary school children, recognizing that significant social change must start with the youngest members of society. It was generally agreed that subject matter mastery was not in itself enough. Educators were concerned about the need for youth to develop a sense of social responsibility. The schools again acknowledged their role in the solution of social problems. The civil rights movement was strong, and it was clear that the schools needed to accept some responsibility for improving race relations. The need for special attention to programs for the disadvantaged and to the very real problems of urban schools was evident. Local control and the neighborhood school became highly controversial issues. It was a period of major organizational change in American schools.

The most significant progress in physical education curriculum development during this period was the increasing interest in human growth and development. The recognition of the need for longitudinal research in motor development and the behavioral sciences, and the growth in popularity of movement education as the vehicle for elementary school physical education were hallmarks of the "new physical education." Increasing emphasis was given to lifetime sports at the secondary level. A few schools experimented with team-teaching and modular scheduling, but these innovations had little continuing impact on physical education. Although social reconstruction was the dominant value orientation in the schools, this orientation was less evident in physical education curricula that still demonstrated preoccupation with competitive athletics and the mastery of sports skills. In many elementary school physical education curricula, high value was placed on individualization and self-direction through movement education programs; but orientation toward self-actualization scarcely penetrated middle school and secondary school physical education.

Professional educators in the decade of the 1970s were especially concerned with attempting to find an optimum balance among the major curriculum elements of the individual learner, the society in which he or she participates, and the subject matter through which the cultural heritage is transmitted and extended. Overall, the dominant value orientation was social reconstruction. There was a concerted effort to improve educational services to the disadvantaged. Equal opportunity, affirmative action, bilingual education, and mainstreaming were all watchwords of concern for the rights of women, the handicapped, and racial and ethnic minorities. Renewed effort was directed toward ecological education, the development of creativity, and a greater commitment to humanistic philosophy. Physical education curriculum designers reflected all of these concerns, but in most instances responded more effectively to the competing demands for accountability and for athletic programs in which the community could take pride.

The professional literature throughout the past half century has championed "education *through* the physical." Statements of curriculum philosophy and program objectives listed in local curriculum guides have emphasized individual development using selected movement learning activities. Curriculum documents have expressed commitment to education of the fully-integrated person through physical activity. In practice, however, the physical education curriculum has been structured with a subject matter orientation. Sports, dance, and gymnastics units have dominated the pages of curriculum guides. Progressions designed to achieve mastery of specific motor performance skills have determined the sequence of unit plans and the content of daily lessons. Many physical educators, facing recent challenges of accountability, have been uncomfortable with the lack of evidence of achievement of subject matter mastery. Few programs have permitted demonstration of clear-cut student achievements, either in fitness measures or sports skill performance, even though curriculum guides have suggested that such outcomes are expected.

Looking back over the years it is clear that the dominant value orientation in physical education curriculum practice has been disciplinary mastery. Concerns for social reconstruction were strong in the World War II era and observable both in the prewar years and in the past fifteen to twenty years. Physical education curricula oriented primarily toward self-actualization, learning process, or ecological validity, have been very few indeed.

Dimensions for Clarifying Physical Education Curriculum Value Orientations

Curriculum theorizers identify three elements as sources for the curriculum. The three factors to be considered are the nature of the individual for whom the curriculum is to provide educative experiences, the nature of the society that has established schools to provide for maintenance and transmission of its cultural heritage, and the subject matter to be learned. In order to examine the existing or desired value orientation in a particular curriculum, it is necessary to ask two questions: (1) What is the value perspective toward personal or individual development, toward social-cultural goals, and toward subject matter content? (2) To what extent is any one of these three elements valued above the other two? Before analyzing particular physical education curriculum models, the curriculum designer needs to clarify his or her own value system and how it determines perspective toward individual development, societal goals, and subject matter content.

Personal or Individual Development

At least three perspectives toward individual development can be identified for consideration. The first of these emphasizes the developmental approach to curriculum design. This perspective relies on the findings of the developmental psychologists and the motor development specialists who have studied sequences in human development and attempted to describe characteristics of motor patterns associated with each stage. From this viewpoint, program planning becomes primarily a matter of *expert diagnosis of individual developmental needs,* and the establishment of activity sequences appropriate to them.

A second perspective emphasizes *self-directed growth* of the individual person. Although the teacher has access to expert knowledge and serves as stimulator, facilitator, and resource person, the student assumes a major role in identifying his or her own goals, in developing individual uniqueness, and in directing personal learning. This perspective emphasizes the student's motivation to progress toward a set of established goals from which he or she chooses those most important and determines a personal level of aspiration. Curricula developed with this orientation demonstrate wide variability both in program content and organization.

From a third perspective, the curriculum designer seeks to facilitate the fulfillment of individual human potential through introduction to the full range of different meanings accessible through participation in movement activity. Students become aware of the broad scope of possibilities for achieving personal fitness, performance skill, and self-actualization; and develop movement behaviors that can be directed successfully toward the search for *personal meaning.* The curriculum planner structures physical education experiences with a view toward broadening horizons and deepening involvement in movement as a component of personal integration.

These three perspectives, and others that might yet be identified, reflect some differences in approach. Curriculum designers who view personal or individual development as the overriding priority all agree that the learner plays a key role in his or her own educational growth and development, that society's primary educational goal is the development of self-directing persons, and that the role of subject content is to serve as the medium for fulfillment of individual human potential.

Social-Cultural Goals

The three major perspectives concerning the role of the school in a democratic society are: (1) the function of the school is to prepare the younger generation for full participation as citizens of their society, (2) the more radical view that the school should be a change agent to achieve equal opportunity for all, and (3) the school should function to reconstruct the existing society by fostering excellence while somehow providing for equality of opportunity. The majority of professional educators have usually been conservative in philosophical outlook. Thus the view of the school's primary function as *preparation for participation in adult society* has typically predominated. This view has been reflected in physical education curricula that emphasize the development of physical fitness as needed for maintaining the body in a highly technological and inactive society, for training for particular jobs or military service, or for enhancing the quality of life over an extended life span. This value orientation also supports curriculum emphases on lifetime sports skills, social dance skills, and excellence in competitive athletics.

In communities where the school is viewed as an agent for social change, the contribution of the physical education curriculum ordinarily emphasizes interpersonal relations and the dynamics of modifying them. Team sports are taught so as to emphasize social interaction and group process skills. The movement activity context is utilized to heighten awareness of other persons, to focus attention on the contributions of individuals with obvious superficial differences, to increase acceptance of ethnic minority group members and persons with varying value systems, and to learn to value individual uniqueness as a social good. The two most prominent contemporary illustrations of the *equal opportunity* value orientation are the efforts now being made to eliminate sex stereotyping and sex discrimination in physical education and sports programs, and the increase of mainstreaming of handicapped individuals in physical education classes. The degree to which these changes are supported or resisted in a particular community provides insight into local attitudes and value orientation.

Democratic societies today share an educational goal that is becoming increasingly difficult to achieve. As the full dimensions of this ideal are recognized, it becomes evident that it is exceedingly difficult to provide *equality for all while stimulating the development of excellence* for those with outstanding abilities and talents. This conflict can be observed in the attempt to provide quality physical education instruction for all, in addition to extensive intramural and club programs for all individuals who desire such opportunities, while developing the full talents of the athletically gifted. Achieving all these goals can seldom be supported by the financial and personnel resources of a single school system. Local compromises are made in accordance with the value orientations of the decision-makers.

If the value orientation of the curriculum is toward the goals of society, the social mission of the school is emphasized in all curricular areas. From this perspective the physical education curriculum is more influenced by the total cultural context and less isolated in its orientation from other subject areas. Physical education curricula adapt to current community concerns and cooperate with desired social changes. Such curricula are likely to be innovative in practice, forward-looking in selecting content, and flexible and experimental in the development of instructional strategies.

Subject Matter Content

One of the most time-honored questions in the study of curriculum is, "what knowledge is of most worth?" There are three popular answers to the question, "what is the proper content of physical education?" There are strong advocates for each of the three major content foci—health-related fitness, play, and human movement.

Those who opt for *health-related fitness* establish their objectives in terms of the components of fitness, and develop programs designed to achieve specific fitness goals. Typical concerns in today's programs are aerobic fitness, muscular strength and endurance, flexibility, and body composition. Curricula highlight various exercise systems, such as obstacle courses, aerobic dance, and circuit and interval training.

Many physical educators take the perspective that the concept of *play* as an essential human activity, or sport as a cultural universal, is the theoretical base for the curriculum. From this perspective the primary goals are: (1) to develop attitudes that will support voluntary participation in physical recreation activities, and (2) to achieve levels of skill development that will permit satisfying participation in appropriate lifetime sports. Curricula designed to achieve these goals emphasize popular activity skills and methodology to stress participant enjoyment.

In recent decades, support for *human movement* as the appropriate subject matter content of physical education has steadily increased. Elementary school movement education programs emphasize basic concepts of: body awareness; space awareness; and effort and relationships through games, dance, and gymnastics activities. Secondary school programs are more likely to stress biomechanical analysis of a particular sport, dance, or aquatics skill.

Curriculum designers who place priority on the subject matter content generally establish competency-based programs that lend themselves to the statement of specific behavioral objectives and evaluation through quantitative measures. Programs are logically organized in terms of the basic concepts of the discipline. Instruction is planned as daily, weekly, and annual sequences. The orientation is toward subject matter, whichever definition of the subject matter is valued most highly.

Summary

Proposed classifications for curriculum theories permit descriptions in terms of value position, major emphasis, focus, and implications for practice. The authors consider value orientation the most significant characteristic for classifying and differentiating among curriculum theories. The classification presented for consideration by the student of physical education curriculum development includes five different value orientations: disciplinary mastery, social reconstruction, learning process, self-actualization, and ecological validity. Each of these value orientations is described and illustrated through a series of curriculum metaphors intended to serve as a lens through which contrasting value orientations can be better perceived and understood.

Since the introduction of physical education into the schools of the United States and Canada, the dominant value orientation in curriculum practice has been disciplinary mastery. The only significant exception to this generalization was during the World War II era when the social reconstruction value orientation was strong. In spite of the philosophy of "education through the physical" as expressed in the professional literature, physical education curricula oriented primarily toward self-actualization, learning process, or ecological validity—rather than subject matter mastery— have been very few indeed.

In order to examine physical education curriculum value orientations, it is helpful to study programs from three dimensions: the major curriculum elements of the individual learner, the society in which he or she participates, and the subject matter through which the cultural heritage is transmitted and extended. Value perspectives toward personal or individual development include reliance upon expert diagnosis of developmental needs, emphasis upon self-directed growth, and commitment to the fulfillment of individual human potential through introduction to the full range of movement meanings. Contrasting orientations toward social-cultural goals place value priorities on preparation for societal participation, equality of opportunity, and the achievement of excellence with equality. Different value orientations, with regard to subject matter content, identify health-related fitness, play, and the analysis of human movement as most important. In translating theory into physical education curriculum models, it is essential that the major alternative value orientations are understood and that the individual curriculum designer clarifies his or her personal value orientation for the physical education curriculum.

References

Association for Supervision and Curriculum Development. 1962. *Perceiving, behaving, becoming.* Washington, DC: The Association.

Eisner, E. W., and E. Vallance, eds. 1974. *Conflicting conceptions of curriculum.* Berkeley, CA: McCutchan.

Giroux, H. A., A. W. Penna, and W. F. Pinar, eds. 1981. *Curriculum and instruction: Alternatives in education.* Berkeley, CA: McCutchan.

Huenecke, D. 1982. What is curriculum theorizing? What are its implications for practice? *Educational Leadership* 39(4) (January): 290–94.

Kliebard, H. M. 1972. Curriculum Theory as Metaphor. *Theory Into Practice* 21(1) (Winter):11–17.

Kliebard, H. M. 1972. Metaphorical roots of curriculum design. *Teachers College Record* 72 (3).

Macdonald, J. B. 1975. Curriculum theory as intentional activity. Paper delivered at Curriculum Theory Conference, Charlottesville, Virginia (October).

McNeil, J. D. 1977. *Designing curriculum.* Boston: Little, Brown.

Orlosky, D. E., and B. O. Smith. 1978. *Curriculum development: Issues and insights.* Chicago: Rand McNally.

Recommended Readings

Metaphors:
    Kliebard, H. M. 1982. Curriculum Theory as Metaphor. *Theory Into Practice* 21 (1) (Winter):11–17.

Classifications for curriculum theories:
    Eisner, E. W., and E. Vallance, eds. 1974. *Conflicting conceptions of curriculum.* Berkeley, CA: McCutchan.
    Giroux, H. A., A. W. Penna, and W. F. Pinar, eds. 1981. *Curriculum and instruction: Alternatives in education.* Berkeley, CA: McCutchan.
    Orlosky, D. E., and B. O. Smith. 1978. *Curriculum development: Issues and insights.* Chicago: Rand McNally.

Value orientation in physical education:
    University of Georgia. 1979, 1981, 1983. Curriculum theory in physical education conference proceedings. Athens, GA: Univ. of Georgia.
    Jewett, A. E. 1977. Relationships in physical education: A curriculum viewpoint. In *The Academy Papers,* 11 (September):87–98. Washington, DC: The American Academy of Physical Education.

Historical perspective:
    American Alliance for Health, Physical Education, Recreation and Dance. 1972. *This is physical education.* Washington, DC: AAHPERD.
    Brown, C., and R. Cassidy. 1963. *Theory in physical education: A guide to program change.* Philadelphia: Lea and Febiger.
    Macdonald, J. B., B. J. Wolfson, and E. Zaret. 1973. *Reschooling society: A conceptual model.* Washington, D.C.: Association for Supervision and Curriculum Development.
    National Commission on Excellence in Education. 1983. A nation at risk: The imperative for educational reform. *Education Week* 2 (31) (April 27).
    Nixon, J. E., and A. E. Jewett. 1980. *Introduction to physical education.* 9th ed. Philadelphia: W. B. Saunders.
    Ulrich, C., ed. 1982. *Education in the 80s: Physical education.* Washington, D.C.: National Education Association.
    Ulrich, C., and J. E. Nixon, eds. 1972. *Tones of theory.* Washington, D.C.: AAHPERD.
    Van Dalen, D. B., and B. L. Bennett. 1971. *A world history of physical education: Cultural, philosophical, comparative.* Englewood Cliffs, NJ: Prentice-Hall.
    Zeigler, E. F., ed. 1979. *A history of physical education and sport.* Englewood Cliffs, NJ: Prentice-Hall.

Translating Theory into Physical Education Curriculum Models

3

Why should physical education programs exist in the schools? What should the physical education curriculum be like? Generally our answers to these questions reflect our relatively narrow personal experiences as students and teachers. Most of you have observed or participated in only a few physical education programs, often located in a single geographic region. Your tendency may be to assume that all physical education programs are like those you have seen. This chapter is intended to introduce you to several alternative ways of designing physical education programs.

The chapter begins with a description of one set of physical education curriculum designs proposed for the 1980s. The remainder of the chapter examines a range of curriculum models that appear in physical education literature. You are encouraged to give serious consideration to each of these alternative approaches to the design of the physical education curriculum.

Physical Education Curriculum Designs for the 1980s
Preschool and Elementary School

From Ann E. Jewett, "Curriculum Designs for fulfilling Human Agendas," in C. Ulrich (ed.) *Education for the 80s: Physical Education,* © 1982 National Education Association, Washington, D.C. Reprinted by permission.

Preschool education is becoming an accepted public service, provided for all children during the two or three years prior to enrollment in an early childhood education program. Learning activities emphasize a combination of perceptual-motor activities, cognitive-developmental tasks, and self-care skills. Movement education activities include body-awareness and spatial-orientation challenges and games, basic motor skills, and creative movement.

All elementary school children need opportunities to participate in movement activity programs twice daily for a total of at least forty minutes. Instructional programs include continuing movement education; ethnic, folk, and creative dance; and new games.

Much of the child's movement curriculum is organized to focus on moving in space and is designed to achieve body awareness, locomotion, object manipulation, and movement expression. Basic locomotor patterns of walking, running, sliding, and jumping are learned, adapted, and refined through imitating, experimenting, solving movement tasks set by teachers, and performing such skills in self-testing, chasing, and rhythmic games. Learning sequences progress to more complex locomotor skills such as galloping, hopping, leaping, and skipping and to advanced forms of propulsion on climbing and hanging apparatus. Students develop more sophisticated concepts of directionality and spatial relationships and better movement control through games emphasizing dodging, chasing, and tagging; through stunts, tumbling, and other gymnastic activities; through folk dance and creative dance; and through simple combatives and weight-training activities. Skating, swimming, and ethnic dances of particular local interest are recommended.

Ball- and object-handling activities involving throwing, catching, kicking, and striking receive major attention. Striking activities requiring foot-eye coordination as well as hand-eye coordination are included. Teachers plan object manipulation challenges using hoops, ropes, wands, and batons, as well as many types of balls and striking implements. Together with continuing attention to increasing efficiency in skill performance, learning sequences are designed for progressive development of strength, balance, agility, flexibility, and circulorespiratory endurance. Elementary concepts of effective body mechanics are included. Modified track and field events are popular.

Popular games are introduced. New games and "friend" games that focus on cooperating with, assisting, and learning to know and enjoy another child are emphasized. Concepts of group interaction, such as partner, team goal, sharing, win-win, teamwork, and leadership, are analyzed.

Curriculum Theory

The curriculum in middle school physical education emphasizes two
major elements, (1) expanded understanding of movement through
refining personal skills, and (2) greater depth of social understanding
through experiences in movement activities of many cultures and in
creating new games. To conduct middle school education programs in
developmental motor performance, each school needs the services of
at least one dance educator, one aquatic specialist, and two general
movement and sport educators. The dance and aquatic specialists
may be shared with other middle schools in the district, depending
upon enrollments. The instructional program includes survival
swimming, sport skills, dance, project adventure, fitness activities, and
new games. Venturesome activities requiring more personal courage
are included. The concept of creating new games is appropriate to all
age levels, but receives special emphasis in middle school programs.
As stated by the New Games Foundation, "New Games is a process.
It's not what you play . . . but how you play. This process begins with
your own enjoyment, extends to an awareness of the other players,
and eventually results in creating some altogether new ways to have
fun."

Many taped programs are available to provide for large group
presentations, or for use by individual students in the learning resource
center. These include innovative movement challenges and fitness
assessment activities. Audio cassettes to assist with out-of-school skill
development are available for individual checkout. Instructional
activities occur in three fifty-minute periods weekly. Two of these
provide for a planned sequential program; the third allows students to
select specific activity skills, field experiences, or needed remedial
work. Most students have approximately three different choices per
year on a seasonal basis. The instructional program is supplemented
by an intramural program directed by a full-time employee with
professional career training in recreation.

Secondary school programs include approximately one hundred hours
of instruction in developmental motor performance at each level. The
core course in the first year is fitness for life. It includes individual
assessment of the key aspects of health-related fitness, self-monitoring
of fitness achievements, guided prescription of exercise, and intensive
participation in selected fitness activities. The program also includes
two skill classes in which the major purpose is the development of
selected movement performance skills. Selections are made by the
individual student on the basis of a desire to become a competent
participant or a more skilled performer.

In the second year the core course is group development through
movement activities in which increased social awareness is sought; the
emphasis is on cooperative games, group choreography, and
community service projects. Large-group sessions, featuring taped

presentations of issues relating to equal opportunity in exercise, sport, and dance programs, are complemented by laboratory-activity sessions in selected sport or dance forms and discussion and analysis of illustrative case studies. In addition to taking the core course, which focuses on the development of individual skills for functioning effectively in groups, each student selects two additional sport or dance skill courses.

The third and final core course emphasizes diverse approaches to seeking personal meaning in movement. Several key approaches are explored: focus on inner awareness through sport; transcendental meditation; pursuit of risk or high adventure; the seeking of effortlessness and excellence in composing or creating movement; and participation in a small-group, wilderness-survival experience. The course concludes with personal assessment and planning for continuing growth in developmental motor performance and life-style patterns to accommodate movement activities within a desired life-style.

Each student in the third-year program selects two additional skill classes. Over the three year period, each has completed instruction in six selected activities beyond the core courses, including at least one cooperative group game activity, one dance activity, and one outdoor activity. Each program also includes successful completion of at least one intramural season and one sport club or dance club season.

Movement, Dance, and Sport is one of six core educational programs within which high school graduation requirements must be met. In addition to the core courses, three instructional units are required: Motor Development in Young Children, The Role of Exercise and Active Recreation in Aging, and International Sport and Dance. A wide variety of elective offerings in the broad field of Movement, Dance, and Sport is available for secondary school credit.

Post-Secondary Education

Students enrolled in college, university, or continuing education programs in physical education are required to participate in fitness appraisal activities at least once in two years. This provides them with current fitness information and instruction in sound self-evaluation techniques, encourages personal goal setting and planning for increasing and maintaining fitness, and offers access to leisure counseling services. Higher education offerings, available at both undergraduate and graduate levels, include the following: interdisciplinary insights into effective movement to meet the demands of new occupational tasks; survival and quality living in underwater communities; exercise and fitness in limited space and in gravity-less environments; impact of popular recreational activities on the biosphere; value systems of other cultures; personal decision-making to influence the shape of one's own future; consensus-seeking skills for creating quality community life; biofeedback analysis; movement notation; holography; worldwide human commonalities; senior citizens as a community resource; and urban futures planning (Jewett 1982, 44–47).

Curriculum Models

Physical education curriculum models are designed to provide a basis for decisions regarding the selection, structuring, and sequencing of educational experiences. Seven physical education curriculum models are discussed. This chapter summarizes basic beliefs or assumptions, identifies conceptual frameworks, and describes designs for implementing the model.

Each of the seven models selected for inclusion in this chapter can be considered a generic category in which more than one specific model might fit. The specific model selected for in-depth analysis illustrates the general category but also has unique characteristics of its own. To the extent possible, the analysis relies directly upon the writings of a major spokesperson for each theoretical model. The review is limited to published materials, rather than local documents. This allows you to examine specific models in greater depth after reading the summary. Though no attempt is made to evaluate each model, issues raised by critics are summarized and comments made regarding factors affecting implementation. After all the models are described, some observations and comparisons are made.

Developmental Education

The developmental philosophy of education is evident in the "education-through-the-physical" approach, which has dominated physical education literature throughout much of the twentieth century. (See chapter 2 for a discussion of physical education value orientations from an historical perspective.) This model sees the enhancement of the development process as the aim of education and of physical education. Human beings are assumed to have common developmental patterns as well as unique characteristics that influence the development process. A nurturing environment is essential for individuals to reach their fullest potentials. It is the responsibility of educators to create such an environment and to guide the development process.

Traditionally, developmental physical education programs employed a multiactivity program of games, sports, dance, and exercise to accomplish broad developmental goals. More recently, models have emerged that organize the physical education program around developmental themes rather than activities, and that emphasize individual differences in the rate of development (Gallahue, Werner, and Luedke 1975; Melograno 1979; Hoffman, Young, and Klesius 1981; Thompson and Mann 1981).

The Project SEE curriculum design (Thompson and Mann 1981) illustrates the developmental education curriculum model. Project SEE was an elementary school physical education curriculum development project funded by the Women's Educational Equity Act and directed by Margaret Thompson of the University of Illinois. Schools from Illinois, Indiana, and Missouri participated in the validation of the holistic developmental curriculum model. The assumptions of this model are summarized in this philosophy statement from the project:

From Thompson, M. M. and Mann, B. A., *Project SEE: Curriculum development,* Urbana, Illinois: Urbana SEE Publications, 1981.

All children regardless of sex, race, ethnicity or possible physical/mental anomalies, have a right to the opportunity of maximum development. Provision of opportunities for maximum development implies a holistic approach in physical education, since all aspects (affective, cognitive, psychomotor) of development are considered interdependent. Inherent in the provision of a meaningful developmentally based physical education curriculum is provision of opportunities to help children learn how to learn, and the provision of environments which are designed and altered to meet the needs of the child. While it is not possible to provide individualized programs for each child in each classroom, it is possible to provide environmental settings, class management techniques, teaching strategies, and variety in learning experiences that take individual differences into consideration. Knowledge of intraindividual and interindividual differences in the various aspects of development as well as in the manner and speed of learning for each child is fundamental to curriculum development. (Thompson and Mann 1981,4)

The Project SEE model identifies the goals of education and of physical education as:

Competence—help the learner use own skills, knowledges, and propensities in positive interaction with the challenges, the people, and the problems of his environment. Help the learner perceive own competence as valid and see self as having the ability to overcome obstacles, master confusions, and solve problems.

Curriculum Theory

Individuality—help the learner toward autonomous functioning characterized by the ability to make choices, develop preferences, take initiative, risk failure, set up an independent course for problem solving, and accept help without sacrificing independence.

Socialization—help the learner develop the ability to engage in relations of mutuality with other people (in work, play, talk, argument, sympathy) so that the self, though unique, does not end up as an isolate.

Integration—help the learner synthesize seemingly disparate elements of experiences through the development of a response system in which thought, feeling, and sensory motor activity are cojoined, and where feeling and empathy are interactive. (Thompson 1980)

The conceptual framework for a developmental education program is derived from research on human development. An overview of developmental stages in each of the domains (cognitive, affective, motor) is used as a scheme to determine what the program should attempt to accomplish. The curriculum planners may rely upon general developmental theories and hierarchies of objectives, or they may use a classification system designed specifically for physical education. Appendix A provides a summary of the developmental theories of Piaget, Kohlberg, Havighurst, Erikson, and Freud and the taxonomies of objectives of Bloom, Krathwohl, Harrow, and Simpson. One or more of these could provide the conceptual framework used to design a developmental physical education program. Also included in appendix A is a summary outline of the taxonomy of objectives for physical education developed by Thompson and Mann (1977). This taxonomy describes six areas of development for which the physical education program is responsible: mental development, social-emotional development, physical development, body handling development, object handling development, and coordinated body and object handling development.

This taxonomy serves as the basis of the conceptual framework for Project SEE. Because of the emphasis upon the holistic nature of the child, domain interaction is considered the keystone of the curriculum. For that reason, objectives and learnings derived from the taxonomy are designated motor-affective (interaction of beliefs, attitudes, values, and motor performance) and motor-cognitive (interaction of knowledge, cognitive processes, and motor performance). Content from the motor-affective and motor-cognitive designations is divided into four topical groups: Self, Movement, Self in Movement,

Figure 3.1
Project SEE curriculum
model
From Thompson, M. M.,
and B. A. Mann. *Project
SEE: Curiculum
development,* Urbana,
Illinois: Urbana SEE
Publications 1981.

Level I

I. Adjusting to learning environment
  A. Body awareness
  B. Space awareness
II. Awareness and appreciation of self and others
  A. Self assessment
  B. Realize personal goals (own)
  C. Movement communication
  D. Awareness of others' abilities
III. Behavior-action responsibility (self/others)
  A. Group strategies
  B. Arbitration-resolution of a social problem
IV. Confidence—Pride in performance: evaluation
  A. Developing realistic movement repertoire
  B. Risk-taking/challenge acceptance
  C. Performing independently/individually

Level II

I. Review—Adjusting to the learning environment
  A. Recognize and accept responsibility for one's own be-havior
  B. Exhibit responsibility toward task performance
II. Recognition of others/reduction of sex and social stereo-types
  A. Awareness of others' achievements
  B. Appreciate achievements/attributes of others
  C. Facilitate achievement for others
III. Establishing realistic goals
  A. Strengths—Weaknesses
  B. Determining/avoiding hazard
  C. Humor/empathy—Laughing at self

and Movement Adaptations to the Environment. Three developmental levels were identified within each of the groupings. The taxonomy was used to develop behavioral objectives at each level.

The curriculum design that was developed is summarized in figure 3.1. This yearly plan describes the topics or units of instruction to be taught to students at each of the three developmental levels. For example, the Level I program begins with a unit on Adjusting to the Learning Environment, then proceeds to a unit entitled Awareness and Appreciation of Self and Others. The units in the yearly plan for the curriculum

IV. Improving and achieving developmental self
   A. Basic skill patterns
   B. Performance strategies
   C. Social implications—Giving and accepting help
V. Adjustments in performance/behavior
   A. Self—Evaluation
   B. Flexibility to novelty in movement experience

Level III

I. Review—Adjusting to learning environment
   A. Conduct/rules/limitations
   B. Pupil involvement in environment structure
   C. Assessment (self/teacher)
II. Physiological aspects of physical education: Values
   A. Self-concept—Compassion/awareness of others
   B. Factors relating to sport skills
III. Skill refinement
   A. Mechanical principles
   B. Applying mechanical principles
   C. Movement generalizations of mechanical principles
IV. Peer communications
   A. Group structures
   B. Establish credibility with peers
   C. Cooperative attitudes (enterprises)
V. Evaluation
   A. Participatory confidence
   B. Confidence to initiate movement experience spontaneously and on command

are derived from the four general topical groupings and emphasize greater concern for the total development of the learner than for development of specific movement competencies.

Remember that a particular curriculum design is just one example of the many ways a physical education program can be developed from the curriculum model. For a more thorough understanding of the developmental curriculum model, examine the Project SEE materials or read *Meaningful Movement for Children* (Hoffman, Young, and Klesius 1981), which is included in the recommended reading list at the end of this

chapter. The approach proposed by Hoffman and his colleagues is similar to that of Project SEE. For an example
of a developmental approach at the secondary level, see
Melograno's *Designing Curriculum and Learning: A Physical Coeducation Approach* (Melograno 1979).

The developmental education model is probably the most
widely endorsed physical education curriculum model. Many
physical education programs have goals consistent with this
theoretical model. However, most of these programs have re-
tained a multi-activity organization and use instructional
strategies that make no provision for individual differences in
development. Frequently, little attention is given to designing
educational experiences that will directly affect specific developmental goals. There appears to be an assumption that development will automatically occur as a result of participation
in games and sports. Critics of the education-through-the-
physical approach have questioned whether physical education can produce the broad developmental outcomes it claims
(Siedentop 1980). They point to a lack of evidence that participation in physical education programs contributes to personal
and social development. The failure to individualize instruction has also been criticized (Lawson and Placek 1981). However, it should be noted that current developmental theorists
attempt to respond to these criticisms by focusing instruction
directly on developmental themes and by accommodating individual differences in development.

Humanistic Physical Education

Macdonald (1977, 17) notes that developmental education
"involves the concept of an elite group (e.g., mature vs.
immature or educated vs. ignorant) that knows the direction
'development' must take and how to guide this process." The
humanistic physical education curriculum model shares the
developmentalists' commitment that physical education
should contribute to the total well-being of the individual, but
stresses the *unique* qualities of each human being. The
prescriptive approach of the developmental model is replaced
by an emphasis upon student self-awareness and choice as
the basis for personal growth.

The work of Hellison (1973; 1978; 1982) is the most
complete description of the humanistic curriculum model in
physical education. Humanistic physical education uses
physical activity to assist the student in the search for
personal identity. It places "student self-esteem, self-
actualization, self-understanding and interpersonal relations

at the center of the physical education teaching-learning act" (Hellison 1978,1). The assumptions of the model are defined as follows:

> (1) Man's major goal in life is to actualize his own potentialities, to become all that he can become, to attain the status of the fully functioning person. Instead of the absence of sickness (negative), psychological health involves for him a high level "wellness" (positive). (2) Each individual has unique potentialities; no two people are the same in needs, abilities, or interests. As such, there is no justification for molding students into some predetermined shape. (3) Individuals must develop a "selective detachment" from their culture in order to avoid mirroring the values of society and thereby inhibiting individual development. (4) How a person feels is more important than what he knows; in fact, how he feels about himself (his self-esteem) and about what he is supposed to be learning will determine whether he will learn anything. Further, individuals with self-esteem difficulties will not be able to strive toward self-actualization to any extent. (5) No one is better able, at least potentially, than the person himself to determine how he best learns and what is most meaningful for him to learn. (Hellison 1973,4)

From D. Hellison, *Humanistic Physical Education*, p. 4. © 1973 Prentice-Hall, Inc., Englewood Cliffs, NJ. Reprinted by permission.

While many humanistic educators believe that goodness is an innate human characteristic, Hellison (1982) reports that he has abandoned this assumption. He proposes that behavior can be categorized either as personal preference or moral imperative. Education provides opportunities for self-reflection to clarify and develop personal preferences and experiences that focus on both affective and intellectual appreciation of moral choices and values. The goals of the physical education program are identified as:

1. To help students make their own self-body-world connection
2. To provide a sense of community
3. To facilitate an active playful spirit (Hellison 1978,3)

The conceptual framework for the curriculum is a system that describes the process of development leading to self-actualization. In *Beyond Balls and Bats*, Hellison identifies four levels of awareness that characterize self-development. In later work, he modifies the model to include the five developmental stages described in figure 3.2. The scope of the program is based on this framework. Experiences are provided that allow individual students to work at appropriate levels.

Risk	1. Toward an initial recognition of the marginal status of most high-risk youth, which includes feelings of powerlessness, extensive use of defense mechanisms, lack of involvement, attempts to discredit anything that appears to be meaningful, the need for immediate "highs" coupled with little deferred gratification, and harmful interpersonal behavior
Involvement	2. Toward involvement in some kind of physical activity—not necessarily learning in a formal sense but at least doing—accompanied by movement toward self-discipline to enable both the teacher and other students to go about their business
Self-direction	3. Toward self-direction that focuses on the development of personal preferences to meet personal needs by (a) interacting with a range of motor skill and exercise concepts and experiences, (b) setting personal goals and being held accountable for one's decisions, (c) developing a sense of process as well as purpose in one's life, (d) developing the courage to stand up for one's own aspirations in the face of peer pressures, and the like
Prosocial	4. Toward prosocial conduct, which is approached as a moral imperative consisting of five qualities: cooperation, group decision-making, helping others, the development of empathy, and learning to "pull one's own weight" in society
Integration	5. Toward the individual's integration of work (with a sense of purpose and process), play, prosocial conduct, and a healthy sense of humor (e.g., to be able to laugh at what one cannot fix), not as a list of items to be checked off one by one as the day or week progresses but as interdependent components to be lived in harmony

Figure 3.2
Framework for humanistic physical education
From D. Hellison, "Philosophy—Back to the Drawing Board," in *Journal of Health, Physical Education, Recreation and Dance*, vol. 53, no. 1 (1982): 43–44. © 1982 American Alliance for Health, Physical Education, Recreation and Dance, Reston, VA. Reprinted by permission.

The design that Hellison describes in *Beyond Balls and Bats* clarifies how this model could be implemented. The program is organized with two days of fitness activities, two days of skills instruction followed by play, and one day of new games and cooperative activities per week. Participation is optional, but students are expected to assume responsibility for the consequences of decisions. Discussions of the levels of awareness help students to increase self-understanding. As students demonstrate adequate self-discipline, they are permitted to develop and implement personal programs (see fig. 3.3). Journals are kept, which help students to focus on their feelings, goals, and behaviors.

Curriculum Theory

Despite the extensive use of the term *humanistic* in educational literature, the humanistic physical education model has not been widely implemented. However, a project sponsored by the governor of Oregon, in which Hellison prepared ten experienced physical educators to implement the model and to conduct workshops for teachers and youth leaders, should increase the impact of the model in that state (Hellison 1982).

One of the major challenges in implementing such a program is a result of its reliance upon the quality of the personal relationship between teacher and students. The teacher does not prescribe and direct learning activities, but facilitates and counsels the student involved in self-directed learning. This process requires a teacher who is authentic and caring. Hellison (1978,67) suggests that "the gym has got to become a comfortable place to be, a sanctuary perhaps, where students feel free to explore their connection to their bodies and to physical activities and where teachers can freely interact with students, caring and sharing who they are and encouraging students to do the same." Teachers accustomed to traditional programs may have difficulty assuming this new role and mastering the personalized instructional strategies required. Administrators may resist extensive student choice and individual programs.

Critics of humanistic education view the concept of self-actualization as lacking in clarity, resulting in an inability to clearly define program objectives (Siedentop 1980). As in the developmental model, concern is expressed about the lack of evidence to support personal and social outcomes (Lawson and Placek 1981). The distinction between education and therapy is described as blurred and questions are raised about the qualification of most teachers to use counseling techniques intended to promote emotional/psychological wellbeing (Siedentop 1980). On the other hand, the attention given to human relations skills and to personalizing instruction is generally viewed as a positive contribution of this model.

Fitness

The inclusion of the fitness approach in a discussion of curriculum models is somewhat problematic due to the absence of a comprehensive, contemporary description of such a model. However, increasing emphasis is being placed on wellness and active lifestyles; therefore we will attempt to examine fitness as a curriculum model. Like the developmental and humanistic models, the fitness approach

II. Connecting personal options to physical activity
choices (draw lines from your goals to those activities
which will help you reach your goals).

Personal options	Physical activity choices
Health:	x Stretching exercises
Aerobics x	x Weight training
Flexibility x	x Push-ups, sit-ups, other
Relaxation x	cals
Weight control x	x Circuit training
	x Jogging
Safety:	x Running-in-place
Speed x	x Interval training
Strength x	x Posture exercises
Self-defense x	x Relaxation/body awareness/
Water safety x	imagery
	x Yoga
Appearance:	x Self-defense
Muscle bulk x	x Karate/kung fu
Muscle shape x	x Boxing
Weight control x	x Wrestling
Posture x	x Swimming skills
	x Swimming fitness
Achievement:	x Trampoline/mini-tramp
Being competitive x	x Gymnastics
Developing courage ... x	x Football
Taking risks x	x Soccer
Developing talents ... x	x Basketball
Feeling better	x Volleyball
physically x	x Track & field
	x Baseball/softball
Play:	x Tennis
Have fun x	x Golf
Be creative x	x Handball
	x Balance exercises
	x Agility exercises
	x Speed exercises
	x
	x
	x

Personal program based on matching physical activity choices & personal options

---

First day:
  First fifteen minutes
    Activity _____

    What I will be doing _____

    _____

    _____

    My goal _____

    How I am going to measure my progress _____

    _____

  Second fifteen minutes

    Activity _____

    What I will be doing _____

    _____

    _____

    My goal _____

    How I am going to measure my progress _____

    _____

---

views physical education as a means to contribute to the well-being of individuals, but such contributions are limited to the area of health. Weber (1968) has defined physical education as "education in its application to the development and care of the body." He describes a physically educated person as one who knows about the effects of exercise on the body and applies this knowledge by exercising. Weber argues that viewing physical education as the science of exercise realigns its values with demonstrably attainable objectives, and emphasizes its unique role in education.

Historically, fitness programs were labelled "education-of-the-physical" and denounced by critics as training, not education. Contemporary programs are not limited to conditioning activities, but have adopted an educational perspective that emphasizes understanding, as well as performance. It is assumed that physical activity is essential to a healthy lifestyle and that the development of such a lifestyle requires: knowledge about the relationship of activity and health; skills in activities with health benefits; and a commitment to the importance of exercise.

The conceptual framework for the program is a delineation of the components of fitness. Many fitness programs restrict the curriculum to the health-related fitness components of cardiorespiratory function, body composition, flexibility, and strength. The scope of the curriculum includes knowledge about how these components are affected by exercise, and physical activities that contribute to one or more of the components. Activities without clear health benefits are omitted from the program. The structure of the curriculum is based on the conceptual framework. Theme units, focused on specific fitness components, are frequently combined with activity units, taught to emphasize health benefits. Progression within the program involves diagnosis of individual performance and development of personal fitness programs to remedy areas of weakness and acquire skills in activities appropriate to individual needs and interests.

The emphasis upon knowledge and understanding has resulted in the publication of many textbooks for use in fitness programs. One example is *Fitness for Life*, developed for secondary school physical education programs (Corbin and Lindsey 1983). Although its authors do not propose that fitness comprises the total physical education program, examination of this publication will give you a good understanding of the conceptual basis of the fitness curriculum model.

Developmental education programs seem to be placing increased emphasis on fitness, but few public school physical education programs seem to aim exclusively for fitness goals. Some college programs have adopted this orientation, and there has been an increase in fitness programs for adult populations. Throughout the country physical educators are receiving specialized training to prepare them to conduct such fitness programs.

Contemporary fitness programs seem to avoid the criticism that they are training and not education, but concerns continue to be expressed that the focus of such programs is too narrow (Lawson and Placek 1981). Siedentop (1980) has suggested that fitness programs, while valuable, are really health education and not physical education. The absence of a clear philosophic statement for the fitness perspective may indicate that most physical educators see fitness as part but not all of the physical education curriculum.

Movement Education

Perhaps the most visible alternative to the traditional "education-through-the-physical" approach is movement education. This model defines the content of physical education as human movement. The purpose of movement education is "the study of the principles which govern the purposeful control of living movement and the acquisition of skill in exerting that control, together with the self-understanding which attends such learning" (Stanley 1969,38).

The terminology of movement education is widely used in physical education literature, but the greatest curricular impact has been upon elementary school physical education. Although a number of authors have discussed movement education in elementary schools, this review will rely upon *Physical Education for Children* (Logsdon, Barrett, et al. 1977) due to the completeness with which it describes both the theoretical orientation underlying such programs and the practical information needed to implement the model. Logsdon and Barrett have expressed some reluctance to label their model *movement education* due to the confusion and misinterpretation surrounding that term. However, the model they describe seems to be an excellent example of the generic category of movement education. Logsdon suggests that movement education is a life-long process of motor development and learning and defines physical education as "that part of movement education which has been designated as a responsible, educational program (subject) in a school curriculum" (Logsdon et al. 1977,11). Logsdon and her colleagues (1977,14) identified six basic beliefs or assumptions upon which the curriculum model is based:

1. The learner is an individual; and his individuality varies from day to day, task to task, and moment to moment.
2. Teachers must respect the integrity of the learner and accept responsibility for the education of this whole being.
3. Teachers need a sincere dedication to each child in order to help him achieve his full potential by permitting him to become an increasingly independent learner.
4. The learner is capable of making decisions, and education is responsible for helping the learner develop the ability to make reasoned and wise choices so that he can adjust his role appropriately as his social and physical surroundings change.

From Bette J. Logsdon, et al., *Physical Education for Children.* © 1977 Lea & Febiger, Philadelphia, PA. Reprinted by permission.

5. Understandings and skills essential to progression can be developed by individuals at different times through different experiences.
6. Physical education, to share meaningfully in the education of the learner, must provide experiences that improve his ability to move, that engage his thought processes, and that contribute positively to his developing value system and to the esteem in which he regards himself and others.

From these beliefs and the definition of movement as the content of physical education, Logsdon and others (1977,17) derive these program objectives for the learner:

1. Move skillfully demonstrating versatile, effective, and efficient movement in situations requiring either planned or unplanned responses.
2. Become aware of the meaning, significance, feeling, and joy of movement both as a performer and as an observer.
3. Gain and apply the knowledge that governs human movement.

The conceptual framework that serves as the basis for decisions regarding movement content is an adaptation of a classification system developed by Laban for the purpose of analyzing and describing movement (Laban and Lawrence 1947). Laban's framework, as adapted by Logsdon and Barrett, is depicted in figure 3.4.

The framework serves to elaborate and expand one's perception of the movement content. It also defines the scope of the physical education curriculum, telling us that in a complete program students will have the opportunity to understand and master each of these dimensions of movement. The structure and sequence of the program are also derived from Laban's work. Laban identified sixteen movement themes that established a progression to be used by teachers of dance in developing movement competence (Laban 1963). Logsdon and Barrett have adapted these themes for each of the areas of content included in the model: educational dance, educational games, and educational gymnastics. The themes, listed in figure 3.5, serve as the basis for designing units of instruction. For each of these themes, objectives and ideas for learning activities are discussed. An example of a unit plan is included in chapter 6.

Movement

Aspects	Dimensions
Body----(what body does)	Actions of the body
	Actions of body parts
	Activities of body
	Shapes of body
Effort----(how body moves)	Time
	Weight
	Space
	Flow
Space----(where body moves)	Areas
	Directions
	Levels
	Pathways
	Planes
	Extensions
Relationship----(what relationships occur)	Body parts
	Individuals and groups
	Apparatus and equipment
	Other types

Figure 3.4
Adaptation of Laban's framework for classifying movement
From Bette J. Logsdon, et al., *Physical Education for Children.* © 1977 Lea & Febiger, Philadelphia, PA. Reprinted by permission.

Educational Dance	Educational Games	Educational Gymnastics
Theme 1: Introduction to the body	Theme 1: Introduction to basic body and manipulative control	Theme 1: Introduction to the body
Theme 2: Introduction to weight and time	Theme 2: Introduction to space	Theme 2: Introduction to space
Theme 3: Introduction to space	Theme 3: Introduction to movement quality (effort)	Theme 3: Introduction to time
Theme 4: The flow of movement	Theme 4: Movement flow	Theme 4: Introduction to relationships of body parts
Theme 5: Introduction to relationships	Theme 5: Introduction to basic relationships	Theme 5: Introduction to weight
Theme 6: Instrumental use of the body	Theme 6: Advanced body and manipulative control	Theme 6: Flow and continuity in movement
Theme 7: The basic effort actions	Theme 7: Introduction to complex relationships	Theme 7: Relationship to others
		Theme 8: Introduction to rhythm

Figure 3.5
Movement themes for organizing and developing movement education content
From Bette J. Logsdon, et al., *Physical Education for Children.* © 1977 Lea & Febiger, Philadelphia, PA. Reprinted by permission.

The movement education model has had a visible impact on elementary school physical education. In many schools, the entire physical education program is based upon the model. However, in other schools, a unit of instruction called "movement exploration" or "basic movement" is included as one component of the program—an approach that should not be confused with the movement education model.

Several issues have been raised by critics of movement education as it has evolved over the past thirty years. Some dispute the definition of movement as the content of physical education, contending that movement outside the context of play loses the meaning inherent in physical education and is less motivating to students. Fear is expressed that the emphasis upon concepts of movement will result in intellectualization of content at the expense of activity. Some feel that movement education relies too heavily on problem solving and exploration strategies, resulting in mediocre, rather than quality, skill performance. Efforts to teach general movement ability as a way to prepare students for new movement situations have been criticized as unsubstantiated claims for transfer of learning (Locke 1969; Siedentop 1980; Lawther 1977).

These critics have addressed the general topic of movement education and have not examined the specific model described by Logsdon and her colleagues. Some of the concerns raised (intellectualization of content, emphasis upon exploration, and claims for transfer) do not seem applicable to the model described in *Physical Education for Children*. In addition, some of the problems cited may result from inadequate implementation of the model rather than from the model itself.

To develop and implement a movement education program requires thorough understanding of the Laban framework and concept of themes. The teacher also needs skill in observing and analyzing movement, and in a range of instructional strategies. Many physical educators may lack the necessary expertise to conduct a quality movement education program. Critics of movement education have acknowledged the positive impact of the emphasis on maximum involvement of all children and the recognition of individual differences. Another accepted strength of the model is its effort to integrate and interrelate the content in games, dance, and gymnastics, and to provide a logical basis for progression in these areas.

Kinesiological Studies

The influence of movement education has been limited primarily to elementary schools. Some secondary school programs have also focused upon the understanding and mastery of human movement, but these programs have tended to use a conceptual framework derived from the disciplinary foundations of physical education (kinesiological studies). Such a curriculum model is described by Lawson and Placek (1981) in *Physical Education in the Secondary Schools: Curricular Alternatives.* They define the subject matter of physical education as ''a unique blend of performance skills and experiences in sport, exercise, dance and contests with that knowledge about performance which is derived from the disciplinary foundations of the field.'' The assumptions of the model and goals for the program are summarized in figure 3.6. Lawson and Placek note the similarity of the assumptions and goals to those underlying elementary school movement education programs.

Lawson and Placek describe the physically educated individual as one who knows how to perform, knows about performance, and possesses the capacity for self-directed learning. Because of this emphasis upon self-directed learning or problem solving skills, the authors have labelled their approach a *process* curricular model. They propose that in a process model, learning should be enjoyable or intrinsically rewarding and should permit students to build upon past experiences to form new perceptions and concepts. To facilitate these outcomes, the model recommends that student-centered learning be directed toward the fundamental ''structure'' of the subject matter. The conceptual framework for the model appears to be a delineation of the components of the problem solving process and of the structure of the subject matter. In other publications, Lawson and Morford (1979) emphasize that physical education is a cross-disciplinary field in which discrete portions of several disciplines are integrated and magnified to examine movement phenomena. Although Lawson and Placek (1981) do not specifically describe the structure of the physical education content, examples of units of instruction include such topics as:

Exercise and fitness
Nutrition, exercise, and cardiovascular disease
Biomechanics
Play, game, and sport
Mind-body unity and aesthetics
Motor learning

Figure 3.6
Assumptions underlying kinesiological studies curricula
From Hal A. Lawson and Judith H. Placek, *Physical Education in the Secondary Schools: Curricular alternatives.* © 1981 Allyn and Bacon, Boston, MA. Reprinted by permission.

1. The primary purposes of secondary school physical education programs are:
   a. To enable students to learn how to move more skillfully.
   b. To enable students to understand the variables which affect and effect their participation in physical and ludic activities.
   c. To assist students with the integration of newly-acquired skills and forms of knowledge with those which were learned previously.
   d. To refine each student's abilities to employ rationally skills and knowledges derived from physical education to real-life problems.
2. The physically educated student should be capable of self-directed learning when formal schooling terminates.
   a. Problem-solving methods (or modes of inquiry) are important forms of content which are to be learned in physical education.
   b. Students should learn how and where to acquire additional resources for problem solving which exist outside the school.
3. The physical education curriculum should be appropriately tailored to each student's needs and interests.
   a. Students' learning should be self-paced and personalized.
   b. Students should be afforded the opportunity to make choices between and among activities and/or problems which they are to address. The process for making choices and both the anticipated and subsequently real consequences of their choices represent content that should be emphasized by physical education teachers.
4. For the most part, forms of knowledge which are to be learned initially by students in physical education are best acquired by experiential learning. Games and sports afford the opportunity for experiential learnings to occur. As such, games and sports should be viewed as educational media in the same ways that games are viewed in other school subjects (e.g., wifn' proof in mathematics, monopoly in economics, etc.).
5. The introduction of appropriate cognitive and affective concepts in physical education can facilitate cross-subject matter application and integration.

Curriculum Theory

In the process of solving problems in these areas, students utilize existing knowledge and acquire new knowledge, which they can apply to their own motor performances. The conceptual framework for the kinesiological studies model is depicted in figure 3.7. Although not all kinesiological studies models emphasize problem solving, this focus upon the process of discovering knowledge is consistent with the discipline-based subject areas of the 1950s and 1960s.

Figure 3.7
Conceptual framework for kinesiological studies From Hal A. Lawson and Judith H. Placek, *Physical Education in the Secondary Schools: Curricular alternatives.* © 1981. Allyn and Bacon, Boston, MA and Hal A. Lawson and W. R. Morford, "The cross disciplinary structure of kinesiology and sport studies: distinctness, implications and advantages," *Quest,* 1979, 31, 222–230. Reprinted by permission.

Components of problem solving (Lawson and Placek 1981):

  Identification of pertinent problems

  Modes for problem solving

  Application of knowledge

  Experience in solving problems

Structure of the subject matter (Lawson and Morford 1979):

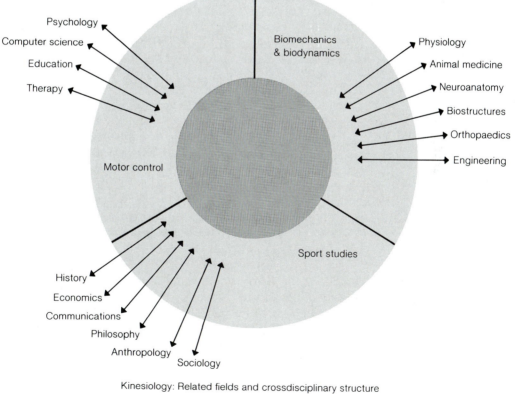

Kinesiology: Related fields and crossdisciplinary structure

Lawson and Placek describe alternative ways in which the curriculum can be organized. One option is to retain an activity organization with an emphasis upon skills instruction, but to integrate disciplinary concepts into the activity units and relate such cognitive information to instruction in other subject matter areas. Such an approach is illustrated in figure 3.8. Another alternative is to organize units around specific concepts; students participate in laboratory experiences involving active learning. But this approach de-emphasizes specific skills instruction (Lawson and Placek 1981,85). Following the introduction to concepts, electives are available that permit the student to develop skills in activities and to pursue more advanced disciplinary knowledge. Lawson and Placek provide a description of a curricular model that includes examples of each of these forms of organization.

Although the Lawson and Placek publication deals only with secondary school programs, the model has been applied to the development of programs for kindergarten through

Figure 3.8
Example of program structure in kinesiological studies model
From Hal A. Lawson and Judith H. Placek, *Physical Education in the Secondary Schools: Curricular alternatives.*
© 1981 Allyn and Bacon, Boston, MA. Reprinted by permission.

Grade 9 Activity	Units in related subjects	Content in conjunction with activity	Basic skills
Soccer-speedball	Cardio-respiratory system (physiology) Graphs (mathematics) Sport in England (European history) Leverage (general science) Situational ethics (human relations)	Evolution of these sports Specificity of training principle Physiological reactions to exercise, pulse rates, and their relation to O_2 consumption and caloric expenditure; introduction to weight control Levers of the body and force production Ethical factors in participation Team plan and cooperative efforts	Goalie play Kicking-passing Trapping Dribbling Heading Shooting Tackling Dodging Strategy, rules Throwing patterns

grade twelve. However, most of the interest in this approach has been in secondary schools. Many secondary schools and colleges have initiated one or two concept units, usually in the area of exercise and fitness, but only a few schools have fully implemented a kinesiological studies program. The publication by AAHPERD of the *NASPE Basic Stuff* series (Kneer 1981) may encourage such an approach. The series identifies basic concepts in each of six disciplinary areas (exercise physiology, kinesiology, motor learning, psycho-social aspects, humanities, and motor development) and illustrates ways in which such concepts can be taught to children and adolescents. Examples of concepts and learning activities identified as appropriate for adolescents are included in figure 3.9. Although the National Association for Sports and Physical Education did not recommend or endorse a particular curriculum model, the applicability of the *Basic Stuff* series to the kinesiological studies model is evident.

Grade 9 Activity	Units in related subjects	Content in conjunction with activity	Basic skills
Tumbling and apparatus Movement exploration Rhythms	Turverein (European history) Gravity (physics) Joint structures and types (general science or biology) Line, space, motion, and color (art and photography)	Mechanical bases of balance and support (a) center of gravity (b) principles of stability Structural-functional limitations in these rolls performance contexts Continuation of training specificity Aesthetics of movement performance	Danish gym-rhythm Ropes, balls, Hoops, music Somersaults Cartwheels Handstands Headstands Arials Handsprings Vaulting Bars
Lead-up games for volleyball	Principles of force production and absorption (general science) Social interaction (human relations)	Continuation of training specificity Force production Angles of projection Games as forms of social interaction	Bump, set, Spike Dig and roll Service Strategy rules

Figure 3.9
Examples of basic stuff
concepts and learning
activities
From M. E. Kneer, et al.,
*Adolescence Basic Stuff
Series II.* © 1981
American Alliance for
Health, Physical
Education, Recreation
and Dance, Reston, VA.
Reprinted by permission.

Exercise Physiology

Inactivity more than food contributes to obesity. There is no evidence that regular exercise leads to the development of obesity because of overstimulation of the appetite. Obese individuals move less throughout the day, but do not necessarily eat more.

Learning Activities:

1. Have each student conduct an investigation of one obese person. Have them record exercise calories burned versus food intake calories for one week. Write up results.
2. Plan vigorous activities and organize the class so that maximum time can be given to activity.
3. Encourage students to be physically active over vacations and weekends.

Psycho-Social

Feelings about our own body image are greatly influenced by social stereotypes. We must acknowledge that there is some stereotyping done by others about each of us based upon how we look. Sheldon suggested three basic body types: endomorphic (spherical), ectomorphic (linear), and mesomorphic (the inverted V or athletic build). The first two shapes are often stereotyped as negative, and the third positive. These generalizations are inaccurate. You can enhance the conformation and capabilities of all body types. Each body type that is appropriately developed will be suitable for a particular sport.

Learning Activities:

1. Identify body types in class. Observe whether the stereotypes fit the somatotype. Discuss.
2. Study the body types of athletes in different sports. Identify common body traits. Encourage participation in sports or positions on teams which most approximate these types.
3. Plan and make available weight training and aerobic dance classes, and encourage students wishing to improve their body image to enroll.

Curriculum Theory

Motor Learning

Cue abbreviation is important to skilled performance. The more complex the movement, the more time is necessary for selecting, planning, and initiating it. "Cue abbreviation" helps to predict and prepare earlier.

Learning Activities:

1. Have class observe a live demonstration or film of a performance. Instruct class to look for cues. Ask what they saw. Repeat several times. Suggest that they look for "telegraphed intentions," common patterns, expected strategy, player characteristics.
2. After several practice games in which the activity is taught, ask class to identify "personal characteristic cues" of classmates, and common patterns.
3. Suggest that students watch for personal cues of selected players while watching televised sporting events.

Motor Development

Muscle size is influenced by the sex hormones and exercise. Muscle size and mass increases with growth and with exercise. Pre-adolescent boys and girls and women do not have the hormone testosterone in sufficient quantity to bring about a large increase in the muscle size with exercise. Strength is not dependent solely on size.

Learning Activities:

1. Where strength is an advantage in a sex-integrated class, post differentiated grading scales based on muscle strength. Examples: weight training, field events, flag football, basketball, soccer.
2. Plan experimental activities in a weight training class to illustrate the concept.

Kinesiology

Spin results when force is applied off the center of the object. The force can be applied by the hands, a racket, or the foot when kicking. The two factors which determine the behavior of the ball are where the force is applied relative to the center of gravity of the ball, and the amount of force applied.

Fig. 3.9 cont.

Learning Activities:

1. Use any ball-type activity. Plan a drill or task which experiments with applying force off-center and with the amount of force. Plan applications of force above, below, and to the sides of the ball. Discuss how spin aids or inhibits performance of skill in the sport being studied and in other sports.
2. Select a variety of objects for experimenting with spin: volleyball, basketball, frisbee, golf ball, softball, and table tennis ball. Practice throwing or striking off center. Watch the spin and note the rebound.
3. Teach the application of force concept to produce spin in the sports where it is a performance factor: tennis, golf, basketball, volleyball, racquetball, softball, and table tennis.

Humanities

Achievement may be based on the comparison with others or self, and personal accomplishment. Most performers acknowledge at least three kinds of achievements in relation to their performance goals:

1. Achievements that are compared with others.
2. Achievements that mark personal progress.
3. Achievements that result in reaching a goal such as running three miles or completing a dance.

Learning Activities:

1. Plan, promote, and reward all 3 type of goals. For example, a volleyball unit may (1) provide a class tournament for comparing with others, (2) provide formative tasks for personal progress, and (3) encourage students to create strategies to reach personal goals.
2. Allow the student to propose his own personal evaluation program for grades.

The implementation of a kinesiological studies model requires that teachers have mastery of performance skills, expertise in the scientific foundations of the field, and the ability to make such information relevant to students. The problem solving process and the use of laboratory experiences require a shift of roles and behavior for both teacher and students.

Critics have expressed many of the same concerns about the kinesiological studies model as were raised about movement education. The use of concept units involving laboratory settings, particularly, has produced objections to the intellectualization of physical education and the deemphasis of activity and play (Siedentop 1980). However, advocates of kinesiological studies point out that knowledge and performance are integrated throughout the program.

Play Education

Curriculum development has been described as a process that provides access to valued forms of knowledge and experience (Peters 1965; Huebner 1970). Some knowledge or experience has instrumental value due to the results it produces, such as health, employability, etc. Other knowledge or experience has intrinsic value due to the qualities that make it an immediately enriching, prized, human activity—regardless of its future or long-range effects. The play education curriculum model views play as an intrinsically valuable activity, which is "at the center of life, an important aspect of human existence." (Siedentop 1980,258). Play is an activity, voluntarily entered into for its own sake, but it is not frivolous or effortless. One learns to play. Complex adult forms of play, such as sport, dance, art, music, and drama, require education in order to participate fully. Physical education is seen as one of several forms of play education and is defined as "any process that increases a person's tendencies and abilities to play competitive and expressive motor activities." (Siedentop 1980,253)

Siedentop (1980,265), the major spokesperson for the play education curriculum model, has summarized the assumptions of the theory:

> First a program theory of physical education must demonstrate that it optimizes the meaning-making potential of the subject matter. Second, there is meaning inherent in playing the activities of physical education. Third, the source of that meaning is revealed most clearly through an understanding of the concept

of play-play rather than physical activity, fitness, or human movement. Fourth, because physical education is a form of play education it must be judged by the degree to which the experiences it provides are educationally valuable, that is, the degree to which they increase subject matter approach tendencies and abilities. Fifth, a definition of physical education should reveal the logical and psychological meaning of the concept and place it properly in its educational context; thus, physical education means any process that increases a person's tendencies and abilities to play competitive and expressive motor activities. Sixth, the mastery of ludus enriches the play experience and requires instruction, skill, training, and socialization; thus establishing play as a valid educational concern. Seventh, and finally, the meaning derived from playing the subject matter of physical education can be best protected and enhanced by a general aim and more specific objectives that are consistent with the definition, and therefore intrinsic to the subject matter itself.

The conceptual framework used as a basis for the curricular model is the typology of play developed by Roger Callois (1961). The scope of physical education is defined as including motor activities in Callois's categories of *agon* (competitive) and *mimicry* (simulative or expressive), but not *alea* (chance). The structure of the program utilizes units focused upon specific play activities, since movement unrelated to the play context is not considered relevant to the subject matter of physical education. The sequence of program content is derived from Callois's suggestion that ways of playing can be arranged on a continuum from *paidia* or spontaneous, carefree child's play to *ludus*, or regulated, complex play requiring increasing amounts of skill, effort, and ingenuity. As individuals develop as players, they become more and more skillful in the movements, rituals, and other features that give meaning to the play experience. The role of play education is to help students acquire such skill that they may engage in the higher levels of play. Siedentop has expanded this idea of progression by developing the hierarchy of program objectives described in figure 3.10.

What does a play education program look like? The content selected is comprised of a range of competitive and expressive play activities, including both traditional and new forms of play. Elementary school programs focus upon "child's play" and developing the basic skills needed for such play. The middle school program is a two-year multi-activity program with the primary aim of exploration and counseling. After sixth grade, students gradually begin to select their own

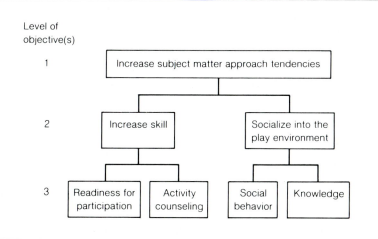

Level of objective(s)

1 — Increase subject matter approach tendencies

2 — Increase skill | Socialize into the play environment

3 — Readiness for participation | Activity counseling | Social behavior | Knowledge

Figure 3.10
Hierarchy of program objectives for play education
From Siedentop, Daryl, *Physical Education: Introductory analysis* 3d. ed. © 1972, 1976, 1980 Wm. C. Brown Publishers, Dubuque, Iowa. All Rights Reserved. Reprinted by permission.

activities, with the program becoming fully elective by grade ten. Beginning, intermediate, and advanced levels of instruction are available and students have the opportunity to concentrate upon one or two activities, if so desired. Community resources are used to expand the number of activities available and a strong intramural and sports club program is conducted. Quality instruction is provided, with the emphasis upon helping participants more fully enjoy the play experience. Creation of a play environment that is positive not coercive is a priority.

Although few physical education programs have publicly endorsed the play education philosophy, in practice some seem to exemplify the characteristics of such a model. Activity-centered programs, which emphasize the development of competence in the activity and allow students to select those activities they wish to pursue, are consistent with this model. If a program aims for mastery and enjoyment of sport and dance activities for their own sakes, it is a play education program. Lawson and Placek (1981) have observed that many lifetime sports programs are based upon a play education model. Some youth sports programs and club sports programs also exemplify the play education model, as do many dance education programs. The aim of most dance programs is mastery and understanding of dance forms. Students learn technique, aesthetic principles, and the choreographic process. They experience several forms of dance, and then may choose to concentrate upon mastery of a particular form.

Instructional programs are generally supplemented by opportunities to participate in a dance club. The emphasis of the program is upon becoming a dancer, not upon using dance as an instrument for personal improvement or physical fitness. Much of the dissatisfaction of dance educators with an affiliation with physical education has been based upon the tendency of physical educators to view dance and sports instrumentally, rather than as intrinsically valuable activities.

The central criticism of the play education model is that play and physical education are essentially different because physical education is not voluntary and is utilitarian rather than nonproductive. Questions are also raised about the relationship between play behaviors learned in youth, and the leisure behavior of adults. Will a student who masters a sport in high school continue to play as an adult? The assumption that increased skill will increase the tendency to play also has been questioned (Lawson and Placek 1981). From a practical point of view, some question the political feasibility of justifying play education to administrators and taxpayers.

Personal Meaning

The personal meaning curriculum model also asserts that, for an experience to be educational, it must have meaning and significance for the individual. The discovery and creation of meaning is viewed as the central task of education. However, in contrast to the play education model, personal meaning can be approached either intrinsically or instrumentally, and the source of meaning in movement is not limited to the play context. The focus may be upon the feelings of joy, pleasure, and satisfaction inherent in the movement experience itself, or upon the use of movement activities to accomplish some extrinsic goal important to the participant. The role of the educator is to analyze potential sources of meaning, to provide a wide range of opportunities, and to respond supportively to the individual's search for meaning.

The search for meaning has received increasing attention in physical education curriculum literature. Johnson et al (1975) have prepared a textbook for college physical education programs that attempts ''to incorporate the identification and application of feelings and emotions into the study of one's personal involvement with sports and exercise.'' Allen (1982) developed a model that describes intrinsic values of movement experiences from a psychological perspective. Kenyon (1968) identifies six types of perceived instrumental values of participation in physical activities: social, health and fitness, vertigo, aesthetic, catharsis, and ascetic. Bain (1978) suggests that these values could serve as the conceptual framework for a personal meaning curriculum in which students choose concept and activity units relevant to their selected goals.

The most thorough description of the personal meaning curriculum model is the work of Jewett and her colleagues (1977) related to the development of the Purpose Process Curriculum Framework. It is important to note that, while a good deal of curriculum research has been directed toward the development of the Purpose Process Curriculum Framework (PPCF), a great deal more attention has been directed toward the PPCF as a conceptual framework, than toward its delineation as a curriculum model. Much scholarly activity has been directed toward theory-building, validation of particular theoretical constructs, definition of elements, and delineation of key concepts. Thus, the theoretical base for this illustration of the personal meaning curriculum model has been the subject of considerable study. It is, therefore, more carefully delineated than most of the other conceptual frameworks that have been used by the designers of physical education curriculum models. However, the refinement of models based on this conceptual framework has been much less extensive than that available to local curriculum planners using some of the other models described in this chapter.

In presentations of the PPCF, physical education is defined as "personalized, self-directed learning, using selected movement learning media to achieve individual human goals" (Jewett and Mullan 1977,1). The framework is based on the assumption that human beings of all ages have the same fundamental purposes for moving. These purposes are unique ways of finding or extending personal meaning through movement activities. Physical education curricula should provide individuals with opportunities to become aware of these possibilities and to develop personal abilities appropriate to their realization (Jewett and Mullan 1977,4). Jewett (1981) has summarized the basic beliefs underlying the Purpose Process Curriculum Framework as follows:

1. Persons are holistic beings, continuously in the process of becoming, who can intend what they will do . . . and for what purpose.
2. The creation and enhancement of meaning is the fundamental concern of education.
3. The primary concern of physical education is the personal search for meaning by the individual moving in interaction with the environment.

4. The basic goals of education are individual development, environmental coping, and social interaction.
5. Process skills are essential learnings.
6. Today's curriculum requires a future orientation.
7. Goal priorities, content selections, and sequence decisions are determined at the local level.

The conceptual framework for the design of the physical education program is the Purpose Process Curriculum Framework described in appendix A. Its two major components are a series of participant purposes for moving and a movement process category system. Twenty-two purposes for moving are identified and grouped into seven major categories. The physical education curriculum, designed at the local level, selects purposes for emphasis based on their significance to the students being served, but all students are provided with experiences leading to the development of the seven major purposes: physiological efficiency, psychic equilibrium, spatial orientation, object manipulation, communication, group interaction, and cultural involvement. Such broad exposure provides the basis for increasing personalization of the program. Jewett (1980a) has suggested that the purposes can be grouped into three value clusters: fitness, performance, and transcendence (fig. 3.11). Personal meaning in movement or physical activity can be sought through any one or any combination of the three.

The content for the personal meaning curriculum is structured in terms of potential meanings for participants. The conceptual framework upon which a personal meaning curriculum is based highlights personal purposes, human intentions, individual incentive motivations, or some other network of personal meanings. In a personal meaning curriculum based on the Purpose Process Curriculum Framework, the structure of the content is derived from both the purpose dimension and the process dimension of the framework. Instruction is usually organized around specific purpose concepts, either by developing theme units (e.g. circulorespiratory efficiency, object projection, movement appreciation) or by teaching sport or dance activity units with an emphasis upon particular purposes or goals (e.g. fitness, teamwork, cultural understanding). The selection of specific content within the unit is based upon an analysis of the subelements of the purpose category and upon the process dimension of the framework.

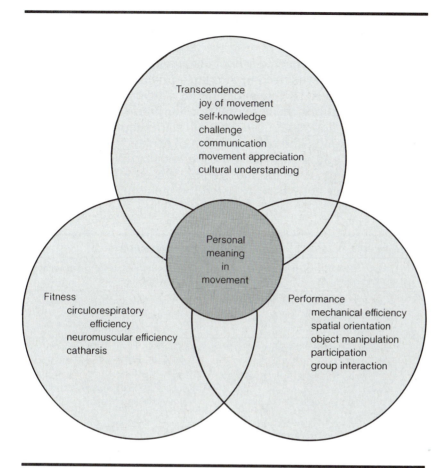

Figure 3.11
Personal meaning value
clusters
From Ann E. Jewett, "The
Status of Physical
Education Curriculum
Theory," *Quest,* 32, 1980,
163–173. © 1980 Human
Kinetic Publishers,
Champaign, IL. Reprinted
by permission.

Personal meaning in a curriculum based on the Purpose Process Curriculum Framework is also sought through a focus on the learning process. The program content is designed to guide students in the processes of learning to move and moving to learn. The process categories of the PPCF describe the ways in which a human being learns movement: perceiving, patterning, adapting, refining, varying, improvising, and composing. These process skills are, themselves, program content to be learned by students. Students not only need to experience each of the processes, but also need to understand and know how to utilize processes to achieve their purposes. The processes also provide a basis for planning and sequencing instructional activities. Teachers can use them to generate objectives for groups or individuals, and as a basis for evaluating student performance (see chap. 5).

Figure 3.12
Curriculum model based
on PPCF
From Ann E. Jewett and
M. R. Mullen. *Curriculum
Design: Purposes in
physical education
teaching-learning.*
© 1977 American Alliance
for Health, Physical
Education, Recreation
and Dance, Reston, VA.
Reprinted by permission.

Jewett has described several models of physical education curricula based on the PPCF. Some are futuristic descriptions (Jewett 1980b) and others describe models developed for implementation in specific school districts (Jewett and Mullan 1977). The PPCF was used to develop a physical education curriculum for a K-12 school district in Calgary, Alberta. Figure 3.12 outlines the core program for grade ten and illustrates the approach used. Students are required to take five units of games and one unit each of fitness, personal development, and dance. Within each subject area, the purpose concepts to be emphasized have been identified. Several possible activities are listed for each subject area.

Subject area	Concepts	Possible activities
Fitness: 1 unit	*Circulo-respiratory efficiency (A-1) self-knowledge (B-5)*	Cross country running, cross country skiing, jogging
Personal development: 1 unit	*Neuro-muscular efficiency (A-3) (balance, agility, co-ordination) challenge (B-7)*	Tumbling, floor routines, apparatus— trampolining
Games: 5 units 2 goal types	*Object manipulation (D)/projection (D-12) reception (D-13)* a) one using the body to manipulate the object b) one using an implement to manipulate the object	Body: a) Basketball, soccer, team handball, flag football, rugby b) Ice hockey, floor hockey, lacrosse, broomball, field hockey
	Group interaction (F)/teamwork (F-17) competition (F-18)	
2 net types	*Object manipulation (D)/projection (D-12) reception (D-13)* a) one net game using the hands to manipulate the object b) one net game using an implement to manipulate the object	a) Volleyball b) Badminton, tennis
	Spacial relationships (C-10)	
1 of: target or combative types	*Target* Object projection (D-12), catharsis (B-6)	Curling, golf, archery, bowling
	Combative Maneuvering weight (D-11), neuro- muscular efficiency (A-3) (agility)	Wrestling, self defense, judo
Dance: 1 unit	Participation (G-20), joy of movement (B-4), clarification (E-15)	Folk dancing, social dancing, square dancing, modern dancing

In developing instructional units for the activities, the process dimension of the PPCF has been used in writing performance objectives. Figure 3.13 illustrates a lesson plan from a grade ten basketball unit that emphasizes the purpose concepts of teamwork and competition and reflects use of the movement process category system in developing objectives.

Basketball

Grade 10: A five lesson unit

Key concepts: Teamwork (17) and Competition (18)

In the game of basketball the concepts of teamwork and competition must be interacting as players learn to cooperate in order to compete effectively.

The concept "offense", as part of the game, develops from ball possession and movement patterns executed to score a basket. The concept "defense" applies to some type of spatial arrangement of players that attempts to deny a score and regain possession. Offense and defense are inverse concepts that have a relationship dictated by the rules.

Sub-concepts

Offense (possession	Defense non-possession)
1. penetration	deny
2. depth	depth
3. mobility	balance
4. width	help

Lesson one

Concepts:

Offense	Defense
1. penetration	deny
2. depth	depth

Skills

1. Fast-break components: rebound, outlet, penetration, fill lanes
2. Defense--one player defense against penetration, against shooter
3. Defense--two player defense tandem and side-by-side
4. Create and use an inverse situation-- *"turnover"*

Figure 3.13
Lesson plan based on PPCF
From Arlene Fay McGinn, ''Conceptual model for games teaching with focus on personal integration.'' Doctoral Dissertation, University of Georgia, Athens GA.
© 1979 Arlene Fay McGinn. Reprinted by permission.

Fig. 3.13 cont.

Potential learning outcomes:

The student will demonstrate the ability to:

1. Examine the activity to have a clear idea of purpose, expectations and way of achieving performance levels. *(perceiving)*
2. Utilize basketball terminology: "offense", "defense", "penetration", "deny."(application-cognitive)
3. Add terms like: "outlet", "head-man", "fill the lanes", "fast break", "read a defense." (comprehension-cognitive)
4. Execute the following components of the fast break with no defense. *(patterning)*
   a) defensive rebound, outlet pass,
   b) fill an empty lane, stay wide,
   c) receive an outlet pass, penetrate mid-court with the dribble,
   d) head-man the ball to the cutter,
   e) follow for a rebound: depth.
5. Execute the following defensive movements: *(patterning)*
   a) one defender--mid-court to deny penetration,
   b) one defender--free throw line to defense cutter,
   c) two defenders--tandem: depth,
   d) two defenders--side by side
6. Refine your movement patterns as you *"read"* the spatial and temporal arrangements of your teammates. *(perceiving, refining)*
7. Adjust and vary your movements to the ball, your opponents, and your teammates in two-on-two game situations. *(adapting, varying)*
8. "Read" possible two-on-two game situation in order to be flexible. *(perceiving, improvising)*
   a) see the ball, see the man in order to predict a pass and create a turnover,
   b) think inverse after a turnover to move immediately into a penetrating pattern,
   c) improvise, use unique or creative moves to gain advantage.

Role of the teacher:

1. To structure the basketball environment so the players could explore, modify and refine movements to solve problems related to concepts of teamwork and competition
2. To present statements in the form of questions to challenge the student to clarify movement patterns
3. To be open to encourage alternative responses from the students
4. To provide feedback that reinforces individuality and diversity

The impact of the Purpose Process Curriculum Framework on curriculum theorizing in physical education has been extensive, but implementation of personal meaning curricula in school physical education programs limited. The early efforts associated with the PPCF, however, have focused on research rather than on the dissemination of the model. Research studies have examined the perceptions of educators and students regarding the value of the purposes, the program content associated with selected purposes, and the teaching strategies associated with developing process skills.

Most of the criticisms of the PPCF relate to a lack of communication concerning its adaptation as a curriculum model. The emphasis to date has been on theory building; very few examples of curricula based on the PPCF have been published. Criticisms have necessarily been directed toward the conceptual clarity, terminology, and definitional precision of the conceptual framework itself. While these are appropriate issues for scholarly debate, from the standpoint of a personal meaning curriculum model, there has been very little examination of its potential for practice, and only limited experimentation with the model in action in schools.

This model has been criticized because it is difficult to use without understanding (1) the conceptual framework, and (2) the relationship between the selection of the participant's purposes for engaging in movement activities and the translation of these purposes into statements of desired program outcomes. A commitment to providing a broad range of experiences leading to the development of all seven major purposes does not, of itself, necessarily result in personalized programs. The current problems are: (1) there are not enough examples in practice to which the interested curriculum planner may be directed, (2) this particular framework cannot be translated into a model that provides a recipe for program development, and (3) its effective implementation depends upon a curriculum planner and teacher knowledgeable both in the art and science of human movement, and in the theoretical basis of the PPCF as a conceptual framework.

All these problems are being addressed by the developers. At the present time, however, the stage of development of the PPCF as a personal meaning curriculum model is considerably less advanced than the level of sophistication of the conceptual framework itself. It is also important to note that this is but one conceptual framework that can be used to develop a personal meaning curriculum model.

Figure 3.14
Summary description of
curriculum models

	Developmental	Humanistic	Fitness
Beliefs	Opportunity for maximum development Development holistic with individual differences Learning how to learn	Individual uniqueness Feelings more important than knowledge Student best determines how and what to learn	Unique role of physical education is its contribution to health
Goals	Competence Individuality Socialization Integration of experience	Self-body-world connection Sense of community Active playful spirit	Knowledge about fitness Skills in activities with health benefits Commitment to regular exercise
Conceptual framework	Developmental characteristics	Stages of development in self-direction	Components of health-related fitness
Program design	Developmental themes	Expanding self-awareness and responsible choice	Knowledge and activities related to fitness

Observations

Many comparisons have been implied in the presentation of physical education curriculum models. However, the models, like apples and oranges, are not strictly comparable. This is primarily a function of the fact that different aspects have been emphasized in the curriculum development process, and that the current models are at different stages of development. Among the models illustrated, only the developmental education, movement education, and personal meaning models reflect a complete, carefully delineated, conceptual framework. On the other hand, the models that provide the most descriptive structure for program organization are kinesiological studies, movement education, play education, and fitness.

A curriculum model includes several elements: clarification of its value base (beliefs and goals); identification of the conceptual framework used to define the elements of the curriculum; and a description of the program design that

Curriculum Theory

Movement education	Kinesiological studies	Play education	Personal meaning
Individual uniqueness Holistic integrity Increasing independence	Experiential learning of knowledge Learning how to learn	Play valuable as source of meaning Quality play requires education	Holistic purposeful beings Education—the creation of meaning Process skills essential
Move skillfully Aware of meaning of movement Knowledge about movement	Move skillfully Knowledge about movement Problem-solving ability	Increase tendency and ability to play by a. increasing skill b. socializing into play environment	Individual development Environmental coping Social interaction
Framework and themes for movement analysis	Structure of discipline	Structure of play	Potential meaning for participants
Movement themes in games, dance, gymnastics	Concepts integrated with activity	Competitive and expressive activities	Learning activities related to purposes and processes

addresses questions of scope, structure, sequence, and instructional process. Figure 3.14 summarizes this information for each of the seven models described in this chapter. Some aspects of this information will be discussed in greater detail in Part 2 of this book.

Each of the curriculum models reviewed makes assumptions about human beings, the role of education in society, and the nature of the subject matter of physical education. An examination of those assumptions reveals some recurring issues. Each model can be analyzed (fig. 3.15) in terms of the value orientations and dimensions discussed in chapter 2, although the proponents of each of the models have not used these terms to describe their models. The judgments are those of the authors of this book and are judgments directed toward the generic models, not necessarily applicable to each specific model selected for illustration, or to any other particular curriculum designer's version of the model. The material that follows discusses this analysis in greater detail.

	Develop-mental	Humanistic	Fitness	Movement Education	Kinesiological Studies	Play Education	Personal Meaning
Dimension: Individual development	Expert diagnosis	Self-directed	Expert diagnosis	Expert diagnosis	Expert diagnosis	Personal meaning	Personal meaning
Dimension: Social-cultural goals	Preparation for society and social change	Social change	Preparation for society	Preparation for society	Preparation for society	Preparation for society	Preparation for society and social change
Dimension: Subject matter content	Movement	Play and fitness	Fitness	Movement	Movement	Play	Movement
Value orientation	Self-actualization	Self-actualization	Disciplinary mastery	Disciplinary mastery and learning process	Disciplinary mastery and learning process	Disciplinary mastery	Ecological validity and learning process

Figure 3.15
Analysis of curriculum models

Individual Development

Most of the models recognize that human beings have both common characteristics and unique individual differences, but the relative emphasis varies. If priority is given to the uniqueness of the individual, personalized instructional strategies and opportunities for student decision-making are provided. Emphasis upon common characteristics and needs is reflected by prescriptive programs and group instruction. The humanistic model exemplifies the personalized approach that permits self-directed growth of the individual student. Both the fitness model and recent developmental models rely upon expert diagnosis and prescription, with an effort to individualize the programs. In the movement education and kinesiological studies models, the subject matter expert retains responsibility for many program design decisions, but the development of the capability for self-directed learning may be viewed as an important program goal. The play education model and the personal meaning model emphasize the student's discovery of meaning in the physical education setting. Both structure a program that will broaden the student's horizons so that the student can select the most meaningful experiences.

All the models seem to share a view of human beings as holistic creatures in which thought, emotion, and behavior are integrated. Any experience affects the total person and educational programs must assume responsibility for cognitive, affective, and motor consequences. This belief in the unity of the person is reflected in each of the models by the development of goals and objectives that relate to each of these domains. However, program goals do reflect a difference in the way the models view human beings and the learning process. Some of the models reflect a commitment to a high degree of transfer of learning from the physical education setting to other aspects of life, while others concentrate on goals and objectives specific to the physical education setting. For example, a narrow, subject matter specific goal might be to develop positive feelings about one's ability to move; a broader, more comprehensive goal might be to enhance total self-concept. The developmental and humanistic models tend to have broadly defined goals. The play education model and the fitness approach specifically limit goals and objectives to those applicable to the physical education environment. The other models can be placed between these two points.

Social-Cultural Goals

Another dimension on which the models differ is the assumptions regarding the role of education in society. In some cases, emphasis is upon preparation for society by transmitting the cultural heritage, or developing the personal qualities needed to successfully participate in the existing society. In other cases, education may be intended to reconstruct society by providing students with the values, beliefs, and abilities to create change. Focus upon social change has tended to emphasize the role of the school in achieving equal opportunity for all. As schools have attempted to provide equal access, they have also struggled with the issue of how schools and society can foster both excellence and equality.

As indicated in chapter 2, the predominant emphasis of most physical education programs has been preparation for society. Of the models reviewed, only the humanistic model could be viewed as endorsing social change rather than preparation for society. Although the emphasis of the humanistic model is personalistic, rather than social, individuals are encouraged to develop "selective detachment" from their culture so as not to mirror societal values and inhibit individual development.

All other models tend to focus upon goals related to preparing the student to become a competent, functioning member of society as it presently exists. In some cases, a model may combine elements of preparation for society with aspects of social change. The personal meaning model assumes that our present world is characterized by continuous social change, which implies deliberate effort by educators to assist in the development of individuals who can create and adapt to change. The movement education and kinesiological studies models also seem to have some potential for both preparation for existing society, and for social change—but it has been less explicitly stated.

Developmental education has an orientation of preparation for society combined with commitment to equal opportunity. Developmental programs emphasizing traditional values of competition and achievement have been described as preparation for the American economic system. However, both Melograno (1979) and Thompson and Mann (1981) have recommended using physical education programs as a means to reduce sexism and racism in society—a reconstructionist position. Play education models generally emphasize preparation for participation in society, but potentially could emphasize social change. Play education programs that include only sport and dance forms that are currently popular in society help maintain the status quo; those that emphasize equal access to play opportunities, or include new play forms (such as cooperative games) might be viewed as change-oriented.

While the authors recognize that specific models within each category may place emphasis upon education as an instrument of social change, the classifications of the generic models in figure 3.15 reflect the emphasis of most physical education curricula upon preparation of the individual for participation in adult society.

Subject Matter Content

The curriculum models also differ in their definitions of the subject matter of physical education. The fitness model limits program content to components of health-related fitness and those activities with health benefits. Play education defines the subject matter as competitive and expressive motor activities. The humanistic model uses both play and fitness activities as means to enhance the development of students.

The other four models (developmental education, movement education, kinesiological studies, and personal meaning) define the content of physical education as human movement. Human movement is a broad definition of the field and encompasses both fitness and play. The study of human movement phenomena includes, but is not limited to, movement that produces health benefits and movement in a play context. The models that use the human movement definition of physical education content also view the process of learning as part of what students are to master. Both the personal meaning model and the kinesiological studies model include process as part of the conceptual framework.

Value Orientation

The identification of the value orientation of a model is based upon an examination of the assumptions related to each of the three dimensions (individual development, social-cultural goals, and subject matter content) as well as the relative emphasis upon each dimension. The conceptual framework is a critical component of a model that permits translation of the beliefs and goals into a program design. Examination of the conceptual framework also provides insight into the value orientation of the model.

Some of the conceptual frameworks are based upon the nature of the subject matter (movement education, kinesiological studies, fitness, play education). The value orientation of resulting curriculum models is primarily disciplinary mastery. Others are derived from the needs and goals of the students (developmental, humanistic). Their value orientation is essentially self-actualization. Personal meaning models are based on the needs of the students, consciously interrelated with the needs of society, and therefore reflect a value orientation of ecological validity. Several of the models also emphasize learning how to learn and are based in part upon a learning process orientation (movement education, kinesiological studies, personal meaning). Because such process-oriented models often emphasize student decision-making, they are sometimes interpreted as having a self-actualization value orientation. Indeed, one of the major impacts of movement education upon elementary school physical education may have been increased attention to the needs and development of the child. However, the goals of both movement education and kinesiological studies (skilled performance and knowledge about movement) seem to reflect a commitment to mastery of content.

Impact of Models on School Programs

A question that usually arises during a review of physical education curriculum models concerns to what extent these models have been implemented in schools. Each of the models has been consciously and deliberately implemented in at least a few programs. Some have been more widely used than others. However, many physical education curricula have been developed by local teachers who were unfamiliar with curriculum models.

What model or models do these locally created curricula resemble? An examination of local curriculum documents and an observation of physical education programs leads to these conclusions:

1. The philosophy statements, goals, and objectives of many programs are consistent with a developmental education model and emphasize broad developmental goals.
2. The program content and organization often consists of games and sports, and is consistent with a play education model. Most exceptions to this generalization occur in elementary schools. (Note: Advocates of play education point out that many current multi-activity programs do not provide sufficient instruction to develop real proficiency in sport and dance.)
3. The elementary school teacher's view tends to be that his/her job is to help children grow—a developmental point of view.
4. The secondary school teacher views his/her job as teaching activities—a play education point of view. (Note: In some secondary schools, the teacher's responsibility is seen as organizing and supervising activity, not as teaching. The physical education program is basically recreational, not educational in nature—an approach that is not consistent with the play education model.)
5. Many college physical education programs seem to exemplify a play education model by emphasizing lifetime sports, although students are rarely counseled regarding the selection of activities. Fitness models and elective programs intended to encourage the development of personal meaning are not uncommon.

Examine these conclusions and do an analysis of programs in your area. Such analysis is an excellent way to clarify your understanding of the models.

Summary

A curriculum theory clarifies the assumptions that underlie an educational program. A conceptual framework used to design a curriculum model reflects a consistent theoretical base. The physical education curriculum models reviewed provide a basis for decisions about the goals, scope, structure, and sequence of the physical education program. The goals described may emphasize (1) the intrinsic values inherent in the experience of physical activity, or (2) the contributions of physical education as an instrument to achieve valued ends extrinsic to the experience itself. Chapter 5 deals more extensively with selection of program goals. The conceptual framework determines the scope of the program or the content to be included. Two options exist for the organization of units of instruction: activity units or theme units. Play education has a firm commitment to activity units, movement education to theme units. The other models permit the option of theme units or activity units in which specific themes are emphasized. Chapter 6 includes examples of both. Sequence decisions are based upon the developmental characteristics of students and the complexity of content. Each of the models addresses these topics to a varying degree of thoroughness. Most of the models also give some attention to the topic of instructional strategies. In some cases specific teaching styles are advocated, while in others instructional process must be inferred from the assumptions and goals of the model. Chapter 7 examines this topic in greater depth.

The examples provided for each of the models illustrate how the model might be implemented. Due to space limitations our descriptions of these models are necessarily brief. You are encouraged to read the original sources for a more thorough understanding. Remember that a curriculum design cannot be exactly duplicated in another setting. Curriculum theories and models are intended, not to provide a recipe, but to stimulate and clarify the thinking of curriculum planners as they make curricular decisions at the local level. Part 2 of this text addresses this decision-making process.

References

Allen, D. 1982. Joy, pleasure and satisfaction in moving: Affective considerations in curriculum design. Paper presented at Annual Convention of AAHPERD. Houston, TX (April).

Bain, L. L. 1978. The state of physical education curriculum. Paper presented at the Curriculum Symposium sponsored by the National Association for Sport and Physical Education. St. Louis, MO (November).

Callois, R. 1961. *Man, play and games.* New York: The Free Press of Glencoe.

Corbin, C. B., and R. Lindsey. 1983. *Fitness for life.* Glenview, IL: Scott, Foresman and Company.

Gallahue, D. L., P. H. Werner, and G. C. Luedke. 1975. *A conceptual approach to moving and learning.* New York: John Wiley.

Hellison, D. 1973. *Humanistic physical education.* Englewood Cliffs, NJ: Prentice-Hall.

Hellison, D. 1978. *Beyond balls and bats.* Washington, DC: AAHPERD.

Hellison, D. 1982. Philosophy—back to the drawing board. *Journal of Physical Education, Recreation and Dance* 53 (1):43–44.

Hoffman, H. A., J. Young, and S. E. Klesius. 1981. *Meaningful movement for children.* Boston: Allyn and Bacon.

Huebner, D. 1970. Curriculum as the accessibility of knowledge. Unpublished paper presented at Curriculum Theory Study Group. Minneapolis, MN (March).

Jewett, A. E. 1980a. The status of physical education curriculum theory. *Quest* 32 (2):163–73.

Jewett, A. E. 1980b. Tomorrow, tomorrow . . . On the optimistic side of pessimism. *Quest* 32 (2):130–42.

Jewett, A. E. 1981. Purpose process curriculum framework. In *Proceedings of the second conference on curriculum theory in physical education,* ed. W. M. Harrington. Athens: Univ. of Georgia.

Jewett, A. E. 1982. Curriculum designs for fulfilling human agendas. In *Education in the 80s: Physical education,* ed. C. Ulrich. Washington, DC: National Education Association.

Jewett, A. E., and M. R. Mullan. 1977. *Curriculum design: Purposes and processes in physical education teaching-learning.* Washington, DC: AAHPER.

Johnson, P. B., W. S. Updyke, M. Schaefer, and D. C. Stoldberg. 1975. *Sport, exercise and you.* New York: Holt, Rinehart, and Winston.

Kenyon, G. 1968. A conceptual model for characterizing physical activity. *Research Quarterly* 39:96–105.

Kneer, M. E., ed. 1981. *Adolesence basic stuff series.* Reston, VA: AAHPERD.

Laban, R. 1963. *Modern educational dance,* 2d ed. Rev. by L. Ullman. New York: Frederick A. Praeger.

Laban, R., and F. Lawrence. 1947. *Effort.* London: Unwin Brothers.

Lawson, H. A., and W. R. Morford. 1979. The cross-disciplinary structure of kinesiology and sport studies: Distinctions, implications and advantages. *Quest* 31:222–30.

Lawson, H. A., and J. H. Placek. 1981. *Physical education in the secondary schools.* Boston: Allyn and Bacon.

Lawther, J. D. 1977. *The learning and performance of physical skills.* Englewood Cliffs, NJ: Prentice-Hall.

Locke, L. F. 1969. Movement education—A description and critique. In *New perspectives of man in action,* ed. R. C. Brown and B. J. Cratty. Englewood Cliffs, NJ: Prentice-Hall.

Logsdon, B. J., K. R. Barrett, M. Ammons, M. R. Broer, L. E. Halverson, R. McGee, and M. A. Roberton. 1977. *Physical education for children.* Philadelphia: Lea and Febiger.

MacDonald, J. B. 1977. Values bases and issues for curriculum. In *Curriculum theory,* ed. Alex Molnar and John A. Zahorik. Washington, DC: Association for Supervision and Curriculum Development.

Melograno, V. 1979. *Designing curriculum and learning: A physical coeducation approach.* Dubuque, IA: Kendall/Hunt.

Peters, R. S. 1965. Education as initiation. In *Philosophical analysis and education*, ed. R. D. Archambault. New York: Humanities Press.

Siedentop, D. 1980. *Physical education: Introductory analysis.* Dubuque, IA: Wm. C. Brown.

Stanley, S. 1969. *Physical education: A movement orientation.* Montreal: McGraw-Hill of Canada.

Thompson, M. M. 1980. Holistic approach to curriculum development. Paper presented at the COPEC Conference on Curriculum Decision-Making in Elementary Physical Education. Kent, OH (November).

Thompson, M. M., and B. A. Mann. 1977. *An holistic approach to physical education curricula: Objectives classification system for elementary schools.* Champaign, IL: Stipes.

Thompson, M. M., and B. A. Mann. 1981. *Project SEE curriculum development.* Urbana, IL: Urbana SEE Publications.

Weber, J. C. 1968. Physical education: The science of exercise. *Physical Educator* 25 (1):5–7.

Recommended Readings

Developmental education:

Hoffman, H. A., J. Young, and S. E. Klesius. 1981. *Meaningful movement for children.* Boston: Allyn and Bacon.

Humanistic physical education:

Hellison, D. 1978. *Beyond balls and bats.* Washington, DC: AAHPERD.

Fitness:

Corbin, C. B., and R. Lindsey. 1983. *Fitness for life.* Glenview, IL: Scott, Foresman and Company.

Movement education:

Logsdon, B. J., K. R. Barrett, M. Ammons, M. R. Broer, L. E. Halverson, R. McGee, and M. A. Roberton. 1984. *Physical education for children.* Philadelphia: Lea and Febiger.

Kinesiological studies:

Lawson, H. A., and J. H. Placek. 1981. *Physical education in the secondary schools.* Boston: Allyn and Bacon.

Play education:

Siedentop, D. 1980. *Physical education: Introductory analysis.* Dubuque, IA: Wm. C. Brown.

Personal meaning:

Jewett, A. E., and M. R. Mullan. 1977. *Curriculum design: Purposes and processes in physical education teaching-learning.* Washington, DC: AAHPER.

Critiques of physical education models:

Lawson, H. A., and J. H. Placek. 1981. *Physical education in the secondary schools.* Boston: Allyn and Bacon.

Siedentop, D. 1980. *Physical education: Introductory analysis.* Dubuque, IA: Wm. C. Brown.

Curriculum Design

Part 2

The emphasis in Part 2 is upon developing your ability to make professional judgments related to program development in physical education. You will be led through the process of curriculum design much as it is experienced by teachers who are responsible for planning school curricula. This is the "how we do it" section. Extensive examples of curriculum materials are included in both the text and in the Appendices. You are encouraged to read further from the list of recommended readings at the end of each chapter.

Chapter 4 sets the tone for process orientation in discussing local considerations in curriculum development. It gives an overview of the process and emphasizes student involvement in planning activities and decision-making. In order to develop a program compatible with the unique characteristics of the local situation, you will need to know how to analyze the community, the educational agency, and the clientele, and you will need to be aware of the legal requirements that apply in your locality. This chapter offers suggestions for conducting these analyses.

Chapter 5 addresses the process of determining goals and objectives for the physical education program. Excerpts from actual curriculum documents are provided in order to permit discussion of the task of establishing program goals within the context of local concern. The process of needs assessment is discussed in some detail. Because our intent is to help you develop the ability to make and justify your own curriculum decisions, the process is emphasized and no attempt is made to provide complete information on the tools or techniques for assessing student achievement. You will need to use the references and readings for more guidance toward developing these competencies. Considerable attention has been directed to the development of objectives. We do not wish to focus upon the skill of stating behavioral objectives, but have chosen to present pertinent information for implementation of the process-oriented approach. Throughout Part 2 we have tried to provide guidance by relating the examples to the theoretical perspectives and models analyzed in Part 1.

Chapter 6 takes the next step in the curriculum development process and focuses on the selection and sequencing of educational activities. Once again, extensive examples are provided from actual curriculum documents. Curriculum design involves decisions about the scope, structure, and sequence of the program content. This chapter discusses how these decisions occur at several levels. It gives examples of structuring curriculum through developmental theme units, movement theme units, and activity units, and makes practical applications—from the district curriculum guide to the yearly plan and the individual unit plan. As you learn to develop these plans and materials you will be taking an important step in the process of translating a curriculum theory into a program in action.

Relationships of program design with instructional methods are discussed in chapter 7. Styles of teaching are illustrated with descriptions of classroom practice. The emphasis is placed upon an examination of the applicability of each of Mosston's teaching styles to the curriculum models discussed in chapter 3. Successful implementation of any curriculum model ultimately depends upon effective teaching. Teaching effectiveness is discussed with the focus on making value judgments consistent with the philosophy and assumptions of the curriculum model selected. As stated earlier, no attempt is made to provide complete coverage of the topics of instructional strategies or teaching effectiveness. The concern is with implementation of the curriculum model. The assumptions and goals of the model have implications for the types of teaching styles to be employed. When the model has been fully implemented, the measurement of outcomes becomes an evaluation, not only of the teacher, but of the assumptions and premises of the model.

The evaluation process in physical education curriculum development is discussed in chapter 8. Evaluation is the final step in the process of curriculum design. Program evaluation procedures are discussed here in terms of relationships with program design. Full treatment of the complex field of evaluation in physical education is definitely not envisioned and you will need to learn much more about this topic through other professional courses, the study of appropriate textbooks, and supplementary reading. Three case studies are presented to provide orientation to the nature of the task. Procedures for student evaluation are summarized. The highlights of teacher evaluation are reviewed. The emphasis is upon alternative models for program evaluation. Desired outcomes models, goal-free models, adversary models, and artistic models have been selected for description and analysis. A number of current concerns relating to the use of qualitative evaluation have been introduced. We hope that, upon conclusion of your study of Part 2, you will have developed confidence in your ability to make the practical curriculum decisions included in the processes of identifying goals, selecting and sequencing learning activities, developing curriculum materials, implementing selected curriculum models through the selection of appropriate instructional methods, and planning for program evaluation.

Local Considerations in Curriculum Development

4

Outline

Curriculum Planning Process

The development of a curriculum involves a process of decision-making regarding the philosophy and goals of physical education and the design of the instructional program. The procedures used to develop curricula vary from one setting to the next, but certain common concerns must be addressed. What follow are descriptions of the process employed in two different situations.

Examples of Planning Procedures

The State Department of Education decided to develop a state-wide guide to assist local school districts in developing quality physical education programs. The steering committee appointed for the project was chaired by a curriculum specialist from a major state university. Members of the committee included physical education teachers from an elementary school, a middle school, and a secondary school, and two district level physical education coordinators. Also included were

State Planning

two university professors and a representative from the state Association for Health, Physical Education and Recreation. The physical education specialist in the Department of Education provided staff support for the group. The steering committee identified a basic philosophy for the guide and determined that the guide would employ a competency approach in which performance objectives for essential competencies would be identified for grades, 3, 6, 8, and 10. The guide would also include information about a wide range of learning activities that might be used by local districts to reach these objectives. A plan was developed to involve approximately fifty public school and university physical educators in identifying the essential competencies. A consultant with expertise in competency-based education met with the group. Then teams, chaired by members of the steering committee, worked to develop performance objectives for each level. The program was piloted in several districts throughout the state. On the basis of the data collected in pilot programs, several modifications in performance objectives were made. The completed document was then released by the Department of Education as the recommended guide for all K–12 physical education programs in the state.

Local District Planning

School board policy in a school district in a mid-size city requires that each instructional area develop a curriculum guide for its program. These guides, once approved by the school board, become official policy of the district. Since no guide existed for the physical education program, the district physical education coordinator was directed to develop one. The coordinator decided that the curriculum planning committee would be composed of physical education teachers from the district and representatives from the community. Two elementary and two secondary school teachers were elected by their colleagues. The community representatives included a representative of the parents' association, a member of the Chamber of Commerce education committee, a recent graduate presently attending the local community college, and a student. The group decided to begin by surveying students and parents regarding their expectations for the physical education program, and by visiting several programs throughout the state that had been identified as being of high quality. Based on the survey and visits, the committee developed a draft of a philosophy statement and circulated it to all physical education teachers in the district for their responses. The committee then proceeded to develop a curriculum design consistent with the philosophy statement. When the overall curriculum design was complete, an open hearing was sponsored by the parents' association to explain the proposal and get feedback from parents and students.

Slight revisions were made as a result of the hearing. The guide was then completed and submitted to the school board. Subsequent to approval by the board, a series of staff development meetings were scheduled for physical education teachers in the district to assist them with implementation of the new program.

_____

Local Curriculum Planning

Curriculum development is, fundamentally, a local responsibility. A curriculum theory can identify a broad philosophy for the program. A curriculum model can provide guidelines for program design. But, ultimately, educators at the state or local level must make curriculum decisions.

There are several advantages to local control of curriculum development (Tyler 1981). Programs developed locally are more likely to be responsive to the unique needs of the community. Modifications and adjustments can be made more quickly than in large scale curriculum projects. Involvement in the curriculum planning process increases educators' commitment to the program and their ability to implement it. Teachers have a critical role in the implementation of any curriculum proposal. Doyle and Ponder (1977) suggest that teachers base their implementation decisions on the perceived practicality of the program. Perceptions of practicality seem to be determined by the teachers' understanding of the proposal as well as its congruence with the situation in which they work. If teachers have assisted in the development of a curriculum, they are likely to have a clearer conception of how it can be implemented, and a vested interest in helping to make it a success. The implementation of any curriculum proposal will reveal unanticipated problems. When those involved in the implementation participate in the curricular decision-making process, their concerns and problems can be identified and responded to.

Despite these advantages of local curriculum planning, several cautions must be noted. Unless curriculum planners have access to curriculum literature and information about other programs, there may be a limited vision of what is possible or a tendency to "reinvent the wheel." Curriculum planning teams need to include someone who is familiar with innovations and current research. Outside consultants or cooperative efforts with university physical education departments are possible solutions to this problem. Another major concern in local curriculum development is the time required. Teachers, especially those who are also coaching, will find it difficult to complete this task in addition to their regular responsibilities. Released time or summer employment to work on program development may be necessary. Time for curriculum development and ongoing program evaluation needs to be built into the educational process.

Local planning of the physical education curriculum is usually the responsibility of a committee comprised of a physical education supervisor and several physical education teachers. Occasionally, the committee will include representation from one or more other groups: administrators, teachers from other subject areas, parents, or students. Physical educators from a university or another school district may be employed as consultants. In some instances, the school district and a local university may initiate a collaborative project in which both school and university personnel are members of the curriculum committee.

The basis for selection of committee members is critical. Participants need to be capable, committed, and have time available for sustained work. There are political considerations as well. Curriculum committees deal with questions of value—of what is important for students to learn. Sociologists have pointed out that such questions are essentially political in nature (Young 1971). Because different groups have different perceptions of what is valuable, participation in the decision-making process is essential if a group's point of view is to be represented. A committee whose members have similar backgrounds (e.g. secondary school physical education teachers from within the district) may share certain values because of similar past experience and professional preparation. Broadening the membership to include representatives of other groups (e.g., elementary teachers, university faculty, parents, students) will create greater diversity of views. Each approach has certain advantages. A homogeneous group with a shared set of values can work toward full implementation of a curricular model without having to compromise aspects of the model to appease various constituencies. A diverse committee will require more time and effort to reach consensus, but may produce more dramatic changes in the curriculum. The curriculum produced, however, may tend to be eclectic, containing elements of various curriculum theories rather than a consistent theoretical base.

Approaches to Curriculum Planning

Once the committee is appointed, how will it proceed with its work? There is more than one alternative in approaching the curriculum planning process. The classic model for the process of curriculum development is the rationale proposed by Ralph Tyler (1949). He suggests that curricular planners have to answer four central questions:

1. What educational purposes should the school seek to attain?
2. What educational experiences can be provided that are likely to help attain these purposes?
3. How can these educational experiences be effectively organized?
4. How can we determine whether these purposes are being attained?

These questions lead to a four-step process for developing a curriculum: stating objectives, selecting experiences, organizing experiences, and evaluating. Tyler describes three sources of objectives: studies of learners, studies of contemporary society, and suggestions from subject matter specialists. Objectives from these sources are to be screened on the basis of local philosophic commitments and psychological research about learning. Learning activities are selected and organized to maximize the efficiency with which objectives can be attained. The Tyler rationale has dominated curriculum planning literature for thirty years. However, considerable criticism has been directed toward the technological ends-means nature of the process (Kliebard 1975b). Identifying objectives before selecting activities promotes the view that the outcome and the activity are separate and that activities are valuable only as a means to an end. Critics argue that the emphasis should be on the quality and worthwhileness of the activity itself (intrinsic values), rather than upon predicted instrumental outcomes (Peters 1965, Kliebard 1975a).

On the basis of observational research, Walker (1971, 1975) suggested that the Tyler rationale does not describe the way curriculum committees actually proceed. He has proposed an alternative model that he calls *curriculum deliberation.* The process of deliberation has also been discussed by Schwab (1969) and Reid (1978). Walker suggests that the first task of a curriculum planning group is to establish a platform or set of common beliefs that will guide it in the planning process. This platform includes statements about aims, but is not a set of objectives. It is a description of assumptions, commitments, and principles. Once the group has reached consensus on a platform, it engages in two processes: construction and deliberation. Construction involves the creation and trial of plans and materials, and is usually assigned to individuals or small subcommittees. The subcommittees develop such materials as scope and sequence charts, statements of objectives, and units of instruction. The materials developed are brought back to the group for review. This review stimulates the group to engage in deliberation. Deliberation consists of discussion of issues and problems in which alternative proposals are considered and debated. The process of deliberation does not proceed in an orderly way, but deals with problems as they arise. Frequently the issues discussed evolve from the materials being constructed. As individuals or small groups develop plans and materials that apply the beliefs in specific concrete ways, points of confusion or disagreement may become apparent. In resolving these issues and problems, the group refers back to its platform. In the process, the platform itself will be redefined, elaborated, and, perhaps, modified.

The product of the curriculum planning process, using either the Tyler rationale or the deliberation model, will be a curriculum guide. The guide will summarize the basic program philosophy and provide information about the scope, structure, and sequence of the curriculum. Although the format of the curriculum guide will vary it will usually include several components: aims and/or objectives, educational activities, materials and resources, and evaluation procedures. In some cases, the guide may include suggested instructional strategies. The amount of detail given and the degree of flexibility in the program will reflect the planning committee's beliefs about teacher and student autonomy. A high degree of structure limits teacher and student choice, while more flexible, open-ended designs place greater responsibility on teachers and/or students (Bernstein 1973).

An effort has been made to make this text useful for planners taking either approach to the curriculum planning process. Chapters are devoted to each of the decision-making components of the process (determining goals, selecting and organizing experiences, and evaluating), but the sequence and emphasis of the Tyler model is not assumed.

This chapter suggests beginning the planning process by focusing upon two tasks: 1) clarification of basic program philosophy and 2) analysis of the local situation. A review of curriculum theories and models is proposed as an effective way to clarify program philosophy or to identify the platform on which the curriculum will be built. An examination of the community, the educational agency, and the clientele provides an understanding of the local environment in which the curriculum structure must exist.

Focusing early efforts upon the clarification of beliefs and an investigation of local needs and constraints has the advantage of postponing specific program decisions until later in the process. This delay can be beneficial. Curriculum planners may have a tendency to support a particular program before thoroughly considering alternatives. Such early closure can be very limiting and reconsideration may be difficult once positions have been publicly adopted. Beginning the curriculum development process with information-gathering will provide a sound basis for later curriculum design decisions.

Clarifying Program Philosophy

As indicated in Part 1 of this book, curriculum design is shaped by the values and beliefs upon which it is based. An important part of the local curriculum planning process is an examination and clarification of the program philosophy of the curriculum planners.

There are several possible approaches to this clarification process. One way to begin is to review alternative curricular models and to discuss the advantages and disadvantages of each. The curriculum committee can read descriptions or visit programs that exemplify various models such as those discussed in chapter 3. One possibility is to assign each member of the committee to be an advocate for one of the models and the theoretical position it assumes. The advocate gains an in-depth understanding of the model and then responds to questions and criticisms of other committee members. This approach to clarifying philosophy has the advantage of requiring careful examination of alternatives. Its disadvantage is that it may seem too theoretical and too time-consuming to teachers with a high concern about practicality. This especially may be a problem if the committee is unable to view examples of the models in action.

In contrast to a systematic study of curricular models, another approach is to go through a series of value clarification experiences under the guidance of a curriculum consultant who can help the group relate its values and beliefs to one or more of the theoretical models. Some examples of such experiences are given in figure 4.1. Although these exercises may seem unrelated to the theories, it is the task of the consultant to introduce information about the models as it is relevant to the discussions. When a direction becomes apparent, the group may want to examine materials or visit programs based on the model or models most compatible with their views. This approach can be very effective, but requires a leader with in-depth knowledge of curriculum theory and skills as a discussion leader.

Figure 4.1
Curriculum value
clarification activities

Critical incidents
   Individual activity:
      Describe the most positive experience you can recall as a student or a teacher in a physical education class.
   Group discussion:
      What was positive about that experience? What does it indicate that you think is important about physical education?
Log a student
   Individual activity:
      Select a student in one of your classes. Observe what that student does in physical education class every day for a week. Keep a log about what you observe. Try to make your log as objective and descriptive as possible.
   Group discussion:
      How would you characterize what you observed? In what ways were the experiences educational? On the basis of what this student did this week, could you justify requiring physical education? Why or why not?
Impossible dreams
   Individual activity:
      Close your eyes and picture in your mind the ideal physical education class. There are no limits on money, equipment, facilities, staff. You are not bound by tradition or administrative controls. It is your fantasy and anything goes.
   Group discussion:
      What was your program like? How did you feel in that situation? Was it exciting? intense? relaxed? reassuring? challenging? Which aspects of your ideal program were the key to its success?

Metaphors

  Individual activity:

  Select a metaphor that you believe captures the essential characteristics of the curriculum. (See chapter 2 for examples.) Write a description that discusses the parallels with the educational process.

  Group discussion:

  What are the theoretical assumptions implied by the metaphor? Are there any parts of the metaphor that do not seem to fit?

Futuristic scenarios

  Individual activity:

  Describe society and education as you think they will exist twenty years from now. What will physical education programs be like?

  Group discussion:

  In what ways do our futuristic programs differ from current physical education programs. What are the implications of the views of the future for the way we plan programs now?

Ranking goals

  Individual activity:

  Identify the three goals you think are most important for a physical education program. Then identify the three you believe are most important to administrators and to students.

Fig. 4.1 cont.

Goals	Importance		
	To me	*To administrators*	*To students*
Health and fitness	_____	_____	_____
Skill/efficiency of movement	_____	_____	_____
Knowledge about movement	_____	_____	_____
Enjoyment	_____	_____	_____
Commitment to participation	_____	_____	_____
Self-understanding and self-esteem	_____	_____	_____
Emotional maturity	_____	_____	_____
Social skills	_____	_____	_____
Understanding heritage	_____	_____	_____
Other (please list):	_____	_____	_____

  Group discussion:

  Do teachers, administrators, and students have similar perceptions of the physical education program? What are the implications of this for curriculum planning? Could someone who observed our current program tell what our goals are?

Another approach to helping the curriculum planners clarify program philosophy is for the group to select one curriculum model to examine in depth in order to stimulate discussion of issues. The intent of this procedure is not to persuade the curriculum committee to adopt the model intact, but to raise questions about it that will help the group clarify its own values and beliefs. After becoming familiar with the model through readings, observation, and discussion, the committee identifies those aspects of the model that could be helpful in their situation. As they discuss and modify, their values and beliefs become increasingly evident. Such an approach has the disadvantage of limiting discussions to one alternative, but it may be more manageable for groups with little previous exposure to curriculum theory.

A similar process is to begin with an evaluation of the strengths and weaknesses of the existing program. The major disadvantage of this approach is that it may not require the group to examine and challenge the overall curriculum goals and the implicit assumptions upon which present practice is based. Effective program evaluation requires prior clarification of the group's definition of quality. Starting with evaluation may encourage tendencies to focus on immediate decisions and to limit consideration of alternatives. It is important to defer planning decisions until the completion of this initial information-gathering stage. The priority at this point is for the curriculum planning group to gain an understanding of its curriculum philosophy and of the community, agency, and clientele it will serve.

The Community

A community is more than a place where people live; it is a group of people who share location, interests, beliefs, and values. Urbanization and population migration have reduced the sense of community in many persons' lives and have created more diversity within communities. Yet each community has unique characteristics and patterns that need to be understood by curriculum developers.

Educators often take it for granted that they understand the community in which they work. However, teachers from outside the community rarely have a thorough understanding of its culture. Longtime residents may suffer from a lack of distance, an inability to step back and see the whole picture. Both groups can benefit from an analysis similar to that conducted by anthropologists visiting another society. The key to such an analysis is unbiased observation and descriptions of values, beliefs, and behaviors. Figure 4.2 outlines questions

Figure 4.2
Community analysis

What Are the Physical Characteristics of the Community?

Find a map of the community and mark the boundaries of the area from which your clients are drawn. Identify those areas that are primarily residential and those that are commercial. Are the residential areas single-family homes or multiple-family dwellings? Do residents own or rent? Mark the location of schools, parks, recreation facilities, libraries, and shopping on the map. How readily can residents get to and from these facilities? Is public transportation available?

Who Lives in the Community?

What is the age distribution of the residents? What is their ethnic and racial heritage? What languages are spoken? Describe their educational background and religious affiliations. How transient is the population?

What Is the Economic Base of the Community?

Where do community residents work? Who are the major employers? What kind of jobs do they have? What is their average income? Do most households have one or more than one person employed? What is the rate of unemployment?

What kind of financial support is provided for public schools? Private schools? Other educational agencies? Recreational agencies? Health services?

What Is the Political System in the Community?

What is the form of local government? Who holds the power? Describe the political voting patterns of the area. Do residents belong to community action groups? Unions? Other organizations with political goals?

What Is the Culture in the Community?

What are the popular recreational activities of residents? Where do residents "hang out"? Who are neighborhood heroes? What are residents proud of? What do they apologize for? What do they disapprove of? What do they hope for? How much crime occurs? Are people fearful of crime?

How are outsiders viewed by residents?

Implications

Describe the implications of this analysis for the curriculum you are developing.

to be answered in a community analysis. Some of this information is available by direct observation, while driving or walking through the community. Other information can be found in the local library or government offices. Some questions require interviewing a sample of community residents. The information recorded should be as objective as possible; the observer should avoid mixing interpretations and opinions with observations. The task of interpreting the community background information is done by the curriculum planning committee. Deriving implications for curriculum from the community analysis requires professional judgment and reflects basic beliefs. If education is viewed as preparation for society, the implications reflect an effort to assist clients in adjusting to their community. If education is viewed as a tool for reconstruction of society, attention is directed to ways in which community conflicts and inequities could be resolved.

How does this relate to a physical education program? An analysis of community recreation patterns is likely to reveal differences in sports participation based on both socioeconomic class and gender (Loy, McPherson, and Kenyon 1978). The preparation-for-society perspective assumes that students should be taught those activities currently popular in their segment of society. If basketball and softball are popular activities in a community, the program teaches these activities so that students can effectively participate in activities that they value and that are readily available to them outside the school. In contrast, the reconstructionist view indicates that physical education programs should attempt to broaden the recreational opportunities available to students by exposing them to nontraditional activities. Providing dance instruction for boys or contact sports for girls might be viewed as a way of changing sex role stereotypes that limit participation patterns. Many aspects of the community have implications for curriculum design in physical education, but the nature of those implications depends greatly upon the committee's underlying view of the role of education in society.

The Educational Agency

In complex societies, education is the responsibility of specialized educational agencies. The public and private school systems are the dominant force, but many other agencies (recreational agencies, business firms, nursing homes, etc.) are now engaged in educational activity. Although this discussion focuses upon schools, a similar analysis of other educational agencies could be undertaken.

A school is a social organization with predictable patterns of interaction, and identifiable power and authority structures. To understand schooling it is necessary, not only to examine the characteristics of individual students and teachers, but also to study the characteristics of the organization itself. Figure 4.3 describes a list of questions to guide the analysis.

Figure 4.3
Agency analysis

Power and Authority
Who are the people who have power?
To what extent is that power seen as legitimate by others?
Is the authority of teachers role-determined (based on their
    position), professional (based on their expertise), or
    personal (based on their "charm")?

Structure
What are the characteristics of the members of the
    organization? (age, gender, socioeconomic background, etc.)
What are the formal and informal sub-groups in the
    organization? (classes, clubs, teams, teachers'
    organizations, etc.)
How tightly controlled are the sub-groups? How much
    autonomy do they have?

Control and Sanctions
What student behaviors do teachers consider acceptable and
    unacceptable?
What behaviors do students consider acceptable and
    unacceptable?
What rewards are given for acceptable behavior?
How is unacceptable behavior treated?

Cohesiveness
What is the attitude of teachers and students toward the
    institution?
Toward the sub-groups?
    Committed—strong loyalty and support
    Calculative—plays the game in order to get along
    Alienated—negative and hostile
What are the rituals and symbols used to increase
    cohesiveness?

Implications
What are the implications of this analysis for curriculum
    development?

One critical aspect of the school as a social organization is the distribution of power and authority. Schlechty (1976) points out that the long-term goal of education is learning, but that the more immediate concern of schools is influencing students to behave in ways considered desirable by the organization. The power to define and enforce behavior is central to the functioning of schools. Power that is accepted by others as being legitimate is called authority. Teachers generally have or seek authority, but their bases for that authority may differ. Role authority automatically accompanies a position; the teacher's power is accepted merely because he or she is the teacher. All teachers, regardless of competence, are afforded a level of compliance. Professional authority is based on a person's expertise; the teacher's power is accepted because he or she has earned the respect of students and colleagues. Personal authority is based upon the teacher's charisma or charm and assumes that students will accept the teacher's authority because they like the person. In general, such personal charm is not viewed as an adequate basis for teacher authority. Traditionally, teachers relied on role authority, an unconditional acceptance of the power of the teacher. More recently in many schools, teachers' authority is not universally accepted, but must be earned on the basis of expertise.

Complex organizations usually operate with a variety of subgroups. These subgroups may be formal or informal, voluntary or involuntary. Membership in subgroups is frequently based upon certain characteristics of the members: age, gender, talent, interests, etc. The larger organization may allow these subgroups considerable autonomy, or it may control them rather tightly. For example, in some schools the teacher has complete control of class procedures; in other schools curriculum, methods, and grading policies may be controlled by the administration.

A characteristic of a social organization is a commonly held definition of acceptable and unacceptable behavior (norms). Complete agreement is not expected, but members generally are aware of the norms. Norms or expectations vary for different roles (principal, teacher, coach, student, athlete, etc.). Members are expected to learn the norms for the role or roles they occupy. A system of sanctions (rewards and punishments) exists to encourage compliance. Such sanctions may include grades, honors, privileges, deprivation, exclusion, or corporal punishment.

The adoption of normative behavior and the effectiveness of various types of sanctions depend upon the attitude of the members toward the organization. Highly committed members, who are loyal to the organization and its purposes, require few sanctions. Calculative members tend to bargain with the system and respond to rewards and punishments. Alienated students are frequently dealt with by using coercion, although it can be argued that such tactics increase hostility toward the school. Organizations make efforts to increase cohesiveness or loyalty to the organization. Frequently these efforts involve the use of rituals or symbols. Athletic events, pep rallies, and school songs are excellent examples of rituals and symbols designed to increase cohesiveness.

An understanding of the organizational characteristics of the school is essential for curriculum developers. Curriculum revisions that involve a change in power relationships or normative behavior require careful planning and implementation if they are to succeed.

The Clientele

Analysis of the educational setting is incomplete without an understanding of the clientele for whom the program is being developed. This understanding can be gained in two ways. Developmental literature can provide a summary of the general characteristics of the age group. Local data-gathering can provide information about the characteristics of the specific population. Both aspects of the analysis are important.

Caution is advised in interpreting the information collected. Both developmental research and local data are generally summarized in terms of group norms or averages. Individuals within the group vary widely from these averages and such variations are normal. To assume that all members of a group possess some characteristics because they belong to the group is an example of stereotyping. Group norms or averages should not become stereotypes. Individual interests and abilities should be expected and encouraged. For example, boys average greater running speed than girls, but some girls run faster than some boys. Both the fast girl and the slow boy are normal, acceptable people, for whom the program should provide appropriate experiences. A second caution is that past performance should not necessarily be interpreted as predictive of future performance. For example, racial or ethnic differences in performance may be due in part to variations in previous experience and opportunity. Programs that equalize instruction and participation for ethnic groups may find that performance differences decrease.

A complete review of developmental literature is beyond the scope of this book. Figure 4.4 provides a brief summary of general characteristics of age groups. Because of the wide variations in rates of development, age is not a very accurate indicator of developmental stage. One should expect to find great differences within these age categories. Additional information on developmental patterns is included in appendix A. Curriculum developers are encouraged to do more

Figure 4.4
General age group
characteristics

Early Childhood (Approximate Ages 3–7)
Physical growth slow and steady; often characterized by long legs and high center of gravity.
Likes to move. Mastery of locomotor skills occurs. Manipulative skills develop more slowly and require lots of practice.
Individualistic orientation indicates preference for playing alone but seeks approval from adults and peers. Gradual development of group play and sharing behaviors.
Gradual increase in attention span but continues to be restless.
Thinking not organized according to logical rules. Understanding of right and wrong largely dependent upon consequences.

Childhood (Approximate Ages 8–12)
Physical growth steady until beginning of puberty, which may occur for girls during this period. Increased strength and endurance, decreased flexibility.
Skills improve, especially manipulative skills and body control.
Peer acceptance important; strong allegiance to the group.
Intellectual curiosity and more complex mental operations evident.
Accepts need for rules.
Greater sex differences in skills and interests appear.

Adolescence (Approximate Ages 13–18)
Sudden growth spurt at puberty. Development of sex characteristics.
Sex differences increase.

extensive reading about the age group of their clientele. In addition, local data should be sought to supplement this information. At this early stage in the curriculum development process, reliance upon available data sources suggested in figure 4.5 seems adequate. Once specific program objectives have been identified, a more complete needs assessment may be conducted (see chap. 5).

Acceptance of one's sexuality a major concern.
Coordination and skill development continue to improve.
Achieving independence from parents and a sense of personal
   identity are central tasks.
Able to deal with abstract thoughts and complex information.
Developing a personal value system.

Adult (Approximate Ages 18–60)
Physical growth ceases. Gradual decline in metabolism rate.
   Physical changes accompany end of child-bearing years.
Physical performance peaks and then gradually declines.
Adopts a work role with one or two career changes likely.
Establishes independent home and family.
Develops avocational interests and lifestyle.
Increased concern about health.
Steadily increasing competence and mental abilities.

Older Adult (Over Age 60)
Physical deterioration and decreased capacity to cope with
   stress.
Motor skill performance changes in style as well as efficiency.
Dealing with death of loved ones and self.
Adjustment to increased free time and retirement from work.
Development of new roles, activities and patterns of
   interaction.

Figure 4.5
Understanding the
clientele: Local data
sources

School Records
Attendance records:
What is rate of absenteeism?
Which students are absent most often?
Health records:
What health problems occur most frequently?
Achievement records:
How does academic achievement compare with
national norms? With other area schools?
Discipline records:
Who gets in trouble for what?
How are discipline problems dealt with?
Extracurricular activities:
Who are the students who participate in various
activities?

Departmental Records
Attendance records:
What is rate of attendance and participation?
Which students are out most often?
Which teachers or activities have highest rates of non-
participation?
Achievement records:
How does fitness performance compare to norms?
What evidence exists regarding cognitive and motor
achievement?
What patterns are evident in the awarding of grades?
Student opinions:
How do students evaluate the physical education
program?
When allowed to choose activities, what preferences do
students indicate?

Other Agencies
Feeder school records:
What content is taught in physical education in feeder
schools?
Recreation:
What organized recreational programs exist for this age
group?
Which students participate in community or private
recreation programs?
What items are big sellers at area sporting goods
stores?
Public health records:
What health problems are prevalent in the community?

Legal Requirements

The final aspect of the background investigation is for curriculum developers to become familiar with laws that place constraints or requirements on the physical education program. Although the laws do not specify program content, they do set limitations that the curriculum must meet.

Physical Education Requirements

Many U.S. states and Canadian provinces legislate that physical education be required of all students in elementary and secondary schools. The law does not usually specify program content, but indicates a minimum amount of time for instruction or minimum number of credits to be earned. The department of education will provide information about the requirements as well as any state or provincial curriculum guidelines.

Title IX

In 1972, the Congress of the United States approved Title IX of the Education Amendments, which states that:

> No person . . . shall, on the basis of sex, be excluded from participation in, be denied the benefits of, or be subjected to discrimination under any education program or activity receiving Federal financial assistance.

The implementing regulations released by the Department of Health, Education and Welfare in June 1975 clarify the application of Title IX to physical education programs. The basic guidelines are that physical education requirements must be the same for males and females, and that physical education classes must be coeducational. The only times when it is legal to separate boys and girls is for instruction dealing with human sexuality and for participation in contact sports. (Separation in these situations is optional, not required.) Title IX does not dictate program content. It requires only that activities offered be open equally to students of both sexes, and that procedures used for assignment of students to classes not discriminate on the basis of sex.

Within classes boys and girls must be treated equally. Students may not be grouped on the basis of sex but may be grouped by ability, providing objective measures specific to the activity are used to determine ability. Responsibilities and privileges, such as equipment manager or team captain, should be assigned without regard to sex. Discipline measures for boys and girls should be comparable.

In light of these requirements, evaluation of performance in physical education poses some unique problems. A single set of standards may be used for evaluation of skills, unless the use of a single standard has an adverse impact on one sex. If one group is disadvantaged, the alternatives are to establish separate standards for males and females, or to use an evaluation procedure that emphasizes individual progress. Evaluating individual improvement, however, is complicated by the problems of unreliability of improvement scores, lack of effort on the initial test, and a ceiling effect on top performers (Safrit 1981). Mastery learning, in which an appropriate criterion (based on initial performance) is identified and students are given multiple opportunities to reach the mark, is another alternative.

Public Law 94–142

Another federal law that affects physical education programs in the United States is PL 94–142, the Education for All Handicapped Children Act of 1975. This legislation is intended to provide a free appropriate public education for all handicapped children. The law specifies that handicapped children should be educated in the "least restrictive environment"; whenever possible, they should be "mainstreamed" or grouped with non-handicapped children. The law does not require that all handicapped children be mainstreamed; that decision is made on an individual basis.

An important aspect of the law is that an individual education program (IEP) must be developed for each handicapped child each year. The IEP is developed by a team, which includes the teacher, the parents, a special education supervisor, and, if appropriate, the child. The IEP must include an assessment of present performance, goals and objectives, special education and regular education services to be provided, and evaluation procedures and criteria.

PL 94–142 requires that physical education be included in the educational program of every handicapped child. If possible, the child should participate in the regular physical education program. However, specially designed physical education instruction should be prescribed in the IEP if appropriate. Such separation should occur only if education in regular classes with the use of supplementary aids and services cannot be achieved satisfactorily.

Physical education departments need to be prepared to assist with the implementation of PL 94–142 by participating in assessment and in the development of IEPs, by making appropriate programmatic adjustments for handicapped students who are mainstreamed, and by providing special physical education for children who need it.

Liability

The assumption of legal responsibility for another person's wellbeing is termed liability. Educational agencies assume such responsibility for students. Officials or employees of the agency may be sued for damage if they are negligent in fulfilling their responsibilities. Negligence can involve *failure to act* (not doing something one should have) or *wrongful action* (doing the wrong thing).

Several aspects of the avoidance of negligence have direct implications for curriculum development. Evidence that the student is physically able to participate should be required, especially in adult fitness programs. Activities should be planned that are appropriate to the age and ability of the students. Documentation of professional endorsement of such activities and of official school board approval of course syllabi minimizes the liability of the individual teacher. Qualified staff must be available for instruction and supervision of all activities included in the program. Teachers are expected to provide correct instruction prior to student participation, particularly in activities with inherent risks. Adequate facilities and equipment must be available. Provisions should be made for appropriate first aid and medical services. Curriculum developers should consider the adequacy of resources in planning a program that meets the legal responsibilities for the welfare of the student. The existence of a well-articulated curriculum and teachers' adherence to that curriculum can provide important protection in the area of legal liability.

Summary

Curriculum development in physical education in the United States and Canada occurs at the local level, enabling the curriculum planners to develop a program that is compatible with the unique characteristics of the local situation. Such compatibility requires a careful analysis of the community, the educational agency, and the clientele, as well as an awareness of the laws impacting the physical education program. As "insiders" in the system, local curriculum planners may have a tendency to skim over this step in the program development process. A careful analysis may provide new insights and raise questions about "taken for granted" assumptions.

References

Bernstein, B. 1973. "On the classification and framing of educational knowledge." In *Knowledge, education and cultural change*, ed. Richard Brown. London: Tavistock.

Brophy, J. E. 1977. *Child development and socialization*. Chicago: SRA.

Doyle, W., and G. Ponder. 1977. "The ethic of practicality: Implications for curriculum development." In *Curriculum theory*. Washington, D.C.: Association for Supervision and Curriculum Development.

Hendricks, J. H., and C. D. Hendricks. 1981. *Aging in mass society: Myths and realities*. Cambridge: Winthrop.

Kennedy, C. E. 1978. *Human development: The adult years and aging*. New York: Macmillan.

Kliebard, H. M. 1975a. "Persistent curriculum issues in historical perspective." In *Curriculum theorizing: The reconceptualists*, W. Pinar, ed. Berkeley: McCutchan.

Kliebard, H. M. 1975b. "Reappraisal: The Tyler rationale." In *Curriculum theorizing: The reconceptualists*, W. Pinar, ed. Berkeley: McCutchan.

Loy, J. W., B. D. McPherson, and G. Kenyon. 1978. *Sport and social systems*. Reading: Addison-Wesley.

Peters, R. S. 1965. "Education as initiation." In *Philosophical analysis and education*, ed. R. D. Archambault. New York: Humanities Press.

Reid, W. A. 1978. *Thinking about the curriculum*. London: Routledge and Kegan Paul.

Ridenour, M. V., ed. 1978. *Motor development*. Princeton: Princeton Book Co.

Safrit, M. J. 1981. *Evaluation in physical education*. Englewood Cliffs: Prentice-Hall.

Schlechty, P. C. 1976. *Teaching and social behavior*. Boston: Allyn and Bacon.

Schwab, J. J. 1969. The practical: A language for curriculum. *School Review* 78:1–24.

Smart, M. S., and R. C. Smart. 1977. *Children: development and relationships*. New York: Macmillan.

Tyler, R. W. 1949. *Basic principles of curriculum and instruction*. Chicago: Univ. of Chicago Press.

Tyler, R. W. 1981. Curriculum development since 1900. *Educational leadership* 38:(May) 598–601.

Walker, D. F. 1971. A naturalistic model for curriculum development. *School Review* 80:51–65.

Walker, D. F. 1975. "Curriculum development in an art project." In *Case studies in curriculum change*, ed. W. A. Reid and D. F. Walker. London: Routledge and Kegan Paul.

Young, M. F., ed. 1971. *Knowledge and control.* London: Collier-Macmillan.

Recommended Readings

Curriculum development process:

Tyler, R. W. 1949. *Basic principles of curriculum and instruction.* Chicago: Univ. of Chicago Press.

Walker, D. F. 1971. A naturalistic model for curriculum development. *School Review,* 80:51–65.

School and community analysis:

Schlechty, P. C. 1976. *Teaching and social behavior.* Boston: Allyn and Bacon.

Developmental characteristics:

Brophy, J. E. 1977. *Child development and socialization.* Chicago: SRA.

Ridenour, M. V., ed. 1978. *Motor development.* Princeton: Princeton Book Co.

Laws:

National Education Association. 1978. *A teachers' reference guide to PL 94–142.* Washington, D.C.: NEA.

U.S. Dept. of Health, Education and Welfare. 1976. *Title IX and physical education: A compliance overview.* Washington, D.C.

Determining Goals and Objectives

5

Outline

The task of establishing goals for the school's physical education program is not an easy one. The problems encountered in translating these program goals into useful statements of objectives can be even more challenging. Since each curriculum committee must deal with these responsibilities, it may be helpful to examine this phase of the process in some detail.

    The opening section of this chapter analyzes program goals, using examples from actual curriculum practice. The next section offers suggestions for conducting a needs assessment to provide the basis for development of a curriculum for a particular local situation. Finally, procedures for developing objectives for the guidance of individual teachers and students are presented.

Program Goals

The following excerpts have been selected from actual curriculum documents to illustrate the relationship of stated program goals to curriculum theory and to exemplify how different value orientations are reflected in actual program goals. Curriculum documents from four different school systems have been selected for study of physical education program goals. You will find it interesting to note such differences as their unique perspectives on the nature of individual student development desired and the type of subject matter content to be emphasized.

Illustrative Local Documents

Examples have been selected from four different educational settings. As you review these, try to analyze the goals in terms of the particular educational setting in which the physical education curriculum is to be implemented, note differences in emphasis, and identify the overall value orientation reflected in the program goals.

The first example is from the Calgary Catholic School District, Calgary, Alberta. The curriculum guide has been prepared in several volumes in accordance with the district organization of grade levels. Each volume is introduced with identical goals, which apply to all grades from elementary school through grade 12. The program guidelines presented in each volume (which do not appear in the following material) include more specific goals and objectives developed for the appropriate age-grade group.

Introduction

Physical Education, an integral part of the total education of the learner, contributes to the development of the individual potential through a variety of movement experiences, functional, expressive and creative. Its overall AIMS are individual development, environmental coping, and social interaction. The ultimate GOAL of physical education is quality and meaningful movement.

The physical education PROGRAM is a sequence of experiences through which the individual LEARNS TO MOVE as he MOVES TO LEARN.

Curriculum Design

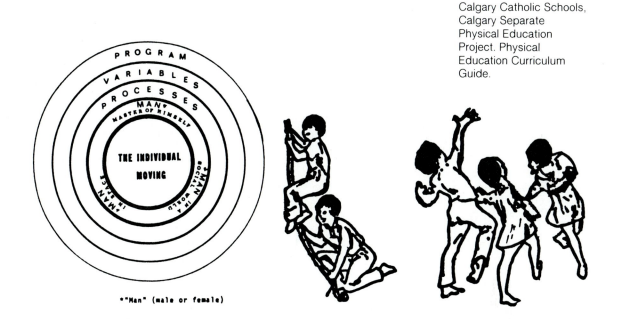

Calgary Catholic Schools, Calgary Separate Physical Education Project. Physical Education Curriculum Guide.

PROGRAM

VARIABLES

PROCESSES

MAN*
MASTER OF HIMSELF

THE INDIVIDUAL MOVING

MAN IN A SOCIAL WORLD

MAN IN A PLACE

•*"Man" (male or female)

Goals

Primary goals for physical education are based on the identification of individual needs along with the assessment of the physical and social environment. The goals require extension into performance objectives and movement learning experiences. No attempt is made to place the goals in order of importance. Subsections under each goal are not meant to be inclusive.

1. Develop as a skillful and efficient moving individual:
   a) Establish and maintain a good physical fitness program that becomes part of a lifestyle.
   b) Demonstrate ability to adapt to and control the physical environment.
   c) Develop skills in relating successfully to others.
   d) Develop a wide variety of movement experiences which will lead to wise and satisfying use of leisure time.
2. Develop understanding and skills in the use of facts, concepts, generalizations relating to human movement:
   a) Learn to adapt, refine, vary and improvise to find solutions to movement problems.
   b) Develop an awareness of the relationship of body movement to the maintenance of physical health and wellbeing.

3. Develop a desire for movement:
    a) Experience joy and satisfaction from movement experiences.
    b) Acquire a positive self-concept through participation in a variety of movement experiences within different environments.
4. Discover new possibilities in human existence:
    a) Recognize current limits of physical exertion.
    b) Identify potential for involvement in active games or newly found sport forms.
    c) Extend resources for finding and/or creating your own activity.

Calgary Catholic Schools, Calgary Separate Physical Education Project. Physical Education Curriculum Guide.

The second example is presented by courtesy of the Gwinnett County Public Schools, a suburban school district in which the population is growing rapidly, facilities are modern, and programs are still expanding. State of Georgia Standards require sixty hours of physical education annually for grades one through eight; the equivalent of one year of daily physical education is required in high school. The district physical education staff is committed to offering a comprehensive program for kindergarten through high school. Recent decisions to implement competency-based education are directly affecting curricula in Georgia schools. The curriculum guide for elementary and middle school physical education is due for revision; the high school physical education curriculum guide is still in the process of completion. The statements which follow have been excerpted from the most recent report to the Board of Education.

The intent of physical education is to encourage students to develop good physical condition, to engage in recreational activities, and to cooperate in team situations. The physical education curriculum follows the developing psychomotor (physical) growth of students. Balance, coordination, and dexterity are all part of physical education. The focus of elementary physical education is movement education with emphasis on motor skill development. Throughout middle and high school individual and team sports are added as they are commensurate with student abilities and interests with emphasis on fitness and life-time leisure activities.

At the elementary level teachers use *Lifetime Health Related Physical Fitness* (AAHPERD) primarily to determine if the Physical Education program is achieving desired goals. A skinfold caliper is used to determine the fat tissue of a youngster's body. Middle school teachers use the *AAHPERD Youth Fitness* to determine student physical fitness. At the high school level, students use *Fitness for Life* in the "Introduction to P.E." (P.E. 100) course. No other print materials are part of the core.

The goals for physical education are for students:

Goals

1. To participate in lifetime sports, hopefully to master one participatory sport.
2. To enable students to use leisure time wisely.
3. To be a good spectator, understand team sports and the necessity to have good sportsmanship.
4. To improve coordination, dexterity, balance and other forms of movement.
5. To exhibit physical fitness and maintain an acceptable level of cardiovascular efficiency and strength.

The preface to the Physical Education Curriculum Guide for Clarke County High Schools appears below. Clarke County is a university community in Georgia, subject to the same state standards as Gwinnett County. The school district is organized in three grade-level groupings—elementary, middle, and high school. Athletics, particularly collegiate and high school football, are a dominant factor in local school and community life.

Introduction

Physical education in the high school is an essential and integral part of the total school curriculum. Physical education has a place in the total curriculum because of values inherent within it as a separate course of curriculum and because of the immense contribution it can make toward enriching the academic curricula.

Because of the technological advances in today's society, there is an increasing amount of leisure time in the daily lives of the average person. Some persons spend more time in avocational pursuits than in their occupational work. Physical education has expanded to teach needed skills and knowledges to pursue many of the leisure sports activities that can be carried over to include lifetime skills.

Physical education is concerned with the whole child—not just the physical aspect. If taught correctly, physical education can contribute immeasurably to the child's total growth and development. The physical education curriculum teaches skills, behaviors and knowledge which are necessary to function at an adequate level of competence enabling each person to be an active, physically and mentally fit individual throughout life.

The words recess, supervised play, and athletics are not terms which are synonymous with physical education. However, they are all a part of the total program of physical education. The classroom instruction phase is the heart of the program. If the greatest values of physical education are to be achieved, teaching must be present in the instructional period.

General Behavioral Objectives

A. Physical fitness: The student will:
  1. Obtain a functional personal fitness level and maintain an optimum degree of muscular endurance and strength, cardiovascular endurance, speed, agility, organic vigor and flexibility.
B. Basic movement: The student will:
  1. Perform basic locomotor, nonlocomotor and combination movements.
  2. Coordinate basic movements with various rhythms.
  3. Develop an appreciation for dance and express creative ideas.
C. Social and emotional: The student will:
  1. Practice self-discipline and self-control.
  2. Accept and adapt to change.
  3. Be physically involved and feel positive about the involvement.
  4. Reflect a cheerful, optimistic attitude.
  5. Obtain and return play items properly.
  6. Take care of equipment.
  7. Abide by rules and show respect for them.

Curriculum Design

D. Values: The student will:
   1. Plan recreational involvement for self and others.
   2. Demonstrate that he or she is a knowledgeable spectator of many sports.
   3. Follow directions.
   4. Know rules and procedures and why they must exist.
   5. Use offensive and defensive strategies in a play situation.
   6. Illustrate or explain the immediate and long-range effects of exercise on the body and several approaches to attaining and maintaining physical fitness.
   7. Know and use safety precautions and protective requirements.

Within each unit taught, more complex and advanced skills should be designed within the class structure to meet the needs of various skill levels present. This should be done to accommodate various skill levels and to maintain interest and enthusiasm since the skills are not taught at proficiency levels (e.g. beginning, intermediate, and advanced).

The last example is selected from curriculum guidelines authorized by the Ministry of Education for the Canadian Province of Ontario. The *Curriculum Guideline for the Intermediate Division: Physical and Health Education* is to be used in developing curricula for students in grades seven through ten throughout the entire Province of Ontario. In Ontario schools, physical and health education is mandatory in the Primary and Junior divisions. In the Intermediate division, courses in physical and health education must be included in the programs of students in grades seven and eight. Credit courses must be made available to all students in grades nine and ten, and students are to be given "all possible encouragement and guidance in making physical and health education an integral part of their program."

The Intermediate Division student needs to understand and to develop positive attitudes towards his or her physical, intellectual, moral, emotional, and social development. Teachers must choose specific objectives that will provide balanced, dynamic programs that will assist in the total development of each individual. These programs should include a wide range of experiences that will provide more for the student than just information and skills.

Introduction

Objectives

A balanced program in physical education is intended to:

encourage and foster the development and maintenance of personal physical fitness;

promote the "joy of effort" in physical activities and provide an element of fun and enjoyment through participation in such activities;

develop a thorough understanding of the principles of movement and foster a greater awareness and appreciation of the various aspects of human physical activity;

help students to learn, manage, and control activities in a variety of situations and assist them in coping with problems of varying intensity;

help students attain levels of skill development that will allow them to participate more competently in physical activities;

provide a wide range of physical activities and experiences, including suitable outdoor activities for each season;

provide for co-instructional programs under the aegis of the school to encourage greater participation and provide competition for students in a suitable and healthy environment;

help students to develop attitudes, concepts, and values that will assist in problem-solving and decision-making in the light of both individual ideals and the customs and mores of the home and the community;

help students develop social skills and attitudes including independence, responsibility, leadership, cooperation, sportsmanship, and an appreciation of the capabilities and limitations of self and others.

Program Components

Seven broad categories of activities make up the physical education curriculum in the Intermediate Division:

physical fitness activities
team sports
individual and dual activities
gymnastics activities
dance
outdoor education
aquatics

Physical fitness must be an integral part of every physical education course at the Intermediate level. Each of the other categories must also be represented in every physical education course in the Intermediate Division in order to create a balanced program. It is recognized that facilities and teacher expertise will affect

Curriculum Design

the depth of treatment in each of the categories. Lack of facilities may preclude an aquatics component. However, where swimming facilities exist in the school, every Intermediate physical and health education student should be involved in the aquatics program.

Any activity or program component (other than those permitted within the rationale of this guideline) can be included only with the express permission of the local board of education. Full courses that concentrate on only one of the seven broad categories, for example, dance or outdoor education, are not within the rationale of this guideline. They are considered experimental courses and must be approved by the appropriate regional office of the Ministry of Education.

The following charts illustrate the continuous nature of the program in physical education from Kindergarten through the Senior Division. In addition, some appropriate major areas of emphasis are indicated for each level of this continuum. The lists are not intended to be prescriptive or all-inclusive.

Sequence

The major emphasis in the early years lies in the development of basic motor skills.

Ontario Ministry of Education, Physical and Health Education: Curriculum Guideline for the Intermediate Division, 1978.

During the Intermediate years, the gross and fine motor skills are developed through a variety of team games, dance, aquatics, gymnastics activities, and some dual and individual sports.

In the Senior Division, the major emphasis is placed on sports and activities that may lead to continuing participation outside of school and in future years. Individual and dual activities should be a major program component at this level.

The preceding curriculum document excerpts were selected to help you examine program goals in terms of the value orientations reflected. In order to examine the value orientation of a particular curriculum, you need to ask two questions: (1) What is the value perspective toward personal or individual development, toward social-cultural goals, and toward subject matter content? (2) To what extent is any one of these three elements valued above the other two?

Value perspectives within each of these three dimensions were discussed in chapter 2. Perspectives toward personal or individual development include reliance upon expert diagnosis of developmental needs, emphasis upon self-directed growth, and commitment to the fulfillment of individual human potential through introduction to the full range of movement meanings. Contrasting orientations toward social-cultural goals place value priorities on preparation for societal participation, equality of opportunity, and the achievement of excellence with equality. The most important value orientations with regard to subject matter content are health-related fitness, play, and human movement. You may wish to return to the analysis in chapter 2 as you consider selected program goals quoted from the preceding illustrations.

Individual Development Goals

Consider the following program goals for students:

1. Improve coordination, dexterity, balance, and other forms of movement.
2. Exhibit physical fitness and maintain an acceptable level of cardiovascular efficiency and strength.
3. Develop an appreciation for dance and express creative ideas.
4. Discover new possibilities in human existence.
5. Promote the "joy of effort" in physical activities and provide an element of fun and enjoyment through participation in such activities.
6. Develop a thorough understanding of the principles of movement and foster a greater awareness and appreciation for the various aspects of human physical activity.

All are taken from the curriculum documents presented at the beginning of this chapter. Each goal emphasizes individual development, yet they all reflect different perspectives toward individual development as a major physical education curriculum goal.

The first two imply a developmental approach. They are apt to be implemented through a curriculum guide based on sequences in human development for which experts prescribe progressions in activities.

The next two goals reflect a belief in self-directed growth. The student in a program with either of these goals is expected to assume some responsibility for the direction and outcomes of his or her own learning. Appreciation results only if the student is personally committed in the learning situation. Expression must be self-initiated. Discovery occurs only if the student is open to experience and actively seeking new possibilities.

The last two of the above goals suggest a personal meaning perspective toward individual development. The curriculum provides a great variety of opportunities. A wide range of learning activities is offered to foster awareness and appreciation within unique learners. Satisfaction and enjoyment in participation come in different activities for different persons.

Social-Cultural Goals

Social-cultural goals for students included within the illustrative physical education curriculum documents are exemplified by those which follow.

1. Develop skills in relating successfully to others.
2. Develop social skills and attitudes, including independence, responsibility, leadership, cooperation, sportsmanship, and an appreciation of the capabilities and limitations of self and others.
3. Plan recreational involvement for self and others.
4. Be a good spectator, understand team sports, and exhibit good sportsmanship.
5. Use leisure time wisely.
6. Participate in co-instructional programs under the aegis of the school to encourage greater participation and to provide competition for students in a suitable and healthy environment.

A re-examination of the goals makes it clear that the social-cultural perspective in all of these programs is one of preparation for participation in the broader community setting. While all of these curriculum guides at least suggest concern for the social development of the students, it is clearly not a major focus in planning any of them. Although the last of the goals implies an acknowledgement of the responsibility to provide equal opportunity to students of both sexes, these guides are typical of most current physical education guides in the United States and Canada in that you must really search for any direct support for equal opportunity goals. Curriculum goals that do express this perspective would be similar to the following:

1. To structure group interaction so as to strengthen race relations.
2. To provide opportunities for handicapped youth to develop and maintain a suitable level of physical fitness through participation in activity settings as supportive to them as to their non-handicapped peers.

Physical education programs that reflect a commitment to achieving both equal opportunity for all and excellence for the most capable are rare indeed. One might expect a program goal like this:

3. To provide differential competitive sports opportunities that consistently challenge the most gifted while motivating full and satisfying participation on the part of the least athletically talented.

Reviewing lists of physical education program goals leads to the conclusion that social-cultural goals are not considered to be of primary importance in very many of today's school districts. When social-cultural goals are stated explicitly, they reflect a perspective of preparation for societal participation, rather than one of social change.

Subject Matter Mastery Goals

Examples of subject matter mastery goals in the illustrative curriculum documents presented above include the following:

1. Achieve a functional personal fitness level and maintain an optimum degree of muscular endurance and strength, cardiovascular endurance, speed, agility, organic vigor, and flexibility.
2. Participate in lifetime sports, hopefully to master one participatory sport.
3. Take part in a wide range of physical activities and experiences, including suitable outdoor activities for each season.
4. Develop understandings and skills in the use of facts, concepts, and generalizations relating to human movement.
5. Learn to adapt, refine, vary, and improvise to find solutions to movement problems.

Curriculum Design

These examples demonstrate each of the three perspectives toward the subject matter of physical education. The first reflects a concern for health-related fitness. The next two emphasize the play perspective. The last two are indicative of a view of human movement as the focus of the physical education curriculum.

Goals Derived from Curriculum Value Orientations

If program goals are selected and carefully stated, with a sincere intent to achieve those goals through planned curricular experiences, the goals are necessarily derived from the prevailing local curriculum value orientation. The preceding discussion focused on illustrations of goals reflecting different perspectives with regard to three dimensions— individual development, social-cultural goals, and subject matter content. Examples were provided within these three dimensions for each of the perspectives for clarifying physical education curriculum value orientations (identified in chapter 2). This analysis can be carried one step further by analyzing any of the same goals within the context of the five general value orientations in curriculum development.

It has already been pointed out that none of the illustrative curriculum documents are derived from a social reconstruction orientation, since there are no stated goals emphasizing social change. Similarly, there is little evidence in these examples of a value orientation of ecological validity; goals derived from this orientation emphasize a personal meaning perspective toward individual development and a striving for excellence with equality in the area of social change. Only the Calgary document shows a commitment to the learning process orientation. On the other hand, all four evidence orientation toward disciplinary mastery (although the degree of emphasis varies) with moderately positive values toward self-actualization coming through in the stated goals of both the Canadian curriculum documents from which excerpts were selected.

Assessment of Needs

Program goals should be established by professional educators working with community leaders, parents, and other representative local citizens. Planning a curriculum to achieve the goals selected requires a local needs assessment process. A comprehensive assessment of current status and resources provides the basis for developing useful curriculum documents, for preparing appropriate curriculum materials, and for translating program goals into instructional objectives.

Importance of Theoretical Orientation

Program goals necessarily reflect the curriculum value orientations of those persons who determine the goals. Consequently, the value orientation predominant in the local community determines the nature and quality of the needs assessment process. The value orientation that led to the selection of the most significant educational goals also

Figure 5.1
Curriculum value orientations and the needs assessment process

Value orientation	Program goals	Information sought	Assessment techniques
Disciplinary mastery	Move skillfully	Skill status	Skill tests/performance ratings
	Knowledge about sports, movement and fitness (applied)	Level of knowledge and understanding	Knowledge tests
	Commitment to active lifestyle	Fitness status Degree of commitment	Medical/fitness tests Attitude inventories
Social reconstruction	Socialization into play environment	Sports competencies Group interaction	Sports skills/knowledge tests Sociometrics
	Commitment to active lifestyle	Fitness status Degree of commitment Participation in recreational physical activity	Medical/fitness tests Attitude inventories Community surveys/ questionnaires
	Equal opportunity	Activity preferences Attitudes, biases, etc.	Interest inventories Attitude inventories/ opinionnaires
	Social responsibility	Leadership skills and cooperative behavior	Ethnographic analysis
Learning process	Move skillfully	Skill status	Skills tests/performance ratings/cinematic analysis
	Knowledge about movement, sports & fitness (biomechanical, exercise physiology, etc.)	Level of knowledge and understanding	Knowledge tests
	Understanding about learning movement	Level of motor development and movement learning abilities	Movement process observation
	Problem-solving ability	Problem-solving skills	Unstructured observation

determines what is to be measured in the effort to plan for reaching these program goals.

Figure 5.1 highlights the impact of value orientations on the needs assessment process. Significant educational goals typical of each value orientation are identified. The chart illustrates variations in the nature of assessment data sought and the appropriate assessment techniques.

Value orientation	Program goals	Information sought	Assessment techniques
Self-actualization	Realization of individual potential (competence, confidence, socialization)	Individual fitness and skill status	Medical/fitness tests/skill tests, performance ratings/ cinematic analysis
		Interests and activity preferences	Interest inventories/attitude inventories
		Self-concept and creative abilities	Self-concept inventories/motor creativity tests
		Level of knowledge and understanding	Knowledge tests
	Integration of experience	Self-assessment and self-direction skills	Goal surveys/satisfaction inventories
Ecological validity	Realization of individual potential (competence, confidence, socialization)	Individual fitness and skill status	Medical/fitness tests/skill tests/performance ratings/ cimematic analysis
		Interests and activity preferences	Interest inventories/attitude inventories
		Self-concept and creative abilities	Self-concept inventories/motor creativity tests
		Level of knowledge and understanding	Knowledge tests
	Outdoor education and environmental protection	Outdoor performance skills	Tests of climbing, rappelling, etc.
	Social responsibility	Leadership skills and cooperative behavior	Ethnographic analysis
	Global perspective	Concepts of alternative futures	Goal surveys/satisfaction inventories/attitude inventories

If the primary value orientation is disciplinary mastery, the program goals emphasize the acquisition of particular motor performance skills and the learning of related knowledges and understandings. It is important to assess student skill levels in throwing, striking, springing; performing gymnastic events, dances, and aquatic tests; and in playing basketball, volleyball, softball, and tennis. Standardized knowledge tests and assessment of understandings in such topical areas as the effects of exercise, stress management, drug abuse, prevention of sports injuries, leisure lifestyles, and the role of exercise in aging, are also needed.

In contrast, if social reconstruction is a key value, program goals highlight equal opportunity in physical education learning. Needs assessment includes inventories of male and female interests and activity preferences, testing of attitudes toward racial and ethnic minorities, analysis of patterns of community participation in recreational activities, and surveys of community attitudes toward public responsibility for health-related fitness.

In a school system with a learning process orientation, program goals focus on perceptual-motor abilities, skill acquisition processes, creative motor performance, problem solving skills, and understanding about learning movement. Needs assessment will emphasize a combination of systematic observation and objective testing and will be especially concerned with evaluation of application, transfer, analyzing, and synthesizing abilities, and all types of process skills.

If the dominant value orientation is self-actualization, curriculum planners select program goals related to development of self-confidence, personal competence, and integration of experience. Needs assessment focuses on: individual interests, motivations and aspirations; evaluation of status and abilities in a broad range of movement tasks; self-assessment and self-direction skills; and the use of self-report techniques.

If ecological validity is the dominant value orientation, program goals focus on the realization of individual potential and excellence, environmental protection, outdoor education, and the development of global perspectives. Needs assessment is extended to: measuring knowledge about the ecosystem and concepts of alternative futures; testing self-concept and creative abilities; and assessing leadership skills and cooperative behaviors.

The theoretical orientation of local decision-makers determines the selection of a curriculum model, influences the choice of program goals, and guides the needs assessment process. The assessment of local curriculum needs is usually a two-level process. The planners first determine what all the children and young people need in order to be useful and fully functioning members of their society; in the second stage the needs of individuals and particular groups of children are assessed in order to determine goals and objectives appropriate to a highly diverse population of unique persons. In this respect, the local theoretical orientation is an important factor. Given a dominant value orientation of disciplinary mastery or social reconstruction, the needs assessment process is directed primarily to the common needs of the local community; the data sought emphasizes follow-up studies, mean test scores, and representative attitude surveys. In an educational system oriented toward self-actualization, learning process, or ecological validity, much more attention is directed toward the assessment of individual needs. Observation, self-assessment, and self-reporting techniques play an important role; a data management and retrieval system that can provide objective test data for and to individual participants also becomes essential. Needs assessment techniques are described in more detail in the following sections.

Instrumentation for Needs Assessment

Assessment of local physical education curriculum needs should be a process tailored to the characteristics of the particular community and its school system. The major types of instrumentation for needs assessment that can be considered by the decision-makers include observation, surveys and inventories, objective tests, and client self-assessment. Each of these can be adapted for use within situations reflecting different value orientations and for implementation of different curriculum models.

The most frequently used assessment techniques are listed in figure 5.2 and described briefly in the following paragraphs. Since assessment and evaluation are not the primary focus of this text, only a few examples of specific assessment or measurement tools are given. Suggested readings for more technical information on the subject are included in the bibliography at the end of this chapter.

Observation	Surveys and inventories	Objective tests
1. Unstructured observation	1. Satisfaction inventories	1. Medical examinations
2. Performance ratings	2. Attitude inventories	2. Fitness tests
3. Systematic observation of movement processes	3. Self-concept inventories	3. Motor performance and sports skills tests
4. Cinematic analysis	4. Sociometric analysis	4. Knowledge tests
5. Ethnographic analysis	5. Goal surveys	

Figure 5.2
Instrumentation for needs assessment

Observation

Informal, unstructured observation has always been a basis for forming opinions about educational needs. In the past half-century, educators have developed a variety of procedures for systematizing observations and increasing the sophistication of observation techniques for needs assessment. Performance rating scales are used to judge skill performance of both groups and individuals. Experienced raters assess the level of play execution and effectiveness of team strategy in such complex sports as basketball and soccer. Individuals are rated for instructional classification in tennis, golf, swimming, and skiing. Championships are determined by expert performance ratings in gymnastics, diving, and synchronized swimming. Dance performance is evaluated through skillful observation by experts. Observation guidelines, checklists, and rating scales designed to evaluate motor performance abilities can all be adapted for use in assessing the needs of physical education curriculum participants.

Motor performance rating scales focus the attention of the observer on the product of motor learning. More recently, educators have been interested in developing techniques for systematic observation of movement processes. In a developmental education curriculum model, it is particularly useful to be able to assess the level of motor development of program participants. Any motor taxonomy can be used as the basis for an observation tool. Unfortunately, not much attention has been given yet to the construction of observation instruments based on a motor taxonomy. Some preliminary efforts have been made to develop this approach to needs assessment using the Movement Process Category System (Jewett and Mullan 1977, 9–10), but much refinement in observation technique is needed before its use in this context is really practical.

In the past three decades, cinematic techniques for observation of motor performance have proven to be exceedingly valuable for both instruction and research.

Curriculum Design

Recording performance on film for visual analysis has the dual advantages of delaying the analysis for the convenience of the observer and of slowing and repeating the performance to permit greater accuracy in judgments. The increasing feasibility of recording and analyzing videotapes is particularly useful for the assessment of individual motor performance and the planning of individually prescribed curriculum experiences. In combination with various electronic aids for measurement, the videotape is also becoming an increasingly effective research tool. It is not unrealistic to anticipate that the development of holography will make three-dimensional pictures available at some time in the future for highly sophisticated observational techniques to be applied to the assessment of motor performance.

Another current development in observation of physical education is the use of ethnographic analysis. Ethnographic procedures have been introduced into the study of personal interaction in schools primarily as a research tool. The observer spends extended periods of time in the classroom environment with no formal observation guide as such. The structure for analyzing and reporting the interaction and describing the learning climate grows out of a large body of observational data. From the standpoint of needs assessment, this approach has potential utility in planning for behavioral change in curricula where social reconstruction, self-actualization, or ecological validity are important values underlying the program goals selected.

Surveys and Inventories

Surveys or inventories are tools frequently used to assess satisfaction with physical education programs. Opinionnaires can be designed to determine the level of overall satisfaction and to identify the particular strengths and weaknesses of local curricula as viewed by participants, parents, college counselors, employers, or citizens in general. Opinions can be sought concerning key educational needs, the relative importance of alternative program goals, or the effectiveness of the program in the achievement of selected goals. Current participants or former graduates can be surveyed as to their degree of satisfaction with their physical education experiences and their recommendations for curricular change.

Another use of the inventory technique is to survey attitudes. If a program goal is to develop desirable attitudes, it is important to determine what the present attitudes of the target population are. Inventories have been designed to assess attitudes toward racial and ethnic minorities, sex stereotypes, moral and ethical behavior in sports, and the importance of regular participation in vigorous physical activity. For example, inventories have been designed to assess an individual's level of commitment to running and other fitness activities (Carmack and Martens 1979; Norton 1982). Administration of such instruments makes it possible to select curriculum materials appropriate to the particular needs identified.

Inventories to assess an individual's concept of self are also available. Typically, this type of instrumentation is used to determine the needs of particular individual participants as opposed to common needs for physical education curriculum planning at the institutional level. Curriculum developers can utilize self-concept measures already validated by psychologists or can develop their own measures to focus specifically on the person's concept of self as a moving human being or as an individual person in a physical activity setting.

Inventories are also used for sociometric analysis. Participants are asked to select other members of the group for partners, for invitations, for companionship, for co-workers, or for particular group roles. Individual choices are analyzed to identify group leaders or isolates, to measure group cohesion, or to describe within-group interaction, climate, or social structure. Such information is useful in assessing needs relative to social interaction.

Another way of using inventories is in identifying the relative importance of potential program goals from the perspective of the participants or of any other concerned group (e.g., parents, classroom teachers, or physical education specialists). Alternative purposes for participating in a physical education program, or in particular categories of physical education program content, or in specific sports, dance or fitness activities are presented to the prospective participants to determine their perceived needs. Responses to such an instrument can provide information of value in assessing both common and individual needs and in selecting appropriate content.

Objective Tests

Many objective tests have been developed and validated for use in physical education. These tests can be used to assess needs, for program evaluation, and for appraisal of student achievement. Objective tests in physical education are directed toward the assessment of status with regard to fitness, motor performance skill, or knowledge.

A thorough medical examination to assess the individual health status of each student is recommended in the year of original entry into the school system and at the fourth grade, the seventh grade, and the tenth grade. Additional fitness tests can be administered regularly by the health and physical education staff; participants can be taught to administer many of these tests themselves or with the help of a classmate. Fitness tests include the traditional tests of muscular strength, muscular power, endurance, and flexibility. Tests of body composition and aerobic work capacity are becoming increasingly important in assessing fitness.

Objective tests of motor performance include tests of perceptual motor development, basic motor patterns, speed, balance, specific sport performance skills, and many standardized sports skills tests. Batteries of such tests can be used: to determine mean levels of motor skill development; to compare local performance scores with state, provincial or national norms; to assess needs for particular program content in the local curriculum; and to identify individuals needing remedial or accelerated programs.

Knowledge tests are employed in assessing needs in physical education as in any other subject area. They are routinely used in testing knowledge of game rules and regulations, terminology, and sports equipment, strategy, and safety. Much greater use could be made of objective testing to assess cognitive skills of application, analysis, and synthesis. Physical education curricula have the potential to develop understandings about the effects of exercise, how fitness is developed and maintained, the management of stress, biomechanical analysis of effective motor performance, common orthopedic injuries in popular sports activities, effects of drug abuse on motor performance, centering and procedures for achieving heightened sensory perception and increased body awareness, techniques for self-directed motor learning, the importance of motor experience in child development, optimum leisure lifestyles, and the role of physical activity in aging. Tests designed to assess the level of understandings in these important areas of knowledge are appropriately included in a comprehensive needs assessment program.

Client Self-Assessment

Client self-assessment can provide information that is not accessible in any other way. The clients can be identified as the student participants in the program, or the concept can be more broadly interpreted to include the parents and the citizens in the community who have a substantial investment in the entire school curriculum. Self-assessment can be directed toward many different aspects of need.

Local program goals should be based on identifiable needs which can give direction in physical education curriculum development. Parents and citizens can participate in identifying needs to be served by physical education; students can assess their individual needs and select personal goals. Interest inventories and activity preferences of students can provide significant input in the selection and sequencing of content.

Students' ratings of their own abilities in motor performance are helpful in classification and course selection; they also provide insight into individual self-concepts. All physical education students should learn to assess their own individual fitness levels. Even young children can learn to take pulse rates, to time exercise performance, and to score simple tests of strength, flexibility, and endurance.

Client self-assessment is a helpful basis for individualizing the curriculum. Given basic information relating to their personal status and needs, students can be guided in establishing task contracts knowledgeably. Computer programs can be devised to organize assessment data and to aid in developing appropriate individual physical education program activities.

Collection and Analysis of Assessment Data

As stated earlier, the collection of assessment data is usually accomplished in two stages. Attention is directed first toward determining the *common needs* of the program participants. The broad structure of the physical education curriculum can then be based on these common needs that provide guidelines for establishing program goals and making initial content decisions. To meet *individual needs* adequately, however, requires supplementary assessment techniques that permit curriculum planners and teachers to individualize and personalize curriculum experiences. This differentiation can be summarized by pointing out that program goals are based on common needs, while instructional objectives should be stated so as to encourage the individual participants to meet their own unique needs.

Common Needs

Professionally prepared physical educators are well informed concerning human developmental needs and have usually received specialized training in motor development and learning. Most have clear commitments relative to the general objectives of physical education. The translation of these general objectives into appropriate program goals requires further assessment of local common needs, using three major sources of information: (1) the values and educational priorities of the local community; (2) the experiences, opinions, and recommendations of former school graduates; and (3) recent and current objective program evaluation data.

It is recommended that an inventory be conducted to determine community priorities concerning the primary goals of the school's physical education program. The physical educators can structure a survey instrument (using a semantic differential or Likert format), basing the items on the key purposes for engaging in movement activities as identified in the Purpose Process Curriculum Framework (Nixon and Jewett 1980, 246–48) or design an instrument based on any preferred comprehensive list of potentially meaningful goals. A representative sample of local citizens should be sought in distributing the inventory. Demographic data to permit analysis of the opinions of appropriate population subgroups should be included.

A follow-up study of recent graduates can be conducted at the same time. If it is a relatively stable community, these two techniques might be effectively combined, although it is helpful to seek opinions and recommendations from recent graduates who have left the community for higher education or for employment opportunities elsewhere as well as those who have remained in the local environment. In any case, it is probably wise to include some of the same items in order to obtain some comparative data. The follow-up instrument should emphasize evaluation of postgraduate program outcomes (including assessment of a personal active lifestyle) as well as individual appraisal of program content and instructional effectiveness, and should seek recommendations for changes in program goals, content, and conduct.

It is suggested that the physical education staff engage concurrently in a thorough study of recent and current program evaluation data. Fitness test scores collected over a two- or three-year period can be analyzed to determine local norms; to determine areas of relative strength and weakness (e.g., upper body strength, abdominal strength, aerobic fitness, flexibility); to identify trends within the local population from one year to the next; and to compare different programs or subgroups within the total school system. Program evaluation data such as mean scores on standardized sports skills tests, numbers of students completing intermediate level qualifications in various activities, and the percentage of students qualifying for local physical education achievement awards are useful in determining particular curriculum changes needed. Data on participation in physical recreation activities, both in school-sponsored recreation programs and in city and county public recreation programs, as well as data on community participation in private club and commercial activities (such as tennis, golf, aquatics, bowling, handball, racquetball, gymnastics, karate, judo, yoga, skating, and health spas), provide information on the level of active participation within the community. Such data can also be analyzed to determine the extent to which individuals are engaging in activities included in school curricula and to determine active recreation needs that are not being met.

The professional staff should propose tentative program goals based on surveys of community priorities, follow-up studies of graduates, and analysis of program evaluation data. A sound procedure is to summarize all the assessment data related to common needs, prepare a report which concludes with recommended goals for the local physical education program, and present recommendations to the board of education in an open meeting scheduled to focus on this phase of the school curriculum. An annual report and review to ensure accurate assessment of current needs should be a continuing aspect of curriculum development.

Individual Needs

Program evaluation data should be collected in ways that are also useful in assessing individual needs whenever possible. Norms, mean test scores, and majority preferences are not particularly helpful in determining the needs of individuals. Consequently, it is important to supplement the program evaluation procedures described above with efforts directed specifically toward individual needs assessment.

Each participant should have a medical examination when entering school and a regularly updated fitness profile. An inventory of personal interests and activity preferences should also be administered. If students are given adequate orientation to the alternative potential program goals, it may also be desirable to offer them the opportunity to participate in setting their individual goals and selecting preferred activities through which the goals can be met. They can identify sports in which they wish to develop performance skill and rate their current skill abilities in these sports. Objective skill test data and skill check sheets should be added to the file. Inventories can be devised to collect this information and the data should become part of the individual physical education profile.

It is recommended that a personal Physical Education Plan (PEP) be developed for each student. The initial medical examination should provide the basis for assessing health status and setting basic fitness goals. An annual fitness evaluation should be provided for all students, leading to the required Individualized Educational Program (IEP) for those students with physical handicaps or learning disabilities. Knowledge and attitude tests designed to evaluate individual progress toward program goals in the cognitive and affective domains might be administered in coordination with medical checkups at the seventh and tenth grade levels in programs following the recommended pattern of medical screening (at school entry, fourth, seventh, and tenth grades). Skill performance data should be added as collected, and individual goals and progress relative to the PEP should be reviewed at least annually.

Development of Objectives

Program goals are developed from general curriculum value orientations. Following a local needs assessment process, it is possible to translate program goals into instructional objectives that can provide guidance to local educators. Educational objectives are formulated in order to assist the teacher with the choice of content and desired learner behaviors for structuring the curriculum and for evaluating the success of an educational program.

Bloom (1956) and Krathwohl (1964) are particularly well known for the taxonomies of educational objectives they proposed for use by educational evaluators and curriculum planners. Almost a quarter-century later, their basic concepts for stating educational objectives in three domains, each including identified categories of learner behaviors, are still widely acknowledged to be useful in educational planning. An early summary of this work of Bloom and his associates by Popham and Baker (1969) follows. It provides a more accurate description of the key concepts of their taxonomic analysis than do more contemporary criticisms.

Popham, W. James and E. I. Baker. *Systematic Instruction*. Englewood Cliffs, NJ: Prentice-Hall, 1970.

. . . In the early 1950s Bloom and a group of his colleagues, primarily college examiners, attempted to set down the kinds of objectives that were commonly being measured in the schools at that time. As a consequence of their analysis, they divided the many objectives treated in the schools into three categories, or as they refer to them, domains. These were the *cognitive domain*, the *affective domain*, and the *psychomotor domain*. The cognitive domain is concerned with the intellectual responses of the learner, as made in performing mathematical solutions, composing an essay, or solving various kinds of "mental" problems. One might substitute "intellectual" or "cerebral" for "cognitive" and describe these kinds of learner behaviors satisfactorily. The affective domain concerns the attitudinal, emotional, and valuing responses of the learner; they are usually classified as interests, attitudes, appreciations, and the like. The psychomotor domain concerns the physical responses of the learner, as made in performing certain types of manipulative operations, athletic endeavors, and so on. . . .

Within each of the domains there are levels, probably hierarchical—although there is some equivocation regarding this point—that attempt to categorize different kinds of learner behavior within each of the domains. One of the problems here, however, is that the levels within the domains that Bloom and his associates have developed deal with essentially internal phenomena. A given overt response might be used, depending upon the situation in which it occurs, to represent very different kinds of internal learner responses. . . . This makes the attribution of objectives to different levels within the taxonomies very difficult, no matter what the domain. However at the very least the various levels within the domains would seem to have some heuristic value, in that they may cause the teachers to try to generate objectives that appear to get at higher levels of learner behaviors.

The development of sound instructional objectives cannot proceed effectively without first clarifying program goals. Physical education program goals are established at the local level, reflect a particular value orientation, and should be frequently reviewed by the professional staff. This process leads to the statement and restatement of one or more series of goals, exemplified by those presented in the following list.

(Jewett 1982) In order to illustrate the process of developing instructional objectives in the remaining sections of this chapter, these goals will serve as the starting point for developing physical education objectives in all three domains.

The overall goals of the *elementary school* physical education curriculum are:

1. Facilitation of optimum motor development through extensive movement experiences.
2. Competence in spatial orientation abilities, including body awareness, consciousness of position in time-space, and identification of a dynamic self-environment of moving objects and other persons.
3. Development of expressive abilities and creative movement.
4. Group interaction skills based on concepts of partner, teammate, group goal, captain, game rules, and sharing.
5. Personal confidence in motor performance based on individual success in meeting progressively more difficult movement challenges.
6. Positive attitudes toward physical education growing out of intensive involvement in meaningful and enjoyable physical activities.

The overall goals of the *middle school* physical education curriculum are:

1. Refinement of personal motor performance skills, providing increasing self-mastery and a broad base for personal recreational involvement.
2. Enhancement of life-activity skills, including efficient body mechanics, survival aquatics, and competencies for the enjoyment of outdoor adventure.
3. Basic understanding of key fitness concepts and personal awareness of individual fitness status.
4. Socialization leading to individual concern for others, cooperative group skills, team involvement, and increased cultural understanding.

The overall goals of the *secondary school* physical education curriculum are:

1. Development of the competencies and the commitment required to achieve individual physical fitness and to plan and maintain personal fitness programs throughout life.
2. Lifetime sports competence enabling the individual to participate in several sports at a personally satisfying performance level in different seasons, climates and circumstances.

Jewett, Ann E. "Program Development." Chapter 7 in *Physical Education and Sport: An introduction.* Earle F. Zeigler (ed.). Philadelphia: Lea & Febiger, 1982, pp. 213–240.

3. Understanding of the major societal roles of the movement arts and sport sciences, the development of democratic group skills through movement activities, and a willingness to modify movement activities and to utilize personal movement skills to create a better global future.
4. Guidance for each individual in seeking personal meaning in movement, through providing for the achievement of effortlessness and excellence in performance, increased awareness and expressiveness, or the pursuit of high adventure in accordance with individual preferences and potentialities.

The overall goals of *adult physical education* are:

1. Achievement and maintenance of long-term health-related fitness, including the abilities to be self-directing, physically independent, and capable of minimizing unavoidable deterioration in physical abilities and capacities.
2. Development of the adult "inner athlete" who seeks active recreation and enhancement of the quality of life through personal fulfillment in challenging and satisfying achievement in physical activity.

Performance as an Indicator of Learning

The majority of instructional objectives in physical education, including most of those derived from the above program goals, are directed toward motor performance. Performance objectives (encompassing motor and other types of performance) emphasize the consequences of instruction. They focus on actual observable changes in pupil behaviors in contrast to the intentions of the teacher. Anticipated student performance can be described in advance. The demonstration of this "terminal" behavior, as it is designated, serves to identify to both student and teacher that the desired learning has in fact taken place. The actual performance of the participant is the indicator of the degree of learning achievement.

A great deal of debate has occurred over "behavioral" and "performance" objectives. Most of this debate focuses on the controversy over the danger of ruling out potentially worthwhile goals that are difficult to measure. The disagreement really centers on whether all educational objectives need to be stated as behavioral objectives. The authors believe that they do not; many of the examples which follow are not stated as behavioral objectives in strict conformity with the criteria popularized by Mager (1962) and others. No one seriously questions, however, that observable or measurable performance is a major indicator of learning in physical education.

Writing Performance Objectives

The specific professional skill of writing performance objectives is an essential tool for both curriculum planners and instructors. In developing the curriculum guide, program goals or long-term educational objectives are usually delineated as performance objectives to be achieved by the end of a unit, a term, or a two- to four-year educational period corresponding to local school district organization. In planning for daily instruction, the teacher must estimate the prior experience and current abilities of the students, and determine what progress can be anticipated during the class period.

The actual mechanics of writing behavioral objectives have been described in detail by Mager (1962). According to Mager, three aspects of anticipated student performance must be specified:

1. The anticipated performance must be clearly described in terms of observable behavior. This criterion implies the use of action verbs in stating objectives.

2. The conditions under which the desired behaviors are to be performed must be stated. Are students to perform the skill in a standardized test setting or in the context of game play? Will students have access to stop watches, skin calipers, universal machines, treadmills, or underwater weighing devices in assessing their own physical fitness?

3. The objective must describe an acceptable level of performance for the anticipated behavior. What range of accuracy scores are to be considered successful? What percentage of trials, ratings, or performances must be satisfactory? What is the minimum acceptable score or the maximum number of errors permitted?

These criteria necessarily lead to the conclusion that behavioral objectives are not appropriate in all situations. However, it is important for physical educators to be competent in writing performance objectives appropriate both to the dominant curriculum value orientation of the educational community within which they are working and to their local program goals.

Motor Performance Objectives

The subject matter content of physical education inherently requires that motor performance objectives will dominate teaching and learning in this field. A motor performance objective incorporates two distinct elements—a purpose element or content focus that reflects a general goal or value orientation, and a description of the desired motor behavior or anticipated motor performance. The use of some type of classification scheme or taxonomy to facilitate sequence in instructional objectives and progression in motor learning is helpful in developing motor performance objectives. Several taxonomies have been proposed for writing motor performance objectives (Simpson 1966; Clein and Stone 1970; Harrow 1972; Jewett and Mullan 1977; Goldberger and Moyer 1982). The PPCF Movement Process Category System (Jewett and Mullan 1977, 9–10) has been selected for further discussion. Because this taxonomy focuses on motor learning as a series of dynamic processes, it is thought to have greater relevance than the others for writing objectives for the development of motor abilities and the learning of motor behaviors.

The Movement Process Category System is based on the assumption that the processes through which one learns movement should be integral parts of curricular planning. Physical education classes will result in improved quality of motor performance for more learners if curriculum planners are thoroughly cognizant of the processes by which an individual learns to facilitate, extend, and fully utilize personal movement capabilities. Movement processes provide a basis for sequencing potential learning experiences and the learning of movement process skills is viewed as an important outcome. The student may be expected not only to improve performance, but also to increase the range of movement abilities. Seven movement process categories have been conceptualized and defined. They are listed as follows with illustrations of physical education instructional objectives directed toward each.

Perceiving

Awareness of total body relationships and of self in motion. These awarenesses may be evidenced by body positions or motoric acts; they may be sensory in that the mover feels the equilibrium of body weight and the movement of limbs; or they may be evidenced cognitively through identification, recognition, or distinction.

In the swimming pool, the student will become aware of the effect that the water has upon the body and upon movement in the water.

While bouncing and catching a tennis ball, the student will become aware of the size and peculiar characteristics of this ball.

The student will swing a softball bat with both arms extended and with the arms close to the body and be able to describe the difference.

Patterning

Arrangement and use of body parts in successive and harmonious ways to achieve a movement pattern or skill. This process is dependent on recall and performance of a movement previously demonstrated or experienced.

The student will hit tennis balls using a forehand stroke.

The student will execute a one-handed layup on the right side of the goal.

The student will perform a legal serve from the ad and deuce courts.

Adapting

Modification of a patterned movement to meet externally imposed task demands. This includes modification of a particular movement to perform it under different conditions.

The student will be able to use the forehand drive on tennis balls which are knee-high, waist-high, and chest-high.

The student will adjust the kicking pattern to perform an instep kick.

While walking on the balance beam, the child will step over a wand.

Refining

Acquisition of smooth, efficient control in performing a movement pattern or skill by mastery of spatial and temporal relations. This process deals with the achievement of precision in motor performance and habituation of performance under more complex conditions.

The student will use legs and arms to increase the height of a jump.

In football, the student will point the toe and kick the leg through the ball to increase the spin on a punt.

The student will hit pitched softballs to right, left, and center fields.

Varying

Invention or construction of personally unique options in motor performance. These options are limited to different ways of performing specific movement; they are of an immediate situational nature and lack any predetermined movement behavior that has been externally imposed on the mover.

The student will project a volleyball upward two different ways using two hands.

The student will pass a basketball to a partner three different ways.

The student will perform two types of tennis serves, employing a different grip for each.

Improvising

Extemporaneous origination or initiation of personally novel movement or combination of movement. The processes involved may be stimulated by an externally structured situation, although conscious planning on the part of the performer is not usually required.

In basketball, the student will be able to throw a ball back inbounds before stepping out-of-bounds.

The student will spontaneously devise a play for a four-on-two offensive fast break.

The student will be able to perform a dismount if balance is lost on the balance beam.

Composing

Combination of learned movement into personally unique motor designs or the invention of movement patterns new to the performer. The performer creates a motor response in terms of a personal interpretation of the movement situation.

The student will plan a balance beam routine using the skills of rolls and balance.

The student will make up a game using the skills of throwing, catching, and running.

The student will design an offensive basketball play using picks and screens.

In practice, curriculum planners determine the scope of physical education curricula by: making priority decisions concerning major emphases; identifying essential curriculum content; clarifying district-wide agreements; and establishing guidelines for planning within each school and within the various administrative units. Teachers develop instructional objectives using elements of human movement as content focus, and process categories to generate educational objectives for particular groups of students. The Movement Process Category System also lends itself to the identification of instructional objectives for individual learners and guides personalized learning toward different processes for a number of individuals learning in a group environment, but not necessarily attempting to achieve the same goal at the same time.

Cognitive Objectives in Physical Education

Bloom and his associates (1956), who proposed the scheme for classifying educational objectives into three categories identified as the cognitive, affective, and psychomotor domains, acknowledged that human behavior is not exclusively of any one function, but a complicated melding of the three domains. Physical educators, as well as teachers in any other subject, must recognize that the three are actually inseparable. Given this limitation, it is still helpful in upgrading the quality of instructional objectives to think about learner behaviors in terms of being primarily in one of the three domains.

The vast majority of instructional objectives in the schools are best classified in the cognitive domain as concerned primarily with the intellectual responses of the learner. They can be ranked in an approximate hierarchy from knowledge at the lowest level to evaluation at the highest. Because of the nature of the subject matter content of physical education, most instructional objectives are best classified in the motor domain as concerned primarily with the physical or motor responses of the learner. Motor performance objectives in physical education have been discussed earlier in this section. It is also important, however, to plan for key cognitive and affective learnings. Cognitive objectives are probably emphasized more in physical education curricula that utilize kinesiological studies models, but are certainly appropriately included in all physical education programs, whatever the particular value orientation or curriculum model.

Examples of instructional objectives at each level of the cognitive domain are listed in the following section. (Definitions of the six categories for classifying objectives in the cognitive domain are included in appendix A.)

Knowledge

The student will be able to identify and name various parts of the racquet.

The student will be able to list selected principles in the prevention of athletic injuries.

The student will be able to state the penalties for various rule violations in basketball.

Comprehension

The student will be able to describe events and influences that have shaped sport in this country.

The student will be able to identify fouls as they occur in a game of soccer.

The student will be able to explain principles of maintaining balance.

Application

The student will understand the rules, strategies, and values of the game of badminton well enough to play a doubles match.

The student will apply knowledge of physiology to the development of a personal conditioning program.

The student will be able to select a jogging shoe, properly designed, constructed, and fitted to minimize foot and leg injuries.

Analysis

The student will be able to analyze the values and varieties of strategies in tennis play.

The student will be able to analyze performance of a balance beam routine to determine possible points of improvement.

Synthesis

The student will be able to utilize a knowledge of psychology to improve performance in middle distance running.

The student will be able to utilize appropriate principles of biomechanics, exercise physiology, buoyancy, and choreography in designing a group synchronzied swimming number.

Evaluation

The student will be able to make judgments about the value of particular exercises, physical activities, and fitness program procedures in programs for senior citizens.

The student will be able to make judgments concerning the
   probable values, possible risks, and potential strengths
   and weaknesses of youth sports programs for
   preadolescent boys and girls.

In practice, the bulk of cognitive objectives in physical
education are stated at the knowledge and comprehension
levels. It is desirable in physical education, as in all subject
fields, to place more emphasis on anticipated outcomes at
higher levels.

Affective Objectives in Physical Education

As stated earlier, the affective domain is concerned with
the attitudinal, emotional, and valuational responses of the
learner. Objectives in the affective domain are directed toward
feelings, interests, and appreciations. Although Krathwohl
and his colleagues (1964) described five categories for
objectives in the affective domain, they are much harder to use
than the six categories of the cognitive domain. It is much
more difficult to identify appropriate observable behaviors. In
particular, it has never been possible to demonstrate that a
hierarchy actually exists among affective learnings.

Although physical education programs are strongly
oriented toward motor performance learnings, there has also
always been considerable interest in the development of
attitudes, appreciations, and values. The particular attitudes
emphasized in a given program vary according to the value
orientation of the curriculum designers and teachers.
Examples of physical education objectives in the affective
domain are listed according to the five categories or levels of
the Krathwohl taxonomy. (Definitions of the categories are
included in appendix A.)

Receiving
The student will explore the sensation of submersing his face
   in water.
The student will experiment with various activities involving
   taking an inverted position in space.

Responding
The student will enjoy participating in activities that involve a
   degree of risktaking.
The student will take turns with a partner.

Valuing

The student will take pride in the cultural movement heritage.

The student will develop a positive self-image relative to
  personal movement capabilities.

Organization

The student will plan and carry out a program for the
  improvement of personal fitness and athletic ability.

The student will develop a code of sportsmanship and be able
  to make consistent interpretations in the many varied
  physical recreation settings in which he or she
  participates.

Characterization by a Value or Value Complex

The student will accept regular physical activity as a way of
  life.

The student will develop a personal philosophical position
  concerning sport and its proper role in society.

Cautions and Concerns

A great deal of emphasis has been placed upon the
identification and clarification of program goals and upon the
importance of well-selected and carefully stated instructional
objectives. Several professional concerns have been implied
and probably need reinforcement, at least for the novice
teacher. Probably most important is a reminder that the
selection of objectives must be among the *first* curricular
decisions at all levels. Since the objectives selected are
fundamental in determining the potential results of any
educational enterprise, it is important to review program goals
frequently to ensure that they accurately represent the
community's real purpose for schooling. Instructional
objectives should offer clear directions for implementing
physical education program goals. Curriculum content must
be chosen with these goals in the minds of the designers.
Instructional strategies must be selected and utilized so as to
maximize the possibilities of achieving, not only daily lesson
objectives, but also long-range program goals.

A parallel concern is the need to avoid becoming
overwhelmed with a ''scientific'' or mechanistic approach to
writing precise behavioral objectives. Some areas of great
educational value do not lend themselves well to precise
measurement. Teachers should never be satisfied to allow
students' learning experiences to be limited to only those in
which the intended outcomes can be precisely described and

objectively tested. Neither should they allow themselves to become slaves to mechanistic series of instructional objectives that blind them to unanticipated teaching opportunities or restrict their creativity in enhancing the quality of the learning environment when "teachable moments" arise.

Another concern is the need to personalize the learning opportunities of students. Well-stated objectives must leave room for teachers to relate learning experiences to the individual interests, abilities, and preferences of students. Remember, also, that instructional objectives are *teacher* objectives. Students should have opportunities to share in determining which performance goals should receive emphasis and in setting standards that are appropriate and realistic for them as individuals. Additional objectives that represent personal goals of particular students should be accommodated within the instructional unit. Opportunities for student choice should be offered whenever such choices can be guided toward the achievement of broad program goals.

It is also important for curriculum planners and teachers to be aware of the impact of the "hidden curriculum" in any school setting. In any physical education class, the students will be learning things beyond those intended. Their learning experiences will be modified by procedures of class organization, groupings of pupils, behaviors of peers, attitudes of teachers, quality of the teaching station, and the supplies and equipment provided. All of these contribute to a "hidden curriculum" that we should continually strive to shape in ways that will support, rather than hinder, achievement of the announced goals and selected objectives.

Summary

Program goals should be established by professional educators, working with community leaders, parents, and other representative citizens. Program goals should be derived from the prevailing local curriculum value orientation and will necessarily reflect particular perspectives concerning individual development, social-cultural goals, and subject matter content.

Planning a curriculum to achieve program goals requires a local needs assessment process. The assessment of local curriculum needs is usually a two-level process. The planners determine first what all the children and young people need in order to be useful and fully functioning members of their society. Secondly, they assess the needs of individuals and particular groups of children. The major types of instrumentation for needs assessment include observation, surveys and inventories, objective tests, and client self-assessment. It is recommended that the professional staff propose tentative program goals based on surveys of community priorities, follow-up studies of graduates, and analysis of program evaluation data.

Following a local needs assessment process, the professional staff should translate program goals into instructional objectives that can provide guidance for local practice. While the majority of objectives in any physical education program will be motor performance objectives, attention should also be given to cognitive and affective objectives. The selection of objectives for a particular physical education program must be among the first curricular decisions in any physical education setting.

References

Bloom, B. S., ed. 1956. *Taxonomy of educational objectives: Handbook I: Cognitive domain.* New York: David McKay.

Bloom, B. S., M. D. Engelhart, W. H. Hill, E. J. Furst, and D. R. Krathwohl. 1956. *Taxonomy of educational objectives: The classification of educational goals.* New York: David McKay.

Carmack, M. A., and R. Martens. 1979. Measuring commitment to running: A survey of runners' attitudes and mental states. *Journal of Sport Psychology* 1:25–42.

Clein, M. L., and W. J. Stone. 1970. Physical education and the classification of educational objectives: Psychomotor domain. *The Physical Educator* 27 (March):27–34.

Goldberger, M., and S. Moyer. 1982. A schema for classifying educational objectives in the psychomotor domain. *Quest* 34 (2):134–42.

Harrow, A. J. 1972. *A taxonomy of the psychomotor domain: A guide for developing behavioral objectives.* New York: David McKay.

Jewett, A. E. 1982. "Program development." In *Physical education and sport: An introduction,* ed. E. F. Zeigler. Philadelphia: Lea and Febiger.

Jewett, A. E., and M. R. Mullan. 1977. *Curriculum design: Purposes and processes in physical education teaching-learning.* Washington, D.C.: AAHPER.

Krathwohl, D. R., B. S. Bloom, and B. B. Masia. 1964. *Taxonomy of educational objectives: Handbook II: Affective domain.* New York: David McKay.

Mager, R. F. 1962. *Preparing instructional objectives.* Palo Alto: Fearon.

Nixon, J. E., and A. E. Jewett. 1980. *An introduction to physical education.* Philadelphia: W. B. Saunders.

Norton, C. J. 1982. Student purposes for engaging in fitness activities. Doctoral Dissertation, Univ. of Georgia.

Popham, W. James, and E. I. Baker. 1969. *Systematic instruction.* Englewood Cliffs: Prentice-Hall.

Simpson, E. J. 1966. The classification of educational objectives: Psychomotor domain. Vocational and Technical Education Grant Contract No. OE-85–104. Washington, D.C.: U.S. Department HEW.

Recommended Readings

Establishing program goals:

American Alliance for Health, Physical Education, Recreation and Dance. 1981. *Essentials of a quality elementary school physical education program.* Reston, VA: AAHPERD.

Association for Supervision and Curriculum Development. 1979. *Lifelong learning: A human agenda.* Alexandria, VA: The Association.

Association for Supervision and Curriculum Development. 1983. *Fundamental curriculum decisions.* Alexandria, VA: The Association.

Jewett, A. E., and M. R. Mullan. 1977. *Curriculum design: Purposes and processes in physical education teaching-learning.* Washington, DC: AAHPER.

Kaufman, R. O., and F. W. English. 1979. *Needs assessment: Concept and application.* Englewood Cliffs: Educational Technology Publishers.

Nixon, J. E., and A. E. Jewett. 1980. *An introduction to physical education.* Philadelphia: W. B. Saunders.

Society of State Directors of Health, Physical Education and Recreation. 1972. *School programs in health, physical education and recreation: A statement of basic beliefs.* Kensington, MD: The Society.

Defining and assessing educational objectives:

Bloom, B. S., ed. 1956. *Taxonomy of educational objectives: Handbook I: The cognitive domain.* New York: David McKay.

Harrow, A. J. 1972. *A taxonomy of the psychomotor domain.* New York: David McKay.

Jewett, A. E., and M. R. Mullan. 1977. *Curriculum design: Purposes and processes in physical education teaching-learning.* Washington, DC: AAHPER.

Krathwohl, D. R., B. S. Bloom, and B. B. Masia. 1964. *Taxonomy of educational objectives: Handbook II: Affective domain.* New York: David McKay.

Krathwohl, D. R., and D. A. Payne. 1971. Defining and assessing educational objectives. In *Educational measurement*, ed. R. L. Thorndike. Washington, DC: American Council on Education.

Mager, R. T. 1962. *Preparing instructional objectives.* Palo Alto: Fearon.

Popham, W. J., and E. I. Baker. 1970. *Systematic instruction.* Englewood Cliffs: Prentice-Hall.

Safrit, M. J. 1981. Evaluation in physical education. Englewood Cliffs: Prentice-Hall.

Instrumentation for physical education needs assessment:

American Alliance for Health, Physical Education and Recreation. 1967. *Sports skills tests.* Washington, DC: AAHPER.

American Alliance for Health, Physical Education and Recreation. 1976. *Youth fitness test manual.* Washington, DC: AAHPER.

American Alliance for Health, Physical Education, Recreation and Dance. 1980. *Health related physical fitness manual.* Washington, DC: AAHPERD.

Barrow, H. M., and R. McGee. 1979. *A Practical approach to measurement in physical education.* Philadelphia: Lea and Febiger.

Baumgartner, T. A., and A. S. Jackson, 1982. *Measurement for evaluation in physical education.* Dubuque: Wm. C. Brown Publishers.

California Department of Education. 1962. *California physical performance tests.* Sacramento: State Department of Education.

Clarke, H. H. 1976. *Application of measurement to health and physical education.* Englewood Cliffs: Prentice-Hall.

Cooper, K. H. 1977. *The aerobics way.* New York: Bantam.

Johnson, B. L., and J. K. Nelson. 1979. *Practical measurements for evaluation in physical education.* Minneapolis: Burgess.

Kenyon, G. S. 1968. Six scales for assessing attitude toward physical activity. *Research Quarterly* 39:566–74.

Manitoba Department of Education. 1977. *Manitoba physical fitness performance test manual and fitness objectives.* Manitoba: Department of Education.

Martens, R. 1977. *Sport competition anxiety test.* Champaign: Human Kinetics Publishers.

Mathews, D. K. 1978. *Measurement in physical education.* Philadelphia: W. B. Saunders Co.

Mood, D. 1971. Test of physical fitness knowledge: Construction, administration and norms. *Research Quarterly* 42:423–30.

Safrit, M. J. 1981. *Evaluation in physical education.* Englewood Cliffs: Prentice-Hall.

Sonstroem, R. J. 1978. Physical estimation and attraction scales: Rationale and research. *Medicine and Science in Sports* 10:97–102.

Stamm, C. L. 1978. Title IX: Implications for measurement in physical education. In *Proceedings of the Colorado measurement symposium.* Boulder, CO: Univ. of Colorado Conference Center.

Texas Governor's Commission on Physical Fitness. 1973. *Physical fitness—Motor ability test.* Austin, TX: The Commission.

Tiburzi, A. 1979. Validation of the construct of physiological fitness, Doctoral Dissertation. Athens: Univ. of Georgia.

Selection and Sequencing of Educational Activities

6

Outline

Curriculum Design

The development of a curriculum is the creation of an environment that provides students with a set of experiences. The experiences or activities are designed not merely to keep students busy but to give them the opportunity to learn something of value. The curriculum designer is like an architect who must select which materials to use and how to structure and sequence them to create the optimum environment. Like architecture, curriculum design involves both science and art. Scientific research provides information about the learning process and about the effectiveness of various instructional strategies. Artistic principles address the human qualities of the program—the intensity, the beauty, and the joy of the day-to-day experience.

Examples from Curriculum Documents

Curriculum design decisions are often summarized in diagrams and charts that depict the scope, structure, and sequence of the program. Such scope and sequence charts generally include both an overview of the total program and a description of units of instruction included in the program at various levels. Examples from two curriculum guides follow. To interpret these materials you need to examine the beliefs and goals of the program, as well as the charts and diagrams included here. The goals of the Calgary program were presented in chapter 5. The rationale for the curriculum from the State of Louisiana is included with the materials in this section.

Calgary Separate Physical Education Project, Calgary Catholic School District, 1977.

From LeRoy Pelletier, et al., *Calgary Separate Physical Education Project,* © 1977 Calgary Catholic School District. Calgary, Alberta, Canada. Reprinted by permission.

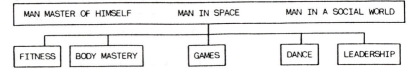

Physical education is made up of subject areas. Each subject area is uniquely different from each other subject area, yet each is related to the others. Each subject area should emphasize different movement within its learning opportunities as well as different human and environmental variables. Each subject area should make a unique contribution to the development of man.

For purposes of program development, five subject areas have been identified:

FITNESS — the basis of all activity in our society — being able to undertake daily physical tasks and engage in physical activity; a "total-fitness"feeling.

BODY MASTERY — managing oneself in movement in varied environments.

GAMES — structural movement activity in which a person or persons on the move, engage in meaningful play with a moving object within the framework of certain rules

DANCE — movement medium for creative experience and expression

LEADERSHIP — group members may be influenced and motivated to achieve common goals through movement activities

MAN MASTER OF HIMSELF	MAN IN SPACE	MAN IN A SOCIAL WORLD

FITNESS	BODY MASTERY	GAMES	DANCE	LEADERSHIP

FITNESS

Assessment:

Pulse test
Flexibility test

Health Related:

Nutrituion
Weight
Relaxation

Programs:

Weight training
Aerobics
Circuit training
Exercise programs

BODY MASTERY

Aquatics:

Canoeing
Diving
Rowing
Sailing
Scuba
Skin diving
Swimming

Cycling:

Gymnastics:

Educational
Olympic

Horsemanship:

Outdoor Pursuit:

Orienteering
Camping
Hiking, etc.

Skating:

Skiing:

Snowshoeing:

Track & Field:

Running
Jumping
Throwing

GAMES

Combatives:

Wrestling
Self Defense

Field Orientation:

Softball
Baseball

Goal Orientation:

Basketball
Football
Field Hockey
Ice Hockey
Soccer
Rugby
Water Polo

Net Orientation:

Volleyball
Badminton
Tennis
Table Tennis

Target Orientation:

Archery
Bowling
Golf
Curling
Pellet Shooting

Wall Orientation:

Racquetball
Squash
Handball

DANCE

Folk:

Modern:

Social:

Square:

Creative:

LEADERSHIP

Instruction & Coaching:

Community leader
Para professional
Certification

Leadership Skills:

Organization
Management

Officiating:

Certification
Referee
Timer
Scorer
Practicum Experience

Sports Medicine:

Trainer
Care of injuries

PROGRAM
VARIABLES
PROCESSES
MAN
MASTER OF HIMSELF
THE INDIVIDUAL
MOVING
MAN IN SPACE
MAN IN A SOCIAL WORLD

From LeRoy Pelletier, et al., *Calgary Separate Physical Education Project,* © 1977 Calgary Catholic School District. Calgary, Alberta, Canada. Reprinted by permission.

Physical Education and Recreation Curriculum Guide (K-10). Department of Physical Education, State of Louisiana, 1980.

Physical education is an integral part of the total education program in Louisiana. Each student needs and is entitled to participate in a comprehensive program of physical activity, taught by a specialist of physical education. A well-planned, sequential program of physical education contributes to the development of fully functioning individuals capable of living healthy, productive lives in our society.

For the optimal learning environment to exist, educators must establish clearly what students are to achieve, how this is to be accomplished, and to what extent the attempts have been successful.

This publication provides a basic list of competencies in physical education for the State of Louisiana and indicates the approximate time at which each should be mastered. The list given is minimum and should be expanded by local systems as permitted by each unique situation.

The process at the local level must include an analysis of various factors that provide valuable insights into the task of curriculum development. It is believed the adoption of performance objectives for physical education statewide can offer guidance for local districts in selecting meaningful content and appropriate methodology for their curriculum.

As shown in the first figure, the successful attainment of the minimum competencies is interrelated with factors such as facilities, teacher characteristics, community and administrative support. It is recognized there is a need for flexibility to accommodate the many aspects of the total environment.

The model presented in the next figure was developed in an effort to provide a framework upon which program objectives and content for each individual school can be based. The framework depicts a basic activity-centered approach that takes into account relevant

From *Physical Education and Recreation Guide,* State of Louisiana, 1980. Reprinted by permission.

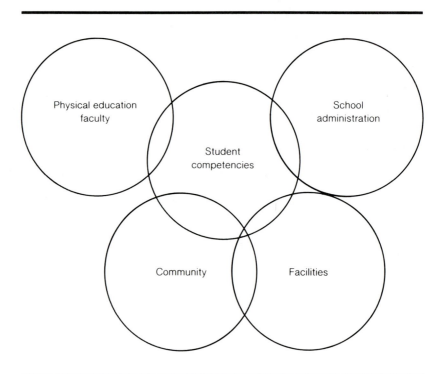

Curriculum Design

From *Physical Education and Recreation Guide*, State of Louisiana, 1980. Reprinted by permission.

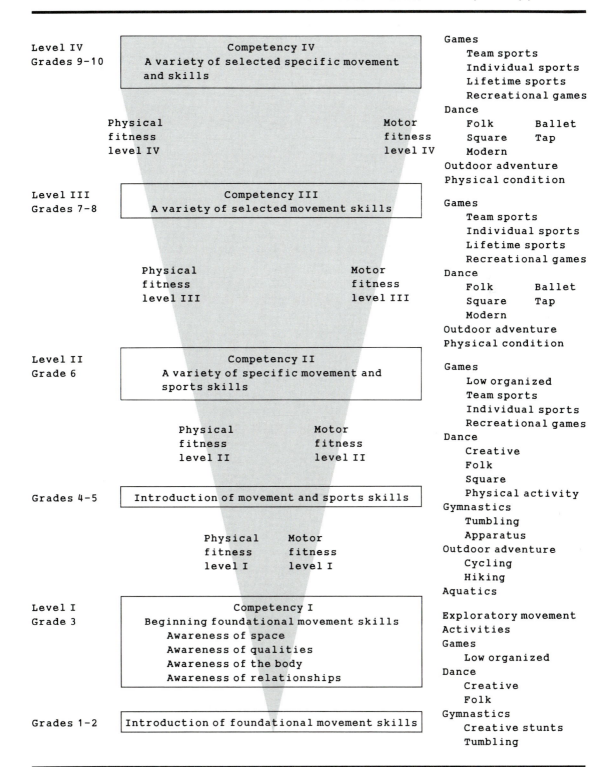

Level IV
Grades 9–10

Competency IV
A variety of selected specific movement and skills

Physical fitness level IV

Motor fitness level IV

Games
Team sports
Individual sports
Lifetime sports
Recreational games
Dance
Folk   Ballet
Square   Tap
Modern
Outdoor adventure
Physical condition

Level III
Grades 7–8

Competency III
A variety of selected movement skills

Physical fitness level III

Motor fitness level III

Games
Team sports
Individual sports
Lifetime sports
Recreational games
Dance
Folk   Ballet
Square   Tap
Modern
Outdoor adventure
Physical condition

Level II
Grade 6

Competency II
A variety of specific movement and sports skills

Physical fitness level II

Motor fitness level II

Games
Low organized
Team sports
Individual sports
Recreational games
Dance
Creative
Folk
Square
Physical activity
Gymnastics
Tumbling
Apparatus
Outdoor adventure
Cycling
Hiking
Aquatics

Grades 4–5

Introduction of movement and sports skills

Physical fitness level I

Motor fitness level I

Level I
Grade 3

Competency I
Beginning foundational movement skills
Awareness of space
Awareness of qualities
Awareness of the body
Awareness of relationships

Exploratory movement
Activities
Games
Low organized
Dance
Creative
Folk
Gymnastics
Creative stunts
Tumbling

Grades 1–2

Introduction of foundational movement skills

From *Physical Education and Recreation Guide,* State of Louisiana, 1980. Reprinted by permission.

Physical education and recreation grade placement

Activity	Grade placement											
	I			II			III			IV		
	K-1	2	3	4	5	6	7	8	9	10	11	12
Movement	+	+	+									
Physical fitness--motor fitness			+			+		+		+		
Dance												
Folk--square					+		+					
Modern												
Team sports												
Basketball					+		+		+			
Football					+		+		+			
Soccer				+		+		+				
Softball					+		+			+		
Volleyball				+		+			+			
Individual and dual sports												
Aquatics												
Gymnastics				+		+		+	+			
Track and field					+		+			+		
Wrestling												
Lifetime sports												
Archery						+		+	+			
Badminton					+			+		+		
Bowling				+			+		+			
Golf						+		+	+			
Tennis				+			+			+		
Park and recreational games												
Outdoor adventure												

Activities required for piloting for each grade level are as designated. Modern Dance, Aquatics, Wrestling, Park and Recreational Games, and Outdoor Adventure are not required as part of the "core" curriculum. However, we would like to establish levels of competencies for these elective activities. Instead of grade competencies, performance objectives in these activities are listed by levels: Level I--(K-3), Level II--(4-6), Level III--(7-9) and Level IV--(9-12). If any activity is taught that is not required but listed as an elective, competencies for that activity at the particular level it is offered should be tested.

characteristics of the learner. Learning activities must be selected and arranged according to each child's developmental level. It should be understood that, due to limited experiences, a student in the Intermediate Stage II may be considered a beginner and will thus be working toward completion of Competency Level I skills. Throughout a student's school years, objectives and content must be paired with individual learner characteristics. Physical fitness and motor fitness aspects of the program are believed to form a basis for successful participation on any level and are thus shown at all levels. The vertical relationship displayed in the framework indicates that each level builds on the level of performance displayed in the previous one.

It is anticipated a more defined sense of direction with predictable outcomes for students will be the result and factor of this guide.

Selection of a Model

Based upon the program philosophy and goals identified, the curriculum committee will select a conceptual framework or model to guide the local design process. The committee may select a conceptual framework that determines the scope of the program content and provides a system for classifying or organizing that content, and proceed directly to the design of a local model. Alternatively, the committee may choose to use an already existing model to assist them in making decisions about what to include and exclude from the program and how to organize content for instruction. If a conceptual framework is selected, it can be used to evaluate whether a specific program is complete; that is, whether it includes all elements identified as essential. Traditionally, many physical educators have used a model that classifies the content of physical education as team sports, individual-dual sports, aquatics, dance and gymnastics, or some variation of this list. The models described in chapter 3 have proposed a number of alternatives for planning a physical education program. Can you identify the value orientations and the type of conceptual framework or model used by the designers of the Calgary and Louisiana curriculum guides?

Selection of a conceptual framework or model is an important decision that will have a major impact upon the nature of the program developed. The framework provides an essential link between the platform or value position underlying the curriculum and the program design. Once the curriculum committee has clarified its conceptual framework and selected a model, they are ready to proceed with what Walker (1975) has called the "production of plans and materials."

Structuring the Curriculum

The first design decision that must be made is how the program content will be built into units of instruction. Dividing content into units has several advantages. It helps students concentrate their attention and, presumably, improve the efficiency of their learning. It gives teachers a planning device that enables them to maintain program continuity and balance. Completion of a unit of instruction provides a mechanism for measuring and recording student progress.

Traditionally in physical education, units of instruction have been organized around specific sport or dance activities, i.e., volleyball, tennis, folk dance, etc. There have been some exceptions, predominantly in elementary school programs, that included units such as body awareness, locomotor skills, and self-testing. Occasionally, secondary school programs have been structured to include such units as fitness or sports appreciation.

The curriculum development process proposed in this book suggests that activity unit structure should not be taken for granted, but that content should be selected and organized according to the curriculum theory and conceptual framework adopted. The following examples should help clarify that process.

Developmental Theme Units

Several of the physical education curriculum models reviewed in chapter 3 perceive curriculum content as selected and structured on the basis of its relevance to human needs and goals. The developmental theme unit illustrates this principle. The organizing center for the unit of instruction is a goal or need of the student. Activities are selected that are perceived to have value in helping the student attain the goal.

Examples of developmental theme units can be found at both elementary and secondary school levels. Hoffman, Young, and Klesius (1981) have described a developmental education approach to elementary school physical education. They identify six developmental themes that serve as the conceptual framework for the program. For each theme, several units of instruction have been developed that contribute to the accomplishment of the overall theme. The themes and the titles of related units of instruction are listed in figure 6.1. In figure 6.2, abbreviated examples of two of the developmental theme units are given. Additional information about learning experiences and evaluation procedures is available in the Hoffman, Young, and Klesius text.

Becoming Aware: Learning About and Establishing Basic Movement Capabilities
1. Developing body image
2. Developing movement potential
3. Developing spatial awareness
4. Developing manipulative abilities

Becoming Independent: Increasing Self-Reliance and Confidence in Moving
1. Following directions
2. Making choices
3. Developing safe behavior
4. Developing courage

Accepting and Expressing Feelings and Ideas: Communicating through Movement
1. Expressing feelings
2. Understanding and accepting feelings
3. Increasing communicative abilities
4. Creating ideas

Accepting Responsibilities and Acting Cooperatively: Sharing the Movement Environment and Respecting and Interacting Productively with Others
1. Developing concern for others and property
2. Developing roles
3. Exploring rules
4. Developing cooperative and competitive behavior

Improving Quality of Response: Refining and Elaborating Movement Capabilities for a Purpose
1. Developing precision
2. Increasing complexity of response
3. Challenging oneself beyond comfortable limits

Drawing Relationships: Comprehending the Significance of Movement in One's Lifestyle
1. Developing healthful patterns of living
2. Understanding environmental influences on movement
3. Developing informed decision-making behavior

Figure 6.1
Developmental themes and related units of instruction
From H. A. Hoffman, J. Young and S. E. Klesius, *Meaningful Movement for Children.* © 1981 Allyn and Bacon, Boston, MA. Reprinted by permission.

Making choices

Planning guide

Objectives

As a result of the learning experiences over time, children will be able to:

1. decide between two alternatives

2. decide between a number of alternatives

3. operate within the limits of the consequences of their decisions

4. create new ideas by combining or selecting activity choices

5. demonstrate understanding that avoiding a decision is simply another form of decision making

Experiences

- making choices between two types of equipment; choosing between two different activities
- choosing suitable equipment for a task; choosing between several activities
- staying involved with a task once chosen; exploring the possibilities that the equipment affords for moving over, under, around
- combining choices to expand the range of alternatives available
- discussions on obstructive behavior focusing on resolution of problems of difficult choices

Understanding environmental influences on movement

Planning guide

Objectives

As a result of the learning experiences over time, children will be able to:

1. explain the influence of the play space on movement, and the influence of the play equipment on the nature of the game

2. describe the effects of varying environmental factors on movement

3. explain the cultural influences on selected ethnic dances or movements

Experiences

- play volleyball or tennis-like games with the net at various heights; conduct games under varying conditions, such as changing the size of the playing area or reducing the number of players
- conduct vigorous activities on days of differing weather conditions, such as high and low pressure days, warm and cold days
- learn contrasting forms of folk dancing, and investigate what influences the development of certain steps or movements

Figure 6.2
Examples of developmental theme units
From H. A. Hoffman, J. Young and S. E. Klesius, *Meaningful Movement for Children.* © 1981 Allyn and Bacon, Boston, MA. Reprinted by permission.

The secondary school physical education program described in Hellison's *Beyond Balls and Bats* also contains examples of the developmental theme approach. Derived from a humanistic curriculum orientation, the program views physical education as a means for personal growth based upon self-awareness and self-understanding. A unit of instruction focusing on self-other awareness is described in figure 6.3.

Regardless of the conceptual framework or model selected, the common characteristic of developmental theme units is a focus upon broadly defined needs or purposes of the individual. Physical education content is selected and organized on the basis of its contribution to the total well-being of the student. In some of these units, all of the learning experiences are selected from one area, i.e., creative dance, games, etc. In other cases, experiences are selected from a

Figure 6.3
Developmental theme
unit: Self-other awareness
From Hellison, D., *Beyond
Balls and Bats.* Copyright
1978 American Alliance
for Health, Physical
Education, Recreation
and Dance, Reston, VA.
Reprinted by permission.

Concepts

How can I help others? Rights of others, worth of others,
   universal sense of community.

Activities

Cooperative games based on the Project Adventure concept;
   for example, games that require all students to move from
   one designated area to another over obstacles without
   touching some areas of the floor, thereby forcing everyone
   into helping roles.

Competitive games with emphasis on cooperation, such as
   awarding one point for certain kinds of passes in
   basketball and two points for a basket (the height of
   frustration for many of my "gunners").

The creation of new games by students, stressing cooperation
   in planning and executing as well as a playful spirit in
   both the creative act and in playing new games.

Skill development situations using students to help other
   students.

variety of activities. The fundamental characteristic of a
developmental theme unit is that the experiences are included
only if they will contribute directly to the goal or purpose, and
the instruction is organized to emphasize that theme.

Movement Theme Units

Both the movement education and kinesiological studies
curriculum models recommend structuring the program
around essential elements of the content area. The conceptual
framework used to organize content in a movement education
program is Laban's system for describing and classifying
movement. The themes derived from the Laban framework
serve as the basis for planning units of instruction. Each
theme selects certain components of the movement framework
and uses those aspects or dimensions to develop skillful
movement in games, dance, or gymnastics. A unit of
instruction organized around one of these themes would
attempt to help students to understand the theme, to perform
skillfully a variety of movements related to the theme, and to
interpret the feelings and meanings associated with the
theme. An example of a unit for educational games focusing
on awareness of the body is described in figure 6.4. Additional
information about the learning experiences is described in
Logsdon et al. (1977).

Major focus

Throwing, catching, with emphasis on specific locomotor skill of jumping.

Content

Body—traveling (general locomotion).
     jumping.
Space—general.
     personal.
     extensions.
Effort—weight (force).
Relationship—individual to individual or small group.
     individual to object.

Appropriate for

Children who can catch and throw with ease working alone and in small groups. They are beginning to be aware of how to create and maintain spaces while moving and are also beginning to adjust effectively the amount of force they use in relation to different situations.

Equipment

A variety of balls (plastic [8 inches]), rubber (5, 7, and 8 inches), volleyballs, basketballs ([junior], sock, yarn, and soft softballs); flat surface; and rebound net.

Area

Indoors, outdoors—medium or large, but with a high ceiling.

Unit objectives

Children should be willing to try to:

1. Throw balls of different types to others who must catch them above their heads and in the air.
2. Catch balls of different types above their head while in the air.
3. Take responsibility for changing the balls they are using throughout the class.
4. Challenge themselves by the selection of ball type as well as the way they are working in the class.
5. Feel the difference between jumping to catch a ball when you *need* to jump and when you do *not* need to jump.

6. Contribute constructively to the group task of designing an original game or modifying a conventional game.

The teacher should be able to:

1. Analyze why specific children are successful or unsuccessful in catching in the air and throwing to make someone else catch in the air.
2. Help children become comfortable in challenging situations.
3. Assist children to redesign their learning experience if they need to be more challenged or less challenged.
4. Alert children to their spacing in relation to the others in the class if they forget to leave enough space.

Ideas for designing learning experiences
    1. *Alone or with one other* (children's choice)
    Throwing (tossing) a variety of balls so you must *catch* it while in the air (jump):

—in places around you above your head (in front, behind, to the sides):
stationary-traveling.
so you must reach to catch it (extension).
—against a wall or flat surface.
—against a rebound net.

    Throwing (tossing) a variety of balls when in the air:

—from different positions around you above your head (in front, behind, to the sides):
stationary-traveling.
—against a flat surface.
—against a rebound net.

    2. *With others* (2–3)
    In a group, throwing (tossing) and catching a variety of balls so that:

—the group is always moving into empty spaces.
—the receiver has to catch the ball while in the air; while in the air *and* reaching for it in different places above the head.
—the thrower tosses the ball while in the air.
—the size of the group or the members change.

Figure 6.4 con't.

In a group (2–3), throwing (tossing) a variety of balls against a flat surface and/or rebound net so that:

—the group keeps shifting positions.
—the receiver has to catch the ball while in the air; while in the air *and* reaching for it in different places above the head.
—the thrower tosses the ball while in the air.
—the size of the group or the members change.

3. *Alone or with others* (2–3) (children's choice)
Select a conventional game and modify it in relation to:

—the content being developed with the children.
—the developmental needs of the children.

Have the children design an original game using the ideas with which they have been working. Let them decide:

—how many will be involved.
—*whether* they wish rules; if so, what.
—*whether* they wish boundaries; if so, what.
—which ball or balls to use.

Most examples of movement theme units are found in elementary school movement education programs. Secondary school programs occasionally use a theme structure, but usually the conceptual framework used parallels the disciplinary areas found in college and university professional preparation programs. High school students are taught units on such topics as exercise and fitness, biomechanics, play, game and sport, and aesthetics (Lawson and Placek 1981). An example of such a unit is described in figure 6.5.

Some critics of the kinesiological studies approach express concern about "intellectualizing" physical education and de-emphasizing movement. Note that movement theme units include movement experiences as the means by which concepts are learned.

Activity Units

Many physical educators may adopt a model that defines the subject matter of the program in terms of various types of games, sports, dance, and exercise activities. Units of instruction are organized around specific activities, and mastery of the activity is the primary goal. The play education curriculum model utilizes such an approach, defining physical education as a process that "increases a person's tendencies

Figure 6.5
Movement theme unit:
Biomechanics
From Hal A. Lawson and
Judith H. Placek, *Physical
Education in the
Secondary Schools:
Curricular alternatives.* ©
1981 Allyn and Bacon,
Boston, MA. Reprinted by
permission.

Objectives

1. Students will be able to estimate the center of gravity of the body in a number of different postural positions.
2. In analyzing various physical and ludic activities, students will be able to identify the factors which are necessary for maintaining balance.
3. Students will be able to recognize different types of spins (or rotations) on balls and will be able to:
   a. explain why the spin resulted in relation to the application of force.
   b. trace the path of the ball both in the air and upon bouncing that is affected by spin.
4. In analyzing various physical and ludic activities, students will be able to apply and explain the applications of Newton's Law of Motion to force production.
5. In analyzing their own performance or the performance of others, with or without film or videotapes, students will be able to identify the sources of performance errors and offer potential solutions which are suggested by mechanical principles.

Content

Week one: Center of gravity and base of support
   Period one: Center of gravity
   Period two: Base of support
Week two: Balance
   Period one: Relationship between center of gravity and base of support
   Period two: Motion
Week three: Spin and angle of rebound
   Period one: Spin on balls
   Period two: Angle of rebound
Week four: Newton's Laws of Motion
   Period one: Newton's First Law
   Period two: Newton's Second and Third Laws
Week five: Force production
Week six: Analysis of errors

and abilities to play competitive and expressive motor activities'' (Siedentop 1980, 253). It should be emphasized that play education is not the same as ''roll out the ball.'' Students do not just play—they are educated to play. The unit includes both instruction related to skills, strategies and rules, and an opportunity to play. An example of an activity unit is described in figure 6.6.

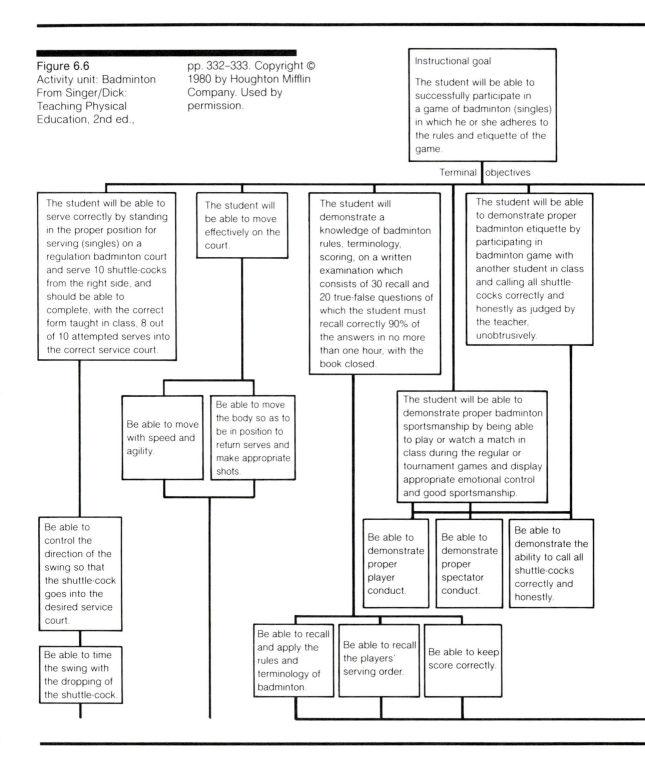

Figure 6.6
Activity unit: Badminton
From Singer/Dick:
Teaching Physical
Education, 2nd ed.,

pp. 332–333. Copyright ©
1980 by Houghton Mifflin
Company. Used by
permission.

Instructional goal

The student will be able to
successfully participate in
a game of badminton (singles)
in which he or she adheres to
the rules and etiquette of the
game.

Terminal objectives

The student will be able to
serve correctly by standing
in the proper position for
serving (singles) on a
regulation badminton court
and serve 10 shuttle-cocks
from the right side, and
should be able to
complete, with the correct
form taught in class, 8 out
of 10 attempted serves into
the correct service court.

The student will
be able to move
effectively on the
court.

The student will
demonstrate a
knowledge of badminton
rules, terminology,
scoring, on a written
examination which
consists of 30 recall and
20 true-false questions of
which the student must
recall correctly 90% of
the answers in no more
than one hour, with the
book closed.

The student will be able
to demonstrate proper
badminton etiquette by
participating in
badminton game with
another student in class
and calling all shuttle-
cocks correctly and
honestly as judged by
the teacher,
unobtrusively.

Be able to move
with speed and
agility.

Be able to move
the body so as to
be in position to
return serves and
make appropriate
shots.

The student will be able to
demonstrate proper badminton
sportsmanship by being able
to play or watch a match in
class during the regular or
tournament games and display
appropriate emotional control
and good sportsmanship.

Be able to
control the
direction of the
swing so that
the shuttle-cock
goes into the
desired service
court.

Be able to
demonstrate
proper
player
conduct.

Be able to
demonstrate
proper
spectator
conduct.

Be able to
demonstrate the
ability to call all
shuttle-cocks
correctly and
honestly.

Be able to time
the swing with
the dropping of
the shuttle-cock.

Be able to recall
and apply the
rules and
terminology of
badminton.

Be able to recall
the players'
serving order.

Be able to keep
score correctly.

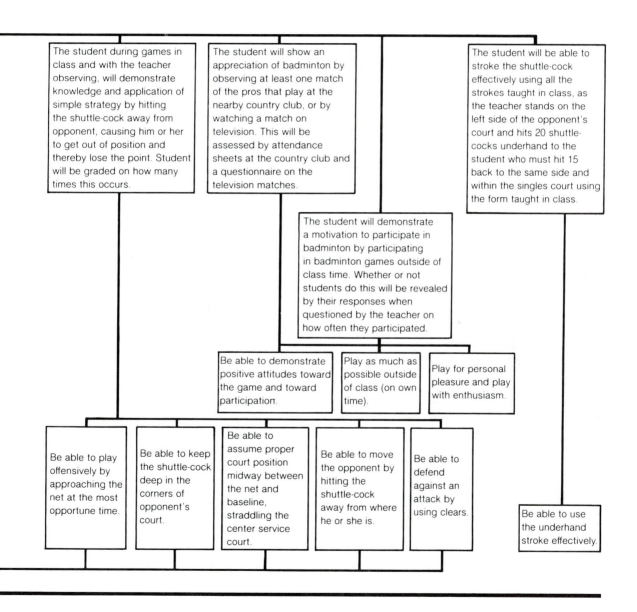

The student during games in class and with the teacher observing, will demonstrate knowledge and application of simple strategy by hitting the shuttle-cock away from opponent, causing him or her to get out of position and thereby lose the point. Student will be graded on how many times this occurs.

The student will show an appreciation of badminton by observing at least one match of the pros that play at the nearby country club, or by watching a match on television. This will be assessed by attendance sheets at the country club and a questionnaire on the television matches.

The student will be able to stroke the shuttle-cock effectively using all the strokes taught in class, as the teacher stands on the left side of the opponent's court and hits 20 shuttle-cocks underhand to the student who must hit 15 back to the same side and within the singles court using the form taught in class.

The student will demonstrate a motivation to participate in badminton by participating in badminton games outside of class time. Whether or not students do this will be revealed by their responses when questioned by the teacher on how often they participated.

Be able to demonstrate positive attitudes toward the game and toward participation.

Play as much as possible outside of class (on own time).

Play for personal pleasure and play with enthusiasm.

Be able to play offensively by approaching the net at the most opportune time.

Be able to keep the shuttle-cock deep in the corners of opponent's court.

Be able to assume proper court position midway between the net and baseline, straddling the center service court.

Be able to move the opponent by hitting the shuttle-cock away from where he or she is.

Be able to defend against an attack by using clears.

Be able to use the underhand stroke effectively.

Figure 6.7
From Ann E. Jewett and
M. R. Mullen, *Curriculum
Design: Purposes and
processes in physical
education teaching-
learning.* © 1977
American Alliance for
Health, Physical
Education, Recreation
and Dance, Reston, VA.
Reprinted by permission.

The emphasis in an activity unit is upon mastery of the sport or dance rather than upon using the activity as a means to accomplish other goals. Note, however, that many programs use an activity unit structure but attempt to incorporate emphasis upon certain developmental goals or concepts within the instruction. For example, the program might include a unit on soccer, with the focus upon interpersonal relationships (teamwork) and understanding of other cultures. A unit on swimming might emphasize overcoming fear, developing

Activity/organizational format	Purpose concept(s)	Process behavior	Specific objectives
III. The serve	C. Spatial orientation: 10. Relationships	A-2 Patterning	A. Take a legal stance which will permit effective motion.
	D. Object manipulation: 12. Object projection	B-4 Refining	B. Refine the serve so that it is repeatedly sent legally to the opponents' court.
	E. Communication: 16. Simulation	C-5 Varying	C. Disguise intent to and direction of serve so that opponents are taken unaware.
	F. Group interaction: 18. Competition	B-3 Adapting	D. Serve with intent of outwitting the opponents.
V. The overhead pass	D. Object manipulation: 12. Object projection	B-4 Refining	A. Refine the overhead pass such that the ball is legally sent to the areas of weakest defense on opponents' court.
	E. Communication: 16. Simulation	C-6 Improvising	B. Mask the movements of passing so that the opponents are unaware of where the ball will be sent.
VIII. The block	A. Physiological efficiency: 2. Mechanical efficiency	B-4 Refining	A. Refine the pattern of blocking so that the jump is accurately timed with the opposing spike, the hands extend higher than the net in front of the ball, and no foul is committed in the process.
	B. Psychic equilibrium: 7. Challenge	C-5 Varying	B. Meet the challenge presented by an opposing spike by attempting to block the ball.

cardiorespiratory fitness, or understanding the biomechanics of force and resistance. Figure 6.7 describes a volleyball unit that focuses instruction on selected purposes and processes from the Purpose-Process Curriculum Framework. Although much of the content is directly related to mastery of the activity itself, volleyball is also being used as a means to understanding purposes and processes fundamental to all movement.

Activity/organizational format	Purpose concept(s)	Process behavior	Specific objectives
	C. Spatial orientation: 8. Awareness	A-1 Perceiving	C. Develop an awareness of the potentials of the body through continued use of the block.
	D. Object manipulation: 13. Object reception	B-4 Refining	D. Refine the block such that spiked balls are legally stopped from crossing the net.
IX. Strategy A. Set to specified spikers	C. Spatial orientation: 10. Relationships	C-3 Varying	A. Alter which spiker is to be set in the light of abilities and game conditions.
	D. Object manipulation		
	E. Communication		
	F. Group interactions: 17. Teamwork		
B. Service placement	D. Object manipulation: 12. Object projection	C-6 Improvising	B. Interpret the defensive alignment and serve accordingly.
	C. Spatial orientation: 10. Relationships		
	E. Communication: 16. Simulation		
C. Screening the service	C. Spatial orientation: 10. Relationships	C-7 Composing	C. Design a legal method of screening the server.
	E. Communication: 16. Simulation		
	F. Group interaction: 17. Teamwork		

Selection of Educational Activities

After identifying the structure of the curriculum, the next step is to select the educational experiences to be included in the program. This involves determining what units of instruction to provide and the general outline of content for each unit. Related decisions include whether specific units of instruction will be required of all students or be made available to students on an optional basis. Certain basic criteria can be employed for making decisions regarding the selection of educational activities. However, the emphasis placed upon each of these criteria will differ, depending upon program philosophy.

Relevance to Goals and Objectives—Can It Get Results?

If the curriculum committee has followed the decision-making process suggested in the Tyler rationale, program goals and objectives will have been identified prior to selecting activities. A fundamental concern in selecting program content is whether the experiences selected can produce the desired results. If the program goal is improved fitness, is the activity sufficiently vigorous to accomplish it? If the program goal is increased proficiency and skill in an activity, are students being provided with adequate instruction, practice, and feedback? If the program goal is movement understanding and versatility, are students having sufficient opportunities to explore and investigate movement? If the program goal is improved social skills, are students being helped to acquire them?

At the planning stages the committee is attempting to select those activities that will be most effective in reaching the goals. Generally they will rely on three sources of information. In some areas research has been done that gives relatively clear answers about how to proceed. Exercise physiologists have determined rather precisely how to produce cardiorespiratory efficiency and muscular strength. Learning research gives some indication of necessary conditions for skill improvement. However, research related to other goals such as attitude change or social development is much less complete. A second source of information is observation and evaluation of existing programs. Although circumstances are never identical in different settings, successful programs can serve as a useful guide in selecting content that will produce results. The final source of information is the expert professional opinion of both the committee and consultants and authors. Their "educated guesses" reflect both professional training and experience.

In addition to considering the effectiveness of an activity in producing desired results, it is important to examine whether it produces any undesirable side effects. For example, a highly competitive evaluation procedure might produce skill development, but it might also increase animosity between students.

The selection of content ultimately reflects a prediction that it can produce the desired goals and objectives. Once the program is implemented, this prediction should be examined using program evaluation procedures (see chap. 8).

Qualitative Aspects of the Experience—Is It Meaningful?

Some educators have argued that education should be viewed, not only as preparation for the future, but as an important part of the present life of students. As such, educational experiences should not be unpleasant activities to be endured because of predicted outcomes, but satisfying experiences that enrich human life independent of long-term consequences. From this perspective, the immediate quality of experiences provided for students becomes a criterion for the selection of educational activities.

Huebner (1966) has suggested that both aesthetic and moral/ethical questions can be asked about the quality of educational experiences. The basic aesthetic question is, To what extent is "living in" this program a pleasurable experience? At the simplest level this may translate into, Is the activity fun? At a more complex level, aesthetic evaluation examines the wholeness, harmony, beauty, and symbolic meaning of the educational experience (Mann 1969). An effort is made to select activities that provide an intense, focused, and meaningful experience for students. Moral/ethical evaluation of educational activity questions the extent to which the experience reflects basic values of justice, equality, and human dignity.

Research has indicated that students have a much more positive attitude toward physical activity than they do toward physical education classes (Keough 1963). Perhaps increased attention to the qualitative aspects of educational experiences would reduce this discrepancy.

Appropriateness for Students—Are They Interested? Can They Do It?

A third concern in selecting curriculum content is the match between the activities and the students. One aspect of this concern is whether students will find the experiences interesting. Assessing student interests can be approached in several ways. The most direct is to administer an interest survey or attitude instrument to the student population. You can also examine polls and surveys administered to a comparable population. Some caution is advised in interpreting student interest data. Students' expressed interests are likely to reflect their previous experiences and cultural influences. This makes it difficult to determine whether they would find a new activity interesting once exposed to it. The dilemma facing curriculum planners is whether to limit the program to existing student interests or attempt to expand those interests.

The second aspect of determining the appropriateness of content for students relates to their readiness to do the activity. Do students have the necessary conditioning, skill, and knowledge for the experience? Is it too difficult or too easy for them? Can it be modified sufficiently to handle the range of performance differences within the student population? Readiness can be estimated on the basis of developmental research and professional judgment, but the needs assessment techniques described in chapter 5 can provide more specific information.

Practicality—Can We Do It?

A major practical concern is the availability of resources necessary to implement the activity. Are facilities and equipment available? Do the teachers have the expertise to conduct the activity? Do they have the time needed for in-service and for planning? Can this experience be implemented with the class sizes in your situation? Is sufficient time available to provide the needed instruction? Can the safety of participants be adequately protected? If resources are not available, inclusion of the learning activity would require acquisition of additional resources. If such recommendations are made, the curriculum planning committee must determine the feasibility of acquiring such resources and develop a plan for doing so.

A second practical concern is the social and political acceptability of the activity. An activity that contradicts local norms of acceptable behavior or requires dramatic changes in the roles of teachers or students may be actively resisted.

Although strategies such as pilot projects, voluntary participation, or slow gradual change may reduce this resistance, this factor of acceptability must be considered.

Sequencing the Activities

The next major curriculum design decision is the order in which the learning activities will be provided. Sequence decisions attempt to provide continuity and progression within each unit of instruction, as well as from unit-to-unit and year-to-year.

Several factors affect sequence decisions. One important influence is the developmental maturity or readiness of the students. Skills requiring highly-developed coordination may not be appropriate for very young children. Strength and size may be prerequisites to learning some skills. Complex strategies may be too abstract for children at early stages of cognitive development.

A second related factor is the interest and motivation of the students. Interest in different activities and topics may peak at certain ages or at different times of the year. Matching program content to these interest peaks may increase student motivation and accomplishment. Within a unit of instruction there may be certain skills or activities that have high student appeal. Introducing such "glamour" activities early in a unit or periodically throughout the unit may be an effective motivational mechanism. In games and sports units, playing the game is usually viewed as highly motivating. For that reason, content may be sequenced so that skills and rules essential to game play are introduced early in that unit. Students are then allowed some game play while mastering more complex aspects of the activity.

A third critical aspect in determining the sequence of learning activities is the identification of skills and knowledges that must be mastered prior to learning the new task. This process of identifying prerequisite skills and knowledges is called *task analysis*. Singer and Dick (1980) give a comprehensive discussion of task analysis, and the activity unit described in figure 6.6 provides an excellent example. Once a task analysis has been completed for each unit of instruction, content is sequenced so that earlier units provide instruction in skills and knowledges prerequisite to mastery of later units.

Certain patterns emerge in the sequencing of physical education curricula. Vertical sequencing decisions deal with the progression of program content from year to year. Some programs are based on a principle of linear progression—that is, the student completes each unit of instruction and then goes on to a new topic without repeating any of the previously accomplished topics. More frequently the program is built upon a principle of spiral progression. The student completes a unit of instruction and then the next year another unit on the same topic is included in the program. The second unit reviews material covered the first year and then "spirals" to a higher level of instruction and includes new material. These spirals may be repeated several times, with each unit including more complex content. It should be noted that careful coordination of progressions from year-to-year is necessary or a spiral curriculum can become mere repetition.

Horizontal sequencing decisions deal with the ordering of content within a semester or year. One basic choice is the use of block units or multiple units of instruction. In a blocked program, all instruction for a period of several weeks focuses on a single activity topic—for example, six weeks of fitness, nine weeks of swimming, or four weeks of spatial awareness. In a multiple unit program, different units are taught simultaneously on different days of the week. For example: Monday and Wednesday might be locomotor skills; Tuesday and Thursday, dance; and Friday, swimming. Each of these approaches emphasizes a different facet of the learning process. Block units concentrate the students' attention and emphasize continuity, while multiple units emphasize variety.

Practical Applications

In a practical sense, curriculum design decisions usually result in written products intended to provide teachers with information needed to plan daily instruction that fits into the total program. The basic document produced, usually by a school district or state planning committee, is a curriculum guide. Each school then develops a yearly plan for its program based on the guide. Plans for each unit of instruction are developed by individual teachers assigned to teach the unit. Teachers use these unit plans as a basis for developing daily lesson plans. Each of these planning documents is discussed briefly in the next section. Examples are included in appendix B. The examples are illustrative and many other possibilities could be devised.

Curriculum Guide

The curriculum guide attempts to clarify the basic theory or philosophy of the physical education program and to provide guidelines for the conduct of the program. Although content and format of the guide may vary, certain types of information are usually included. Most guides include a rationale that summarizes the philosophy of the program. Frequently this rationale is accompanied by a listing of the goals or objectives of the program. Examples of rationale statements are included in chapter 5 and in appendix B. You are encouraged to examine them to determine what curriculum theory the rationale seems to endorse.

A second component commonly included in the curriculum guide is a scope and sequence chart. This chart usually identifies which units of instruction are to be included in the program at various levels. The levels may be based upon age and/or grade or upon student performance. The guide may identify specific units that must be included in the program or may provide guidelines indicating suggested emphasis or balance, but allowing the school to select specific activities within those guidelines. Examples of scope and sequence charts are included in the introduction to this chapter and in appendix B.

Another element included in most curriculum guides is a resource section that provides information to assist teachers in planning units of instruction. The format and amount of detail varies greatly. In some cases the emphasis is placed upon specifying performance objectives for the activity. Some guides merely provide a listing of skills or concepts to be included in the unit and references where teachers might get additional information. Others provide detailed information about the content and, in some cases, examples of learning activities useful in teaching the unit. Appendix B includes excerpts from several resource units illustrating various approaches.

In addition to these basic components, curriculum guides may contain other types of information. Some include a summary of the developmental characteristics of students. Recommended instructional strategies and organizational techniques may be discussed. Policies regarding evaluation and grading may be included. In some cases, such topics as equipment and facilities or safety and liability may be addressed.

The kind of information included in the guide and the degree of specificity reflect basic philosophy and assumptions about the prospective students and about the teachers who will implement the program. Guides that are more flexible and less detailed permit more autonomous decision-making by teachers and/or students. Such autonomy places greater responsibility on the teacher and requires both professional expertise and extensive time commitment to develop a quality program. However, any curriculum ultimately depends upon individual teachers for implementation. Teachers use the curriculum guide in preparing specific plans for their particular schools.

Yearly Plan

The first task at the school level is developing a yearly plan for the program. This is usually an administrative responsibility of the physical education department chair. The yearly plan indicates the number, length, and title of the units to be taught throughout the year. Unit length may vary from two weeks to one semester (sixteen–eighteen weeks). Frequently units coincide with six or nine week grading periods, but the basis for determining length should be more than convenience. The length of the unit should provide reasonable opportunity for accomplishing objectives. For certain simple concepts (e.g., orientation to basic gymnasium rules) or activities with relatively few skills (e.g., bicycling), a two or three week unit of daily instruction may be sufficient. However, mastery of complex concepts or activities may require much longer periods of instruction. Consideration might also be given to flexible unit length. For example, students who have achieved unit objectives after four weeks might begin a mini-unit in another activity while other students complete the full six week unit.

Some schools develop prescribed programs in which all students have the same units of instruction. Others have a selective program in which students may choose from a range of activities. These options may be unrestricted or may be limited to choices that fall into certain categories (e.g., one team sport, one individual sport, one dance, etc.).

The manner in which students are grouped for instruction also varies. Students may be assigned to groups on the basis of age or ability. (Title IX requires objective measures specific to the activity being taught if ability groups are used. The law also prohibits assignment on the basis of sex except in contact sports. See chapter 4 for discussion.) Students may select groups on the basis of interest. Each teacher may be assigned a class of "normal" size or two teachers may be assigned to team teach a larger group. Class sizes may vary according to activity. It is possible that students not be assigned to any group, but rather that the program utilize an open gym concept in which students work independently and all teachers are available to supervise and assist. Decisions described in the yearly plan are a critical step in developing a program that reflects the curriculum theory expressed in the guide. The consistency of the actual program with the curriculum guide may depend upon the clarity of the material in the guide and the degree to which teachers at the school level endorse the basic curriculum philosophy.

Unit Plans

The final step in the curriculum planning process is the development of unit plans by the teacher assigned to teach a unit. Such planning is the link between the curriculum design and the instructional process. The unit plan provides the framework for day-to-day instruction. The most abbreviated form of unit plan is simply a calendar of activities to be taught. Usually this calendar is supplemented by the identification of objectives and evaluation procedures. The objectives describe the level of performance that students should accomplish by the end of the unit. Evaluation procedures specify the instruments and process that will be used to evaluate the progress of students. Other information that may be included in the unit plan is a list of available resources and materials and plans for any special events to be included in the unit (field trips, demonstrations, guest instructors, etc.).

A unit plan for individualized instruction differs from one for group instruction. (See chapter 7 for a discussion of instructional strategies. For a comprehensive explanation of planning for individualized instruction, see Heitmann and Kneer 1976.) The individualized unit plan identifies the tasks or modules to be included in the unit and indicates whether the tasks are required or optional and the sequence in which they must be mastered. For each task, materials are developed describing objectives, alternative learning activities, and evaluation procedures. These materials are used by students for self-directed learning, with guidance and assistance from the teacher. A system is devised for assessing student entry behavior, selecting tasks appropriate for each student, and recording student progress. Class management procedures are developed that permit individual students to be working on different tasks simultaneously. The calendar for the unit specifies only marker events, such as orientation, initial assessment and personal planning, and final evaluation. Throughout the remainder of the unit students work at their own paces on those tasks included in their personal programs.

Teachers may decide to involve students in the planning of the unit of instruction. In individualized instruction this frequently happens during the initial assessment stage when the student's personal program is being developed. The teacher, rather than diagnosing and prescribing, may give the student responsibility for selecting objectives and learning activities. Student participation in the planning process may be less frequent in group instruction, but Cassidy and Caldwell (1974) describe procedures for building a unit with a group of students.

Examples of unit plans for group and individualized instruction are included in appendix B. Because of the limitations of space, these materials are abbreviated.

Summary

Curriculum design involves decisions about the scope, structure, and sequence of program content. As indicated in figure 6.8, these decisions occur at several levels—the curriculum planning committee, the physical education administrator for the school, and the individual teacher. Written documents record the decisions made and serve as a resource for planning daily instruction. The curriculum guide for a state or province or a school district includes a rationale, a description of scope and sequence of program content, and resource materials to assist teachers in planning. The school's yearly plan identifies specific units to be taught and time allocated to that instruction. The unit plans developed by teachers determine content and procedures for instruction. At each level, certain criteria or principles influence design decisions. The development of these plans and materials is an important step in the process of translating a curriculum theory into a program in action.

Figure 6.8
Development of
curriculum documents

Level	Person(s) responsible	Curriculum documents
District or state	Curriculum planning committee	Curriculum guide: Rationale and goals Scope and sequence Resource materials
School building	Department chair	Yearly plan
Class	Teacher	Unit plan

References

Cassidy, R. F., and S. F. Caldwell. 1974. *Humanizing physical education.* Dubuque: Wm. C. Brown.

Heitmann, H. M., and M. E. Kneer. 1976. *Physical education/instructional techniques: An individualized humanistic approach.* Englewood Cliffs: Prentice-Hall.

Hellison, D. 1978. *Beyond balls and bats.* Washington, DC: AAHPER.

Hoffman, H. A., J. Young, and S. E. Klesius. 1981. *Meaningful movement for children.* Boston: Allyn and Bacon.

Huebner, D. 1966. Curricular language and classroom meanings. In *Language and meaning,* ed. J. B. Macdonald and R. R. Leeper. Washington, DC: Association for Supervision and Curriculum Development.

Jewett, A. E., and M. R. Mullan. 1977. *Curriculum design: Purposes and processes in physical education teaching-learning.* Washington, DC: AAHPER.

Keough, J. 1963. Extreme attitudes toward physical education. *Research Quarterly* 34: 27–33.

Lawson, H. A., and J. H. Placek. 1981. *Physical education in the secondary schools.* Boston: Allyn and Bacon.

Logsdon, B. J., K. R. Barrett, M. Ammons, M. R. Broer, L. E. Halverson, R. McGee, and M. A. Roberton. 1977. *Physical education for children.* Philadelphia: Lea and Febiger.

Mann, J. S. 1969. Curriculum criticism. *Teachers College Record* 71: 27–40.

Siedentop, D. 1980. *Physical education: Introductory analysis.* Dubuque: Wm. C. Brown.

Singer, R., and W. Dick. 1980. *Teaching physical education: A systems approach.* Boston: Houghton Mifflin.

Walker, D. F. 1975. Curriculum development in an art project. In *Case studies in curriculum change,* ed. W. A. Reid and D. F. Walker. London: Routledge and Kegan Paul.

Recommended Readings

Cassidy, R. F., and S. F. Caldwell. 1974. *Humanizing physical education.* Dubuque: Wm. C. Brown.

Heitmann, H. M., and M. E. Kneer. 1976. *Physical education/instructional techniques: An individualized humanistic approach.* Englewood Cliffs: Prentice-Hall.

Singer, R., and W. Dick. 1980. *Teaching physical education: A systems approach.* Boston: Houghton Mifflin.

Implications of Curriculum Models for Instruction

7

Outline

The seventh grade children at Smilie Middle School are beginning a unit on soccer. One of the skills included in the soccer resource unit in the curriculum guide is the instep (top of the foot) kick. Ms. Franklin and Mr. Rodriguez each developed a lesson to teach the instep kick to their classes. Descriptions of their lessons follow:

Ms. Franklin begins class with several demonstrations of the instep kick. She emphasizes that the nonkicking foot should be even with the ball and the kicking leg drawn well back in the preparation phase. She instructs students to watch the ball, snap the leg forward, and contact the ball with the top of the foot, then follow through with the kicking leg. After the demonstration, the students work with partners practicing the instep kick while Ms. Franklin observes and makes corrections.

Mr. Rodriguez organizes his class into partners and asks each pair to practice kicking the ball to each other so that it stays low to the ground and then so that it lofts into the air. After they have worked on this for several minutes, he asks the students what they did to produce the different results. Answers include attention to where the ball was contacted and which part of the foot was used to contact the ball. (Some students used the inside of the foot for the low kick and the instep for the lofted kick.) He asks them if it is possible to use the instep kick for both. They try it briefly and most, but not all, answer affirmatively. Mr. Rodriguez then asks the partners to increase the distance between them and try to increase the speed and distance of both the low and the lofted kick. After several minutes of practice, Mr. Rodriguez briefly mentions and defines the terms range-of-motion, velocity, and force. He asks what changes the students made to increase speed and distance. They indicate that bringing the leg back farther, increasing the speed of the leg coming forward, and more follow-through helped. He asks if any students are having difficulty with missing the ball or not having it go where it was aimed. They discuss possible solutions and then resume practice. Mr. Rodriguez assists those students with persistent problems by helping them analyze the source of the problems.

The lessons taught by Ms. Franklin and Mr. Rodriguez both dealt with the instep kick in soccer, but the teaching styles employed differed greatly. To what extent did the differences in teaching methods alter the content and outcomes of the experience? Were the lessons taught more or less compatible with a particular curriculum model?

The successful implementation of any curriculum model ultimately depends upon an instructional process that translates the design into action. The curriculum model identifies what will be taught and the goals of the program. Instructional decisions determine how the teaching-learning process will be conducted. For implementation to be successful, the instructional process must be consistent with the philosophy of the model and effective in attaining its goals.

In general, the individual teacher is responsible for instructional decisions. However, certain teaching styles or approaches may be essential to the effective implementation of a particular curriculum model. For this reason, the curriculum planners must attempt to ensure that teachers have both the ability and the commitment to use the appropriate styles of teaching.

Styles of Teaching

Early discussions of teaching styles or approaches focused on an attempt to find the one best way to teach. More recently, educators have suggested that no single style is best under all circumstances. The effectiveness of various styles differs depending upon the goals to be attained, the type of learning task, and the characteristics of the students. In order to plan and carry out effective instruction with differing goals, tasks, and students, teachers need to learn a range of teaching styles.

Classifications of teaching styles or models have been proposed as a basis for extending understanding of the instructional process and as a means for assisting teachers in developing a repertoire of styles (Joyce and Weil 1972). In physical education, the most widely used classification of teaching styles is the spectrum of styles developed by Mosston (1981). Mosston has described teaching as a chain of decision-making, which involves pre-impact (planning), impact (during the lesson), and post-impact (evaluation) decisions. The spectrum of teaching styles analyzes and classifies teaching styles according to who makes decisions in each phase— teacher or learner. Mosston suggests that no one style is superior to another, but that each style can be used to accomplish a particular set of objectives that differ from those accomplished by the other styles. Teachers need to understand both the assumptions and goals of each style and the procedures for using each. The teacher then has the capability of selecting those styles that are appropriate for the students being taught and the curriculum model being implemented.

This chapter examines the applicability of each of Mosston's teaching styles to the curriculum models discussed in chapter 3. Before beginning that analysis, you will need to study the following section, which gives a brief description and an example of each style. You also are encouraged to read Mosston's book for a more complete understanding of the spectrum of styles.

A. Command Style

All decisions are made by the teacher. The teacher describes or demonstrates a model for the student to emulate, then gives command signals to direct the student's practice. The student responds only when directed to do so by the teacher and the teacher evaluates the success of those responses in terms of their similarity to the prescribed model. (See fig. 7.1.)

B. Practice Style

As in the command style, the teacher explains or demonstrates a model of performance and all students perform the same practice tasks. However, students perform the practice tasks at their own pace, while the teacher circulates and gives private, individual feedback. If the practice tasks are complex, the teacher may prepare task cards to assist the student in remembering what to do and how to do it. (See fig. 7.2.)

In physical education, the command style can be seen in a variety of activities. For example:

1. Short episodes of a "single" movement such as standing at attention. This calls for a particular body posture performed in a particular location and maintained for a particular length of time. And all this is done by the learner in response to a specific stimulus (command signal) by the teacher.
2. A series of movements *predesigned* in a particular sequence, such as a routine in gymnastics, a dance performance, a folk dance. Here, too, each movement is performed according to a model following a particular sequence of commands. (In the case of floor exercises or dance routines, the music becomes the surrogate giver of commands.)
3. An entire sport, such as crew. Particular postures are designated, particular movements are called for by each participant, and all must be coordinated by the rhythm provided by the coxswain.

Name _____   Style B
Class _____   Task sheet # _____
Date _____   S.S./M.T.

Basketball: Dribbling

To the student: Your task is to practice the following skills as described and as demonstrated.

Logistics:
1. All the basketballs are in the bin in the N.W. corner of the gymnasium.
2. At the end of the episode, return all the balls to the appropriate bin.
3. You will have _____ minutes for the tasks.

Tasks:
1. Dribble the ball with the right hand, bouncing it to knee level, ten times in a row (a set).
2. Dribble the ball as before, three sets of ten, with ten-second intervals between sets.
3. Repeat #1 with the left hand.
4. Repeat #2 with the right hand.
5. Dribble the ball with either hand between any two points while walking ten steps.
6. Repeat #5 with light jogging.

C. Reciprocal Style

The teacher explains or demonstrates the task to be learned and the criteria for successful performance. During the practice phase, the students work in pairs in which one student is the doer who practices the task and the other is an observer who gives feedback to the doer. The teacher provides the observer with a checklist of criteria to use in evaluating the doer's performance. The teacher's role during practice is to be available to assist the observer but not to usurp the observer's responsibility. (See fig. 7.3.)

D. Self-Check Style

The initial portion of the lesson is the same as in styles A, B, and C: the teacher explains or demonstrates the task and the criteria for successful performance. However, during the practice phase the students assume responsibility for identifying and correcting their own errors. A criteria card, similar to that used in the reciprocal model, is developed to assist the students in this process. During practice, the teacher does not evaluate student performance, but attempts to help students sharpen their self-analysis skills. (See fig. 7.4.)

E. Inclusion Style

In the first four styles, the students are presented a task with a single standard of performance. In the inclusion style, the teacher designs and presents one task with multiple levels of difficulty. The students decide at which level of difficulty to begin. During practice they assess their own performance and decide when to proceed to the next level. The teacher's role is to respond to and assist the student with the decision-making and self-analysis process. (See fig. 7.5.)

F. Guided Discovery

This style crosses what Mosston has labeled the discovery barrier. Unlike the previous direct styles in which students are told how to perform, this style requires the students to discover a selected skill or concept by responding to questions. The teacher develops the series of questions, incorporating a sequence of small steps that slowly and gradually lead the student to the desired response. At each step the teacher asks a question, reinforces the response, and provides additional clues if necessary. Questions should be designed so that they elicit a correct response, which leads to the next question. (See fig. 7.6.)

Figure 7.3
Reciprocal style (C)
From M. Mosston,
*Teaching Physical
Education.* © 1981
Charles E. Merrill
Publishing Co.,
Columbus, Ohio.
Reprinted by permission.

Name _____   Style A B Ⓒ D
Class _____
Date _____
Partner _____

Archery task and criteria sheet

Instructions for the observer:

Communicate to the doer about how he or she is performing the task (use the "Things to look for" column).

Make positive statements to doer first.

Examples of feedback statements:

"You are gripping the bow correctly, but remember not to grip it too tightly."

"You are nocking the arrow exactly as the criteria describe."

"The elbow of your drawing arm is in line with the arrow."

"Now I will check to see if you are using the same anchor point."

Task 1: Each doer, shoot six arrows.
Switch roles after each round of six arrows.

	Things to look for	Yes	No
Stance--	Stand astride shooting line, feet apart at shoulder width, body in comfortable position with straight posture.		
Grip--	Fit handle in "v" formed by thumb and index finger, bow felt in upper part of hand. Grip should not be tight.		
Nocking--	Nock arrow with cock feather facing away from bow, arrow between first and second fingers, string resting along first joint of all three fingers that grip string.		
Draw--	Keep bow arm and wrist straight without being rigid, drawing arm, shoulder, and upper back muscles do the drawing. Keep elbow of drawing arm in line with arrow.		
Anchor--	Draw until string touches another point on face (check to ensure that anchor point is the same each draw).		
Release--	Release by relaxing fingers, allowing string to roll off the fingers. Hold bow hand relaxed but steady during release and follow through.		

Curriculum Design

Name _____   Style A B C Ⓓ E

Class _____

Date _____

Squash--High lob serve

Task: Practice 10 high lob serves from the right service
box and 10 from the left service box.

Note the following steps, or the position of the task.

After the performance, check each step of the criteria.

Criteria:

	Service box	
	Right side	Left side
Starting position		
1. Stand as near to the center "T" as possible, with one foot inside the lines of the service box.	_____	_____
2. Hold the racket low and point the left shoulder at the spot on the front wall where the ball is aimed.	_____	_____
The swing		
1. Toss the ball up about 2 inches, well in front of the body.	_____	_____
2. Keep wrist firm and swing arm forward to meet the ball directly ahead of the body at about knee level.	_____	_____
3. Contact point is under the ball so it will lift upwards.	_____	_____
Follow-through		
1. The racket, arm, and shoulder all follow the ball, allowing a long, high, deliberate follow-through.	_____	_____
2. Ball should contact the front wall as high as possible and have a rising, arching effect after leaving it.	_____	_____
3. Ball should fall perpendicularly to a length of the court.	_____	_____

Figure 7.4
Self-check style (D)
From M. Mosston,
*Teaching Physical
Education.* © 1981
Charles E. Merrill
Publishing Co.,
Columbus, Ohio.
Reprinted by permission.

Golf

To the student:

1. Select an initial level and circle the number you expect to do.
2. Do the task and blacken out the number of the actual performance.
2. Compare your execution of the task with the performance criteria.
4. Decide whether to repeat the task at the same level or at a different level.

The chip shot (criteria):

Did you--

1. Stand with your feet close together?
2. Bend your knees slightly, as though starting to sit?
3. Contact the ball off your left heel?
4. Follow through along the path of the ball, keeping the left wrist firm at contact?
5. Refrain from letting the club head pass the left hand?
6. Keep the flight of the ball low?
7. Hit to a predetermined spot and have the ball roll to the cup?

The task: Choose a distance (either line A, B, or C) and a target area (either the large or the small). Take 10 chip shots, and record the number of times you hit the target area.

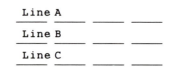

Distance	Large target									
A	1	2	3	4	5	6	7	8	9	10
B	1	2	3	4	5	6	7	8	9	10
C	1	2	3	4	5	6	7	8	9	10

Distance	Small target									
A	1	2	3	4	5	6	7	8	9	10
B	1	2	3	4	5	6	7	8	9	10
C	1	2	3	4	5	6	7	8	9	10

Figure 7.5
Inclusion style (E)
From M. Mosston,
*Teaching Physical
Education.* © 1981
Charles E. Merrill
Publishing Co.,
Columbus, Ohio.
Reprinted by permission.

Subject matter:	Shot put
Specific purpose:	To discover the stance for putting the shot.
Question 1:	"What is the main purpose of putting the shot in competition?"
Anticipated answer:	"To put it as far as possible."
Question 2:	"What is needed to achieve distance?"
Anticipated answer:	"Strength, power!" (Teacher's response, "Correct!")
Question 3:	"What else?"
Anticipated answer:	"Speed!" ("Good," says the teacher.)
Question 4:	"In the total motion of putting the shot, *where* should the power and speed reach their maximum?"
Anticipated answer:	"At the point of release!" ("Correct!" responds the teacher.)
Question 5:	"Where would be the point of minimum strength and speed?"
Anticipated answer:	"At the stationary starting position!" ("Very good," says the teacher.)
Question 6:	"In order to achieve the maximum strength and speed at the point of release, how far from this point should the starting position be?"
Anticipated answer:	"As far as possible!" ("Correct!")

Comments: This is the rationale behind the starting position presently used by the top shot putters. If the answer to question No. 6 is not readily given, an additional step must be taken--"In order to gain maximum momentum should the body and the shot travel a short or a long distance?" then, "How long?" From this point on, physical responses are called for.

Question 7:	"If the point of release is at this line in front of your body, what would be *your* starting position which fulfills the requirements of response No. 6?"
Anticipated answer:	Here some students might stand in a wide stance with the shot resting someplace on the shoulder. (The balance requirement becomes clear immediately, and some sort of straddle position is usually offered.

Figure 7.6
Guided discovery style (F)
From M. Mosston, *Teaching Physical Education.* © 1981 Charles E. Merrill Publishing Co., Columbus, Ohio. Reprinted by permission.

Figure 7.6 cont.

If this is not apparent you may ask, "Are you well balanced?" and wait for the new physical response.) However, others may take the concept of "maximum distance" from the point of release quite literally and attempt to stretch out the arm holding the shot; here you intervene with another question.

Question 8: "Since the shot is quite heavy, can the arm do the job alone, or could the body help?"

Anticipated answer: "The body could help!" (The student has already felt the weight of the shot and the awkwardness of holding it in the outstretched hand.)

Question 9: "Where could you place the shot in order to get maximum push from the body?"

Anticipated answer: "On the shoulder!" ("Correct!")

Question 10: "In order to gain maximum momentum, do you place your body weight equally on both legs?"

Anticipated answer: "No. On the rear leg!" ("Correct!")

Question 11: "What should the position of this leg be to gain maximum thrust from the ground?"

Anticipated answer: "Slightly bent!" ("Yes!")

Question 12: "Now, what would be the position of the trunk to fulfill the conditions discovered above?"

Anticipated answer: "Slightly bent (and twisted) toward the rear leg!" ("True!")

Teacher: "Good! Does this position seem to be the starting position we were looking for?"

G. Divergent Style

In contrast to the convergent thinking in guided discovery in which students "discover" a pre-selected response, the divergent style involves problem solving in which more than one possible solution exists. The teacher designs and explains a problem that is relevant to the subject matter and to the readiness and experience of the students. The learner

Problems to Solve on the Balance Beam

Let us begin with problems involving movements on the balance beam. This activity was selected because of its pliability of content; despite some fundamental common arrangements of movements, the entire experience of learning to use the balance beam for the development of balance, grace, and beauty of movement is composed of endless alternatives. Alternatives exist in practically every balance beam position, movement, or sequence.

Phase 1—Getting On (Mounts)
1. Can all the parts of the body be used for getting on?
2. Which parts cannot be used?
3. What is the maximum number of body parts that can be used for the mount (which mounts?) at the same time?
4. For the same mount (which one?), what is the minimum number of parts needed?
5. One part of the body less than maximum?
6. Two parts less than maximum?
7. Other number of parts less?
8. One part of the body more than minimum?
9. Can you get on the beam with maximum area of the body touching the beam?
10. Can you get on with minimum area of the body touching the beam?

Figure 7.7
Divergent style (G)
From M. Mosston,
*Teaching Physical
Education.* © 1981
Charles E. Merrill
Publishing Co.,
Columbus, Ohio.
Reprinted by permission.

identifies alternative responses to the problem and evaluates the responses in terms of their adequacy in solving the problem. (See fig. 7.7.)

H. Going Beyond

This style resembles the divergent style, except that the student now initiates the process by identifying a problem to be solved. The teacher assumes a supportive role that involves asking questions for clarification and giving assistance as needed.

Although the styles described by Mosston involve varying amounts of student decision-making, all of them except style H generally involve a group instruction format in which all students are working on the same task or problem. The teacher normally initiates the process by explaining or demonstrating the task in the direct styles or presenting the problem to be solved in the discovery styles.

An alternative to group or cohort instruction has been called individualized or personalized instruction (AAHPER 1976). The assumption underlying individualized instruction is that individual students in the same class have different needs and abilities and should, therefore, work on different learning tasks. Because it is not feasible for the teacher to explain or demonstrate a different task to each student when he/she is ready for it, individualized instruction requires the development of instructional materials that can explain the task to the student, assist the student in participating in

School: Inner City High School
                 Chicago, Illinois
Facilitator: Marian E. Kneer

Activity: Badminton

Description:
   The course was taught by a university professor with extensive public school experience to a class of 35 senior girls with no previous badminton experience. The school is in a deprived neighborhood with meager facilities and equipment (three singles-width courts with 3 feet of space between wall and end line, 17 racquets, and 12 shuttlecocks). The course consisted of fifteen lessons of 10-minute periods.

Objectives:
  1. Students will be able to play a doubles game in badminton.
  2. Students will be able to execute all major badminton strokes with 50 percent accuracy and consistency.
  3. Students will be able to pass rules test with 70 percent or better accuracy.
  4. Students will be able to share equipment and help each other as evidenced by class conduct.
  5. Students will enjoy badminton as evidenced by their eagerness to play and reluctance not to participate.

Diagnosis:
   Students were asked to respond to a questionnaire concerning their ability. No skill or knowledge tests were given as summative evaluation.

Prescription:
   A schedule for all fifteen lessons was posted, along with directions.

Curriculum Design

meaningful learning activities, and provide guidelines for the evaluation of performance. These instructional materials usually rely on a variety of media including written instructions, audiovisual materials and, more recently, microcomputers. Heitmann and Kneer's *Physical Education/ Instructional Techniques: An Individualized Humanistic Approach* (1976) provides an excellent guide to the planning and implementation of individualized instruction. (See fig. 7.8 for an example.)

Schedule:

Day 1	Explain plans and diagnose.
Day 2	Conferences, play, and begin work on skills.
Days 3-7	Each student spent one-third time playing, one-third time practicing, and one-third securing information from pictures on learning module.
Days 8-15	One-third of time was spent playing in tournament and two thirds working on learning modules.

Guidance:

Ten learning modules were developed, placed on posters, and taped on the wall. A module was developed for each of the following topics:

Equipment, lines, courts	Smashes
Clears	Defensive play
Drives	Offensive play
Net shots	Game play
Service	Rules

Evaluation:

Each learning program was valued at 5 points. Attendance was rewarded by granting a point each day the student was present. The maximum number of points possible was 65. Grades were based as follows:

A = 45 +
B = 38 +
C = 31 +
D = 24 +

Figure 7.8 cont.

Sample module:

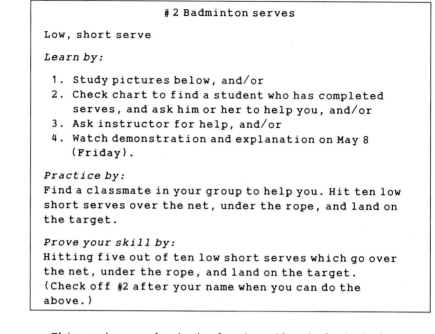

2 Badminton serves

Low, short serve

Learn by:

1. Study pictures below, and/or
2. Check chart to find a student who has completed serves, and ask him or her to help you, and/or
3. Ask instructor for help, and/or
4. Watch demonstration and explanation on May 8 (Friday).

Practice by:
Find a classmate in your group to help you. Hit ten low short serves over the net, under the rope, and land on the target.

Prove your skill by:
Hitting five out of ten low short serves which go over the net, under the rope, and land on the target. (Check off #2 after your name when you can do the above.)

This system was kept simple since the students had never experienced the process before, had never learned to share equipment, and had low reading ability.

It should be noted that individualized instruction may incorporate either a direct or a discovery style. Instructional packets or modules that specify the task to be learned and the practice activities to be completed are direct and tend to resemble Mosston's styles B (practice), C (reciprocal), or D (self-check), depending upon who is given the responsibility for evaluating the student's performance. Materials that allow the student to determine the difficulty level at which to begin utilize style E (inclusion). Programmed learning materials, using a series of questions with reinforcement for correct answers and branching if errors are made, resemble guided discovery. Instructional materials that pose a problem to be solved exemplify the divergent style. Independent study options in which students design and implement their own problem solving process fit into style H. (One might suggest that the group instruction version of style H occurs when a group of students identifies a problem they wish to solve and then works together to find a solution.) The spectrum of teaching styles can, therefore, be used to classify and describe either group or individualized instruction.

Instructional Strategies for Alternative Curriculum Models

How does a teacher decide which of the teaching styles to learn and to use? The selection of a teaching style depends upon the goals to be attained, the type of task, and the characteristics of the students. Each of the curriculum models is based upon certain assumptions about what goals the program should accomplish, the nature of the subject matter, and what students are like and how they learn. For this reason, certain teaching styles are more compatible with each of the curriculum models.

Two factors seem to influence selection of teaching styles along the decision-making dimension of Mosston's spectrum. The type of task is one of these factors. The direct styles (A–E) are generally preferred for teaching specific knowledges or motor skills. Discovery styles (F–H) are often advocated for teaching concepts, for eliciting creative responses, or for helping students "learn how to learn." The other factor influencing selection of styles A through H is the student's perceived capability for decision-making. Most would agree that certain students are less capable than others of assuming decision-making responsibility (i.e., younger students, highly anxious students, or students with low self-discipline). However, curriculum models vary in their general expectations of students' ability to handle decision-making and autonomy.

This expectation of decision-making capability is also likely to influence selections of group or individualized instruction. Individualized instruction requires confidence in students' capability for self-direction and also reflects a strong belief that individuals have unique needs that are less effectively met in a group instruction setting. Teachers who choose group instruction usually do not deny the existence of individual differences, but believe that students share many common needs and that differences can be adequately accommodated in group settings.

The physical education curriculum models described in chapter 3 address the topic of instructional strategies to various degrees. In some cases, specific teaching styles are advocated. In others, instructional strategies must be inferred from the assumptions and goals of the model.

The developmental education model aims for a broad range of developmental goals. Because of this broad range, such models usually advocate a variety of teaching styles, including both direct and discovery approaches. However, the teacher as the developmental expert retains responsibility for selecting and sequencing the learning tasks. Most developmental programs in physical education have employed group instruction based on common developmental patterns of children. Despite acknowledgement of individual differences, both Project SEE (Thompson and Mann 1981) and Hoffman, Young, and Klesius (1981) describe group instruction procedures.

The humanistic physical education model emphasizes the unique characteristics of individuals and views the individual as the person most able to determine what and how to learn. Because of these basic assumptions, the model relies heavily upon individualized instruction and personal goal-setting. However, Hellison (1978, 1982) recognizes that some level of self-discipline must be attained before a student is able to function in an autonomous fashion without interfering with the rights of others. Until the student attains such self-discipline, direct teaching styles may be necessary.

The fitness model generally involves a prescriptive approach in which direct teaching styles are used to communicate knowledge about fitness and to implement programs to improve fitness. Traditional fitness programs set similar standards for all students, but some contemporary programs have developed personalized goals and programs. Some of these programs employ a style similar to the inclusion style in which all students perform the same tasks, but at different levels of difficulty. A few fitness programs have developed individualized instruction materials, allowing different students to work on different components of fitness. In some cases, particularly in adult fitness programs, participants select the fitness "problem" they wish to solve, then seek information to assist them in designing a program to reach this goal (style H).

One of the basic beliefs specified in the movement education model is that the learner is capable of making decisions and that education is responsible for helping the learner develop the ability to make wise choices (Logsdon et al.

1977). Historically, the use of discovery or problem solving models has been associated with movement education programs. In the Logsdon, Barrett, et al. work, teachers and students are viewed as mutually responsible for decision-making but decision-making is described as a continuum without labeling or categorizing of patterns of teaching behaviors. Logsdon, Barrett, et al. suggest that the absence of labels encourages greater fluidity in teaching behavior and that the wider the range of teaching behaviors teachers have, the greater the likelihood that they will be effective teachers. Emphasis is also placed upon the teacher's ability to observe and respond to what occurs in the learning environment.

The kinesiological studies model emphasizes development of the capability for self-directed learning as a primary goal of the physical education program. Understanding of movement concepts, as well as skillful movement, are important goals. Both common developmental characteristics and individuality are recognized as important. Because of these beliefs, this model emphasizes the use of problem-solving or discovery teaching models. Lawson and Placek (1981, 85) state that, "Problem-solving methods (or modes of inquiry) are important forms of content which are to be learned in physical education." While teachers in kinesiological studies programs do use direct teaching styles, this emphasis upon learning how to learn places great importance on the use of discovery styles.

The play education model described by Siedentop (1980) places high priority on the teaching of specific skills and knowledges needed to participate in a particular activity. While there is a counseling component that assists students in selecting appropriate activities, most instruction is focused upon acquisition of specific skills, knowledges, and social behaviors. For that reason, direct teaching styles are generally advocated and instruction is delivered in group settings to students with similar interests.

The personal meaning curriculum model defines physical education as personalized, self-directed learning (Jewett and Mullan 1977). Although human beings share certain common purposes for moving, the search for meaning is a highly personal quest. Jewett (1982) has suggested that elementary school teachers use a variety of instructional methods with a particular emphasis upon discovery styles. Middle school students should have opportunities for selection among alternative educational activities and should be given opportunity for self-direction and personal creativity. Instructional procedures in secondary schools should emphasize individual assessment, personal goal-setting, and opportunities for individualizing and personalizing learning. Jewett also proposes that students should gain understanding and competence in the processes for learning movement: perceiving, patterning, adapting, refining, varying, improvising, and composing. Such mastery requires appropriate instructional processes ranging from direct to discovery styles.

Although few of the curriculum models recommend a single instructional approach, certain teaching styles may be viewed as an integral part of a curriculum model. If the model is to be implemented in a local setting, the teachers in that school must have the skills to effectively use the recommended teaching styles.

Teaching Effectiveness

Successful implementation of any curriculum model ultimately depends upon effective teaching. A curriculum guide is a meaningless document unless the ideas incorporated in the curriculum design are reflected in the instructional process. Concerns about the quality of public education have produced increased interest in the evaluation and improvement of teaching effectiveness. Such procedures require a value judgment about "what is good teaching?". These value judgments need to be consistent with the philosophy and assumptions of the curriculum model and with the results of research on teaching.

Definitions of teaching effectiveness and approaches to research on teaching have changed during the past several decades. Medley (1979) has identified four phases in the research on teacher effectiveness: (1) characteristics of effective teachers, (2) effective methods of teaching, (3) behaviors of effective teachers, and (4) competencies of effective teachers. Each of these phases is described briefly in the next section. In addition, an alternative approach that views teaching effectiveness from a moral and aesthetic perspective is discussed.

Characteristics of Effective Teachers

The earliest research on teacher effectiveness attempted to identify the characteristics that differentiate effective teachers from those who are less effective. In general, teachers were classified as effective or ineffective on the basis of opinions or judgments by students or administrators. Following such classification, comparisons were made of the traits of the two groups. In some cases, the comparisons involved measurement of personality, mental abilities, academic achievement, attitudes, and other such variables. More frequently, researchers relied upon pupils, administrators, or experts to generate a list of characteristics that could be attributed to those teachers whom they perceived to be good teachers.

Several problems exist with this approach to research on teaching effectiveness. The first and most basic is that those teachers who seem to be good teachers may or may not actually be more effective in helping students learn. This is particularly problematic when you examine how the decision was made regarding who is effective. Students have extensive exposure to teachers, but lack the professional expertise that may be needed for such a judgment. Administrators have professional expertise, but often have only limited time to observe each teacher. Neither group may be able to reliably determine which teachers are truly most effective.

A second major problem is the generality and limited usefulness of the traits identified. Such lists often include such characteristics as good judgment, self-control, considerateness, enthusiasm, magnetism, leadership, and cooperation (Medley 1979). Teachers who want to use this information to improve their own teaching have a difficult time knowing what specific behaviors to change in order to improve in one of these categories. In addition, the results are often inconsistent from one study to the next.

Effective Methods of Teaching

As researchers became discouraged with efforts to identify traits or characteristics of effective teachers, a form of research called the "methods experiment" appeared. In this approach, two or more classes were taught by different methods and students' gains in achievement were compared across the classes. In physical education, some methods experiments used teaching styles from Mosston's spectrum of styles. The intent of the methods experiment was to find which method is superior in producing learning, changes in attitudes, or other variables of interest. The results of such experiments were often inconclusive (no significant difference existed between the methods) or contradictory (results from one study differed from those of another). Teachers and administrators, seeking to know the best way to teach, find little helpful information in this research.

Several aspects of the research design limited its usefulness. Often only a small number of teachers and classes were used in an experiment and no estimate could be made whether different teachers using the same method would get similar results. Usually the teachers in the experiment were not observed on a regular basis to verify that they were using the specified method. Some "drift" may have occurred, which blurred the distinctions between the two methods being tested. Some problem also existed in interpreting the results of the comparison. If differences in effectiveness were found, those aspects of a particular method that were responsible for its success could not be identified. The methods experiment made an important contribution in identifying student learning as the criterion for teacher effectiveness, but researchers were still trying to describe good teaching without entering classrooms.

Behaviors of Effective Teachers

A significant breakthrough occurred in teaching-effectiveness research in the early 1960s, when researchers began to observe in classroom settings to identify characteristic behaviors of teachers who effectively produce student learning. Such research, called *process-product research*, looked for stable patterns of behavior that differentiate most effective teachers from less effective teachers. This research differs from the early research comparing effective and ineffective teachers in two ways. First the identification of good teachers was based upon measured gains in student learning rather than upon the opinions of students or administrators. Second, instead of focusing upon personal traits and qualities of teachers, this research tried to specifically identify how effective teachers behave in the classroom by observing them in that setting.

Much of this research focused upon teaching behaviors that produce achievement in basic academic skills, and, to a lesser extent, motor skills. In some cases, the research also examined positive attitudes toward school and self as criteria for effectiveness. In general, this research identifies the following characteristics of effective teaching (Siedentop 1983, 41–42):

1. High percentage of time devoted to academic content
2. High rates of on-task behavior among students
3. Appropriate matching of content to student abilities (success-oriented learning)

4. Development of a warm, positive climate
5. Development of class structures that contribute to Item 2, but do not violate Item 4

While these characteristics of good teaching might apply to any teaching style, the research indicates that direct instruction has been most frequently associated with high rates of learning time.

> Direct instruction refers to academically focused, teacher directed classrooms using sequenced and structured materials. It refers to teaching activities where goals are clear to students, time allocated for instruction is sufficient and continuous, coverage of content is extensive, the performance of students is monitored, questions are at a low cognitive level so that students can produce many correct responses, and feedback to students is immediate and academically oriented. In direct instruction, the teacher controls instructional goals, chooses materials appropriate for the student's ability, and paces the instructional episode. Interaction is characterized as structured, but not authoritarian. Learning takes place in a convivial academic atmosphere. The goal is to move students through a sequenced set of materials or tasks (Rosenshine 1979, 38).

Effective teaching in programs aiming for basic skill achievement seems to be direct teaching, which is efficiently organized so that students get high levels of practice on tasks of appropriate difficulty levels.

Several cautions seem necessary in interpreting and applying these results. As noted previously, the characteristics of effective teaching (high time on task, success-oriented learning, warm positive climate) could be incorporated into any teaching style. The research may indicate that this is more difficult for teachers to do with individualized and discovery teaching styles because of the complexity of these approaches and teachers' relative unfamiliarity with them. Teachers who are skilled in these teaching styles may find them equally or more effective than direct teaching.

Caution also seems appropriate in assuming that direct teaching is equally effective for all students. Research that examined the effectiveness of different teaching behaviors for different types of students (aptitude-treatment interactions) finds that certain characteristics of the student may make a difference in how they respond to particular teaching styles (Cronbach and Snow 1977). Characteristics such as ability, socioeconomic class, gender, anxiety, locus of control, and learning style may influence which method is more effective for a particular student. Proponents of individualized instruction argue that this may necessitate adjusting the teaching style to the individual student's needs and characteristics.

Another concern in evaluating teaching effectiveness in terms of student outcomes is that many of the curriculum models have goals other than basic skill achievement. If the program aims for social or emotional development, self-awareness, understanding of concepts, problem solving skill, joy of movement, or commitment to an active lifestyle, it may be much more difficult to measure the effectiveness with which such outcomes are produced. Peterson (1979) suggests that open styles of teaching, involving more student choice and individualization, may surpass direct instruction in improving students' attitudes toward school and toward their teacher, and in promoting students' independence and curiosity. She concludes that, "if educators want to achieve a wide range of educational objectives and if they want to meet the needs of all students, then neither direct instruction alone nor open-classroom teaching alone is sufficient."

Competencies of Effective Teachers

As process-product research revealed the complexity of teaching effectiveness, a new approach to the research emerged. Rather than searching for stable patterns of behavior that characterize all effective teaching, researchers are addressing the question of what skills or strategies teachers should use under what circumstances in order to be maximally effective. The conception of effective teaching, which underlies this approach, is that good teachers have a large repertoire of teaching skills and make wise decisions about when to employ these skills.

The research based on this assumption differs from traditional process-product research in several ways. Variability in teachers' behavior, which was ignored in the search for stable patterns of behavior, is now being examined. Researchers are interested in how teachers select the "right approach" for the "right student" at the "right time." The teacher is viewed as a decision-maker and researchers are studying teachers' thinking to determine how effective teachers make decisions before and during instruction (Borko et al. 1979; Clark and Yinger 1979). The research includes the concept of reciprocal causality, which assumes that not only do teachers affect students, but that students affect the way teachers teach (Doyle 1979). Attention is given to student characteristics and the effect these characteristics have on teacher behavior, and on the effectiveness of various teaching styles (Brophy and Evertson 1981).

Most of the process-product research employed systematic observation in which specific behaviors in pre-selected categories were recorded. Some of the recent research uses what Doyle (1979) has called an ecological approach, in which naturalistic description is used to record detailed accounts of events occurring in classrooms, and the relationship of the observed behaviors to the environment.

At this time it is not possible to discuss trends in the results of this fourth phase of research on teaching effectiveness. One risk of this approach is that research that addresses multiple variables and interactions among those variables may be so complex that teachers will have difficulty in interpreting and applying the results. Gage (1978, 20) suggests that, while science can guide teachers in becoming effective, in complex situations the teacher as artist must make professional judgments about the best way to teach.

Quality of the Experience Provided

Although most of the research on teaching has defined good teaching in terms of its results, another way of looking at teaching effectiveness is the extent to which the teacher creates a "liveable" educational environment, consistent with the value system embodied in the curriculum model. Huebner (1966) suggests that educational environments have moral and aesthetic qualities that may be just as important as their technological efficiency in attaining specified outcomes. Eisner (1983) suggests that teaching is an art and a craft in which the teacher's creativity and artistry represents the ideal of educational performance. Both argue that examination of the process of education is just as important as evaluation of the products or outcomes.

Evaluation of teaching effectiveness, from a moral perspective, involves examination of the basic values reflected in the day-to-day interactions between teachers and students. Does the teacher recognize and protect the dignity of each individual student? Are principles of fairness and compassion applied to all students? Do instructional practices provide for both the common needs and the individual differences of students? Is the gymnasium a pleasant, safe world for students? Does each student have the opportunity to learn something of value? These questions imply that, regardless of the curriculum model or teaching style, the good teacher is one who is humane in dealing with students. It should be noted that such concern with humane treatment of students is not limited to the curriculum model that has been labeled the humanistic model.

Evaluating teaching from an aesthetic perspective requires examining the artistry of the teacher in creating an educational experience that is involving, exciting, and meaningful to students (Barone 1983). Are students interested and motivated to learn? Does the intensity of the lesson build to a climax, then finish with a sense of closure on completion? Are students emotionally, as well as cognitively and motorically, engaged in the lesson? Is the student actively involved in drawing personal meaning from the experience? When teaching effectiveness is viewed from the moral and aesthetic perspectives, the quality of the experience assumes an importance equal to that of the quantity of time on tasks and measurable student performance.

Staff Development

The research on teaching reveals a profile of the effective teacher as a professional who has a range of teaching competencies or styles and who knows when and how to use these competencies to promote student learning. Not all of these teaching skills will have been mastered during undergraduate teacher preparation. Staff development activities are important to enhance the continued growth of teachers. Such staff development activities are particularly essential when a new curriculum model is being implemented. Curriculum revisions often require teachers to teach new content or new teaching methods. The curriculum planning committee should provide the needed staff development activities to help teachers acquire the abilities needed.

The most common form of staff development is the in-service workshop or lectures on topics of interest to teachers. In general, these in-service programs are perceived as having little value or impact upon educational practice (Yarger, Howey, and Joyce 1980). Efforts to improve the quality of staff development have focused upon the design of more comprehensive, theoretically based programs. Three different approaches regarding staff development are identified as: instructional development, psychological development, and organizational development (Howey and Bents 1979).

The instructional development approach specifies skills or content to be learned by teachers, and then establishes a program to help them acquire those skills. Frequently an analogy is drawn between the development of teaching skills and the development of motor skills (Joyce and Showers 1982; Siedentop 1983). The process involves goal setting and extensive practice and feedback until the skill or competency is mastered. Joyce and Showers (1982) emphasize the importance of "coaching" teachers as they attempt to incorporate a newly acquired skill in their own classes. The skill acquisition perspective emphasizes specific instructional goals for staff development and sustained comprehensive programs that enable the teacher to master the skills identified.

The psychological development approach expands the view of staff development to include not only acquisition of professional skills but also the personal growth of teachers (Willie and Howey 1980). Developmental theorists have placed increasing emphasis on developmental changes that occur throughout adulthood. All adults, including teachers, must deal with a series of life events that affect both their personal and professional functioning. Psychological growth may result in more advanced cognitive styles characterized by more abstract thinking, greater creativity and flexibility, increased ability to deal with complexity and stress, and greater empathy. In research by Hunt, teachers at more advanced developmental stages were rated as more effective teachers and more capable of using a variety of teaching styles (Hunt and Sullivan 1974). Programs designed to promote developmental growth provide teachers with opportunities to assume new roles and to discuss and reflect upon the meaning of these experiences. Continuity and personal support are emphasized and attention is given to personal as well as professional concerns. Both the content and the format of the program are matched to the developmental level of the individual teacher.

The third perspective that can be adopted in planning a staff development program is that of organizational development (Roark and Davis 1981). Organizational development is an emerging field that attempts to make an organization more effective in accomplishing its task and to improve the quality of life for those who work in it. Several issues are typically addressed. Goal alignment attempts to identify and resolve incompatibility in the formal and informal goals of the organization and its individual members. Task and process analysis involves examining the extent to which the activities of the organization are consistent with task accomplishment. Other issues that are examined include the availability of valid information and the opportunity to make informed choices and personal commitments. Staff development programs based on this perspective focus less upon the development of individual competence and more upon organizational competence. Activities are planned that increase communication, improve group effectiveness, and create an open problem solving climate.

Regardless of the approach taken, effective staff development programs have several characteristics in common. Teachers are involved in the planning and execution of the program and see it as relevant to their needs. The program is ongoing and involves a significant time commitment. The staff development activities are experiential and an adequate support system is provided as changes are incorporated into the system.

Summary

The implementation of any curriculum model requires that teachers devise instructional strategies that effectively translate the model into action. The assumptions and goals of the model have implications for the type of teaching styles to be employed. Staff development activities may be needed to help teachers learn to use the teaching styles compatible with the model.

Each curriculum model attempts to describe an environment that provides a valuable educational experience for students. The effective teacher is one who can design and conduct instructional activities that make that environment a reality. When the model has been fully implemented, the measurement of student outcomes becomes an evaluation, not only of the teacher, but of the assumptions and premises of the model.

References

American Alliance for Health, Physical Education and Recreation. 1976. *Personalized learning in physical education.* Washington, DC: AAHPER.

Barone, T. 1983. Education as aesthetic experience: "Art in germ." *Educational Leadership* 40 (4): 21–26.

Borko, H., R. Cone, N. Atwood-Russo, and R. J. Shavelson. 1979. Teachers' decision-making. In *Research on teaching: Concepts, findings and implications*, ed. P. L. Peterson and H. J. Walberg. Berkeley: McCutchan.

Brophy, J. E., and C. M. Evertson. 1981. *Student characteristics and teaching.* New York: Longman.

Clark, C. M., and R. J. Yinger. 1979. Teachers' thinking. In *Research on teaching: Concepts, findings and implications*, ed. P. L. Peterson and H. J. Walberg. Berkeley: McCutchan.

Cronbach, L. J., and R. E. Snow. 1976. *Aptitudes and instructional methods.* New York: Irvington Publishers.

Doyle, W. 1979. Classroom tasks and student abilities. In *Research on teaching: Concepts, findings and implications*, ed. P. L. Peterson and H. J. Walberg. Berkeley: McCutchan.

Eisner, E. W. 1983. The art and craft of teaching. *Educational Leadership* 40 (4): 4–13.

Gage, N. L. 1978. *The scientific basis of the art of teaching.* New York: Teachers College Press.

Heitmann, H. M., and M. E. Kneer. 1976. *Physical education/instructional techniques: An individualized humanistic approach.* Englewood Cliffs: Prentice-Hall.

Hellison, D. 1978. *Beyond balls and bats.* Washington, DC: AAHPER.

Hellison, D. 1982. Philosophy—Back to the drawing board. *Journal of Physical Education, Recreation and Dance* 53 (1): 43–44.

Hoffman, H. A., J. Young, and S. E. Klesius. 1981. *Meaningful movement for children.* Boston: Allyn and Bacon.

Howey, K., and R. Bents. 1979. A general framework for induction and continuing teacher education. In *Toward meeting the needs of the beginning teacher*, ed. K. Howey and R. Bents. Minneapolis: Midwest Teacher Corps, Network.

Huebner, D. 1966. Curricular language and classroom meanings. In *Language and Meaning*, ed. J. B. Macdonald and R. R. Leeper. Washington, DC: Association for Supervision and Curriculum Development.

Hunt, D., and E. Sullivan. 1974. *Between psychology and education.* Hinsdale: Dryden Press.

Jewett, A. E. 1982. Program development. In *Physical education and sport: An introduction*, ed. E. F. Zeigler. Philadelphia: Lea and Febiger.

Jewett, A. E., and M. R. Mullan. 1977. *Curriculum design: Purposes and processes in physical education teaching-learning.* Washington, DC: AAHPER.

Joyce, B., and B. Showers. 1982. The coaching of teaching. *Educational leadership* 40 (1): 4–10.

Joyce, B., and M. Weil. 1972. *Models of teaching.* Englewood Cliffs: Prentice-Hall.

Lawson, H. A., and J. H. Placek. 1981. *Physical education in the secondary schools.* Boston: Allyn and Bacon.

Logsdon, B. J., K. R. Barrett, M. Ammons, M. R. Broer, L. E. Halverson, R. McGee, and M. A. Roberton. 1977. *Physical education for children*. Philadelphia: Lea and Febiger.

Medley, D. A. 1979. The effectiveness of teachers. In *Research on teaching: Concepts, findings and implications*, ed. P. L. Peterson and H. J. Walberg. Berkeley: McCutchan.

Mosston, M. 1981. *Teaching physical education*. Columbus: Charles E. Merrill.

Peterson, P. L. 1979. Direct instruction reconsidered. In *Research on teaching: Concepts, findings and implications*, ed. P. L. Peterson and H. J. Walberg. Berkeley: McCutchan.

Roark, A. E., and W. E. Davis Jr. 1981. Staff development and organization development. In *Staff development/organization development*, ed. E. Dillon-Peterson. Alexandria: Association for Supervision and Curriculum Development.

Rosenshine, B. 1979. Content, time and direct instruction. In *Research on teaching: Concepts, findings and implications*, ed. P. L. Peterson and H. J. Walberg. Berkeley: McCutchan.

Siedentop, D. 1983. *Developing teaching skills in physical education*. Palo Alto: Mayfield.

Siedentop, D. 1980. *Physical education: Introductory analysis*. Dubuque: Wm. C. Brown.

Thompson, M. M., and B. A. Mann. 1981. *Project SEE curriculum development*. Urbana: Urbana SEE Publications.

Willie, R., and K. R. Howey. 1980. Reflections on adult development: Implications for inservice teacher education. In *Staff development and educational change*, ed. W. R. Houston and R. Pankratz. Reston: Association of Teacher Educators.

Yarger, S. J., K. R. Howey, and B. R. Joyce. 1980. *Inservice teacher education*. Palo Alto: Booksend Laboratory.

Recommended Readings

Dillon-Peterson, B., ed. 1981. *Staff development/organization development*. Alexandria: Association for Supervision and Curriculum Development.

Heitmann, H. M., and M. E. Kneer. 1976. *Physical education/instructional techniques: An individualized humanistic approach*. Englewood Cliffs: Prentice-Hall.

Mosston, M. 1981. *Teaching physical education*. Columbus: Charles E. Merrill.

Siedentop, D. 1983. *Developing teaching skills in physical education*. Palo Alto: Mayfield.

Evaluation in Physical Education Curriculum Development

8

Outline

Evaluation is a process of asking questions and making judgments based on current answers (often incomplete or tentative) to those questions. This chapter proceeds by raising key questions appropriate to evaluation in physical education curriculum development and then offering partial responses to those questions. Comments are designed to stimulate your thinking toward better evaluative practice in physical education.

How do you go about evaluating a physical education curriculum? What is the purpose of evaluation? How is student evaluation used to make curriculum decisions? How can teacher evaluation contribute to program improvement? How can we evaluate the overall merit of the curriculum?

Curriculum Evaluation in Process

How do you go about evaluating a physical education curriculum? Look first at three selected examples of how it's being done.

Central High School is preparing for a regional accreditation. The head of the Physical Education Department calls a faculty meeting to discuss plans for the self-study. He suggests that the faculty may wish to proceed as they did the last time and describes the plan followed previously.

"Our first step was to get out the curriculum guide and to review the objectives to see whether they still fit what we were trying to do." The program goals as stated in the curriculum guide were listed on a sheet of paper and distributed to each staff member to rate from "strongly agree" to "strongly disagree," with an invitation to add any other objectives that should be considered. These responses were compiled, and the staff was reassembled to achieve consensus on the goal statements and to agree on a procedure for evaluating student achievement of the program goals.

The goals emphasized fitness, lifetime sports, attitude toward physical activity participation, and knowledge about the variables that affect performance. The staff agreed to conduct schoolwide testing, using the AAHPER Youth Fitness Test, and determined that their standard would be the sixtieth percentile, based on national norms. They decided to evaluate achievement of the other goals in terms of student grades based on a system used by all instructors. "That's when we adopted the present grading system in which we give thirty points for skill, twenty points for knowledge, twenty points for dress, ten points for effort, and twenty points for participation on task." Four skill tests and one or more knowledge tests are given in each major activity. Skill and knowledge portions of the grades are used to determine how many students meet minimum standards in each sport.

"Since dress, effort, and participation on task were each graded by subtracting points from an initial total, we figured that the average number of points subtracted per class gave us a pretty good indication of the general attitude toward participation. It was not too difficult to carry out this evaluation." Each instructor administered fitness tests in all classes in September and in March and submitted class grades, by activity, at the end of each unit for computer analysis in the departmental office.

Most of the physical education faculty members appear to be satisfied with this general approach, although there are a few suggestions for modification. Mr. Bond suggests that the new AAHPERD Health-Related Fitness Test should be substituted, and that the group should develop its own school norms. Ms. Clinton thinks

Curriculum Design

more weight should be given to actual sports performance and that the group should seek a better system for evaluating it. Ms. Nakamura indicates concern for what she perceives to be an essentially negative approach toward assessing attitude. This leads to a somewhat lengthy discussion and the group agrees to meet again to consider restatement of psychosocial goals, and to discuss whether attitude objectives are important enough to include evaluation in this area as a part of the overall curriculum evaluation.

The physical education staff of the **Lake County Elementary Schools** are meeting with their local administrators to plan for evaluation of the physical education curriculum. For nearly a year they have been the recipients of federal funds channeled through the State Department of Education to promote curricular innovation. They have been offering a program utilizing a particular National Distribution Network model, and are required to report certain evaluation data in applying for continuation funds. The planned evaluation procedure is essentially a mastery learning approach. The movement education curriculum, conducted in accordance with the innovative model, is evaluated through the identification of specific performance skills included in checklists to be used for recording the progress of each individual child throughout the year. Checklists include such items as slide, gallop, skip, jump over a rope using two-foot take-off and landing, jump "front door" into a moving rope, rope climb alternating hands and feet, catch a playground ball with two hands below the waist, trap a soccer ball with one foot, one-hand underhand softball throw to partner, clap a rhythmic pattern, create a movement sequence, forward roll, walk backward on low balance beam.

The physical education specialists have consulted with the classroom teachers involved and are satisfied that individual class records are current and that progress of the children toward meeting the specified goals will be more than satisfactory at the end of the academic year. They hope to be able to demonstrate higher levels of achievement in mastery of these skills from grade to grade and from year to year. However, they also wish to broaden the curriculum evaluation.

Ms. James expresses interest in determining whether the movement education model actually results in more positive concepts of self, as claimed. They agree to set up a schedule of interviews with parents to assess parent satisfaction with the program, as well as parents' opinions concerning their child's self-concept, movement competence, and enjoyment of physical activity. The group also decides to experiment with a simple technique of asking each child to rate daily their satisfaction with the physical education class from "didn't like it at all" to "lots of fun."

Mr. Sanchez points out that they ought to check on whether students have maintained the same levels of fitness, since they are now devoting so much less time to fitness exercises and testing. The group agrees to administer the state fitness test battery in May and compare the scores with those recorded a year ago. They also plan to survey the middle school physical education teachers for the next two years to seek their evaluations concerning subsequent sports performance of the students who have experienced movement education compared with those who completed elementary school prior to this program change.

Specific plans are made for the monthly staff development workshops for the remainder of the year, and for the fall teacher in-service physical education meetings. Plans include clinics on use of appropriate evaluative techniques, as well as orientation to new curriculum materials and teacher-led sessions on selected instructional techniques. The fall workshop is to provide for orientation of new teachers to the physical education curriculum model and focus on involvement of the total staff in long-range plans for continuing evaluation of the physical education curriculum.

The **Cedar City** physical education secondary school curriculum committee is holding an organizational meeting. The committee consists of six teachers, the Director of Physical Education, four senior high school physical educators, and one each from the elementary and junior high school staffs. Three years ago, the Board of Education approved a proposal for major curriculum revision submitted by the Director of Physical Education. Substantial funds were allocated for released time for teachers, purchase of new equipment, printing and distribution of curriculum guides, and staff development workshops for implementation. The elementary school curriculum has been planned and field tested, guides have been published, and all teachers have been using the revised curriculum guides for at least a year. Last year the junior high school curriculum committee developed and pilot tested its initial materials; a preliminary guide is in the hands of junior high school physical education teachers for field testing this year. The Cedar City Physical Education Director opened this meeting by pointing out that the focus in planning needs to be shifted now to the senior high school program.

The Director, serving as chair of the committee, has reminded the committee members that a community survey was conducted four years ago to determine overall program goals for physical education in Cedar City. The survey instrument was based on the purposes of the Purpose Process Curriculum Framework; the professional staff used these purpose concepts to establish program goals for elementary school, junior high school, and senior high school at that time. A follow-up of the community survey last year showed that community priorities had not changed much, except that there is even greater concern for developing fitness and teamwork than was expressed four years ago. The efforts of the senior high school curriculum committee are directed toward program improvement in meeting objectives relating to physiological efficiency, self-knowledge, joy of movement, object manipulation, space awareness, spatial relationships, communication, teamwork, competition, leadership, and participation.

The chair has also reviewed the decisions that led to the selection of five subject areas for physical education curriculum development throughout the secondary school (grades 7–12): fitness, body mastery, games, dance, and leadership. The committee has now reached the point in the agenda where they are considering evaluation standards and strategies prior to making more specific decisions concerning the particular content and instructional sequences for structuring the senior high school physical education curriculum. The Manitoba Physical Fitness Performance Test is already being administered three times annually throughout the school system (September, December, and May); the group wants to continue to use this test battery in order to collect evaluative data comparable to scores already on record.

Considerable discussion of the problems of setting meaningful standards for motor performance skill finally leads to the decision to state the program goal in terms of achieving a beginning or intermediate competency in a given number of lifetime sports as a senior high school physical education curriculum completion requirement. Such a requirement could be structured to ensure evaluation relating to object manipulation, neuromuscular efficiency, teamwork, and competition. The group recognizes that it will be a long-term effort to establish beginning and intermediate standards for each sport included in the curriculum, and that other members of the faculty will need to be involved in this effort.

As the discussion continues it becomes clear that two major evaluation strategies will be important. Those goals that lend themselves to the statement of specific objectives and the use of objective testing procedures will be evaluated by use of standardized testing to the extent feasible in order to establish clearly defined goals and to collect data that permit comparison, generalization, and communication to the Board of Education, parents, and the general public. Objective measures will require supplementing, however, in order to meaningfully evaluate individual progress toward such purpose goals as self-knowledge, joy of movement, participation, and leadership. The group makes a tentative decision that, beyond fitness and sports competency testing, they will make the individual instructor responsible for individual guidance and evaluation within the class setting. Personal goal-setting and self-evaluation will be encouraged. Students will be assisted in selecting appropriate challenges and developing realistic task contracts. Individual profiles and progress reports will be kept and will follow the student to a new instructor. The instructor will be expected to recommend appropriate activities to students whose performance in a particular subject area is below average.

"Brainstorming" about how to evaluate group interaction leads to suggestions for observation teams that might systematically describe both student interaction and teacher instructional behaviors. Inventories to assess student attitudes toward competition, responses toward certain leadership styles, enjoyment of various types of physical activities, could be used. Follow-up data on voluntary participation in physical recreation activities, membership on sport teams, participation in races and other athletic events, would be of interest. Surveys could be directed toward recent high school graduates, as well as present students. Ideas are flying and the committee members are startled when the director interrupts their productive interaction with suggestions as to how they might prepare to continue their planning during next week's meeting.

Purposes of Evaluation in Physical Education

The curriculum process in physical education is an ongoing cycle of planning, implementation, and evaluation. Evaluation serves many purposes in physical education: classification, diagnosis and guidance, motivation, reporting progress, and program improvement. Since our focus is on evaluation as a component of curriculum development, its primary purpose in this context is program improvement. Sound pedagogical practice dictates assessment of the effectiveness of any program at frequent intervals in order that needed modifications can be made. Modifications may be needed in the curriculum plan, in the instructional strategies being used to implement that plan, or, in many cases, in both curricular and instructional practice.

When the purpose of evaluation is overall program improvement, the data on individual student achievement constitute only a portion of that needed. Evaluators must assess the nature and impact of the "hidden" curriculum, as well as the outcomes of the planned curriculum. What factors, other than the intended curriculum content and the planned instructional techniques, are affecting the actual experience of the students? Are class regulations and management routines affecting the quality of the educational experiences in unintended ways? What can be determined concerning the quality of the educational climate and the interpersonal interaction among students and teacher?

Evaluation for purposes of program improvement need not be limited to seeking data concerning how more students can achieve the existing standards in reaching present goals. It may also be directed toward possible changes in program objectives or the modification of existing program standards. An assessment directed toward program improvement also needs to evaluate the program in relation to the needs of the particular community and the special priorities of the local citizens who support the schools and who should accept responsibility for the quality and effectiveness of all local educational programs.

Student Evaluation

It is generally agreed that data on student achievement are needed to assess the effectiveness of a physical education program. Evaluation is viewed as a continuous, ongoing, integral part of the educational process. Measurement (the concrete, identifiable, quantifiable phase of evaluation) is an important aspect of the evaluation of student achievement. A complete evaluation program, however, goes beyond the aspects that are capable of accurate assessment through the use of valid and reliable measuring instruments, and encompasses varied approaches to assessing pupil behavioral changes, curriculum efficiency, and teacher effectiveness. The evaluation of student progress and achievement includes appraisal of knowledges gained, motor performance skills mastered, gains and losses in the state of health-related fitness, and changes in affective behavior.

A planned program of student evaluation uses both formative and summative evaluation. These terms have come into general usage in physical education evaluation during the last decade. The basic distinction between the two types of evaluation is that formative evaluation takes place throughout the instructional period, while summative evaluation occurs upon completion of the instructional unit. Formative evaluation is designed to assess student performance during the learning period in order to formulate or revise instructional objectives or techniques. Summative evaluation is directed toward the assessment of the sum total of student achievement at the conclusion of an instructional program. Thus summative evaluation emphasizes the product or learning outcome, whereas formative evaluation places more emphasis on guidance of the learning process.

Two other terms, frequently used in discussing evaluation of student performance, are norm-referenced evaluation and criterion-referenced evaluation. Norm-referenced evaluation is based on the concept of the curve of normal distribution. Given a large number of test scores, these scores will be normally distributed in accordance with a bell-shaped curve, with the majority of scores falling in the middle range, and fewer scores distributed at the high and low extremes. For purposes of norm-referenced evaluation, a table of norms is established, based on the scores of all those who comprised the norming group. Thus the individual's score or grade depends upon comparison of his or her score with all those who have taken the test in the past or all of those who are part of the group who took the test at the same time, depending upon what group was used to determine the norm.

In criterion-referenced evaluation, specific descriptions of desirable performance are spelled out as the evaluative criteria. Performance objectives are used to assess the student's level of performance at any point during the instructional sequence. When the student masters the criterion behavior, the objective has been met. Student achievement is evaluated in reference to an established criterion, rather than relative to the performance of others.

Formative evaluation emphasizes criterion-referenced evaluation. Summative evaluation tends to rely more heavily on norm-referenced evaluation, but often includes criterion-referenced evaluation procedures as well. Both formative and summative evaluation have a place in evaluating student achievement. If evaluation is to serve purposes of guidance, motivation, and facilitation of learning, more emphasis should be put on formative evaluation. A key principle for evaluating students is planning evaluation procedures according to the important objectives of the local physical education program. Determine, specifically, what is important to evaluate, and then find the best techniques for assessing appropriate student accomplishments. In most programs, this will lead to a focus on fitness and motor performance testing. Since active participation in physical activity programs will be maintained only if positive attitudes are developed, attention should also be given to evaluating affective learnings. Knowledge is important, primarily, as it is likely to modify behavior, and should be evaluated with this in mind.

A common concern is the question of how much time should be devoted to evaluation of student achievement. Most physical educators believe that insufficient time is allotted for the instructional program, making it difficult to make a judgment concerning how much of this time is well-spent in testing. In this connection it is well to remember that measurement produces only quantitative information; evaluation is the value judgment placed upon available data. The judgment about time devoted to testing and other types of performance assessment is really dependent upon the degree to which the data gathered are effectively used in making value judgments for guiding students and improving the program.

Specific tools and techniques available for student evaluation are numerous and diverse. Most tests and other types of instruments used for evaluation are also used for assessing student needs. A number of these are discussed in chapter 5. If you are interested in reviewing this topic, you may choose to return to the section on instrumentation for needs assessment. Additional information is also available in the readings at the ends of both this chapter and chapter 5.

Teacher Evaluation

Evaluation in physical education is focused on student achievement, teacher effectiveness, or overall program success. Now that you have reviewed evaluation of student achievement, identified specific student accomplishments for evaluation, and considered the alternative procedures for assessing student achievement, shift your attention to the teacher. Try to think of yourself as an individual professional being evaluated.

Teacher evaluation should be viewed in the context of its contribution toward program improvement. The focus of teacher evaluation should be on helping the individual teacher to do a quality job as a professional educator. While evaluation by supervisors, students, peers, and outside experts can help in a systematic study of a teacher's professional performance, the teacher must also be engaged in continuing self-evaluation. Evaluative techniques can best include both product measures and evaluation of the process. It is important to give sufficient attention to process evaluation in a continuing evaluation plan designed for long-range program improvement. Above all, everyone involved needs to be reminded that the teacher alone is not wholly responsible for the success of the educational endeavor. He or she should feel accountable to the board of education (as the representative of the local community) for a conscientious, caring professional performance, recognizing and working within local limitations toward maximum and continuing personal professional growth.

Why are Teachers Evaluated?

The purposes of teacher evaluation in physical education can all be viewed within the perspective of program improvement as a major focus for physical education evaluation. Three subpurposes can be noted. The first of these is to determine whether individuals are qualified to be certified or licensed to teach. Public policy requires some type of screening and evaluation at the time of initial certification and again, following a probationary period, to determine that performance meets the standard justifying permanent certification for tenure.

A second reason for teacher evaluation is as a basis for salary increases or promotion decisions. Evaluation for certification purposes focuses on whether the teacher possesses minimum essential qualifications. When evaluating teachers for decisions based on meritorious performance, a judgment relative to quality of teaching performance is implied. The individual's performance is expected to be somewhat above the minimum standard; in some instances, the evaluation results in a decision concerning the extent to which this teacher exceeds minimum standards, and may be reported in one of several categories indicating different quality levels or degrees of excellence in performance.

A third reason for evaluating teachers is to assist the individual teacher in improvement of job performance. Teacher evaluation should be directed toward helping the individual teacher increase personal effectiveness and should lead toward overall program improvement by helping them do their assigned jobs better. Evaluation designed to stimulate individual professional growth must be based on identifiable criteria that are useful in the diagnosis of typical performance and in guidance of the individual teacher being evaluated. Teacher evaluation programs in different settings vary widely according to which of these three subpurposes they are designed to serve.

How Should Teachers be Evaluated?

The answer to this question depends, in large measure, upon how we define effective teaching or a competent teacher. In general, there are two major approaches, product evaluation and process evaluation. Various patterns combining elements of both are also possible.

Product evaluation is the type traditionally used. Product evaluation bases the judgment concerning teaching effectiveness on observed gains in student learning. A long-standing example is the evaluation of teacher competence based on student performance in the New York State Regents examinations, in which high school students throughout the state take a single standardized examination in a subject matter area such as English literature, algebra, or American history. A contemporary example is teacher evaluation based on average classroom scores on standardized tests of reading and mathematics. A physical education example is the evaluation of teacher competence based on the scores their students earn on the AAHPERD Health Related Physical Fitness Test or on a battery of standardized sports skills tests.

Procedurally, there are at least three ways to conduct product evaluation. A standardized test can be administered as a pre-test and then administered again at the end of the instructional unit or the year's work in physical education. Results of the two testings can then be compared. A second procedure is product evaluation based on standardized tests with well-established norms; student achievement is judged in relation to the norms selected, rather than on before and after student performance. A third approach, which is becoming increasingly popular, is known as competency-based education. Achievement standards are carefully defined in advance. The students work to meet these standards, or to master the learning tasks prescribed. Upon completion of instruction, the teacher is evaluated according to the number of students who have succeeded in fulfilling the competencies, or in terms of the percentage of competencies mastered by the average student.

Competency-based education and evaluation are more popular with legislatures, boards of education, and administrators than with teachers. Many teachers do not view student learning as the major criterion for determining teaching effectiveness. Teachers are likely to value process criteria above product measures. Process evaluation of teaching usually depends on some type of observational technique. Observation may be focused on specific teacher personal characteristics and technical skills, such as demonstration procedures, classroom control, and techniques for individualizing instruction. Presently in vogue are a variety of observation systems that focus on student activity and how time is used within the instructional period. This is based on the rationale that the student must be actively involved with the subject field content if desired learning is to occur.

Most systematic efforts toward process evaluation of physical education teachers during the past twenty years have been directed toward descriptive analytic analysis of social interaction in the physical education class. Several observation systems have been designed: studying verbal interaction among students and teachers; categorizing teacher pedagogical moves as initiatory, reflexive, or neutral; classifying the target of the teacher's attention in terms of a single individual, a small group, or the entire class; clarifying the nature of discipline or the locus of control; or assessing the nature of the classroom climate or quality of rapport between students and teacher. In addition to a variety of instruments that have been validated for studies of teacher behavior, any individual teacher can develop an informal plan to focus on any specific aspect of his or her own behavior that is to be evaluated. To answer the question of how teachers should be evaluated, it is probably reasonable to expect some combination of several relevant evaluative techniques, including both assessment of student achievements, and studies of teacher behavior in the instructional role.

Who Should Evaluate Teachers?

School administrators, or staff personnel identified as supervisors, are usually charged with the official responsibility for evaluation of teaching performance. These individuals have an obligation to work with teachers in clarifying evaluative criteria to be used. Teachers can expect that they will base judgments on an adequately representative sample of individual performance, and that they will seek different kinds of evidence as a basis for evaluative judgment. The supervisor should assume responsibility for sharing evaluative data directly with the teacher, and for using this information to provide guidance for the teacher's professional growth.

In some situations, students are asked to contribute to the evaluation of teaching performance. Student ratings can be helpful in the context of different kinds of assessment data. It is important, however, that student opinions of teachers be utilized to add a perspective to the evaluation, and not substituted for a more thorough, objective evaluation by supervisors and other mature adults.

Peers are sometimes brought into evaluation for either of two reasons. A colleague may be in a better position to evaluate the teacher's performance in relation to given educational objectives, and may be much better able to communicate helpful conclusions for the assistance of the teacher evaluated. If an important personnel judgment, such as tenure or promotion, is to be based upon the evaluation, peer evaluation (as part of the total) may be more equitable.

Some current plans for teacher certification and evaluation include participation by subject matter specialists and pedagogical experts on the evaluation team. Thus, if the teacher is to be certified on the basis of demonstrated competencies, a team of experts may be identified to make judgments concerning teacher competence. At the initial certification level, the panel may include the student-teaching supervisor from the teacher education institution, the cooperating teacher in the school setting, and a representative of the state department of education, who has completed a special training program. For permanent certification, the teacher with some full-time experience might be evaluated by a panel consisting of a school administrator, a peer teacher in the same subject matter field, and one or more trained representatives of the state department of education.

Who evaluates the teacher depends upon the purpose of the evaluation. In the last analysis, the teacher's self-evaluation is the most important and will have the greatest long-range value. Every teacher should become a student of teaching effectiveness and an evaluator of personal teaching performance.

For What Are Teachers Accountable?

Much has been said and written about educational accountability. While everyone agrees that the public school should be accountable to its constituency for meeting reasonable standards in fulfilling its educational mission, there is much controversy both in setting standards and in determining how the achievement of standards will be demonstrated. When the question of accountability is directed toward the individual teacher, it seems a reasonable expectation that the teacher will have a genuine concern for and attempt to establish positive interaction with each student for whom he or she has an assigned responsibility. The individual teacher is accountable to his or her classes to provide access to key content in the subject matter area, to give guidance in identifying other resources to challenge the student's learning, and to provide opportunity and support for the student to achieve maximum self-directed growth and learning. Beyond these responsibilities, it is probably not reasonable to hold teachers accountable for highly specific student learning outcomes without reference to the readiness of the student's abilities or the resources available to the teacher.

It would probably be wise to ask what other things we hold teachers accountable for, in addition to academic productivity. Teachers today are typically accountable for performing many managerial tasks and for carrying out a variety of miscellaneous professional responsibilities, in addition to the instructional role we regard as central. Job analysis studies, or studies of how teachers spend their working hours, show that only approximately one-third of their time is spent in activities directly related to academic instruction. Teachers typically spend one-third to one-half of their time in management duties, and one-fifth to one-third of their total working time in other types of miscellaneous professional responsibilities. If we wish to raise our expectations in terms of academic accountability, it may be necessary to examine closely how teachers must function in typical school settings, and to consider whether there are better ways to give emphasis to the full utilization of their potentials as professionals.

Program Evaluation

Program evaluation is primarily concerned with establishing direction for program improvement. It is directed toward the local board of education and the local citizenry, as well as the professional staff. It is designed to win support from educational authorities and taxpayers for the local schools, and to gain greater financial input for current community educational needs and desired future curriculum developments.

Program evaluation usually includes evaluation of student performance, but evaluators are likely to be more interested in group means than in individual student scores because the evaluation report will be submitted to the school's total clientele, rather than providing a progress report to the individual parent. Program evaluation may also include teacher evaluation, but will focus more directly on the success of particular innovative instructional strategies or the effective utilization of particular curriculum materials than on the individual professional growth of the teacher. Thus program evaluation has a broader scope than either student evaluation or teacher evaluation alone. It tends to emphasize progress toward long-range community educational aims, rather than short-term gains. Special effort is usually directed toward evaluating student learning in terms of real world criteria.

In recent years there has been increased public interest in program evaluation. In periods of unusual economic pressure, all public servants face greater demands for accountability. Under these conditions there is a tendency for educational administrators to attempt to preserve the status quo, and to ignore newer approaches to educational evaluation. This is particularly unfortunate at a time when some promising new approaches to educational evaluation are gaining acceptance.

Many curricularists believe that we should resist the pressure to rely upon the time-honored quantitative methods of research and evaluation, and give more attention to the use of qualitative methods and nonscientific approaches to the evaluation of educational practice. As Willis (1978) points out, there is no such thing as an "objective" educational evaluation; program evaluators can view quantitative and qualitative procedures as complementary. This is a controversial issue that will be discussed in more depth in the next section. In the paragraphs that follow, we also consider different program evaluation models and their potential applications in evaluating physical education curricula.

Is Evaluation to Strengthen Ends or Means?

The principal purpose of program evaluation should be improvement of the curriculum. McNeil (1981, 267) identifies some of the specific improvements that might be addressed.

> Scores or descriptive terms that summarize learner performance give study groups the opportunity to see the strengths and weaknesses of their programs. . . . Study groups also discuss the reasons for a curriculum's strengths and weaknesses. Members try to explain results in terms of particular learning opportunities, time spent on an objective, the ordering of activities and topics, the kinds and frequency of responses from learners, the grouping patterns, and the use of space and interactions with adults. Explanations are verified by seeing whether all the data lead to the same conclusion. Plans are made to modify the curriculum in light of deficiencies noted and the cause of the deficiencies.

Evaluation should be used to strengthen both ends and means. A thorough program evaluation can be expected to identify certain student needs that are not being met. The identification of these unmet needs provides direction to curriculum planners in establishing additional goals, or in stating new or more specific instructional objectives. Often new objectives are actually more important than those initially selected. When this occurs, the curriculum is improved by directing sharper focus toward more significant educational concerns. The ends themselves are strengthened.

Results of program evaluation can also be used to strengthen means. They may identify areas in which learning activities do not provide sufficient variety or repetition to permit the generalization of important concepts. They may pinpoint activities on which too much time is spent in relation to student accomplishments fostered. They may highlight specific activity or theme units in which student participation is limited by insufficient equipment or practice space. They may identify instructional difficulties such as too much teacher talk, use of outdated curriculum materials, insufficient technological aids, inefficient class management, or lack of skill in providing verbal feedback. They may help to make explicit certain aspects of the "hidden curriculum" that adversely affect student learning. In all of these ways, program evaluation can be utilized to improve the curriculum through pointing to ways in which means can be modified and strengthened. It is not a question of strengthening ends *or* means; both should be the focus of program evaluation.

Which Evaluation Model Shall We Use?

Different program evaluation models are used for different purposes. Different evaluation models are appropriate for different curriculum value orientations. Certain physical education curriculum models dictate the use of a particular evaluation model; others permit the program evaluator more options. The four types of program evaluation models discussed have been selected because they have distinctive characteristics that allow description and differentiation. The models selected (desired-outcome models, goal-free models, the adversary model, and artistic models) are not precisely defined, and these four are not viewed as exhaustive categories. Many variations and combinations of these and other types are possible.

Desired-outcome models have dominated practice in curriculum evaluation since the point at which educational evaluation became a recognized area of professional specialization. Tyler's view of evaluation has strongly influenced curriculum development and research since the publication of *Basic Principles of Curriculum and Instruction* in 1949. During the period from 1960 to 1980, with both taxpayers and funding agencies calling for more systematic evaluation, accountability, and cost effectiveness, desired-outcome models continued to flourish. These models emphasize responsible selection of desired outcomes and systematic determination of the extent to which objectives are actually being realized.

Tyler described a three-step procedure. The first step is clearly defining program objectives. This is followed by identifying situations that will give students opportunities to express the behaviors implied by the statement of objectives. The final step in the procedure is examining available evaluation instruments and selecting or devising tools appropriate for the particular assessment task. Techniques for evaluating physical education knowledge, motor performance skill, student fitness achievement, and desired attitudes or affective learnings are discussed in chapter 5. Program evaluation using a desired-outcomes model often includes research on teacher effectiveness directed toward establishing relationships between particular teacher behaviors and selected desired outcomes. Evaluative designs include standard experimental designs (such as pretest–posttest–control group designs), interrupted time series designs, and longitudinal follow-up studies.

The primary focus of the desired-outcomes model is actual student achievement. The major advantages are that criterion referenced measurements can be obtained with regard to specific objectives, and the findings can be reported to the lay public in terms meaningful to the average citizen. Research data can illuminate the comparative values of alternative curriculum materials or the relative effectiveness of various tactics of instruction. Evaluation based on specific objectives provides helpful feedback for rational curriculum decision-making.

On the other hand, evaluation is limited to those desired outcomes that can be precisely stated, and for which relatively objective measures exist or can be developed. This may lead to the oversimplification of educational aims, and to ignoring very important concerns that cannot be evaluated adequately through a desired-outcomes model. It is also very difficult to ensure a representative sampling of student behaviors upon which to base evaluative judgments. Furthermore, there are problems inherent in placing too much emphasis on the proper statement of behavioral objectives; it can be argued that they are inappropriate for certain types of student responses, that they may overemphasize the trivial, that students may be manipulated, that teacher creativity and spontaneity are restricted, and that the potential for desirable educational experiences to emerge from the teaching-learning situation is limited. The approach tends to overvalue efficiency and to be insensitive to the process and to the humanistic aspects of the educational environment.

It has already been pointed out that different program evaluation models are used for different purposes. Most of the physical education curriculum models described in chapter 3 suggest some variation of the desired-outcomes model for program evaluation. Fitness models, kinesiological studies models, developmental education models, movement education models, and play education models all emphasize clarification of desired curriculum outcomes, and tend toward prescription of program content. Although the desired-outcomes model is clearly the one most frequently advocated in physical education, there appears to be little documentation in the literature of comprehensive systematic evaluation studies of physical education curricula.

Indeed, there is considerable reason to question whether there is sufficient evaluation of any type in physical education curricular practice. Perhaps it is appropriate to note that a major assessment plan, identified as National Assessment of Educational Progress (NAEP), includes plans for the assessment of each of ten study areas—reading, literature, music, social studies, science, writing, citizenship, mathematics, art, and career and occupational development. Physical education is obvious by its omission. It is no more difficult to assess progress in physical education than in citizenship; physical education cannot be viewed as less "academic" than art or music; physical education is not as new to the school program as career education. Must we conclude, therefore, that physical education is not yet acknowledged as an important "study area" in the school curriculum?

Goal-free models were developed to meet some of the criticisms of desired-outcomes models, and to offset the weaknesses resulting from a singular focus on prespecified goals. Scriven (1972) popularized goal-free evaluation as a model that shifts attention beyond intended outcomes only to concern for all relevant effects. Curriculum planners who assume the responsibility for establishing statements of desired outcomes may, as program evaluators, overlook other types of achievement. They may be unaware of emerging new priorities, or even miss unanticipated harmful side effects. The goal-free model attends to all relevant effects within a given evaluative context.

In order to evaluate all relevant effects, more and varied measures are needed. Program evaluators employing goal-free models usually follow a checklist and use a wide variety of techniques. In addition to relatively objective measures, indicators of change in learners may include teacher-made devices, interviews, self-evaluation measures, sociograms, projective devices, and semantic differential scales. Creative indicators may be found in learners' products and self-reports. The evaluator may give particular emphasis to classroom observation and attend to such data as absences, disciplinary actions, anecdotal records, and assignments.

The primary value of goal-free models is that the evaluation is likely to be much more thorough, complete, and representative. It results in a broader picture of the program's operation and effects. The major disadvantages are that one is apt to rely too heavily on subjective perceptions, or that the range of evaluative devices may be insufficient to ensure that all relevant effects are actually identified.

Responsible, goal-free evaluation has been little used in physical education. Among the models discussed in chapter 3, the humanistic curriculum model is probably most likely to make use of goal-free evaluation. Curricula developed within the personal meaning model may also seek data on relevant effects beyond the achievement of desired goals. In both humanistic and personal meaning models, the program evaluator normally uses some combination of the typical performance tests, administered in accordance with desired-outcomes models, and other more creative approaches to the collection and analysis of evaluative data.

Educational evaluators continue to seek alternatives to the desired-outcomes model. A recent innovation that uses a process-oriented design is the *adversary* model. Levine (1974) is the primary advocate of this model, which casts evaluators in juristic roles. The model borrows extensively from judicial procedures, highlighting defense and prosecution teams of evaluators, and simulating actual courtroom procedures.

The evaluation is planned in detail. Two teams of evaluators are identified. One team serves as advocates for the curriculum being evaluated, while the opposite team is designated as adversaries, directed to attack it. Roles may be determined by coin toss; both teams are expected to prepare arguments thoroughly in advance. The opposing teams present arguments before a jury and even conduct cross-examinations.

The adversary model is attractive in its use of a fair and just procedure, and its appearance of submitting all claims to an appropriate test. It is probably best suited to evaluation of an innovative program that departs significantly from typical practice. On the other hand, it has the disadvantage of requiring that the issue be framed in terms of two options. It is also expensive, in terms of both time and expert personnel. Since its introduction, it has won only limited support. Popham and Carlson (1981) have identified six major weaknesses or deficits: disparity in prowess of the opposing proponents, fallible arbiters, excessive confidence in the model's potency, difficulties in framing the proposition in a manner amenable to adversary resolution, decision-maker bias, and excessive costs. The model appears to hold very little promise for physical education curriculum evaluation.

An *artistic* model of educational evaluation has recently emerged. This alternative appears to have potential for broader support, particularly from the reconceptualists. The model has been developed primarily by Eisner and his students, particularly Donmoyer, McCutcheon, and Vallance. Using the artistic model, the curriculum is viewed as a work of art; the evaluative process is analogous to artistic criticism. The curriculum evaluator attempts to assess educational experiences offered to students as an art critic would assess a painting or a dance. Donmoyer (1981, 352) describes what the "evaluator as artist" does as follows:

> Clearly he or she focuses on aspects of curriculum that are often obscured by the methodologies and/or reporting procedures of other evaluation approaches. Because the evaluator as artist illuminates idiosyncracy, the process of curriculum, and the qualities of the curriculum process, and because he or she uses theory as an aid to perception and action, he or she should provide a valuable supplement to information of other evaluators working with other evaluation models.

The qualitative orientation of the artistic model, the emphasis placed on more fully describing the subtleties of the total curricular experience, and the fact that the evaluator is his or her own evaluation instrument, magnify certain traditional curriculum evaluation problems, and create some new ones. Donmoyer identifies seven major problems: the problem of time, the problem of personal description, the problem of metaphor, the problem of plot, the problem of distance, the problem of logistics, and the problem of a theoretician-practitioner gap. As Donmoyer points out, the very humanity that is the artistic evaluator's strength also poses unique problems.

Donmoyer suggests that the curriculum evaluator using this evaluation model adopt a primarily formative role, carefully seek to attune himself or herself to the particular school situation, and work within a context of clinical supervision. Time is required to give feedback, and to permit sufficient interaction with the practitioners whose work is being evaluated. It is also suggested that the practitioner who is the subject of artistic criticism should control release of this information to decision-makers or to any other individual. In Donmoyer's (1981, 360) words, "Only if these suggestions are adhered to, can the evaluator as artist's work be ethically desirable, politically possible, and practically useful."

It has also been pointed out that the artistic model of educational evaluation is relatively new. It has not yet been widely used in any subject matter area, and certainly rarely, if at all, in physical education. It is proposed that a physical education curriculum developed in accordance with a perspective of ecological validity might be an appropriate vehicle for exploring the use of an artistic model of educational evaluation.

Quantitative Evaluation or Qualitative Evaluation?

Qualitative evaluation is a relatively recent development in education. Until very recently all respectable educational evaluation was quantitative in that it was based upon scientific approaches, the use of numerical analysis, and empirical verification. Modern curriculum evaluation acknowledges two major approaches: (1) quantitative studies that emphasize numerical analysis of the most easily observed and empirically verifiable characteristics of the environment, and (2) qualitative studies that are directed toward broader consideration of observed characteristics and the perception and description of specific qualities identified as personal forms of meaning. The evaluator in quantitative studies tends to investigate a world viewed as largely determinant and nonproblematic. Qualitative evaluation includes the personal determination of the qualities of an indeterminant world, and involves a process of qualitative problem solving.

The major force that led to the development of qualitative methods in educational evaluation is the recognition by many that scientific and quantitative methods alone are inadequate for studying some of the most important concerns of those responsible for curriculum development. Many curriculum specialists consider that laboratory research methods are too limiting, and that methods are needed that permit observation of what naturally transpires without intervention by experimenters. A more flexible and naturalistic approach to inquiry increases the likelihood of developing theory that is effective for understanding schooling and teaching. Many basic educational questions dealing with personal meaning and social significance simply cannot be asked or answered through quantitative methods alone.

Willis (1978) has provided the first book devoted entirely to the use of qualitative methods in educational evaluation. Since the presentation of qualitative evaluation in this chapter is necessarily superficial, the Willis publication is highly recommended for in-depth study of this topic. Willis describes the processes of qualitative evaluation as description, disclosure of meaning, and judgment. In both quantitative and qualitative forms of evaluation, description begins with direct observation. In quantitative evaluation, the evaluator ordinarily approaches the setting with an observation guide and preconceived plan for selecting data to be reported. In qualitative evaluation, the critic has a greater range of observed characteristics from which to select for description. Often categories for recording observations are not specified in advance. Descriptions may even be extended to include perceived qualities of the situation that are personal forms of meaning not subject to public verification.

In quantitative evaluation, inferences about meaning are usually in terms of statistical significance; in qualitative evaluation the inferences about meaning focus on broader kinds of educational and personal significance. The evaluator's use of judgment is a key distinction in the two types of evaluation. Quantitative evaluation, on the whole, accepts little responsibility for identifying or making explicit the value basis of the critic. In qualitative evaluation it is absolutely essential that the value basis for judgments be made explicit.

The methodological techniques of qualitative evaluation reflect the dominant interest of the evaluators. These interests may be aesthetic, personal, or political. "The aesthetic interest is concerned primarily with how people develop meaning in response to the particulars of the external world as embodied in individual and collective forms" (Willis 1978, 14). Its principal concern is the integrity of form and meaning. This approach to educational evaluation has been described as the artistic model in the preceding section.

The personal interest in curriculum criticism is primarily concerned with how the individual develops meaning as a function of his or her own experience, in contrast to the emphasis on meanings about the external world. The perceptions, attitudes, and values of specific individuals, as they relate to different personal meanings, are emphasized. The political interest, by contrast, is primarily concerned with the uses for which meanings are intended and to which they are put. Those reconceptualists who have been identified as Marxists exemplify the political interest in qualitative evaluation.

Clearly the best programs of curriculum evaluation use both quantitative and qualitative evaluation. It is not a question of which type of evaluation should be used; it is desirable that both types be used, since they use different techniques for asking and answering different questions. Both types of evaluation are empirical in that they begin with observation of phenomena. Both forms depend directly on the personal meaning brought to the setting by individual evaluators. Consequently, there is no such thing as "objective" educational evaluation, but the differing approaches and types of data upon which to base judgments suggest a strong case for both quantitative and qualitative evaluation as complementary processes.

Almost all systematic curriculum evaluation in physical education to date has been quantitative in nature. It is suggested that quantitative methods are more appropriate for curricula in which the value perspective of disciplinary mastery predominates. If achievement of the types of goals envisioned when viewing the curriculum from other perspectives is to be assessed, quantitative evaluation must be supplemented by qualitative evaluation methods. Of those curriculum models described in chapter 3, humanistic and personal meaning models need to rely more heavily on qualitative evaluation methods than do the other models. The use of qualitative methods is more congruent with goal-free and artistic models of educational evaluation than with the adversary or desired-outcomes model. Both forms of evaluation should be used in a complementary fashion, regardless of the evaluation model selected.

Summary

How do you go about evaluating a physical education curriculum? It seems appropriate to return to this initial question. Although the question remains somewhat open-ended, certain generalizations are possible. Curriculum evaluation includes evaluation of student achievement, teacher effectiveness, and overall program success. Both formative and summative evaluation procedures can be used effectively in appraising changes in student knowledges, motor performance skills, health-related fitness, and affective behavior. Techniques for evaluating teacher effectiveness can best include both product measures and evaluation of the process.

Program evaluation can be conducted according to many different models. At the beginning of the chapter, we eavesdropped on three different curriculum evaluation planning sessions. You may wish to return to these descriptions now to see how they incorporated the approaches and techniques examined throughout the chapter. The Central High School physical education faculty was working with a desired-outcomes model to plan for evaluation of a program built with a kinesiological studies design. The Lake County staff extended evaluation of their movement education curriculum through a goal-free model, planning for examination of not only intended outcomes achieved, but of all relevant aspects of the educational experience. The Cedar City physical educators also used a goal-free model, but they were involved in the third phase in the development of a K–12 curriculum built via a personal meaning model. Figure 8.1 summarizes these illustrative local program evaluation plans.

All of these educators planning evaluation activities to improve local physical education programs are free to select from a vast array of assessment tools. All should consider both quantitative and qualitative approaches in asking key evaluation questions. Although local variations are infinite, the curriculum evaluation process usually involves six steps: (1) clarification of local value orientation, key program goals, and major emphases for the physical education curriculum; (2) selection of an evaluation model, organization of the evaluation team, and assignment of roles and tasks; (3) selection and/or creation of evaluative instruments, tools, and techniques; (4) assessment of student needs, status, and gains; (5) study of the instructional process in progress; and (6) making judgments, reports, and recommendations for program improvement.

	Central High School	Lake County Elementary Schools	Cedar City High School
Curriculum model	**Kinesiological studies model**	**Movement education model**	**Personal meaning model**
Program goals	Fitness Lifetime sports Attitude toward participation Knowledge about performance	Move skillfully Knowledge about movement Positive self-concept	Physiological efficiency Self-knowledge Joy of movement Object manipulation Space awareness Spatial relationships Communication Teamwork Competition Leadership Participation
Evaluation model	Desired outcomes	Goal-free	Goal-free
Evaluation techniques currently in use	Fitness test Skill tests Knowledge tests	Skill checklists	Fitness performance test Skill tests Knowledge tests
Additional student evaluation needed	Evaluation of sport performance Attitude evaluation	Self-concept Enjoyment Fitness test Teacher opinionnaire	Lifetime sports competencies Personal goal-setting and self-evaluation
Evaluation of instructional process	(none planned)	Parent interviews Staff development workshops	Observation and analysis of teacher behavior and teacher-student interaction
Recommendations focus	Accreditation self-study	Proposal for continuation funding	Curriculum guide revision

References

Donmoyer, R. 1981. The evaluator as artist. In *Curriculum and instruction: Alternatives in education*, ed. H. A. Giroux, A. W. Penna, and W. F. Pinar, 342–46. Berkeley, CA: McCutchan.

Levine, M. 1974. Scientific method and the adversary model. *American Psychologist* (September): 666–77.

McNeil, J. D. 1981. Evaluating the Curriculum. In *Curriculum and instruction: Alternatives in education*, ed. H. A. Giroux, A. W. Penna, and W. F. Pinar, 252–69. Berkeley, CA: McCutchan.

Popham, W. J., and D. Carson. 1981. Deep dark deficits of the adversary evaluation model. In *Curriculum and instruction: Alternatives in education*, ed. H. A. Giroux, A. W. Penna, and W. F. Pinar, 271–80. Berkeley, CA: McCutchan.

Figure 8.1
Plans for program evaluation

Scriven, M. 1972. Pros and cons about goal-free evaluation. *Journal of Educational Evaluation* (December): 73–76.

Willis, G., ed. 1978. *Qualitative evaluation: Concepts and cases in curriculum criticism.* Berkeley, CA: McCutchan.

Recommended Readings

Program evaluation:

Association for Supervision and Curriculum Development. 1983. *Fundamental curriculum decisions.* Alexandria, VA: The Association.

Bloom, B. S., J. T. Hastings, and G. F. Madaus. 1971. *Handbook on formative and summative evaluation of student learning.* New York: McGraw-Hill.

Giroux, H. A., A. W. Penna, and W. F. Pinar, eds. 1981. *Curriculum and instruction: Alternatives in education.* Berkeley, CA: McCutchan.

Kaufman, R. O., and F. W. English. 1979. *Needs assessment: Concept and application.* Englewood Cliffs, NJ: Educational Technology Publishers.

Safrit, M. J. 1981. *Evaluation in physical education.* Englewood Cliffs, NJ: Prentice-Hall.

Tyler, R. W. 1950. *Basic principles of curriculum and instruction.* Chicago: Univ. of Chicago Press.

Willis, G., ed. 1978. *Qualitative evaluation: Concepts and cases in curriculum criticism.* Berkeley: McCutchan.

Worthen, B. R., and J. R. Sanders, eds. 1973. *Educational evaluation: Theory and practice.* Belmont, CA: C. A. Jones.

Tools for evaluation in physical education:

Barrow, H. M., and R. McGee. 1979. *A practical approach to measurement in physical education.* Philadelphia: Lea and Febiger.

Baumgartner, T. A., and A. S. Jackson. 1982. *Measurement for evaluation in physical education.* Dubuque, IA: Wm. C. Brown.

Johnson, B. L., and J. K. Nelson. 1979. *Practical measurements for evaluation in physical education.* Minneapolis, MN: Burgess.

Mathews, D. K. 1978. *Measurement in physical education.* Philadelphia: W. B. Saunders.

Safrit, M. J. 1981. *Evaluation in physical education.* Englewood Cliffs, NJ: Prentice-Hall.

Evaluation of teaching:

Anderson, W., and G. T. Barrette, eds. 1978. *What's going on in gym: Descriptive studies of physical education.* Newtown: Motor Skills: Theory Into Practice.

Association for Supervision and Curriculum Development. 1983. *Effective schools and classrooms: A Research-based perspective.* Alexandria, VA: The Association.

Dunkin, M. J., and B. J. Biddle. 1974. *The study of teaching.* New York: Holt, Rinehart and Winston.

Gage, N. L. 1978. *The scientific basis of the art of teaching.* New York: Teachers College Press.

Joyce, B. R., and M. Weil. 1972. *Models of teaching.* Englewood Cliffs, NJ: Prentice-Hall.

Nixon, J. E., and L. F. Locke. 1973. Research on teaching physical education. In *Second handbook of research on teaching,* ed. Robert M. W. Travers, 1210–42. Chicago: Rand-McNally.

Part 3

Curriculum Issues and Concerns

Part 3

In Part 3 we hope to stimulate integration of what you have learned concerning the curriculum process in physical education. The theoretical concepts established in Part 1 are applied to the practical activities of curriculum design in Part 2. Not all of the problems are solved, however. Realistically, many controversial issues and debatable concerns remain. In Part 3 we try to help you to examine both practical and theoretical issues and concerns.

Chapter 9 focuses on those issues and concerns of a more practical nature. The chapter opens with an example of the type of practical situation with which you are likely to be faced. Because we believe that curriculum change involves politics (in gaining administrative support and the acceptance of those who will implement the program), the chapter describes some of the possible strategies. Practical problems of particular concern in the physical education setting relate to instructional conditions, individual differences, scheduling, relationships with athletics, and accountability. As you struggle with the process of curriculum development in your own local setting you may need to address many of these concerns.

In chapter 10 we turn to theoretical issues and concerns and conclude with a series of brief position statements dealing with philosophical and theoretical issues that affect curriculum development in physical education in important ways. The topics discussed have been selected to stimulate your interest in developing a carefully considered position on a variety of theoretical issues. At this point you should have the background and the understanding to take your own position on important curriculum issues and to defend it with a sound theoretical rationale and appropriate practical arguments. We hope you will enjoy debating important issues and concerns with your professional colleagues in physical education.

Practical Issues and Concerns

9

The physical education staff at East Bay High School is discussing a proposed revision of their physical education program. In the proposed program, entering tenth grade students would participate in a four-week orientation unit that includes assessments of their abilities and interests, followed by counseling on activities that might seem appropriate for them. Each student, with the assistance of the orientation instructor, would then select units of instruction for the remainder of the year.

The chair of the planning committee has just presented the general plan being proposed by the committee. The whole staff is now discussing the length of units of instruction to be included in the selective program. Ms. Brown, who has been at the school for a long time, wants to continue with the two- or three-week units that they have used in the past, arguing that variety and exposure to many activities is important. Mr. Tate is presenting the planning committee's view that units should be eight weeks in length in order to permit real mastery of the content. He argues, "It's better to learn a few things well than to be exposed to a lot of things." Mr. James, the head basketball coach, has been silent throughout the discussion. Suddenly, he interjects, "What am I going to do to keep them busy for eight weeks?" Another teacher responds, "You keep your basketball players busy for longer than that." James replies, "Yes, but that's my sport— and they want to be there!" After further discussion, the group chooses to delay the decision until its next meeting.

The planning committee, in reflecting about the discussion, identifies four concerns that may be contributing to some teachers' reluctance to accept eight-week units:

1. Concern about the need for additional preparation for longer units
2. Insecurity about teaching more advanced material
3. Concern that students may get bored with less variety
4. Concern that teachers may get bored with less variety

What strategies might the committee employ to address these concerns?

Curriculum design involves a process of developing and implementing a quality program. Frequently, individuals participating in the curriculum design process will hear comments that "This sounds good but it won't really work— it's just not practical." Such concerns must be addressed. Individuals' perceptions of the practicality of a proposal seem to be a major determinant of their willingness to implement it (Doyle and Ponder 1977).

Practical problems are fundamentally political issues, related to the availability of resources and support, and to the power and influence needed to gain such access. Curriculum development is a process of planned change. Curriculum developers need to understand the politics of curriculum change in order to enhance the probability of successful implementation of the curriculum design.

Politics of Curriculum Change

Curriculum change involves two fundamental political processes: (1) gaining administrative support to assure that necessary approvals and needed resources will be available, and (2) gaining the acceptance of those who will implement the program. Because success in each of these areas is essential, the curriculum planning committee must address, not only curriculum design questions, but issues related to the politics of curriculum change.

The foundation of that process is an understanding of the educational agency for which the program is being developed. The analysis described in chapter 4 is a good beginning. The committee needs to know the power structure of the school system and, particularly, the official approval process for the proposed curriculum. In addition, it is important to identify the constituencies or subgroups who will be concerned about the program, and to analyze the norms, values, and dynamics of each group.

Research on change in social institutions has indicated that most groups include individuals who can be classified as innovators and those who can be described as resistors— based upon their characteristic reactions to change (Morrish 1976). Innovators tend to be younger and better-educated than resistors, but the committee should be cautious about assuming this to be universally true. It is also important to identify the leaders of each group. Frequently leaders cannot be labeled as either innovators or resistors, but tend to suspend judgment until they have more information.

A pattern that often emerges when a new idea is introduced is that innovators immediately endorse it while resistors oppose it. After a period of time, the leader or leaders make a judgment based on additional information (perhaps on the trials by the innovators). If the leaders endorse the idea, their support may gradually persuade the resistors (who tend to respect the leaders but who are influenced very little by the innovators whom they see as people who will try anything new). From this scenario, it seems clear that the curriculum committee must attempt to gain support from the leaders of the various constituencies or subgroups. While the endorsement of the innovators may be welcomed, it is usually not sufficient to gain the widespread support necessary for full implementation.

Winning the support of both the power structure and the various constituencies involves developing a program that can be "sold," and devising effective strategies for "selling" it. Havelock (1973) suggests that educational innovations can be evaluated on each of three dimensions that influence the probability of successful implementation:

1. Practicality. Is it practical in our situation? Do we have the staff, time, facilities, equipment, and money to implement the idea?
2. Workability. Will it get results? If we do implement it, will it produce the benefits claimed?
3. Acceptability. Is it acceptable to the people involved? Does it conflict with the norms and value systems of students, teachers, administrators, or parents?

As the planning committee is developing the curriculum design, there needs to be a constant check on how well the proposal meets each of these three criteria. No proposal will be perfect on all three counts, but major problems should be addressed during the planning stage so as to facilitate the implementation process.

Devising a strategy to secure approval and acceptance of a curriculum proposal is an important part of the curriculum development process. There are two fundamentally different approaches to implementing a curriculum: power and persuasion. In the power approach, the committee secures the approval of top-level administrators, who use their power and authority to require that the program be implemented. In the persuasion model, the planning committee attempts to convince those responsible for implementation to adopt the curriculum design, but the ultimate decision to accept, reject, or modify rests with the implementors. Each of these approaches has certain advantages and disadvantages.

The power approach permits immediate systemwide change. In cases where persuasion is ineffective or too slow, such an approach may be viewed as a necessity. Legislation mandating equal educational opportunity, regardless of race, ethnicity, sex, or disability, exemplifies the use of the power approach to curriculum change. Teachers' implementation of a mandated change depends partly upon their acceptance of the legitimate authority of administrators to prescribe such change, and partly upon the system of sanctions that exists to ensure compliance. The use of power can produce compliance, but unwilling acquiescence has certain costs. Effective enforcement may require an extensive monitoring system, along with administrative ability and willingness to reward and punish. The atmosphere of threat may create anxiety and lower productivity. Compliance may be superficial, masking a subversive resistance that dooms the mandated program to failure. Generally, when a power approach is employed, it is followed by an effort to counter these concerns and problems by persuading constituents of the validity of the mandate.

Because of the problems inherent in the power approach, many curriculum planners prefer to use the persuasion model. This model relies upon a dissemination strategy, in which teachers and key support groups are provided with information to convince them of the proposal's merit. Implementation is often incremental and gradual, rather than total and systemwide. The dissemination strategy includes decisions about which individuals to target first, and what information and experiences to provide these individuals. Early efforts are generally directed toward selected innovators and key leaders who are well-respected throughout the system. Approaches to selling them on the proposal vary, but all need to take into account the stages through which individuals typically progress in the process of adopting an

Phase:	Assistance:
Awareness Initial exposure to the idea Passive interest	Information which is brief, interesting, easy to understand, and positive Try to instill curiosity
Interest Active information-seeking Open attitude, undecided	Additional, more specific information as requested Group discussion to gain information and air doubts
Evaluation "Mental trial" of the innovation	Information showing applicability in the individual's situation Demonstration in the home environment
Trial Use on a small scale or "pilot" basis	Training on how to implement; Support and encouragement Assistance in interpreting successes, failures
Adoption Decision to adopt	Continued training as needed Assistance, support services to deal with problems encountered
Integration Innovation used until it becomes routine	Reminders, follow-up questionnaires, recognition

innovation (Havelock 1973). As individuals progress through these phases, they need different kinds of information and assistance. Six phases and some of the types of strategies that might be applicable at each stage are described in figure 9.1. Individuals must be allowed to progress through all of the phases at their own paces. Most people need time to think things over before they make a change that affects their lives in a significant way. Rejection of the new program can occur at any stage. The curriculum committee needs to develop an implementation plan that is carefully designed, but also flexible enough to respond to unforeseen circumstances.

Two aspects of the persuasion process deserve special comment. Much of the dissemination literature assumes that the innovation or program has been fully developed before it is "marketed" to teachers. An alternative is to involve the teachers during the development process by allowing them to provide input, react to proposals, or field-test ideas. Such broad-based involvement is likely to produce greater receptiveness to the curriculum developed. A second concern in the persuasion process is the tendency to rely solely on rational arguments, disregarding the fact that the people make decisions on both rational and emotional bases. The dissemination process needs to reflect sensitivity to people's values, concerns, and insecurities.

Figure 9.1
Phases of the process for adoption of an innovation From R. Havelock, *The Change Agent's Guide to Innovation in Education.* © 1973 Educational Technology, Englewood Cliffs, NJ. Reprinted by permission.

Planning for the process of implementation is just as important as planning an elegant curriculum design. Such a plan requires an understanding of the politics of curriculum change, as well as strategies for dealing with specific practical concerns. The worksheet described in figure 9.2 may assist you in developing such a plan.

Practical Concerns

Designers of physical education programs must deal with several recurring practical concerns. Strategies must be developed to alleviate problems, or to minimize their impact on the quality of the program. Unfortunately, simple solutions do not exist for some of the problems, but careful consideration may permit identification of workable options.

Instructional Conditions

A quality physical education program requires reasonable class sizes and adequate facilities and equipment. Classes of seventy students, two or three classes in a single gymnasium, or three playground balls to teach a whole class ball skills, are examples of the type of inadequate instructional conditions that exist in some schools. Two responses to such problems are possible. One possibility is to mount a campaign to secure the added resources to solve the problem: more teachers, more teaching stations, or more equipment. The other option is to devise strategies that improve the quality of the program without a major infusion of additional resources.

Developing a strategy to secure additional resources requires convincing administrators that the change will be cost-effective; that the benefits produced will be worth the money expended. The proposed benefits could include such things as reduced absenteeism, fewer discipline problems, fewer injuries, and improved learning. Projecting specific benefits is generally more persuasive than vague generalities about improved learning conditions. Comparison data from other schools with more favorable conditions, or standards from professional organizations, may be used to support your case.

While getting more resources is clearly the most desirable solution, it is not always feasible in school districts with financial difficulties. Improving the program with existing resources may be the only alternative. In large classes, the use of aides or student leaders may make instruction possible.

Figure 9.2
Worksheet for planning
curriculum change

General description of proposed change:

Evaluation on dimensions affecting probability of success:

Practicality

Workability

Acceptability

What constituencies will be affected by the change?

Who are key figures whose support is needed?

Official approval required   Highly influential

(Note: Some names may appear on both lists.)

Anticipated concerns of key figures:

Concern   Strategy for dealing with
                               concern

Activities that allow mass participation may be selected, rather than activities that produce a lot of waiting for turns. Students may be scheduled for fewer class sessions per week in order to make more reasonable class sizes. If additional teaching stations are needed, unused space such as hallways or classrooms may be used for instruction in activities that can be accommodated there. Inadequate amounts of equipment for a whole class may require station teaching, in which different groups are doing different activities. Program modifications can be made to emphasize activities that require little equipment.

Deciding whether to aim for new resources or to focus upon improvement with present resources is a difficult choice. The success of a campaign for more resources often depends upon the public's perception of the quality and value of the program. It may be necessary to improve the quality under existing circumstances before going to the public for more money. At the same time, such measures to "make do" with inadequate resources should not be mistaken for satisfaction with the status quo.

Individual Differences

Differences in ability and interest among individuals in a class have always existed, but one of the effects of coeducation and mainstreaming in physical education classes has been to expand this range of differences dramatically. Successful implementation of coeducation and mainstreaming is partially dependent upon overcoming the stereotypes and biases of teachers and students. However, success may also depend upon providing the teacher with solutions to the practical problem of individual differences in ability and interests.

There are several ways of dealing with, or minimizing, individual differences in a class. Students may be grouped by ability as long as an objective measure specific to the activity is used to determine ability. Allowing students to choose activities of interest to them may also result in groups with fewer differences among individuals. Although such grouping procedures provide one solution to the problem, some would argue that this practice is not consistent with the intent of coeducation and mainstreaming.

Another approach to minimizing the effect of individual differences is to redesign the program to emphasize activities in which previous experience or size-strength differences do not advantage or disadvantage individual students. Emphasis upon noncompetitive activities, or activities that are unfamiliar to all students, may be a way to equalize students and simplify the instructor's task. The growing popularity of activities such as yoga and korfball might be attributed to this phenomenon. The emphasis upon learning of concepts might also be viewed as a means for designing a program applicable to students of widely-varying skill levels.

The final approach to dealing with individual differences is to use teaching styles or methods that accommodate those differences. Teachers who rely predominantly upon traditional command or practice styles (see chapter 7) may need to learn other methods. Adjusting expectations for individual performance (inclusion style), using "buddies" to help others learn (reciprocal style), or setting up problems that individuals can solve in their own way (divergent style) seem particularly useful. In some cases, instruction may need to be individualized so that different students can work on different tasks within the same class. The school system can assist teachers with this process by providing necessary staff development activities and the time and resources needed to do the instructional planning.

Scheduling

Developing a schedule for a physical education program involves decisions about time allocation and distribution, as well as procedures for assigning students to specific classes. Time is a valuable resource in a school. Recent research has indicated that one of the best predictors of student achievement in an area is the amount of time allocated to that subject area (Borg 1979). Generally, professional organizations have recommended two-hundred-fifty minutes of physical education per week, distributed over three or more days, for middle school and secondary school students (Society of State Directors of HPER 1972; AAHPER 1977) and one-hundred-fifty minutes per week for elementary school students (AAHPERD 1981).

Many states or provinces mandate a number of minutes per week, but it is not uncommon for schools to fail to comply. In elementary schools, the absence of an adequate program is often the result of the lack of a sufficient number of physical education specialists, and the inability or unwillingness of classroom teachers to assist with the conduct of the program. A supervised recess may be substituted for an organized physical education class. In secondary schools, the time allocation for physical education may be diminished by the substitution of health education, driver education, or extracurricular activities such as band or athletics.

Strategies for securing a full time allotment for physical education require distinguishing the purposes of the program from those of recess, health education, driver education, or extracurricular activities. What are the goals and objectives of the physical education program? Can those goals and objectives be met by recess, band, athletics, etc.? The second aspect of eliminating substitutions for physical education is securing the resources needed to provide a program for those not presently served. If all students had a daily physical education program, how many teachers and teaching stations would be required? Are these resources presently available? Securing an adequate time commitment for the program is an essential precondition for a quality program.

Decisions regarding the distribution of time include both the length of the class session and the number of sessions per week. The desirable number and length of sessions depends upon both the characteristics of the students and the goals to be attained. A minimum of three sessions per week seems necessary if the program attempts to improve fitness levels. Acquisition of motor skills also requires adequate practice time distributed over several days each week.

The most common procedure for assigning students to physical education classes is by grade level. However, as middle and secondary schools are developing selective programs, new procedures are being used. In one approach, students are assigned to physical education during a certain class period, much as they were previously. The physical education staff then develops a range of options for that class period (the number dependent upon the number of teachers and teaching stations available) and registers students for the option of their choice. (See Alternative A in figure 9.3.) Such registration may occur at the beginning of each new unit or once each semester. A second approach also described in figure 9.3 involves identifying a range of options for each class period, which may differ from period to period. The schedule is published and students select the hour they will take physical education, based upon the activity choices available that hour. Such a system greatly expands the number of choices available to each student, but requires cooperation and support from administrators and counselors responsible for scheduling. With the expanded use of computers, such scheduling procedures should become more feasible.

	Alternative A	Alternative B
Period 1	Aerobics Tennis Folk dance Soccer Swimming	Jogging Beginning tennis Modern dance Soccer Beginning swimming
Period 2	Aerobics Tennis Folk dance Soccer Swimming	Aerobic dance Beginning tennis Tumbling Flag football Intermediate swimming
Period 3	Aerobics Tennis Folk dance Soccer Swimming	Weight training Intermediate tennis Folk dance Volleyball Lifesaving
Period 4	Aerobics Tennis Folk dance Soccer Swimming	Jogging Intermediate tennis Gymnastics Basketball Scuba diving
	Students are assigned to a class period.	Students select class period and activity.
	Physical education faculty registers students for option of their choice.	Computerized scheduling is handled by central administrative offices.

Relationship with Athletics

Historically, physical education and athletics have been integrally related at both a theoretical and practical level. Competitive sports programs were viewed as an extension of the physical education instructional program, designed to provide athletically talented students with an opportunity to develop their full potential. At the practical level, the programs shared facilities and were generally conducted by individuals who served as both teachers and coaches.

Many problems have developed with the conduct of athletic programs in the United States, and with the relationship between athletics and physical education. Athletic programs often appear to have abandoned their educational goals for an emphasis upon winning and entertainment. Physical education programs are frequently viewed as "feeder" programs, designed to identify and develop potential talent for athletic teams. As athletic programs

Figure 9.3
Approaches to selective program scheduling

expand, the availability of facilities for physical education classes and for intramurals may decrease. In some cases, students are allowed to substitute athletics for physical education throughout middle and secondary school. Because of the visibility of athletic programs, administrators emphasize the need for success in these programs. Administrative concern for and support of physical education programs often appears to be nonexistent.

Another major problem is role overload and role conflict, which physical educators experience as they attempt to be both teacher and coach (Locke and Massengale 1978). Adequate performance in each of these roles requires considerable time and energy and somewhat different professional skills. A common response to such role conflict is to select one of the roles as the primary role and devote most of one's time and attention to it. Because of the high value placed on athletics in our society, coaching most often becomes the primary role, and teaching is often neglected. Public recognition, pressure from parents, and emphasis by administrators, all tend to reinforce this decision.

The development and implementation of a quality physical education program requires attention to these problems. What are the educational goals of the athletic program? Are these consistent with the goals of the curriculum model adopted for the physical education program? What should be the relationship between the two programs?

Several possibilities for the relationship between physical education and athletics seem to exist. One alternative, seen in many colleges and universities, is a total disassociation of the two programs. The programs are philosophically and administratively separate, and employ different individuals in teaching and coaching positions. A second possibility is the historical view of the athletic program as an enrichment experience for athletically talented students. Athletes accomplish the basic goals and objectives of physical education in the regular instructional program and also participate in athletics. The responsibility for physical education and athletics rests with the physical education staff and the focus of the athletic program remains educational. The third possibility is that athletics be viewed as a component of the physical education program, designed for high ability students. Athletics substitute for physical education because the goals and objectives of the programs are identical. Clearly this third option is not feasible with most curriculum models unless the purpose and conduct of athletic programs is drastically revised. However, athletics that follow the club sports format might be considered to exemplify the higher levels of the play education model. Identifying the appropriate relationship between physical education and athletics is an issue that must be addressed.

An equally difficult problem may be to develop strategies for helping teachers/coaches to deal with role conflict in ways that do not diminish the quality of the physical education program. Such strategies can concentrate on three areas: (1) increasing the teacher's/coach's ability to fulfill the teaching role, (2) minimizing the time demands of handling both jobs simultaneously, and (3) increasing the rewards and recognition associated with quality teaching.

While teaching and coaching require similar abilities, many aspects of the two jobs differ. Teachers need to know a wider range of subject matter; they must communicate with and motivate students with various abilities and interests; and they should be able to organize large groups of students for effective instruction and practice. Teachers/coaches lacking any of these abilities may need assistance if they are to become effective teachers.

A second critical aspect of dealing with role conflict is helping teachers/coaches deal with the excessive time demands of their jobs. Staff development on time management techniques, less demanding teaching assignments during heavy coaching seasons, and support services and assistance for teachers/coaches may be ways to approach the problem.

Perhaps even more important is the establishment of a system of rewards and recognition for quality teaching. The rewards associated with athletics are very potent and visible. A support system of students, parents, colleagues, and, if possible, administrators who care about the quality of the physical education program needs to be established. The mechanisms used to develop such support have varied. Examples include special events such as demonstrations, inter-class competition, total school field days, rope jump-a-thons, award days or ongoing public relations projects to make the parents and community aware and supportive of the program.

Accountability and Public Support

Throughout the United States, schools and other educational agencies have experienced increasing financial difficulties. Simultaneously, there has been a loss of confidence in the schools based upon concerns about declining test scores and lack of basic computational and literacy skills.

These forces have created pressure for accountability in educational programs. Financial support is viewed as contingent upon evidence that a particular program produces results.

Traditionally physical education programs have been held less accountable than many other subject areas in the school. With the exception of fitness tests, no standardized achievement tests are administered regularly. Administrators often view the physical education program as recreational rather than instructional. Grading procedures in physical education classes are usually based upon participation, rather than performance, and neither students nor their parents receive reports of student progress related to educational goals.

In general, it could be argued that the absence of accountability reflects the marginal status of physical education (Hendry 1975). Subject areas that are perceived as central to the mission of the school are evaluated and examined regularly. While the absence of accountability, and the resultant professional autonomy, might be viewed as benign in times of economic plenty, it becomes a political risk when schools are faced with the prospect of budget cuts.

Gaining public support for physical education seems to require convincing the community that physical education has values that are an essential component of education and that the physical education program in their specific school system produces the desired results. Such efforts need to be ongoing and cannot be successful unless a quality program exists. It is a tactical error to wait until the program is attacked to begin efforts to gain support. It is an even more fundamental error to wait until the program is attacked to begin building a program that deserves to be saved.

Summary

The development of a quality physical education program involves, not only the theoretical process of creating a curriculum design, but the practical process of implementing the design. Practical issues and concerns relate to gaining support and securing the resources necessary to make the program a success. Because of the political nature of these concerns, curriculum developers need to acquire an

Curriculum Issues and Concerns

Process issues:

Should we use the power or persuasion approach to changing
our program?
How and when should the physical education teachers be
involved in the planning process?

Resources issues

Should we seek additional resources (teachers, facilities,
equipment) or try to build a quality program with what we
have?
Should physical education teachers also coach?
Should staff development activities for teachers be required or
optional?

Program procedure issues

Should students be assigned to classes or select classes?
Should we use ability grouping?
Should athletics (or band, driver education, health education)
substitute for physical education?
Should students receive grades based on performance rather
than participation?

understanding of the political process of change in a social
institution. Physical educators also need to address specific
practical problems of particular concern in the physical
education setting.

Several practical issues confronting physical educators are
identified in this chapter. An issue is, by definition, a question
to be disputed, a topic on which consensus is lacking. As you
struggle with the process of curriculum development in your
own local setting, many of these issues may arise. Figure 9.4
provides examples of some of the questions you may need to
address.

Figure 9.4
Examples of practical
issues in physical
education curriculum
development

References

American Alliance for Health, Physical Education and Recreation.
1977. *Assessment guide for secondary school physical
education programs.* Washington, DC: AAHPER.
American Alliance for Health, Physical Education, Recreation and
Dance. 1981. *Essentials of a quality elementary school
physical education program.* Reston, VA: AAHPERD.
Borg, W. R. 1979. Time and school learning. *Newsletter: Beginning
Teacher Evaluation Study* (March):2–7.

Doyle, W., and G. Ponder. 1977. The ethic of practicality: Implications for curriculum development. In *Curriculum theory.* Washington, DC: Association for Supervision and Curriculum Development.

Havelock. R. 1973. *The change agent's guide to innovation in education.* Englewood Cliffs, NJ: Educational Technology Publications.

Hendry, L. B. 1975. Survival in a marginal role: The professional identity of the physical education teacher. *British Journal of Sociology* 26:456–76.

Locke, L. R., and J. D. Massengale. 1978. Role conflict in teachers/coaches. *Research Quarterly* 49:162–74.

Morrish, I. 1976. *Aspects of educational change.* London: George Allen and Urwin.

Society of State Directors of Health, Physical Education and Recreation. 1972. *School programs in health, physical education and recreation: A statement of basic beliefs.* Kensington, MD: The Society.

Recommended Reading

Havelock, R. 1973. *The change agent's guide to innovation in education.* Englewood Cliffs, NJ: Educational Technology Publications.

Theoretical Issues and Concerns

10

This text concludes with a series of brief position statements dealing with philosophical and theoretical issues that affect curriculum development in physical education in important ways. Each issue is phrased as a question. We attempt to present eleven issues in a similar format, identifying the nature of the concern or the significance of the issue, analyzing and comparing the major differing viewpoints expressed in the professional literature, and summarizing a personal perspective or position with regard to the issue or concern discussed.

Five of these position statements have been contributed by other physical educators, in response to our invitations. Their papers are appropriately identified in the text.

Up to this point, this text has been designed to acknowledge all predominant value orientations, to describe each of the well-developed physical education curriculum models, to present a broad spectrum of instructional models, and to recognize different approaches to evaluation—without reflecting unduly the personal biases of the authors. However, the issues selected for discussion in this chapter are important because they do indeed involve different value positions, conflicting opinions and philosophies, and continuing controversy. The position supported in each case is only one of two or more which might be equally well-supported by its proponents. As a knowledgeable student of curriculum you are encouraged to read each position statement, weigh the arguments presented, and attempt to formulate your own position on the issue. As a professional educator who will have a responsibility for developing physical education curricula for others, you may wish to write your own position statement on one or more of these theoretical issues and concerns.

Who Should Control the Curriculum?

The question of who should control the curriculum is one of the most heatedly and frequently debated issues among those who profess a major concern for public education. The overall concern encompasses several subissues: (1) decision-making by professional educators versus decision-making by the lay public; (2) local versus state and federal control; and (3) the role of the student and the individual teacher in selection of curriculum content versus the role of administrators and curriculum specialists. Each of these three subissues is addressed briefly in examining the larger issue.

Many important decisions in the realm of public education are made by professional educators—school superintendents, building principals, supervisors, curriculum directors, staff assistants to these administrators, department heads, and teachers. Vesting curriculum decision-making with professional educators is based on the rationale that these persons have completed four or more years of professional preparation in education, are certified as specialists in their particular subject matter fields, and have acquired considerable additional expertise through their collective years of experience in carrying out the work of the schools. It is argued that they are the acknowledged educational experts and thus competent to make the soundest curriculum decisions. They are knowledgeable about the aims and goals and the history of public education. They have greater understanding of the functioning of the schools and what is possible and reasonable to do within the school environment than any other group of citizens. They know their subject fields, and are familiar with the key concepts and knowledge that constitute important content. Certified teachers have studied child or adolescent development (or both), psychology of learning, and instructional methods appropriate to their special fields. They are expected to be familiar with contemporary textbooks, specialized professional journals, current instructional materials, and recently developed instructional technology. Since school administrators, teachers, and other professional educators are the best qualified to make educationally sound curriculum decisions, and will be entrusted as well with the major responsibilities for implementing these decisions, these professional educators should be expected to play the primary role in curriculum decision-making.

The extent to which professional educators should serve as agents for social change is a complex issue directly related to one's value orientation. A traditional view of the school's mission places the emphasis on transmitting knowledge to the younger generation and preparing them to function successfully in the existing society. From this perspective, the teacher or curriculum planner who seeks social change is in direct conflict with the doctrine that politics has no place in the public school. The educator who views the school as an agency for social change clearly expects to play a larger role in control of the local curriculum. Some who are committed to particular significant social changes believe that it is an educator's responsibility to take leadership in effecting these changes.

On the other hand, it must be acknowledged that public education is a key factor in the American dream and that citizens of the United States have made a tremendous investment in the schools of America. Therefore, it is argued, the schools belong to all citizens and the lay public has both the right and the responsibility to control the curriculum. How else can the public be assured that the schools will educate future citizens in ways that will lead to achievement of the nation's goals? How else can we expect that the next generation will be prepared to preserve our most cherished traditions, or to build the kind of society we want to become? Viewpoints such as these lead many citizens to insist that the board of education should determine such things as what level of mathematics competency should be required of all students graduating from high school, which approach to the teaching of reading should be used in the elementary schools, at what grade level foreign language study should be introduced, and how much physical education should be required. In some communities, lay citizen committees have claimed authority to select the health textbook series, to approve school library acquisitions, to establish budgets for school music or interscholastic athletic programs, to investigate the use of standardized achievement tests, or to choose school administrators. All such activities are based on the rationale that the public should control curriculum decisions that are important in determining whether the schools offer the kinds of programs which they want for the children who will become tomorrow's citizens.

The history of education in the United States reflects the establishment of many state systems, rather than a single national ministry or federal system (which is the pattern in much of the rest of the civilized world). In this country, school attendance regulations, mandated curriculum content, and certification requirements for teachers are all controlled at the state, rather than the federal level. At the same time, the local school district maintains the legal responsibility for providing and supporting schools for its population. Over the years, however, it has become increasingly evident that local districts must be assisted by both state and federal funds, since it is impossible even to approximate equal opportunity for children in vastly different communities due to extremely unequal resources. This dilemma has led to greater dependence upon state and federal funding, but with continued determination to maintain local control of public education.

Generally, local governments and boards of education have asserted their control of the schools primarily in the area of curricular decision-making. Only when legislation or national policy mandates curriculum practice are these decisions beyond local control. Some examples of this are coeducational physical education, as directed by Title IX, and mainstreaming of the handicapped, as mandated by PL 94–142. When such curriculum requirements become a part of official public policy, local school authorities have no alternative but to conform or to give up supplementary state and federal funds essential to the operation of local schools. Philosophically, one can make a convincing argument that local citizens are best informed about the needs of their community, and are the most competent group to make sound curriculum decisions. However, when the state or federal government determines that the greater good of the greater number requires a particular curriculum requirement, local curriculum decision-makers are overruled.

Another subissue in the broad area of control of the curriculum is the question of who should select curriculum content. Should the curriculum specialists who are responsible for preparation of local curriculum guides, and the administrators who approve local manuals and publications determine the specific content of the curriculum? Should the individual teacher who must develop instructional units for each of his or her own courses and prepare the daily lesson plans select the actual subject matter content at this level? It is difficult to achieve any philosophical consensus on this matter, but it is probably realistic to attempt a degree of local consistency through cooperative development and district-wide distribution of local curriculum guides. District-wide acceptance of a local curriculum guide is essential to effective articulation of the curriculum between elementary and middle school units, or between middle schools and high schools. Central administrative and staff leadership is probably essential for achieving district-wide acceptance of a curriculum guide. At the same time, involvement of teacher representatives is a necessary condition of effective implementation. In the final analysis, the operative curriculum will be the one that is effected through the individual teacher's plans and instructional behaviors, regardless of the recommended activities in the curriculum guide.

What is the desirable role of the individual student in the selection of curriculum content? It stands to reason that professional educators are more competent to select curriculum content than children or immature youth. On the other hand, does the individual's self-knowledge and need to develop the skills of self-direction sometimes outweigh professional experience and judgment? Is a high school student better able to identify personal academic needs than his or her teacher or the curriculum director? Should the curriculum planners develop several options for achieving curriculum goals and permit the student to select from among the options in accordance with personal interests? Can individual choices be provided within the required physical education course? Should the elementary school child be offered any role in selection of curriculum content? These are all questions to be resolved at the local district level.

The logical conclusion concerning control of the curriculum is that it is necessarily a process of group sharing. Because public education is indeed central to American democracy, equal access for all to a quality education is viewed as a fundamental right of every American. Thus curriculum development must be a cooperative enterprise. All citizens have the right to participate in determining the goals of

American education. That right is accompanied by the responsibility for systematic evaluation to assess the effectiveness of the schools in serving the nation's best interest.

At the same time, the citizenry must be willing to rely upon the professional integrity and competence of those who are educated specifically to be teachers and educational administrators. Professional educators carry the major responsibility for selection of appropriate subject matter content, for making decisions concerning sequence and structure of the curriculum, for choosing the best instructional materials and technological aids, and for determining the most effective teaching strategies.

Parents and school and public officials can be expected to give input concerning local needs, aims, and assessments of school programs. The students themselves should be encouraged to contribute to the effectiveness of the curriculum through identification of personal needs, interests, and goals; through individual selection from among available program alternatives; through development of skills of self-direction; and through responsible feedback regarding their school experiences to assist in improving local curricula for those students who succeed them. Thus the control of the curriculum does not rest entirely with professional educators, although their role should be one of strong and effective leadership.

What Are the Boundaries of "Curriculum?"

Candace J. Norton, State Department of Education Atlanta, Georgia

Curriculum is most often used to describe an array of courses offered by a school. It has also been defined as all of the experiences of a learner in an educational setting. Goodlad (1979) has described curriculum as a generic term having formal, operational, and experiential subclasses.

All of these subtypes are various ways of describing particular dimensions of the total concept of curriculum, which also embraces sociopolitical, technical, and professional processes of creating and delivering various curricula. There is no single definition of the word curriculum; therefore, no general boundaries exist. What are the implied boundaries of the formal, operational, and experiential curricula?

The formal curriculum is a prescribed course of study, usually officially sanctioned in the form of a curriculum guide, or an adopted set of curriculum materials or texts. In physical education, the formal curriculum can be linked with the

Curriculum Issues and Concerns

concept of education about movement, in which movement is a subject to be studied. In principle, the study of movement in the formal curriculum encompasses work and play, art and science, medicine and health, and sport and recreation, as well as education. Movement can be studied as a theoretical body of knowledge in its own right—as an "object" of study. Education about movement is concerned with rational movement knowledge that can be presented in a discursive, communicable manner. The dimensions in the formal curriculum are explicit and well-defined.

The operational curriculum is what actually occurs in learning situations. The operational curriculum refers to observable teacher and participant behaviors. It may or may not resemble the formal curriculum. Rational movement knowledge is not only presented for its own sake, but as a vehicle through which educational purposes can be fulfilled. At times the purposes of the operational curriculum are implicit (or hidden) as well as explicit, making the boundaries difficult to map. Efforts to create reliable observational methodology have been substantial, but dissatisfaction with research directed toward the operational curriculum continues.

The experiential curriculum is what is experienced by the participant in the educational setting. In physical education, the movement itself is experienced as educative in its own right. Through engaging in the activity, the mover comes to understand the meanings inherent in the activities themselves as well as the mover's own personal meanings. Student perceptions of the subject matter, the teacher, and the various interactions are all part of this curricular domain. The dimensions of experiential curriculum are within the learner, implicit and hard to specify.

The formal, operational, and experiential aspects of total curriculum are subclasses, which are not mutually exclusive, but overlapping and interdependent. These dimensions of curriculum are conceptually discrete, but functionally related, like a triangle having different points of emphasis that come into prominence at different times. Physical education must be seen "not only as a field of study and as having instrumental value, but as worthwhile activity to be engaged in for its own sake" (Arnold 1979, 178). For the curriculum implications of the concept of movement to be grasped adequately, the boundaries must be broadly construed, specifically recognizing the formal, operational, and experiential aspects of the world of learning.

What Responsibilities Have Physical Educators for Shaping the "Hidden Curriculum?"

The curriculum of an educational institution reflects the expressed values and deliberate decisions of educators regarding what is to be taught and what is to be learned in that institution. These values and decisions are reflected in the program design developed in the curriculum planning process. However, the operational curriculum, or the program as implemented, includes both this planned curriculum and a second "hidden curriculum" comprised of unplanned and unrecognized values taught and learned through the process of schooling. These implicit values, communicated to students through the context of the learning environment, may or may not be consistent with the explicit philosophy of the program.

How are the silent messages of the hidden curriculum communicated to students? Teachers model their value commitments by their behavior (e.g. choosing or avoiding participation in movement). Of particular importance are teachers' interactions with students (e.g. differentially praising or criticizing the high- and low-skilled, the attractive and unattractive, boys and girls). The way in which the class is organized also sends messages to students (e.g. working alone, assisting a less-skilled partner, choosing to work with friends, assigning teams by ability). The kinds of learning activities (e.g. cooperative versus competitive practice situations) and evaluation procedures (e.g. grading on attitude, attendance, or performance) also communicate values to students. Many educators have argued that the persistent messages included in the hidden curriculum of the school have a more powerful impact on students than the planned curriculum.

Considerable debate has occurred regarding whether the hidden curriculum is functional or dysfunctional, harmless or harmful. Some writers have proposed that the hidden curriculum teaches social norms and values necessary for the transition from childhood to the adult world. It is argued that students need to learn to exist in an impersonal work setting, compete for rewards, and strive for long-range goals, and that the hidden curriculum is the mechanism by which they learn these values. Others have criticized the process of schooling as stressing control, distrust, and conformity, and serving as a vehicle for unjustified differential treatment of students on the basis of race, social class, or sex.

Clearly the hidden curriculum has the potential for either positive or negative effects. The critical issue seems to be whether the values communicated by the hidden curriculum are consistent with values endorsed in the planned curriculum. Discrepancies between implicit and explicit values seem to exist for one of two possible reasons.

In the first case, educators may be unaware of the difference between stated values and the values implied by their behavior. Increasing the level of awareness of one's behavior will require coping with any dissonance caused by conflicts between explicit and implicit values. A second explanation for the discrepancy between the stated program philosophy and the hidden curriculum assumes that educators are aware of this discrepancy, but view it as necessary. The objectives and philosophy of the physical education program may be viewed as primarily a political effort to win support from administrators and taxpayers, while the conduct of the daily program reflects the real values of the teachers involved.

The authors believe that effective curriculum planning and educational accountability require that teachers attempt to shape a hidden curriculum that is consistent with the values endorsed in the planned curriculum. Such an effort first requires consciousness-raising, in which the teacher attempts to evaluate the implications of previously unexamined behavior. Procedures and routines once taken for granted are examined for their impact on students. Contradictions between the planned curriculum and the hidden curriculum are identified. The second stage in this process is the attempt to resolve conflicts. Such resolution may involve changing either the planned curriculum or the hidden curriculum. The individual teacher whose personal values differ from those in the official curriculum may work to modify the program. In other cases, the teacher who discovers that teaching practices are undermining efforts to accomplish important educational goals will face the challenge of changing habits and routines. Ultimately the power of the operational curriculum depends on the consistency of the planned and hidden curricula.

What Is the Primary Function of Curriculum Theorizing?

One of the major obstacles to the appreciation of curriculum as a field of scholarly activity is the confusion concerning the role of curriculum theory and theorizing. If we accept the distinction between the two terms that was presented in chapter 1, theories in general attempt to define, describe, and explain sets of related phenomena; in addition, theories may be used to make predictions about the nature and interaction of related phenomena. It is suggested that, "If we had curriculum theories they could guide the work of teachers, researchers, curriculum developers, policy makers, administrators, and other educators." (McCutcheon 1982, 20). Theorizing, the activity preliminary to the production of a theory, is appropriate for practitioners at all levels. Theorizing can be directed toward organizing and guiding the work of the curriculum theorist, toward focusing and designing the work of the curriculum researcher, or toward establishing goals and guidelines for the curriculum planner. What should be the primary function of physical education curriculum theorizing?

Certainly there are several acceptable answers to this question. Probably the most popular position is the view that the purpose is to describe the ideal physical education program. The theorizing focuses on the detailing of a proposed program. The proposal deals with content, aims, and educational approaches, and provides specific justification for why the proposed program would be good and should be adopted as the physical education curriculum. In short, the primary function of theorizing is to rationalize curriculum programs by describing what constitutes an ideal physical education program. The LaPorte study (LaPorte and Cooper 1973) might be identified as the classic example of this view of the function of physical education curriculum theorizing. Many current physical education publications that deemphasize theory and deal with curriculum in "practical" terms, tend to reflect this type of theorizing.

A second function of curriculum theorizing that is acknowledged by physical educators is that the primary purpose is to describe a sound procedure for making a curriculum. This type of theorizing "*rationalizes procedures* for curriculum construction or curriculum determination, rather than rationalizing the program itself" (Walker 1982, 63). The well-known Tyler rationale (Tyler 1950) encourages the curriculum planner to raise four key questions and to build the curriculum by generating systematic answers to these questions. The step-by-step procedure to be implemented by the Tyler rationale results in the statement of objectives, the selection of learning experiences, the structuring or organizing of these experiences, and evaluating them. Many curriculum writers, both historical and contemporary, espouse some systematic procedure for developing a curriculum. Their recommendations are based upon a type of curriculum theorizing that emphasizes the importance of the *procedure* used for curriculum development, in contrast to justifying a particular concept of the ideal program. Typical current examples can be noted in proposed procedures for individualizing the curriculum or for application of technology to curriculum construction.

A third view of the function of curriculum theorizing stresses understanding the curriculum in operation. How does it work? How can we explain what actually happens in practice? Theorizing in this mode seeks explanations that can provide the directive force for the efforts of practitioners. It raises questions about the interactions of persons in their educational environments, about the relationship of the curriculum plan to actual class occurrences, and about the contextual variations that modify the experiences of individual class participants. The function of theorizing is to understand the *real* curriculum—to explain what actually occurs in the educational setting, rather than to describe the ideal program or to describe the best procedure for making a good curriculum.

A fourth perspective identifies the primary function of curriculum theorizing as predicting the results of potential alternatives. The theorizer analyzes a variety of approaches for curriculum practice and attempts to predict the probable results and anticipate the comparative success of each alternative. Theorizing is primarily concerned with studying social and economic trends, biological and medical developments, and technological and environmental projections, and then predicting their educational implications. Theorizing is a process of identifying relevant trends, examining logically alternative curriculum approaches, and evaluating the future impact of particular educational decisions.

A fifth function, considered by some to be the primary function of curriculum theorizing, is to generate new curricular options designed to lead cultural changes. This is the goal of many of the reconceptualists. From this perspective, theorizing becomes a highly creative process, emphasizing conceptualizing and seeking new ways of looking at curricular phenomena. This view has given rise to increased interest in phenomenological analyses and ethnographic studies. The purpose of the theorizer is to help us see things in a new light, to interpret educational alternatives from a perspective external to our usual professional roles, and to create curricular options that have the potential for genuine social change.

In response to the challenge to identify the primary function of physical education curriculum theorizing in the 1980s, five functions of general curriculum theorizing have been discussed: (1) to describe the ideal curriculum; (2) to describe a sound procedure for building a curriculum; (3) to understand the curriculum in operation; (4) to predict the results of potential curricular alternatives; and (5) to generate new curricular options designed to lead cultural changes. All five are legitimate functions. The only defensible conclusion is that the primary function depends upon the role of the theorizer and the ultimate goal toward which curriculum change is addressed.

If the theorizer is a district curriculum director, the primary function is apt to be description of an ideal program to provide a model for physical educators in the system and to communicate key concepts of physical education to the community. It may well be clarification of a sound procedure for curriculum development to assist curriculum planners in different educational settings within the district to build appropriate and effective curricula systemwide. The theorizer whose role is focused on curriculum research is more likely to view the explanation of curricular phenomena or the understanding of the curriculum in operation as the primary function of his or her theorizing. Only the individual who engages in theorizing at some distance from actual classroom practice can justifiably select the generation of new options or the prediction of potential success of new alternatives as the *primary* function of personal theorizing. Given the current state of the art in physical education curriculum theorizing, it seems reasonable to conclude that, for most of us at present, the primary purpose of theorizing should be to improve the physical education curriculum through description, explanation, and communication to those both within and outside our profession whose lack of understanding of the theoretical base of physical education appears to place a genuine limitation upon both immediate and long-range educational progress.

Science or Art?

Leslie Lambert,
University of Georgia

Preparing students for tomorrow has historically been a primary goal of educational systems and, until recently, the future for which we prepared was reasonably predictable. As a result, the curriculum emphasized the acquisition of precise skills and particular subject matter. Now, with nuclear

Curriculum Issues and Concerns

weaponry, transformative discoveries in science, and the knowledge explosion, we find ourselves in the midst of a rapidly changing world. We cannot keep pace with these changes in a traditional way. This paper addresses an important issue confronting the field of curriculum—should we study curriculum as an art or as a science as we thoughtfully address current realities?

Curriculum positions span the spectrum from scientific to aesthetic. Control-oriented and technology curricula (Eisner and Vallance 1974) are relatively value-free approaches centered around efficiency of learning. They tend to be dominated by scientific methodology. The self-actualization approach assumes a more individual value-full posture and places more emphasis on aesthetic concerns. Critical analyses of our basic assumptions about people, learning, and conceptions of our world are primary, and require us to give attention to both scientific and aesthetic forms of knowledge. As a result, synthesis and balance prove to be practical and necessary.

Many people, including both scientists and philosophers, recognize the need for such balance. They realize that our reasonings are both logical and intuitive, both precise and imaginative. No one questions the significance of scientific thought. However, intuitive, aesthetic modes are equally essential, though greatly neglected. While rational thought is linear, highly focused, and analytic, meaning cannot be achieved without the meshing of aesthetic, responsive modes. Therefore, each, in isolation, is disastrously incomplete.

Gary Zukav wrote:

> (W)e are approaching the end of science. . . . The "end of science" means the coming of Western civilization, in its own time and in its own way, into the higher dimension of human experience. (Zukav 1979, 316)

Perhaps Pinar (1978) was referring to this phenomenon when he claimed that what we need in our world is a paradigm shift. We need to get beyond the traditional and totally explainable and grow upward toward newer and broader perspectives. The intention should not be to leave everything behind, but rather to find exciting links between the old and rich new horizons, thus gaining a larger world view.

To achieve a more encompassing world view, personal beliefs and values blend into educational and societal ones. Pauwels and Bergier (1964) emphasize that some scientists are effecting personal and societal changes based on insights and discoveries in their laboratories. It is becoming increasingly clear that whole concepts cannot be understood when studied only as parts. There are major scientific ideas, for example, that complement each other and allow for greater understandings when studied together. Even more interesting, many scientific insights have uncanny links with long believed poetic and mystical descriptions of nature. At times, science is simply uncovering facts that have long been sensed by humans in nonexperimental, aesthetic ways.

Lyall Watson wrote:

> You can collect as many seawater samples as you like, but none will contain, nor tell you anything about the tide. You can dissect as many living organisms as you can lay your hands on, breaking them down into their subatomic components, and still find no answers. Life is a pattern, a movement, a syncopation of matter; something produced in counterpoint to the rhythms of contingency; a rare and wonderfully unreasonable thing. (Watson 1979, 332)

Relationship is the axis for everything. Neither something nor someone can be isolated from its context and be completely understood. The practice of fragmenting and isolating those things that are meant to be flowing, dynamic, and whole needs to be changed.

Ilya Prigogine's (1980) Nobel prize winning dissipative structures theory has tremendous potential in our field of curriculum studies. Though the basis for the theory is chemical, the concepts it supports are much more pervading. Prigogine, whose background is in the humanities, shows how nature makes exhausting efforts toward higher orders of life. In doing so, he contrasts open and closed systems. Very simply, an open system is one with continuous exchange of energy with the environment. This type of system is a dissipative structure—very organized and whole, yet always in process. In order to sustain itself there must always be movement. As movement occurs, the parts interchange, thereby creating a new whole, a higher order. With this phenomenon occurring over and over, each subsequent order is more integrated than the one before.

Prigogine relates this theory beyond the laboratory to society. He points out that, historically, small creative groups of people have been the impetus for major change, pushing society to view itself differently. Societies are very cohesive, dissipative structures, and can experience tremendous shifts toward higher order. What is obvious in Prigogine's ideas is a strong world view based heavily upon pluralism and unlimited new realities not confined within traditional linear parameters.

These authors and others in the scientific realm are recognizing the need for bridging the gap between the scientific and the aesthetic. Within the field of curriculum, there are several theorists who are equally concerned. Macdonald (1975) expresses the need for bringing control and understanding together—science and the aesthetic, if you will. He suggests that this could be best accomplished through critical curriculum theory and theorizing. "It is an attempt to subjugate, in a sense, the technical praxis of control with the free floating theory of hermeneutics." (Macdonald 1975,4). Aoki (1983) recognizes the necessity of relationship between the analytic and interpretive modes, and suggests the dialectical curriculum orientation. The authors of this text propose ecological validity as a powerful and unprecedented approach to curricular understanding. In doing so, these theorists are suggesting a dissipative structure, a whole confluent concept that allows for further and greater enlightenment. Cultural, historical, economic, scientific, political, personal, and aesthetic ingredients evolve together toward a new consciousness and more meaningful curricular insights.

It is evident that our beliefs and practices are often incongruent. We know about balance, about bridging gaps—holistic medicine, ecology, dissipative structures theory, etc.—all of these offer more integrated ways of understanding, but we ignore or simply pay lip service to them. We know about hermeneutic understanding, the need for greater knowing, yet we continue to stagnate in mediocre, worn out ways of providing learning experiences and, beyond that, living life.

In summary, we need to quit choosing sides—one end of the spectrum or the other. Rather, the need exists to reevaluate our basic beliefs within the context of the world around us. Neither scientific nor aesthetic theory is complete. The most practical and necessary needs are for synthesis, integration, and balance. But how do we pull together two such different components? To exist at one end of the issue or the other is easy; the true challenge lies in bringing them together.

Is Eclecticism Acceptable in Lieu of a Consistent Theoretical Base?

Observation of current practices in physical education program development reveals clearly that most programs are not built on a consistent theoretical base. Instead they have been constructed by selecting what appear to be the best elements from various sources. The combining of various program elements in this manner results in an eclectic curriculum. Is eclecticism a sound approach to curriculum development? Are there any truly convincing reasons for giving serious attention to the theoretical base that underlies the physical education curriculum in any given setting? Is there any real justification for emphasizing theoretical consistency in preference to eclecticism?

Those who suggest that eclecticism in formulating the theoretical base for curriculum is a reasonable and acceptable alternative point out that no genuine theory of physical education has yet been developed, that no consensus exists in physical education curriculum theorizing, and that we are still a long way from the establishment of sound curriculum theory. Thus, we should not divert our energies on a relatively nonproductive cause, but should focus our time and effort on the obviously important demands of curriculum development and instructional practice and get on with the job. In short, in these times of economic stress and strict accountability, we can't afford too many philosophers.

It is also argued that physical educators have an extremely important obligation to society to transmit to each new generation essential knowledges, understandings, and skills relating to human development and motor performance. It is asserted that a consistent theoretical orientation is not necessary for effective performance of the task. In fact, too much attention to philosophical arguments or undue concern for a consistent theoretical base may actually impede progress in achieving the primary goals of physical education.

Probably the most plausible argument of those who prefer to take an eclectic position relative to physical education curriculum theory is the belief that none of the major theoretical positions that have been described is entirely satisfactory. If something is wrong with each theoretical alternative identified, why not select the best from each proposed theoretical construct? Why not choose the preferred features of each potential theory and have the best of all possible worlds? Those who believe in this approach are quick to point out that there has never been any empirical evidence that a consistent theoretical basis for the physical education curriculum improves educational practice.

The proponents of theoretical consistency, on the other hand, believe that eclecticism is unacceptable, that one cannot hold an eclectic theoretical position since eclecticism is inherently atheoretical. A series of disparate elements cannot serve as a theory to unify the phenomena to be examined. In the absence of a consistent theoretical base, there is actually no theory at all.

Those who support the need for theoretical consistency argue that it is not reasonable to expect that a physical educator can be involved in any significant way in advancing knowledge of human movement phenomena without an identifiable theoretical orientation as a working base. Physical education research, conducted in the human performance laboratory or in the gymnasium, must be designed within a consistent theoretical framework. The predominant emphasis on teaching traditional subject matter, whether it be sports skills or health-related fitness, is in itself a value position that should be examined.

The primary need for a consistent theoretical base is that it is required in order that theory function as a guide to the curriculum planner and the teacher. Only with a consistent theoretical orientation does the teacher gain control over the direction of learning activities. Theoretical consistency in selection of curricular goals, choice of physical education learning activities, instructional strategy decisions, and evaluative procedures is essential to educational achievement. The teacher who has no clearcut purpose or direction is at best ineffective, at worst a tool of those who are the real decision-makers.

It is the conviction of the authors that eclecticism is not acceptable in lieu of a consistent theoretical base. Curriculum theorists must acknowledge and understand a variety of theoretical orientations. The right of individual professionals to make personal selections of the theoretical base upon which to build the local curriculum is not questioned. But eclecticism is a "cop out." In practice it becomes a shift from one position to another or a "glue-together" curriculum using a bit of this and a bit of that. Neither of these practices will permit the potential impact of the physical education curriculum to be realized. Eclecticism is a rationalization to avoid examination of one's theoretical position. It is argued that the conscientious physical educator who finds none of the already identified theoretical orientations acceptable is free to develop yet another theoretical base for curriculum development. He or she may consider elements of previously established or proposed theories; but they must be selected, conceptualized, and related in ways that result in a consistent theoretical base. Given this approach, theorizing will lead to additional alternatives. Those who disagree will work from different theoretical perspectives, but each will function from a consistent theoretical base.

Is There Any Genuine Physical Education Curriculum Theory?

Is there really any physical education curriculum theory? This is a question frequently asked by academics and professional physical educators. If so, what in the world is it? Definitions were offered in chapter 1; but the question was not addressed as a theoretical issue. In the following paragraphs, the issue will be explored as a theoretical concern by offering tentative answers to five interrelated questions: (1) Is there any curriculum theory? (2) Is there any theory in physical education? (3) Is there any physical education curriculum theory beyond general curriculum theory? (4) Is there any physical education theory other than physical education curriculum theory? (5) What is physical education curriculum theory?

Does a legitimate curriculum theory actually exist? If a theory is defined as a set of related statements explaining some series of events, or a coherent group of general propositions used as principles of explanation for a class of phenomena, the term cannot be applied precisely in the study of curriculum. But, clearly, scientific theory should not be the model for curriculum theory; nor should the model for aesthetic criticism serve as the model for curriculum theory. As Walker points out, curriculum theories are theories of practice (1982, 64).

> They attempt to rationalize practice, to conceptualize it, to explain it, but all deal with practice, rather than with some purely natural phenomenon of universal scope, such as the sciences, natural and social deal with. . . . Curriculum theories are like theories in law, or business, or journalism, or social work, criminal justice, or city planning, not like theories of sociology, psychology, physics, chemistry, biology.

Yes, curriculum theory is an acceptable construct, if broadly defined to include the activity of theorizing that leads up to the production of a full-blown theory. Yes, there is curriculum theory,

> loosely construed, which involves careful scholarly thought leading to many different formulations, and describes a body of activity whose purpose is generally to illuminate the workings of the curriculum. (Vallance 1982, 8)

Given this interpretation, curriculum theory exists as an important area of scholarly activity.

Is there any physical education theory? The development of physical education theory has been a professional concern in the United States for at least a quarter of a century. The "Design Conference" and the "Theoretical Structure Project" in the 1960s were major cooperative efforts to build physical education theory (Ulrich and Nixon 1972). Metheny was a major contributor to both of these efforts; her work was probably the first systematic theoretical analysis of the discipline of human movement. The first comprehensive formulation of theory in physical evaluation was the 1963 classic written by Brown and Cassidy entitled *Theory in Physical Education: A Guide to Program Change.* This work presented two major components, a theoretical analysis of the field of knowledge of physical education and a more pragmatic school program development component.

It is generally agreed that physical education theorists are building theory to define, classify, and describe human movement phenomena, and to establish relationships among these phenomena. Most of the theory-building to date has focused on classifying disciplinary areas for scholarly study and research. It is interesting to note that Zeigler's 1982 taxonomy presents five "subdisciplinary areas of our field" and three "subprofessional or concurrent professional components" (Zeigler 1982, vi-vii). The subdisciplinary areas are identified as (1) background, meaning, and significance; (2) functional effects of physical activity; (3) sociocultural and behavioral aspects; (4) motor learning and development; and (5) mechanical and muscular analysis of motor skills. The subprofessional areas are (1) management theory and practice, (2) program development, and (3) measurement and evaluation. While the current level of theorizing in physical education and the degree of sophistication of many theory-building efforts can be justifiably criticized, there is no doubt that a body of physical education theory does exist and that physical education theorists have made substantial progress during the past decade.

Is there any physical education curriculum theory beyond general curriculum theory? The answer to this question is a definite yes. While there is considerable overlap in theoretical elements describing the professional and general education aspects of the physical education curriculum and of the broad general curriculum, physical education has its own unique discipline. Curriculum theory in physical education is necessarily concerned with defining, classifying, describing, and relating human movement phenomena—a vast area of human experience that is of little interest to the general curriculum theorist. Theorizing about movement, fitness, and sport, and the significance of these concepts for planned educational experiences, is clearly the domain of physical education curriculum theory.

Is there any physical education theory other than physical education curriculum theory? This is probably the most difficult question of the series. To the extent that curriculum theory is interpreted in the broad sense that has been intended in this text, and to the extent that physical education is viewed as a professional field, it follows that there is no physical education theory other than physical education curriculum theory. Taking the broader view, it might be better to refer to our theorizing as theory of physical education. Clearly our theories are theories of practice; like other curriculum theories, they draw more heavily from philosophy, psychology, sociology, and anthropology than from other established disciplines.

On the other hand, it can be argued that the discipline of physical education has generated some theory that should be distinguished from the curriculum theory of practice. This position is almost impossible to support, however, as long as we continue to identify our field as physical education. A professional orientation is inherent in the label of physical education. To be sure, scholars have theorized about, and in some instances proposed, theories of meaning and movement, motor learning, neurophysiological bases of movement, motivation for maximal performance, participant socialization, exercise addiction, and motor development. But all of these can be encompassed within any general theory of physical education. Scholars who have been interested in theory of physical education have usually developed their work from a philosophical or sociological base and are most often identified as curriculum theorists.

So what *is* physical education curriculum theory/theory of physical education? It is still not an easy question to answer. The most comfortable position available is the conclusion that there is indeed physical education curriculum theory, and that its concern with human movement phenomena makes it unique within the scope of general curriculum theory, but that the phrase *physical education curriculum theory* probably describes nothing different than physical education theory, which encompasses sub-theories concerning specific phenomena within the general rubric of human movement phenomena.

In the twenty years between Brown and Cassidy and Zeigler we have come full circle in our concepts of theory of physical education. A theory is still viewed as

> a conceptual structure based on a set of interrelated concepts which has for its purpose: (a) the tentative *description* of an event, object, or idea; (b) the tentative *description of relationship* between two or more variables . . . ; (c) the tentative *explanation* of the cause and effect relationship between two or more variables . . . and (d) the tentative *prediction* of the occurrence of an event or activity based upon the acquisition of warranted evidence. (Ulrich and Nixon 1972, 6)

In their theory of physical education, Brown and Cassidy included both the disciplinary and the program development components. Zeigler makes his case for five "subdisciplinary" and three "subprofessional" dimensions of sport and developmental physical activity. These authors share a common perspective with many other physical education theorists of the 1960s, 1970s, and 1980s, that these areas provide the basis for conceptualizing theory of physical education or physical education curriculum theory.

What Is the Role of the Curriculum Specialist in the Academic Discipline?

Over the course of the past one hundred years, an information base has been developed about human movement phenomena, especially within the contexts of sport, dance, and exercise. The past thirty years have marked the most productive period in that development, with scholars and researchers applying the rigorous standards of philosophical and scientific inquiry to their efforts to gain information. This progressively academic endeavor has been accompanied by the contention that there is now a legitimate discipline focused upon human movement studies; a discipline that is organized according to a

Elizabeth S. Bressan, University of Oregon

formal theoretical structure for understanding human moving. Theoretical structures operate within disciplines as frameworks for thinking by defining the concepts and content germane to the discipline, and by endorsing certain modes of inquiry and criteria for verification of information. The structure adopted by the members of a discipline serves to identify what will be studied and how it will be studied.

The role of the curriculum specialist in physical education within the creation of the structure of the discipline of human movement studies has not been cultivated. The greatest inhibiting factor to specialists' involvement may be the perception that any work associated with curriculum is concerned with the application of sound professional practices, rather than the discovery of abstract theoretical perspectives on knowledge. The efforts of curriculum specialists, even those who specialize in theorizing, is not considered to be sufficiently removed from the specific demands of an educational setting to allow the cultivation of a universal situation-independent view, essential for the conceptualization of a structure for academic knowledge. The task of *taking theory,* generated by academicians, and *translating it into practice,* defines the prevalent conception of the role of the curriculum specialist in relation to the academic discipline.

It is ironic that curriculum specialists would not be accorded—or, for that matter, would not pursue aggressively—a more active role in designing the structure of the discipline. Of all individuals involved with the study of human moving, those who work in curriculum may have the greatest investment in how the total discipline is defined and organized. Schwab (1974) has suggested that all educators have an intimate concern for the structure of their respective disciplines, since it is that structure that defines many of the elements in the subject to be taught, and determines the type and range of information about that subject that will be gathered. Because the structure determines the nature and extent of our knowledge base about human moving, it profoundly affects all of our decision-making about the physical education experience. If that knowledge base is simplistic, partial, or inaccurate, our decisions will reflect such qualities.

There is another dimension to the role of the curriculum specialist within the discipline that must be taken into account. The structure of a discipline proposes a pattern of priorities for inquiry, suggesting that certain questions about a subject are more central or important to the overall mission of the discipline. With this pattern, there is the assignment of preferential status to individuals who work to answer these central questions. These priorities are manifested in the amount of time allocated in undergraduate and graduate programs of study, hiring patterns of faculty within universities, and the entire scheme of recognition and reward that sustains members of the discipline. If the tasks of the curriculum specialist are relegated to those of a "receiver and translator" of information, it should be expected that academic status and recognition of efforts will not be substantial.

There are two kinds of structural patterns currently competing for predominance in organizing the study of human moving. The first kind of structure follows a parent-child metaphor, where traditional academic disciplines such as physiology, psychology and sociology are regarded as the sources from which an interdiscipline or crossdiscipline is formed. This "new" discipline inherits the theories and modes of inquiry of the identified "parents." Franklin Henry (1964, 1978) has been a spokesman for this position, which partitions our body of knowledge into units called subdisciplines that parallel the established disciplines in the academic community, e.g., physiology . . . of exercise; psychology . . . of sport. The chief criticism of this approach is that the borrowing of theories and modes of inquiry from other disciplines results in a conglomeration of insights, rather than a coherent body of knowledge. The information gathered from the physiological perspective, for example, is not compatible with the information gathered from the sociological perspective. Facts discovered within different perspectives cannot be related to each other because they are expressed using different concepts and criteria for verification.

The curriculum specialist within the parent-child metaphor is accorded the monumental task of translating the information garnished by the separate subdisciplines into some sort of guidelines for professional practice. Because each subdiscipline works with the concepts and language of its parent, the curriculum specialist is left to decode and decipher. Each subdiscipline's dependence on its intellectual parent precludes any input on redesigning structure from members in any other subdiscipline or professional field.

The second structural pattern follows a sibling metaphor, where two related yet separate disciplines are proposed; one an academic discipline concerned with theoretical descriptions and explanations, and the other a professional discipline concerned with the accomplishment of educational objectives in practical situations. VanderZwaag (1983) presents this sort of division in his suggestion that there should be a discipline of sport studies and a profession of sport management. While others have expanded the focus of their models well beyond the limits of sport, the dual discipline approach still precludes the involvement of curriculum specialists in the structuring of inquiry in the academic discipline, since such specialists are considered professionals whose concerns are restricted to the professional discipline.

The fundamental problem with both the parent-child and the sibling metaphor is that they rely on borrowing definitions and modes of inquiry from other disciplines rather than attempting to design a coherent structure by examining their unique focus of interest, e.g. human movement. Because any structure of a discipline is supposed to provide a comprehensive framework for thinking, a grand design for relating bits of information to each other until finally a pattern for understanding emerges, the strategy of borrowing structures is inappropriate. It results in the proliferation of disparate pieces of information that can, at best, be related to aspects of other pieces of information, but never to a coherent whole. This problem becomes one of fragmentation, both in our knowledge base and among those individuals involved in the discipline.

The fragmentation manifested in the structure of our discipline will probably be perpetuated unless some cataclysmic event occurs to break the inertia. Those individuals accorded the highest status in the discipline are usually specialists within a subdiscipline. They have neither the background nor the disposition to regard human moving as an integrated phenomenon. Their patterns of intellectual allegiance and esteem are rooted with the established parent disciplines. Although curriculum specialists are seldom accepted as potential theoreticians by academicians, they are more accustomed to looking at human moving in an integrated fashion. They have a good deal of practice in looking at human performance from many different perspectives, since they have been relegated to the role of translator for so many years. They are probably more flexible in their thinking, due to the need to design responsive programs within a variety of settings. Most important of all, however, is that they may be the only members of the discipline/profession who have been formally taught how to theorize, how to create designs, and how to relate complex considerations into coherent patterns of relationship.

Until individuals involved in curriculum begin to assert their insights and cultivated talents within the academic discipline, it is unlikely that substantial changes will occur in the structure of our academic discipline. While there would be numerous political considerations in any attempt to launch such a reorganization, there is little point in pursuing plans for implementation until an actual proposal is made. The continued submission of variations of the parent-child or sibling model is likely as long as academicians struggle with this structure. It is only with the imaginative and holistic approach of the curriculum specialist that a reconceptualization is probable. The rewards for such an effort could range from establishing a base of information that relates directly to performance in movement (rather than some obscure reference calling for practitioners to "apply it") to a setting of priorities in research where some of the most pressing questions about human moving might be answered (rather than some questions seen as important within another discipline). Although the structuring of academic inquiry is not often listed among the tasks of a curriculum specialist, the need for active theoretical expertise and skill in design suggests that the time may have come for active professional intervention.

To What Extent Should Theory Be Grounded in Practice?

Wilma M. Harrington, University of Georgia

In order to determine the extent to which theory should be grounded in practice, we must examine the function and utilization of theories. In an earlier position paper, theories in physical education are described as theories of practice that are "used to define, classify, and describe human movement phenomena and to establish relationships." It can also be said that, in the broadest perspective, curricular theories provide insight into "what is," "what could be," and "what should be." Each of these extends the function of theories.

Curricular theorizing can be described as identifying valued activity. In answering the questions "what is?", "what could be?", or "what should be?", a value set is implied. In order to define, classify, and describe, some value must be placed on certain aspects of the phenomena of interest to determine what will be defined, classified, and described. Therefore, we must ask whose values are to be used.

Generally, when we examine theories of the "should be" and "could be" varieties, the values made explicit and those implied are those of the theorist. When we examine "what is," it usually becomes obvious that the values present are those found in actual practice. The question arises, "Can we address only one perspective and provide a valid description, definition, or classification of the phenomena for study?"

One of the major criticisms leveled at attempts to apply theories in the school setting is that theories have no relationship to practice. Utilizing the actual context of schools to generate and verify curriculum theory answers this criticism. These approaches also allow us to determine the degree of match between theoretical values and contextual values, which have the greater influence on practice.

The recent trend in educational research, which focuses on generation of grounded theory, has directed attention to the necessity for entering the real world of schools in order to develop theories about schooling. Grounded theory relies on descriptive categories that emerge from a selected situation where representative phenomena of interest have been observed.

The concept of grounded theory definitely implies that the requisites for formulating explanations or descriptions are found in "what is." This proposition makes explicit the need to understand that "human behavior is completely influenced by the context in which it occurs and often has more meaning than its observable facts" (Wilson 1977, 253). Any theory that attempts to describe and classify practice, or affect it, must reflect the context of the behaviors making up practice.

Observations of what occurs in practice can be used as a means of verifying theory, as well as for generation of theory. Activity based on supposition has little value if there are no grounds to support that it does or can occur. Naturalistic inquiry, which is used in the social sciences as a means of theory verification, allows us to determine the extent to which "what is," purported as desirable practice, in fact occurs in the real world.

It also allows for the verification of "what should be" and "what could be." This assumes that one of the aims of theorizing is to affect practice. If the conditions, consequences, and values that permit theory to have an effect on practice have not been delineated as a part of the process, then a major relationship has been ignored. Theories that define what should or could exist, but do not address the determinants for them are exercises in futility.

To what extent should theory be grounded in practice? Theory should be grounded in practice to the extent that the explicit value positions take into account the context and conditions of representative situations. Practice or the real world may be used to generate or verify theory. The use of either approach provides a means for determining the match between supposed and actual values, which is essential for theory to provide a basis for practice. The definitions, descriptions, and classifications of the phenomena of interest must at some point in the theorizing process demonstrate some relationship to what occurs in actual practice in order for them to be accepted as valid.

To What Extent Is Instructional Theory Independent of Curriculum Theory?

Is educational theorizing an activity within which curriculum and instruction are indistinguishable? Are there curriculum theories that can explain, describe, and/or predict distinct from instructional theories with similar goals? Is a school program based on both curriculum theory and instructional theory, either of which may be studied separately, although the two must have congruent value orientations?

One answer to these questions is that curriculum includes instruction; consequently, instructional theory does not exist as a separate entity, but is encompassed within curriculum theory. This view is typical of those who define curriculum broadly. If curriculum is the study of "what should constitute a world of learning and how to go about making that world," (Macdonald 1977, 11) its theoretical base necessarily includes instructional elements. If curriculum is viewed as theory to be implemented through instruction, it is quickly evident that the theory cannot readily be separated from the practice.

From a position that the focus of the curriculum should be on the person in a unique social environment, it must be acknowledged that curriculum theory and instructional theory are inseparable. Educational theory must be dynamic and changing over time. Only a holistic approach to theory is consistent with this perspective. Different "realms of meaning" (Phenix 1964) can be conceptualized, but this does not generate instructional theories to be disassociated from curriculum theories. It simply suggests the possibility of different approaches to facilitate the search for meaning, with each avenue for theorizing relating elements of both curriculum and instruction.

It is becoming increasingly popular to define *curriculum* as the educative agency's plan and *instruction* as the delivery system for putting the plan into action. Accepting this distinction makes it reasonable to attempt to generate *either* curriculum theory or instructional theory. In fact, a growing number of scholars identify their field of study primarily in one of the two areas.

Points of differentiation between curriculum theory and instructional theory, in accordance with this position, include the focus of the theory, the decisions it is designed to facilitate, the questions toward which it is directed, and the predictions it attempts. Curriculum theory is designed to facilitate decisions concerning scope, structure, and sequence; instructional theory directs more attention to classroom methodology. Categories of curriculum questions include values, goals, content, and evaluation. Categories of instruction questions can be listed as strategies, materials and learning resources, teaching behaviors, teacher-learner interaction, class management, and assessment. Curriculum theory attempts to predict the impact of structured experience on instruction; instructional theory attempts to predict the impact of instruction on educational outcomes.

Those who urge separate identification of curriculum and instruction tend to build curriculum theory on the assumptions of philosophy, sociology, and psychology; instructional theory relies primarily on the foundation knowledges of motor development, motor learning, motor control, and motor behavior. Curriculum theory is likely to have a value-based prescriptive emphasis; instruction theory is usually scientific and descriptive in nature. Modes of inquiry also differ. Quantitative modes predominate in instructional inquiry; qualitative modes are much more common in curriculum inquiry. Curriculum research uses such holistic, naturalistic approaches as phenomenology, attitude inventories, and contextual validation; instructional research usually deals with designated episodes and relies heavily on experimental and quasi-experimental approaches.

The extent to which one views instructional theory as independent of curriculum theory depends primarily upon the chosen definitions of curriculum and instruction. But, irrespective of definition, there certainly is no clearcut distinction between the two. In theory or practice it becomes a matter of emphasis or focus. We cannot separate completely the quality of the plan from the quality of the implementation. It is impossible to separate people into parts. "Domains of experience" is a figure of speech and not an accurate description of the inner life of a human being, whether we are speaking of the planners or the learners. Thus, we must conclude that we cannot separate curriculum theory from instructional theory or theory from practice, although it may sometimes be useful to focus on one or the other. Our educational goal is a whole greater than the sum of its parts. Curriculum, instruction, and evaluation all blend together in the educational endeavor, in physical education as in any other subject matter area.

What Kind of Physical Education Curriculum Research Is Most Needed?

Catherine D. Ennis, University of Wisconsin

When solutions are sought to existing curriculum problems, the results of curriculum research are likely to be discussed only when all other possibilities have been exhausted. This may be attributed to a belief on the part of practitioners and administrators that present research in curriculum has little resemblance to or consequence for the practice arena. In fact, some physical educators may question whether curricular research is a viable means of dealing with curriculum problems at all. For many other disciplines and professions, research is a central focus of existence. Medical professionals who are not well informed on research advances soon have little need for waiting rooms. When physical educators disclaim the usefulness of curriculum research it may not be the credibility of research as a problem solving tool that is being questioned, but the focus of the research approach that is under attack.

Two approaches to curriculum research are considered within this paper. The first approach investigates a specific curricular concern from a single perspective. The second approach investigates the same concern from a variety of perspectives. For example, the question of who controls physical education curriculum decisions in school systems might be analyzed in the first approach by collecting questionnaire data from a sample of teachers. Within the second approach, the control of curriculum decisions might be identified using not only teacher questionnaires, but also questionnaires from physical education supervisors, principals, local, state, and federal curriculum directors, and lay persons. Furthermore, selected class observations and follow-up interviews with representatives of each group may provide additional information in understanding the intricate nature of curriculum decision making.

It is important to note that both research approaches may be either empirically or descriptively based and both may use quantitative or qualitative methods for collecting and analyzing data. However, the first approach is unidimensional, basing administrative and policy decisions on one indicator. The second approach is multidimensional, considering several perspectives when identifying sources of information on a given concern.

When the unidimensional research approach is used in physical education curriculum, researchers focus on one aspect of curriculum planning, implementation, or evaluation. Curriculum may be studied from the perspective of theorists, teachers, or students. It may be analyzed as it is conceptualized by the teacher, operationalized in the gymnasium, or experienced by the student. Researchers, at times, make claims for the generalizability of their results to the theory and practice of physical education. But are these studies generalizable? Can the complex relationships of people, context, and methodology that compose the existing physical education curriculum ever be simplified into a tight study? Can a single aspect of curriculum be better understood by isolating it from the environment in which it exists?

Advocates of a multidimensional approach to curriculum research think not. These researchers argue that narrowly-focused studies do not produce relevant information concerning complex existing curricula. Decker Walker (1973) addresses this concern in the article, "What Curriculum Research?". Walker urges a broadening of focus, allowing knowledge from a variety of sources to enlighten overall understanding. Holman (1980) suggests that our examination of individual curriculum "trees" give way to a more complete investigation of the "forest." She continues this metaphor by identifying an educational ecosystem as a way of providing meaningful results for relevant decision making. These authors suggest that curricula be studied from a more complex or multidimensional perspective to provide information that practitioners and policy makers can utilize.

Of course efforts of this magnitude are also criticized. The availability of resources and the extent of the overall commitment to curricular research is questioned continuously (Walker 1973). However, several theorists and researchers have sought to design and to conduct studies from this perspective. The multidimensional approach simultaneously considers a variety of research perspectives within a single design. These researchers propose to grasp the magnitude of the endeavor by focusing on one curricular concern as it is analyzed from several different curricular perspectives.

Fenwick English (1980) proposes the concept of "curriculum mapping" to focus on the amount of time spent in academic activities. By analyzing the time teachers spend on developing concepts, skills, and attitudes, English identified complex content emphases in the existing curriculum. Goodlad, Klein, and Tye (1979) propose a series of curricular domains from which to view the existing curriculum. In the technical reports of *A Study of Schooling in the United States,* Goodlad (1982) suggests data collection strategies in each domain to provide a multidimensional perspective on school curriculum. In physical education, Bain (1974) describes the hidden curriculum from the vantage point of the context, the teacher, and the student. Her study emphasizes the relationships among these constructs, which compose the hidden curriculum in physical education. Advocates of a multidimensional approach to curriculum research believe that the complexity of their research is dictated by the complexity of the phenomena under study.

It is evident that efforts to understand and improve the existing physical education curriculum must go beyond the study of isolated components to an analysis of the total curriculum. Multidimensional research approaches address the curricular complexity through an analysis of differing perspectives on planning, implementation, and evaluation. For future curriculum research to be of use to practitioners, it is imperative that it consider the multiplicity of concerns that impact on the existing physical education curriculum. We can no longer allow our curriculum solutions to be dwarfed by the magnitude of the problems.

Additional Theoretical Issues and Concerns

Selection of the eleven issues to be discussed on the preceding pages reflect the judgment of the authors as to important contemporary questions being debated among physical education curriculum specialists. The choices were admittedly somewhat arbitrary. Many other theoretical issues and concerns are just as relevant for your study, analysis, and decision-making. No list of important issues and concerns can be exhaustive. You and your colleagues have undoubtedly engaged in debating other current physical education curriculum issues. The authors encourage you to develop your own position statements on those issues of most concern to you at the present time.

References

Arnold, P. J. 1979. *Meaning in movement, sport and physical education*, London: Heinemann.

Aoki, T. T. 1983. A dialectic between the conceptual world and the lived world: A way of understanding communal life. Paper presented at the symposium Exploring Settings as Source for Global/Community Curriculum, AERA Conference, Montreal.

Bain, L. L. 1974. Description and analysis of the hidden curriculum in physical education. Doctoral dissertation. Madison, WI: Univ. of Wisconsin.

Brown, C., and R. Cassidy. 1963. *Theory in physical education: A guide to program change.* Philadelphia: Lea and Febiger.

Eisner, E. W., and E. Vallance. 1974. Five conceptions of curriculum: Their roots and implication for curriculum planning. In *Conflicting conceptions of curriculum*, ed. Elliot W. Eisner and Elizabeth Vallance. Berkeley: McCutcheon.

English, F. 1980. Curriculum mapping. *Educational Leadership* 37:558–59.

Goodlad, J. I. 1982. A study of schooling: A series of introductory descriptions. In *A study of schooling in the United States*, ed. J. I. Goodlad. Technical Report Series, No. 1, ERIC, ED 214 871.

Goodlad, J. I. 1979. *Curriculum inquiry.* New York: McGraw-Hill.

Goodlad, J. I., M. F. Klein, and K. A. Tye. 1979. The domains of curriculum and their study. In *Curriculum inquiry*, ed. J. I. Goodlad. New York: McGraw-Hill.

Henry, F. 1964. Physical education: An academic discipline. *Proceedings* of the 67th Annual Conference of NCPEAM (January 8–10):6–9.

Henry, F. 1978. The academic discipline of physical education. *Quest* 29:13–29.

Holman, E. L. 1980. The school ecosystem. In *Considered action for curriculum improvement.* Alexandria, VA: Association for Supervision and Curriculum Development.

Kerlinger, F. N. 1979. *Behavioral research: A conceptual approach.* New York: Holt, Rinehart and Winston.

Kuhn, T. 1970. *The structure of scientific revolutions.* Chicago: Univ. of Chicago Press.

LaPorte, W. R., and J. M. Cooper. 1973. *The physical education curriculum (A national program).* Columbia: Lucas Brothers.

Macdonald, J. B. 1975. Curriculum theory as intentional activity. Paper presented at The Curriculum Theory Conference, Charlottesville, Virginia.

Macdonald, J. B. 1977. Values bases and issues for curriculum. In *Curriculum theory*, ed. Alex Molnar and John A. Zahorik, 10–21. Washington, DC: Association for Supervision and Curriculum Development.

McCutcheon, G., ed. 1982. *Theory Into Practice.* 21 (1) (Winter).

Pauwels, L., and J. Bergier. 1964. *The morning of the magicians.* New York: Stein and Day.

Phenix, P. H. 1964. *Realms of meaning.* New York: McGraw-Hill.

Pinar, W. 1978. The reconceptualization of curriculum studies. *Journal of Curriculum Theorizing* 10 (3).

Prigogine, I., 1980. *From being to becoming.* San Francisco: W. H. Freeman.

Schwab, J. 1974. The concept of the structure of a discipline. In *Conflicting conceptions of curriculum,* ed. E. Eisner and E. Vallance, 162–75. Berkeley: McCutchan.

Tyler, R. W. 1950. *Basic principles of curriculum and instruction.* Chicago: Univ. of Chicago Press.

Ulrich, C., and J. E. Nixon. 1972. *Tones of theory.* Washington, DC: AAHPER.

Vallance, E. 1982. The practical uses of curriculum theory. *Theory Into Practice* 21 (1) (Winter):4–10.

VanderZwaag, H. 1983. Coming out of the maze: Sport management, dance management and exercise science. *Quest* 35: 66–73.

Walker, D. F. 1973. What curriculum research? *Journal of Curriculum Studies* 5:58–72.

Walker, D. F. 1982. Curriculum theory is many things to many people. *Theory Into Practice* 21 (1) (Winter):62–65.

Watson, L. 1979. *Lifetide.* New York: Simon and Schuster.

Wilson, S. 1977. The use of ethnographic techniques in educational research. *Review of Educational Research* 47 (1) (Winter):245–65.

Zeigler, E. F., ed. 1982. *Introduction to physical education and sport.* Philadelphia: Lea and Febiger.

Zukav, G. 1979. *The dancing wu li masters.* New York: William Morrow.

Epilogue

This volume opened with a scenario. It was entitled "The Movement for Life Curriculum 2035 A.D." You may have felt that some of the specifics were patently improbable. You may have experienced some distaste for certain aspects of the future portrayed for physical education and for persons living in the sort of world envisioned.

By this time you are keenly aware that no one of us has a corner on ideas for creating a better future. You know that many individuals should be giving input to the curriculum process in physical education. You have learned that our best hope for more effective education requires that we target some changes sooner than a half century in the future. You know that an unlimited number of possible scenarios can be written. We close this book with an alternative scenario.

Human Wellness and Satisfaction 2001 A.D.*

* Portions of this scenario have been adapted from an unpublished paper by Keith Radford.

The time:	October 31, 2001
The place:	House of Representatives, Washington, D.C.
The occasion:	A speech to a Joint Session of the U.S. Congress by the Chair of the President's Commission on Quality of Life in support of legislation to establish a federal Department for Human Wellness and Satisfaction.
The setting:	The Commission was appointed over two years ago. The initial report submitted to the President in February, 2000 included eight major recommendations, some of which are already being addressed.

Mr. Vice-President and Members of the Congress, I am deeply appreciative of this opportunity to address you and to urge your support of PL 110–999. This legislative proposal represents the very heart of the recommendations of the President's Commission on Quality of Life. The establishment of a federal Department for Human Wellness and Satisfaction, with adequate funding and appropriate congressional and executive agency support, will permit us to give needed attention to writing the scenario for this nation's future and to our immediate and near-future responsibilities essential to the enhancement of the quality of life for all American citizens.

The Commission has already published a summary of the preliminary fact-finding activities, which resulted in identification of the major problems to be addressed. We have traveled extensively, though selectively, in our efforts to become familiar with institutions, governmental arrangements, research and development projects, and creative approaches to the solutions to these problems, both in the United States and in other countries. We have requested and been granted the opportunity to share selected findings and conclusions with you.

It is clear that our immediate focus must be upon fostering a higher level of positive health-related fitness for the entire population. This goal must be achieved as the basis for all other efforts to increase the potential for human wellness and satisfaction and to raise the quality-of-life index in this country. It was my personal privilege to visit the United Kingdom as a part of the Commission's study of ongoing national efforts to raise quality standards of living; I will report some of the highlights of this study. Other members of the Commission will report on significant developments and innovative plans in Australia, Canada, Scandinavia, West Germany, Switzerland, Japan, South Korea, Brazil, Panama, Nigeria, and Kenya.

Technological, economic, and educational developments in the United Kingdom, coupled with an enormous and growing burden on the national Health Services, led the British Human Maintenance and Satisfaction Department (HMSD) to commission the Smith and Johnson Report, which appeared in 1996. The successful utilization of solar power, together with the electrical energy derived from harnessing the power of the seas surrounding the United Kingdom, accelerated the trend of decentralization of both business and education. By 1995 education was mainly conducted through computer programs in homes. Many businesses had already decentralized to the point where the majority of the work force ceased to commute to the marketplace. Solar technology, together with the need to conserve fuels, further heightened this process.

Today the United Kingdom is characterized by a sprawling electronic home industry. Almost all manual labor is efficiently completed by machine or robot. Even in the home the doors and lights are monitored by a central computer, which negates the necessity to raise an arm to open a door or switch on a light. The disintegration of almost all of the major cities and the trend toward underground housing gave me the impression of being in a giant landscaped garden. The further development of the pneumatic subway delivery system has created a country of self-sufficient single or multi dwellings. Thus the advancements in solar energy, together with the stabilization of both the population and the family, has led to nuclear family units that are not only self-sufficient, but often also psychologically isolated. Eliminating the need to leave the dwelling to work, bank, shop, or pursue entertainment created major problems. Statistics published by His Majesty's Stationary Office show that the stabilization of the population, together with a very low birth rate, has led to a significant increase in the average age of the population. All requirements concerning forced retirement have been abolished, not only because they were seen to be discriminatory, but also of necessity, as the elderly are now viewed as a valuable part of the work force.

The Smith and Johnson Report showed that at all ages the vast majority of the population were below the recognized fitness norms established by the HMSD. Health costs had mushroomed because of the poor condition of the young, the rapid deterioration of the middle aged, and the precarious position of the aging. Personal satisfaction measures revealed that the majority of the population felt alienated and isolated; the number of suicides associated with what has been colloquially dubbed "the stir-crazy syndrome" had the HMSD extremely concerned.

It had been felt that the many individualized computer movement maintenance programs available to the general population would be sufficient to provide the necessary tools to maintain physical efficiency and promote good health. Unfortunately the majority of the population seemed to find the programs passé, uninteresting, or even boring. While a significant minority of the population appeared to follow a sound maintenance program in their leisure hours, the vast majority did not take advantage of either the programs or the facilities. Smith and Johnson also brought to light the fact that many young people had trouble socializing, relating to their peers, and developing the skills necessary to make social encounters pleasurable.

Implementation of the general recommendations of the Smith and Johnson Report has led to some major changes in lifestyle in the United Kingdom.

1. All children are required to attend educational centers once every seven days for regular monitoring, assessment, and further guidance in achieving the objectives of their individualized education programs (IEPs). Scheduling is flexible to allow parents to attend with them at least once a month.

2. Human Maintenance and Satisfaction (HMS) Centers have been established throughout the country to facilitate participation in individually monitored maintenance programs.

3. Beginning at four years of age, all children are required to attend HMS Centers for two days out of every seven. The programs feature movement activities that emphasize both cooperation and competition. I observed two novel approaches. The first is a weightless chamber for the enjoyment of touch pursuit games and rotational skills. The second is the concept of a fantasy adventure unit where cooperative and competitive situations may be planned and pursued. I understand that this is also used for survival skills and catharsis activities. Individuals above eight years of age are encouraged to specialize in at least one individual activity of their choice per year and required to demonstrate movement and cognitive proficiency commensurate with their maturation.

4. Shortly after their initial establishment the HMS Centers were enlarged and modified to provide more adequately for the adolescent and adult populations. All individuals are now required to prove competency in a safety skills program. One of the new approaches to maintenance is the use of heavy gravity environment to improve physiological efficiency. In this environment every physical movement is difficult, so that any activity provides a training effect in that it builds strength and improves circulo-respiratory functioning.

5. The Smith and Johnson report provided evidence that the population perceived a need for more human contact and companionship outside the family. Activities appropriate to older youth and to groups of mixed ages were added. The Centers now provide for social amenities, as well as indoor and outdoor pursuits.

6. Special Adventure Activity Centers have now been established throughout the country to extend the services of HMS Centers and to increase the interest and participation of the adult population. The AACs are oriented toward activities

that emphasize physical challenge, such as scuba diving, rapelling, karate, and triathlon competition.

7. The lack of fitness and/or opportunity for physical recreation among the aging was a major concern expressed in the Smith and Johnson Report. The aged are now encouraged, not only to attend the HMS Centers to participate in vigorous activity programs with their peers, but also to become involved with programs encompassing persons of all ages.

8. All participants are urged to set personal maintenance goals. Each HMS Center staff is expected to provide a range of activities sufficiently broad to offer personal satisfaction, enhance motor performance, and improve physiological and psychological efficiency levels among all segments of the population.

The HMS Centers have definitely contributed toward a higher level of wellness in the United Kingdom. Its citizens have had to deal with some of the same economic and social problems that beset us; they have had to face some of these problems sooner, before they posed an equal threat to the quality of life in our country. I believe we can gain from their experience as we shape some new alternatives of our own. Some of the specific recommendations to the U.S. Secretary of Human Wellness and Satisfaction which will appear in the Commission report include the following:

1. The Department (DHWS) will be responsible for assisting State Departments of Education to establish local Wellness Centers throughout the nation. Wellness education will be viewed as an integral part of public education. Centers will be established in every public elementary school as curricula are revised to meet today's and tomorrow's needs. The British experience has convinced us that we want to maintain our present system of public schools. The Commission has recommended that schools continue to operate on a five-day, forty-hour week, eleven-month schedule. However, a minimum of 25 percent of each student's school time will be assigned for Wellness Center activities. Wellness Centers will be accredited by State Departments of Education; they will be financed by local taxes and state funding based on average daily attendance. Building construction costs will be borne by State transportation and luxury taxes (fuel, highway tolls, airline mileage, space shuttle vouchers, liquor, cigarettes, cable TV, lottery, professional sports, etc.) and federal funds on a matching basis. Overall administrative responsibility will be assigned to certified health and physical educators; all program staff will be required to meet appropriate state

licensing standards. Wellness centers, although located in or adjacent to elementary schools, will provide programs and services for persons of all ages and will be accessible to all local citizens.

2. The curriculum in Developmental Motor Performance (still called physical education in sixteen states) will continue to be required of all students entering elementary schools at age four until completion of the fourteen credit requirement. Secondary students who have completed the DMP curriculum will enroll in Movement for Life programs until graduation from high school. Developmental Motor Performance and Movement for Life programs will be conducted in Wellness Center facilities. It is anticipated that these programs will be similar to the best of today's offerings.

The youngest elementary school children will continue to emphasize movement education activities that include body awareness and spatial orientation challenges and games, basic motor skills, and creative dance. Older elementary children will engage in continuing movement education; ethnic, folk, and creative dance; new games and friend games. They will learn basic movement notation, beginning game terminology and rules, and elementary biomechanical and physiological principles using the computer software now available. The instructional program in the middle school should include survival swimming, sport skills, dance, project adventure, fitness activities, and student-created games. Audiocassettes and computer diskettes available both for school and home use provide excellent support for self-directed fitness assessment, sport skill development, and innovative movement challenges.

Good secondary school programs will continue to emphasize fitness for life, group development through movement activities, and the personal search for meaning in movement. The fitness for life curriculum includes individual assessment of the key aspects of health-related fitness, self-monitoring of fitness achievements, guided prescription of exercise, and intensive participation in selected fitness activities. The core course in group development through movement activities seeks increased social awareness, emphasizing cooperative games, group choreography, community service projects, and discussion and analysis of social issues. Media segments focusing on panel discussions of exploitation of athletes, amateurism in sports, and drug abuse among professional athletes exemplify topics of current interest. Several key approaches to seeking personal meaning in movement, which will continue to be used, include focus on inner awareness through sport, pursuit of high adventure, composing or creating movement, and the seeking of excellence in a favorite sport. All secondary programs will include skill development experiences in physical recreation activities of individual choice, and will culminate in a personal assessment and planning for lifestyle patterns to accommodate movement activities. Most of the skill development will be stimulated and monitored by individually selected computer programs, and then refined and extended in group activity settings provided at school or through outside community agencies.

3. Federally supported and operated Environmental Recreation Centers will be established in every state. We are indeed fortunate that federal land use policy was reversed in 1984 to reestablish the primary goals of conservation and environmental protection. As a result, we have preserved areas throughout the country in which these centers can be located. They will operate programs in hunting and fishing, skiing, mountain climbing, surfing, kayaking, ice-sailing, marine biology, forest renewal, desert wildlife, and other regionally feasible activities. The Environmental Recreation Centers will be charged with certain environmental protection responsibilities, and participants will be required to volunteer minimum service to appropriate state environmental protection projects. These facilities and their programs will be staffed by employees of the U.S. Park Service and by qualified leisure counselors and recreation program leaders employed by the State Quality of Life Department. Programs will be designed to emphasize adult and family recreation.

4. A network of Quality of Life Centers (QLCs) will supplant our present local public recreation programs and coordinate many of the existing diverse health and social agency programs. We believe that a system of Wellness Centers whose programs are well coordinated with the public schools, supplementing their fitness education activities through other types of centers, will serve America's needs better than the plan currently in operation in the United Kingdom. The QLCs will provide a broad spectrum of leisure activities, including programs in all popular physical recreation activities. They will be responsible for recruiting and training individuals for global sport teams and for participation in international sports, gymnastics, and dance festivals. Their staffs will include clinical psychologists, family counselors, group therapists, and social integration

specialists, who will provide direct assistance to participants of all ages, interests, and skill levels, and refer them to Wellness Centers, to Environmental Recreation Centers, or to particular public health or social agencies as appropriate. Research and development directed toward enhancement of life quality will be an assigned function of the Quality of Life Centers.

5. Each Quality of Life Center will be responsible for making adequate provision for services to older Americans. They will be directed to plan for continuing education, recreation, and social activity programs; to provide appropriate services both to the young old and the old old; to maximize opportunities for interaction in groups of all ages and in activities requiring varying levels of fitness.

6. Every U.S. citizen will be expected to carry out a personal health maintenance program throughout life. The Wellness Centers will be charged with the responsibility for making the needed services available and for promoting these programs. We believe that the centers will be more effective if they are allowed to focus on this one objective in contrast to the British system. Adults in the work-force will be encouraged toward active participation and acceptance of responsibility through requirements of all government employees to demonstrate annually a minimum level of fitness and required safety knowledge. Employers in the private sector will be required to pay health maintenance taxes for employees on their payrolls who do not meet these same standards annually.

Ladies and gentlemen, it will not be easy for the leaders of this nation to implement these recommendations. But you have seen the Commission's fact-finding report, published on April 15, 2000. As Aldous Huxley once said, "Facts do not cease to exist just because they are ignored." The quality of life in these United States will certainly continue to deteriorate unless something is done. The first step is federal acceptance of responsibility for giving leadership to action plans designed to focus attention on health-related fitness for everyone and to enhance the quality of life for the entire population. This requires legislation to establish a federal Department of Human Wellness and Satisfaction and the allocation of funding essential to meet the challenge. As our legislators, you have it within your power to ensure that we take that first giant step. Members of the Congress, I thank you for your attention.

As a student of the curriculum process in physical education, you have been developing your personal understanding of the exciting potential of good education in the field of physical education. You have learned to ask some of the right questions and have developed curriculum decision-making skills. Hopefully, you are ready to write your alternative—and better—scenario for the physical education curriculum.

Appendix A
Developmental Information and
Conceptual Frameworks

Stages in Development
Taxonomies
    The Cognitive Domain
    The Affective Domain
    The Psychomotor Domain
    Physical Education
Purpose-Process Curriculum Framework

Stages in Cognitive and Personality Development, Birth through Adolescence

Age (Approximate)	Cognitive development Piaget	Moral judgment Kohlberg	Developmental progressions Test Content
0–1	*Early sensorimotor stage* Reflexes Early circular reactions Coordinating secondary schemas	*Early pre-moral stage* Completely egocentric No moral concepts	*Simple baby tests* Alertness Visual tracking
1–2	*Late sensorimotor stage* Object permanence Tertiary circular reactions Rudimentary thought	*Pre-moral stage* Fear of punishment, egocentric hedonism	*Baby tests* Sensorimotor schemas Primitive cognitive schemas
2–6	*Preoperational stage* Use of imagery, memory Conditioning, role learning Skill development Egocentric cognitive development Egocentric language development Gradual assimilation of schemas to one another	*Early conventional morality* Develops gradually as hedonism and egocentrism give way to desire to please parents and significant others "Good boy," "good girl" stage	*Basic skills, persistence* Memory span Association, role learning Direction following Vocabulary Factual knowledge Persistence, sustained attention Complex sensorimotor schemas

From *Child Development and Socialization* by J. E. Brophy. © 1980 St. Martin's Press, and reprinted by permission of the publisher.

Developmental tasks Havighurst		Personal-social development Erikson	Psychosexual stages Freud
PHYSICAL/INTELLECTUAL TASKS *Infancy* Eye-hand coordination Sensory discrimination Simple motor skills	*SOCIAL PERSONAL TASKS* *Infancy* Learning to eat solid foods Achieving emotional stability	*Trust vs. mistrust* Dependence on caretakers for consistent good care, especially feeding	*Oral stage* Successful feeding leads to optimism and security Problems lead to insecurity, hostility, mistrust
Toddlerhood Walking Talking Increasing self-reliance and independence	*Toddlerhood* Controlling body elimination Adjusting to socialization demands Beginning social play	*Autonomy vs. shame, doubt* Need to adjust to toilet training and other socialization demands while retaining sense of autonomy Danger of lasting sense of shame and self-doubt otherwise	*Early anal stage* Toilet training problems can lead to conflicts about compliance vs. resistance to external demands, messiness vs. obsessive neatness
Early childhood Skill learning and general bodily control Fine muscle control Developing and refining concepts of social and physical reality Learning about sex differences, developing an accurate body concept Learning through exploration, manipulation, play	*Early childhood* Learning cultural rules and expectations Learning about right and wrong Learning about sex roles Relating emotionally to family members and, later, to others, such as relatives and peers	*Initiative vs. guilt* Need to adjust to rules i.e. appearance, dress, behavior, without losing sense of initiative, curiosity, desire to explore and enjoy without becoming intolerably guilty or inhibited Developing sense of right and wrong which controls behavior, but without going too far and becoming guilt-ridden	*Late anal stage* Possible problems related to refusal to let go of possessions Later penuriousness, possessiveness *Phallic, Oepidal Stage* Exhibitionism, pride in body and skills Later repression at Oedipal stage leading to sex typing, conscience development

Age (Approximate)	Cognitive development Piaget	Moral judgment Kohlberg	Developmental progressions Test Content
6–12	*Stage of concrete operations* Continued schema assimilation, establishment of stable structure Attainment of conservations, reversibility, other logical operations Ability to use concrete operations for thinking and problem solving	*Advanced conventional morality* Gradual change in orientation from pleasing specific people to upholding rules and laws, maintaining authority Generalizing from specific situations to general rules of behavior	*Level I skills* More advanced problem solving requiring associative learning and direction following Logical operations as applied to familiar content Concrete similarities and differences More difficult vocabulary, memory, and knowledge items
12+	*Stage of formal operations* Reduced dependence on presence of objects and/ or imagery for thinking Development of advanced logical and mathematical schemas Ability to comprehend purely abstract or symbolic content	*Post-conventional morality* Development of abstract moral philosophies; legalistic morality based on ideas about rights and privileges Development of sophisticated moral code including ability to distinguish morality from legality	*Level II skills* Abstract and symbolic problem solving Abstract similarities and differences Difficult analogies, induction, deduction, and math problems Information processing and "problem finding" tasks

Developmental tasks Havighurst		Personal-social development Erikson	Psychosexual stages Freud
Middle childhood Mastering three R's at school Learning to learn through reading and other informative activities Learning basic facts of sciences and humanities Distinguishing fact from fantasy Learning through hobbies and recreational activities	*Middle childhood* Relating to teachers and other unfamiliar adults Achieving independence within the family Meeting expectations of peers, reference groups Developing conscience and self-regulation of behavior Coping with sex role expectations and other external pressures Developing frustration tolerance	*Industry vs. inferiority* Facing and meeting family, peer, and school expectations successfully, producing enjoyment of learning and practicing childhood skills Coping with frustration and failure without developing generally low self-esteem and sense of inferiority	*Latency* Repression of childhood sexuality, freeing energy for concentration on tasks of childhood, both intellectual and social-personal
Adolescence Mastering philosophy, higher mathematics, other abstract fields Mastering conceptual and theoretical aspects of sciences and humanities Learning about and being able to apply knowledge needed for adaptation in general and one's occupation in particular	*Adolescence* Adjusting to bodily changes, new emotions Achieving gradual independence from adults Questioning old values and reaffirming them or finding new ones Achieving intimate personal relationships Ultimately choosing mate, vocation, and life philosophy	*Identity vs. role diffusion* Need to question old values without sense of dread or loss of identity Need to gradually achieve new, more mature sense of identity and purpose *Intimacy vs. isolation* Need to learn to share intimacy without inhibition or dread, paving way for deeply satisfying personal relationships	*Genital stage* Infusion of new energy into system at adolescence temporarily breaks up stability, makes possible development of new, more mature personality, which includes mature sexual and intimacy relationships

The Cognitive Domain Taxonomy

1.0 Knowledge
    1.1 Knowledge of specifics
    1.2 Knowledge of ways and means of dealing with specifics
    1.3 Knowledge of universals and abstractions
2.0 Comprehension
    2.1 Translation
    2.2 Interpretation
    2.3 Extrapolation
3.0 Application
4.0 Analysis
    4.1 Analysis of elements
    4.2 Analysis of relationships
    4.3 Analysis of organizational principles
5.0 Synthesis
    5.1 Production of a unique communication
    5.2 Production of a plan or proposed set of operations
    5.3 Derivation of a set of abstract relations
6.0 Evaluation
    6.1 Judgments in terms of internal evidence
    6.2 Judgments in terms of external criteria

The Affective Domain Taxonomy

1.0 Receiving (Attending)
    1.1 Awareness
    1.2 Willingness to receive
    1.3 Controlled or selected attention
2.0 Responding
    2.1 Acquiescence in responding
    2.2 Willingness to respond
    2.3 Satisfaction in response
3.0 Valuing
    3.1 Acceptance of a value
    3.2 Preference for a value
    3.3 Commitment
4.0 Organization
    4.1 Conceptualization of a value
    4.2 Organization of a value system
5.0 Characterization by a value or value complex
    5.1 Generalized set
    5.2 Characterization

From *Taxonomy of Educational Objectives: The Classification of Educational Goals: Handbook II: Affective Domain* by David R. Krathwol, et al. Copyright © 1964 by Longman, Inc. Reprinted by permission of Longman, Inc., New York.

Harrow's Taxonomy of the Psychomotor Domain

1.00 Reflex movements

Action elicited without conscious volition in response to some stimuli; flexing, extending, stretching, and making postural adjustments; provides base for movement behavior.

1.10 Segmental reflexes

1.20 Intersegmental reflexes

1.30 Suprasegmental reflexes

2.00 Basic-fundamental movements

Inherent movement patterns based on combination of reflex movements; patterns provide starting point for improvement of perceptual and physical abilities; basis for complex skilled movement.

2.10 Locomotor movements

2.20 Non-locomotor movements

2.30 Manipulative movements

3.00 Perceptual abilities

Interpretation of stimuli from various modalities so that adjustments can be made; includes auditory, visual, kinesthetic, tactile, and coordinated perceptual abilities.

3.10 Kinesthetic discrimination

3.20 Visual discrimination

3.30 Auditory discrimination

3.40 Tactile discrimination

3.50 Coordinated abilities

4.00 Physical abilities

Characteristics which, when developed to a high degree, provide the learner with a sound, efficiently functioning body; organic vigor essential to the development of highly skilled movement.

4.10 Endurance

4.20 Strength

4.30 Flexibility

4.40 Agility

5.00 Skilled movements

Degree of efficiency in performing a complex movement task; consists of a vertical and a horizontal continuum; based upon inherent movement patterns.

5.10 Simple adaptive skill

5.20 Compound adaptive skill

5.30 Complex adaptive skill

6.00 Non-discursive communication
   Movement expressions that are part of a movement
   repertoire; movement interpretations that include any
   efficiently performed skilled movement; movement
   patterns designed to communicate a message to the
   viewer; ranges from facial expressions through
   sophisticated choreographies.
   6.10 Expressive movement
   6.20 Interpretive movement

From Simpson, E. J., "The Classification of Objectives, Psychomotor Domain" in *Illinois Teacher of Home Economics*, Vol. X, No. 4 (1966/1967), pp. 110–144. © Copyright (1966/1967) *Illinois Teacher of Home Economics*, Champaign, Il. Reprinted by permission.

Simpson's Taxonomy of the Psychomotor Domain

The classification scheme prepared by Elizabeth Simpson for *The Illinois Teacher of Home Economics* (1966–67) is presented here in its entirety. It should provide you with a more complete understanding of psychomotor behaviors and their relation to each other.

1.0 Perception—This is an essential first step in performing a motor act. It is the process of becoming aware of objects, qualities, or relations by way of the sense organs. It is a necessary but not sufficient condition for motor activity. It is basic in the situation—interpretation—action chain leading to motor activity. The category of perception has been divided into three subcategories indicating three different levels of the perception process. This level is a parallel of the first category, receiving or attending, in the affective domain.

    1.1 Sensory stimulation—Impingement of a stimulus or stimuli upon one or more of the sense organs.

        1.11 Auditory—Hearing or the sense of organs of hearing.

        1.12 Visual—Concerned with the mental pictures or images obtained through the eyes.

        1.13 Tactile—Pertaining to the sense of touch.

        1.14 Taste—Determine the relish or flavor of by taking a portion into the mouth.

        1.15 Smell—To perceive by excitation of the olfactory nerves.

        1.16 Kinesthetic—The muscle sense; pertaining to sensitivity from activation of receptors in muscles, tendons, and joints.

The preceding categories are not presented in any special order of importance, although, in Western cultures, the visual cues are said to have dominance, whereas in some cultures, the auditory and tactile cues may pre-empt the high position we give the visual. Probably no sensible ordering of these is possible at this time. It should also be pointed out that "the cues that guide action may change for a particular motor activity as learning progresses (e.g., kinesthetic cues replacing visual cues)."

    1.1 Sensory stimulation—Illustrative educational objectives.
Sensitivity to auditory cues in playing a musical instrument as a member of a group.

Awareness of differences in "hand" of various fabrics.

Sensitivity to flavors in seasoning food.

1.2 Cue selection—Deciding to what cues one must respond in order to satisfy the particular requirements of task performance. This involves identification of the cue or cues and associating them with the task to be performed. It may involve grouping of cues in terms of past experience and knowledge. Cues relevant to the situation are selected as a guide to action; irrelevant cues are ignored or discarded.

    1.21 Cue selection—Illustrative educational objectives.

    Recognition of operating difficulties with machinery through the sound of the machine in operation.

    Sensing where the needle should be set in beginning machine stitching.

    Recognizing factors to take into account in batting in a softball game.

1.3 Translation—Relating of perception to action in performing a motor act. This is the mental process of determining the meaning of the cues received for action. It involves symbolic translation, that is, having an image or being reminded of something, "having an idea," as a result of cues received. It may involve insight which is essential in solving a problem through perceiving the relationships essential to solution. Sensory translation is an aspect of this level. It involves "feedback," that is, knowledge of the effects of the process. Translation is a continuous part of the motor act being performed.

    1.31 Translation—Illustrative educational objectives.

    Ability to relate music to dance form.

    Ability to follow a recipe in preparing food.

    Knowledge of the "feel" of operating a sewing machine successfully and use of this knowledge as a guide in stitching.

2.0 Set—Set is a preparatory adjustment or readiness for a particular kind of action or experience. Three aspects of set have been identified: mental, physical, and emotional.

2.1 Mental set—Readiness, in the mental sense, to perform a certain motor act. This involves, as prerequisite, the level of perception and its subcategories. Discrimination, that is, using judgment in making distinction, is an aspect of mental set.

    2.11 Mental set—Illustrative educational objectives. Knowledge of steps in setting the table. Knowledge of tools appropriate to performance of various sewing operations.

2.2 Physical set—Readiness in the sense of having made the anatomical adjustments necessary for a motor act to be performed. Readiness, in the physical sense, involves receptor set, that is, sensory attending, or focusing the attention of the needed sensory organs, and postural set, or positioning of the body.

    2.21 Physical set—Illustrative educational objectives. Achievement of bodily stance preparatory to bowling. Positioning of hands preparatory to typing.

2.3 Emotional set—Readiness in terms of attitudes favorable to the motor acts taking place. Willingness to respond is implied.

    2.31 Emotional set—Illustrative educational objectives. Disposition to perform sewing machine operation to best of ability. Desire to operate a production drill press with skill.

3.0 Guided response—This is an early step in the development of skill. Emphasis here is upon the abilities which are components of the more complex skill. Guided response is the overt behavioral act of an individual under the guidance of the instructor or in response to self-evaluation where the student has a model or criteria against which he can judge his performance. Prerequisite to performance of the act are readiness to respond, in terms of set to produce the overt behavioral act and selection of the appropriate response must be made in order to satisfy the requirements of task performance. There appear to be two major subcategories, imitation and trial and error.

3.1 Imitation—Imitation is the execution of an act as a direct response to the perception of another person performing the act.

    3.11 Imitation—Illustrative educational objectives. Imitation of the process of stay-stitching the curved neck edge of a bodice.
Performing a dance step as demonstrated.
Debeaking a chick in the manner demonstrated.

3.2 Trial and error—Trying various responses, usually with some rationale for each response, until an appropriate response is achieved. The appropriate response is one which meets the requirements of task performance, that is, "gets the job done" or does it more efficiently. This level may be defined as multiple-response learning in which the proper response is selected out of varied behavior, possibly through the influence of reward and punishment.

    3.21 Trial and error—Illustrative educational objectives.
Discovering the most efficient method of ironing a blouse through trial of various procedures.
Determining the sequence for cleaning a room through trial of several patterns.

4.0 Mechanism—Learned response has become habitual. At this level, the learner has achieved a certain confidence and degree of proficiency in the performance of the act. The act is a part of his repertoire of possible responses to stimuli and the demands of situations where the response is an appropriate one. The response may be more complex than at the preceding level; it may involve some patterning in carrying out the task.

    4.1 Mechanism—Illustrative educational objectives.
Ability to perform a hand-hemming operation.
Ability to mix ingredients for butter cake.
Ability to pollinate an oat flower.

5.0 Complex overt response—At this level, the individual can perform a motor act that is considered complex because of the movement pattern required. At this level, skill has been attained. The act can be carried out smoothly and efficiently, that is, with minimum expenditure of time and energy. There are two subcategories: resolution of uncertainty and automatic performance.

5.1 Resolution of uncertainty—The act is performed without hesitation of the individual to get a mental picture of task sequence. That is, he knows the sequence required and so proceeds with confidence. The act is here defined as complex in nature.

5.11 Resolution of uncertainty—Illustrative educational objectives.
Skill in operating a milling machine.
Skill in setting up and operating a production band saw.
Skill in laying a pattern on fabric and cutting out a garment.

5.2 Automatic performance—At this level, the individual can perform a finely coordinated motor skill with a great deal of ease and muscle control.

6.0 Adaptation—Altering motor activities to meet the demands of new problematic situations requiring a physical response.

6.1 Adaptation—Illustrative educational objectives.
Developing a modern dance composition through adapting known abilities and skills in dance.

7.0 Origination—Creating new motor acts or ways of manipulating materials out of understandings, abilities, and skills developed in the psychomotor area.

7.1 Origination—Illustrative educational objectives.
Creation of a modern dance.
Creation of a new game requiring psychomotor response.

Physical Education Taxonomy

From Thompson, M. M. and B. A. Mann, An Holistic Approach to Education Curricula: Objectives Classification System for Elementary Schools. © 1977 Stipes Publishing Co., Champaign, Il. Reprinted by permission.

1.0 Mental development
    1.10 Knowledges and understandings of the human body
        1.11 Body parts and body segments
        1.12 Differentiation among body parts and segments
    1.20 Knowledges and understandings of movement patterns and skills
        1.21 Patterns and skills terminology
        1.22 Purpose and use of skills
        1.23 Pattern and skill continuity
    1.30 Knowledges and understandings of mechanical principles of movement
        1.31 Locomotion
        1.32 Body parts
        1.33 Propulsion of objects
        1.34 Receipt of objects
    1.40 Knowledges and understandings of physiologic factors
        1.41 Factors important to human movement
        1.42 Physiologic functioning and physical activity
        1.43 Factors of physical fitness
    1.50 Knowledges and understanding of rules and strategies
        1.51 Rules and/or performance regulations for specific activities
        1.52 Strategies for specific activities
        1.53 Safety factors related to rules and strategies
    1.60 Knowledges and understandings of common/related concepts
        1.61 Art
        1.62 Language arts
        1.63 Mathematics
        1.64 Music
        1.65 Science
        1.66 Social science
2.0 Social-emotional development
    2.10 Appreciation and acceptance of physical activity
        2.11 Enjoyment in physical endeavor
        2.12 Effects of physical activity
        2.13 Participation in movement activities
        2.14 Achievement of skill and success in movement activities
        2.15 Non-verbal communication through movement

2.20 Values of positive self-concept
    2.21 Abilities and limitations
    2.22 Body image
    2.23 Self-discipline
    2.24 Self-direction
2.30 Values relating to others
    2.31 Competition
    2.32 Cooperation
    2.33 Abilities and limitations of others
    2.34 Values and value systems of others
    2.35 Behavior of others
2.40 Concepts regarding groups
    2.41 Variety in group structures
    2.42 Work in variety of groups
        2.421 Decision-making
        2.422 Contribution
        2.423 Identification
2.50 Values related to the development of humor and empathy
    2.51 Incongruent behavior in self and others
    2.52 Incongruity potential
    2.53 Incongruity assignment appropriateness
3.0 Physical development
3.10 Agility
    3.11 Stop and start
    3.12 Change direction
    3.13 Change levels
3.20 Balance
    3.21 Static
    3.22 Dynamic
3.30 Coordination
    3.31 Eye-hand
    3.32 Eye-foot
    3.33 Speed
3.40 Endurance
    3.41 Cardiovascular
    3.42 Muscular
3.50 Flexibility
    3.51 Neck
    3.52 Trunk
    3.53 Limbs
    3.54 Extremities
3.60 Kinesthesis
    3.61 Non-locomotor and locomotor tasks
    3.62 Object handling tasks
    3.63 Varying environments

3.70 Rhythm
    3.71 Self imposed
    3.72 Externally imposed
3.80 Strength
    3.81 Arm strength
    3.82 Leg strength
    3.83 Total body strength
3.90 Power
    3.91 Arm power
    3.92 Leg power
4.0 Body handling development
    4.10 Sensori-motor abilities
        4.11 Body awareness
        4.12 Body in relation to space
        4.13 Body in relation to surrounding objects
        4.14 Discrimination
            4.141 Auditory
            4.142 Visual
            4.143 Tactile
            4.144 Kinesthetic
    4.20 Non-locomotor patterns and skills
        4.21 Total body
        4.22 Body parts and segments
    4.30 Locomotor patterns and skills
        4.31 Propulsion
        4.32 Absorption
    4.40 Combining locomotor and non-locomotor patterns and skills
        4.41 Arm movements
        4.42 Segmental movements
    4.50 Combining locomotor, non-locomotor and body awareness
        4.51 Laterality
        4.52 Balance
    4.60 Movement communication
        4.61 Imitative
        4.62 Expressive
        4.63 Interpretative
5.0 Object handling development
    5.10 Sensori-motor abilities
        5.11 Visual discrimination
        5.12 Auditory discrimination
        5.13 Tactile discrimination
        5.14 Kinesthetic discrimination

Purpose-Process Curriculum Framework

Key Purpose Concepts

I. Individual development: I move to fulfill my human developmental potential.
   A. Physiological efficiency: I move to improve or maintain my functional capabilities.
      1. *Circulo-respiratory efficiency.* I move to develop and maintain circulatory and respiratory functioning.
      2. *Mechanical efficiency.* I move to develop and maintain range and effectiveness of motion.
      3. *Neuro-muscular efficiency.* I move to develop and maintain motor functioning.
   B. Psychic equilibrium: I move to achieve personal integration.
      4. *Joy of movement.* I move to derive pleasure from movement experience.
      5. *Self-knowledge.* I move to gain self-understanding and appreciation.
      6. *Catharsis.* I move to release tension and frustration.
      7. *Challenge.* I move to test my prowess and courage.
II. Environmental coping: I move to adapt to and control my physical environment.
   C. Spatial orientation: I move to relate myself in three dimensional space.
      8. *Awareness.* I move to clarify my conception of my body and my position in space.
      9. *Relocation.* I move in a variety of ways to propel or project myself.
      10. *Relationships.* I move to regulate my body position in relation to the objects or persons in my environment.
   D. Object manipulation: I move to give impetus to and to absorb the force of objects.
      11. *Maneuvering weight.* I move to support, resist or transport mass.
      12. *Object projection.* I move to impart momentum and direction to a variety of objects.
      13. *Object reception.* I move to intercept a variety of objects by reducing or arresting their momentum.

From A. E. Jewett and M. R. Mullan, *Curriculum Design: Purposes and processes in physical education teaching-learning.* © 1977 American Alliance for Health, Physical Education, Recreation and Dance, Reston, VA. Reprinted by permission. (Concepts have been rephrased to accommodate to current language usage. Developed primarily through group study from 1970 through 1976 with the leadership of Ann E. Jewett, University of Wisconsin, Madison, and University of Georgia, Athens. Major contributors: Iris Bliss, Donald K. Brault, Gretchen A. Brockmeyer, Peggy A. Chapman, Sheryl L. Gotts, Wilma A. Harrington, Laura J. Huelster, L. Sue Jones, Sandra M. Knox, Douglas F. Knox, Marilyn J. LaPlante, Marie R. Mullan, Alison Poe, Sarah M. Robinson, Gail Royce, Lee Smith, Charles L. Wuerpel.)

III. Social interaction: I move to relate to others.
   E. Communication: I move to share my ideas and feelings with others.
      14. *Expression.* I move to convey my ideas and feelings.
      15. *Clarification.* I move to enhance the meaning of other communication forms.
      16. *Simulation.* I move to create an advantageous image or situation.
   F. Group interaction: I move to function in harmony with others.
      17. *Teamwork.* I move to cooperate in pursuit of common goals.
      18. *Competition.* I move to vie for individual or group goals.
      19. *Leadership.* I move to motivate and influence group members to achieve common goals.
   G. Cultural involvement: I move to take part in movement activities which constitute an important part of my society.
      20. *Participation.* I move to develop my capabilities for taking part in movement activities of my society.
      21. *Movement appreciation.* I move to become knowledgeable and appreciative of sports and expressive movement forms.
      22. *Cultural understanding.* I move to understand, respect, and strengthen the cultural heritage.

Movement Process Categories

A. *Generic movement:* Those movement operations or processes which facilitate the development of characteristic and effective motor patterns. They are typically exploratory operations in which the learner receives or "takes in" data as he or she moves.
   1. *Perceiving:* Awareness of total body relationships and of self in motion. These awarenesses may be evidenced by body positions or motoric acts; they may be sensory in that the mover feels the equilibrium of body weight and the movement of limbs; or they may be evidenced cognitively through identification, recognition, or distinction.

2. *Patterning:* Arrangement and use of body parts in successive and harmonious ways to achieve a movement pattern or skill. This process is dependent on recall and performance of a movement previously demonstrated or experienced.

B. *Ordinative movement:* The processes of organizing, refining, and performing skillful movement. The processes involved are directed toward the organization of perceptual-motor abilities with a view to solving particular movement tasks or requirements.

3. *Adapting:* Modification of a patterned movement to meet externally imposed task demands. This would include modification of a particular movement to perform it under different conditions.

4. *Refining:* Acquisition of smooth, efficient control in performing a movement pattern or skill by mastery of spatial and temporal relations. This process deals with the achievement of precision in motor performance and habituation of performance under more complex conditions.

C. *Creative movement:* Those motor performances which include the processes of inventing or creating movement which will serve the personal (individual) purposes of the learner. The processes employed are directed toward discovery, integration, abstraction, idealization, emotional objectification, and composition.

5. *Varying:* Invention or construction of personally unique options in motor performance. These options are limited to different ways of performing specific movement; they are of an immediate situational nature and lack any predetermined movement behavior which has been externally imposed on the mover.

6. *Improvising:* Extemporaneous origination or initiation of personally novel movement or combination of movement. The processes involved may be stimulated by a situation externally structured, although conscious planning on the part of the performer is not usually required.

7. *Composing:* Combination of learned movement into personally unique motor designs or the invention of movement patterns new to the performer. The performer creates a motor response in terms of a personal interpretation of the movement situation.

Appendix B
Curriculum Planning Documents

Rationale and Goals
    Delta School District
    Manitoba Department of Education
    Ohio Department of Education
Scope and Sequence Charts
    Manitoba Department of Education
    Ohio Department of Education
Resource Units
    Flag Football, British Columbia Ministry of Education
    Grade 5 Games, Calgary Catholic School District
    Badminton, Louisiana Department of Public Education
    Grade 7 Fitness, Manitoba Department of Education
    Grade 6 Games, Toledo Public Schools
Yearly Plans
    Lyons Township High School
Unit Plans
    Group Instruction—Grade 9 Archery
    Individualized Instruction—Grade 5 Track and Field

Rationale and Goals

Delta School District

Programme Philosophy

The Delta Physical-Health Education Programme should:

1. Provide students with the understandings, attitudes and abilities required to consciously maintain physical-health throughout life;
2. Prepare students to make reasoned choices when selecting exercises, physical activities and health habits;
3. Provide a rationale for encouraging participation in extra-curricular and community programmes;
4. Provide students with the opportunity to develop gross and fine motor skills;
5. Provide students with the opportunity to improve and maintain physical fitness;
6. Provide learning experiences which are directly related to objectives contained in other curriculums;
7. Determine how each student's progress in the affective, cognitive and psychomotor domains will be evaluated;
8. Integrate learning from the affective, cognitive, and psychomotor domains;
9. Provide a variety of active, enjoyable, and safe ways for students to learn;
10. Accommodate a wide variety of learning and performance abilities.

Programme Goals

1. Students will have the knowledge and ability to develop and maintain physical fitness through adult life.
    1.1 Students will have experienced the process of developing and maintaining physical fitness.
    1.2 Students will be able to apply the principles of training and conditioning to the design of personal exercise programmes.
    1.3 Students will be able to apply their knowledge of exercise and physical fitness to improve their performance in specific sports.
2. Students will be able to apply their knowledge of biomechanical principles to the effective performance of fine and gross motor skills.
    2.1 Students will be able to perform effectively a wide variety of fundamental movement skills.

2.2 Students will be able to apply knowledge of the principles of balance and stability to skilled performance.

2.3 Students will be able to apply knowledge of the principles of force production, force application, and force absorption to skilled performance.

2.4 Students will be able to apply knowledge of the laws of motion to skilled performance.

2.5 Students will be able to apply knowledge of projectiles to skilled performance.

2.6 Students will be able to apply knowledge of biomechanical principles to analyze performance skills.

3. Students will be able to apply knowledge of the body's systems to their participation in physical activity, and to maintenance of physical-health.

3.1 Students will be able to apply knowledge of the musculo-skeletal system, the cardio-vascular system and the respiratory system to participation in physical activity, and to maintenance of physical health.

3.2 Students will be able to apply their knowledge of the thermo-regulatory system to participation in vigorous physical activities.

3.3 Students will be able to apply knowledge of good health habits to their personal lives.

4. Students will be able to apply knowledge of behaviors, organization, rules and strategies to performance in selected physical activities.

4.1 Students will be able to apply knowledge of appropriate behavior to performance in selected physical activities.

4.2 Students will be able to apply knowledge of organization and rules to performance in selected physical activities.

4.3 Students will be able to apply knowledge of strategies to performance in selected physical activities.

Manitoba Department of Education

Rationale

Two needs identified in the mid-seventies have directly contributed to the development of the new K-12 Physical Education curriculum. The first, defined in a Department of Health and Welfare document entitled, *A New Perspective on the Health of Canadians,* is the need to deal with the health problems which lead to tremendous financial costs and personal losses. Many of these problems can be traced to inadequate physical activity. The second, identified as a result of public discussion, is the need to develop leisure-time activities that can provide a change of pace, a source of relaxation, and an opportunity to re-energize.

These increasingly complex challenges demand a vigorous response. Since each individual must assume the responsibility for choosing a personal lifestyle, the physical education program provided in our schools must prepare students to make rational decisions. In this way, the physical education programs can contribute significantly in assisting students to select lifestyles conducive to good health. To accomplish this aim, teachers of physical education must maintain sensitivity to the needs and interests of students and society.

It is imperative that the physical education program not only contribute to students' present levels of health and fitness but also prepare them for lifelong involvement in meaningful physical activities which will enhance the quality of their lives. Therefore, the physical education program must foster the development of habits which will be practiced throughout life. These habits will help prevent many health problems, help people cope with the stress and strain of modern life, and encourage people to develop healthful leisure-time pursuits.

Simply stated, the primary aim of the physical education program from kindergarten through senior high schools in Manitoba is

> To help students develop and participate in a purposeful, physically active lifestyle, which will enable them to experience a more enjoyable quality of life—today and tomorrow.

Learning Goals and Related Objectives

The learning goals of physical education are the general statements of the skills and attitudes that students are to develop. These goals are constant throughout the K-12 physical education program; however, at each stage, the objectives which prepare students to reach these goals vary. Such variance is necessary because of the developmental stages of maturation and learning.

The child/student should demonstrate an increasing ability to:

1. Develop physical well-being.
2. Develop desired movement patterns through the neuromuscular system.
3. Express ideas, thoughts, and feelings with confidence through physical activity.
4. Develop an independence in pursuing physical activity throughout life.
5. Develop safety and survival practices.
6. Develop positive social interactions through a variety of physical activities.

Ohio Department of Education

Structured Overviews of Beliefs, Goals and Objectives

From Marion Sanborn and others, *Elementary School Physical Education.* © 1978 Ohio Department of Education, Columbus, OH. Reprinted by permission.

Belief A.
"Moving about" or investigating in a challenging physical setting is basic to children understanding themselves and their environments.

Goal A1.
Children need time to "move about" or explore, with a great deal of freedom, the physical education environments.

Objectives:
Children need time:

A1.1 To get a feel for the size, shape, and boundaries of the physical education environment.
(Environmental)
A1.2 To explore the various kinds of climbing and gymnastic apparatus.
(Apparatus)
A1.3 To explore with many different kinds of small equipment.
(Small Equipment)

Goal A2.
Children need opportunities to "move about" with equipment and/or in environments of their choice.

Objectives:
Children need opportunities:

A2.1 To choose the equipment with which they wish to work.
(Equipment Choice)
A2.2 To structure their environment for themselves and for others.
(Environment Choice)
A2.3 To choose to work independently or with other children.
(Social Choice)
A2.4 To stay with a task of their choice.
(Task Choice)

Belief B.
In the physical education environment, children need to feel comfortable moving in the presence of others and to cooperate with others.

Goal B1.
Children need to develop both an acceptance and a trust of others in movement activities.

Objectives:
Children need:

B1.1 To consider the limitations and safety of others and to expect the same consideration from others.
(Mutual Trust)
B1.2 To develop an awareness of the differences and similarities of their classmates.
(Awareness)
B1.3 To develop a sympathetic concern for the feelings and needs of others.
(Concern)
B1.4 To value contributions of others and of themselves.
(Valuing)

Goal B2.
Children need to grow in ability to function as contributing members of a group.

Objectives:
Children need to be able:

B2.1 To share.
       (Sharing)
B2.2 To move in a variety of relationships with one or more
       persons.
       (Relationships)
B2.3 To cooperate with others in solving mutual problems.
       (Cooperation)
B2.4 To recognize conflict and work toward its resolution.
       (Conflict)
B2.5 To identify qualities of others and use them for the
       benefit of the group.
       (Qualities)

Goal B3.
To make appropriate decisions individuals must be aware of
choices of behavior and action.

Objectives:
Children need:
B3.1 To learn that there are many ways to solve a problem, to
       secure a goal, and to reach an objective.
       (Problem Solving)
B3.2 To realize that there are a number of choices of behavior
       available to them in movement activities.
       (Behavior Choices)
B3.3 To learn to anticipate possible consequences of different
       behavior choices and to accept responsibility for their
       choices.
       (Anticipation-Responsibility)
B3.4 To be able to cooperate with both teammates and
       opponents in competitive activities.
       (Cooperation-Competition)

Belief C.
**To gain control over themselves and their environments,
children need experiences which challenge them to develop
movement abilities and skills.**

Goal C1.

Children need to be able to utilize the elements of space, time, effort and flow to increase their movement repertoire and to enhance the quality of their movement.

Objectives:
Children need:

C1.1 To understand and move in self space and general space; to move into general space going forward, backward, sideways, diagonally, and up and down, using high, medium and low levels, and using a variety of ranges (wide-narrow, long-short, far-near) and planes. (Space)

C1.2 To move at different speeds, to accelerate and decelerate and to differentiate between sudden and sustained movement. (Time)

C1.3 To judge and apply efficient amounts of effort needed for different tasks. To feel, maintain, and relax muscle tension at appropriate times. (Effort)

C1.4 To understand the difference between bound and free movement and demonstrate fluency and restraint while in movement. (Flow)

C1.5 To use different combinations of space dimensions to provide variations in body shapes. (Control)

Goal C2.

Children need opportunities to increase awareness of their bodies and to expand their movement potential.

Objectives:
Children need:

C2.1 To be able to identify parts of the body and to control their movement in space. (Body Parts)

C2.2 To understand and be able to make different body shapes—straight, curved, bent, and twisted—and combinations of these shapes. (Body Shapes)

C2.3 To be aware that their trunks and other body parts can stretch, bend, twist, turn, swing, sway, push, pull, lift, and fall.
(Nonlocomotor Movement)

C2.4 To be able to balance in a variety of postures, using different body parts as the base of support, to maintain balance while moving.
(Balance)

C2.5 To be aware of the sides of the body and to know left from right.
(Laterality)

C2.6 To develop ability to project laterality away from the body into the spatial environment.
(Directionality)

C2.7 To develop an awareness of body location in space in relation to the total space and to objects and other people occupying that space.
(Spatial Awareness)

C2.8 To be able to travel through space by rocking, rolling, steplike actions, sliding and flight actions for the purpose of developing basic locomotor movements.
(Locomotor Movements)

Goal C3.
Children need to learn to control their bodies in different ways in a variety of situations.

Objectives:
Children need to be able:

C3.1 To support their body weight on different body parts in many situations.
(Support)

C3.2 To absorb the force of their body weight safely from both on- and off-balance positions.
(Give)

C3.3 To link movements together smoothly.
(Sequences)

C3.4 Children need to manage themselves by mounting and dismounting, and moving over, under, around and through a variety of small and large equipment.
(Management)

C3.5 To respond to different rhythmic patterns.
(Rhythm)

Goal C4.
Children need experience controlling (using and accommodating force with) a variety of objects.

Objectives:
Children need to be able:

C4.1 To send objects by rolling, tossing, throwing and slinging.
(Send)

C4.2 To receive objects by catching and trapping.
(Receive)

C4.3 To hit, strike and kick different objects using different body parts and implements.
(Strike)

Goal C5.
Children need confidence in their ability to meet the requirements of new movement challenges.

Objectives:
Children need:

C5.1 To determine what is required in a new situation and to assess the skills and abilities they already possess that will enable them to perform safely.
(Judgment)

C5.2 To realize that performance modifications may be needed to achieve success in a specific task.
(Trials)

C5.3 To set their goals in accordance with their own past performance rather than in relation to other children.
(Goals)

C5.4 To realize that while ability to perform should increase with age, it does not improve at an even rate (plateaus, regressions, and spurts can be expected).
(Uneven Improvement)

C5.5 To realize that fear is natural and that courage is facing fear and trying to overcome it sensibly.
(Courage)

Goal C6.
Children need to be able to use movement creatively for purposes of expression and communication.

Objectives:
Children need:

C6.1 To be able to use locomotor and nonlocomotor movements, as well as gestures, to express feelings and ideas.
(Expressing)

C6.2 To be able to move creatively in response to different stimuli: sound, light, color, form, and a variety of manipulative materials.
(Stimuli)

C6.3 To be able to select and link movements in sequence.
(Sequencing)

C6.4 To have opportunities to create their own games and dances.
(Creating)

C6.5 To be able to modify games.
(Modifying)

C6.6 To be provided with an environment that will encourage them to create their own movement challenges.
(Self-Challenge)

Goal C7.
Children need opportunities to develop understandings and skills specific to traditional dance and sport forms in their cultural settings.

Objectives:
Children need:

C7.1 To be provided opportunities to develop understandings and movement skills characteristic of dance patterns.
(Dance)

C7.2 To be provided opportunities to develop understandings of and skills specific to traditional sports and games.
(Sports)

Belief D.
Children will grow in appreciation of movement as they realize the meaning movement has in their lives.

Goal D1.
Children need to become aware of movement as a total experience.

Objectives:
Children need:
D1.1 To increase physical awareness of movement.
(Physical Awareness)
D1.2 To be aware of the relationships between movement and emotions.
(Emotional Awareness)
D1.3 To develop an aesthetic appreciation of movement.
(Aesthetic Awareness)

Goal D2.
Children need to realize the effect movement has on their lives.

Objectives:
Children need to realize:

D2.1 That movement is a means of maintaining life.
(Sustaining Life)
D2.2 That movement helps them to investigate and acquire knowledge.
(Investigation)
D2.3 That movement skills already mastered can be used in new situations.
(Skill Transfer)
D2.4 That moving for pleasure is sufficient reason for moving.
(Pleasure)
D2.5 That movement is a means of communication.
(Communication)

Belief E.
Understanding and applying movement principles and strategies will increase effectiveness of movement.

Goal E1.
Children need to understand that stability is related to the size and shape of the base of support, the level and weight of the object and the center of gravity.

Objectives:
Children need to know that:

E1.1 Generally speaking, the larger the base of support, the greater the stability.
(Size of Base)

E1.2 Stability can be increased by balancing body parts over the base of support.
(Balance)

E1.3 Stability can be increased or decreased by changing the shape of the base of support.
(Shape of Base)

E1.4 Stability can be increased by lowering the body over the base of support, thus lowering the center of gravity.
(Center of Gravity)

E1.5 To maintain stability, the proper amount of tension must be maintained in appropriate body parts.
(Tension)

Goal E2.

Children need to understand and apply the principles involved in efficiently controlling force.

Objectives:

Children need to know that:

E2.1 Force can be increased by moving more body parts in rhythmic sequence in the desired movement.
(Rhythmic Sequence)

E2.2 Force can be increased by using the opposite arm and leg which allows for an increase in the length of levers and in trunk rotation.
(Opposition)

E2.3 Force can be increased by transferring weight from the back to the front foot when sending an object (sending) and the effect of on-coming force (receiving) can be decreased by shifting weight from the front to the back foot—letting the body "give" in the direction of the force.
(Weight Transfer)

E2.4 Force is most effective when applied through the center of an object and should usually be applied in the direction of the target.
(Point of Contact)

E2.5 Greater force and speed can be achieved if the action of the body is allowed to continue after the point of release or contact.
(Follow Through)

Goal E3.
Children need to understand that the flight of projectiles is influenced by force, gravity, spin and angle of contact.

Objectives:
Children need to know that:

E3.1 The speed and distance an object travels is determined by the amount of force applied.
(Force)

E3.2 The path or trajectory of an object will be influenced by the point of release or contact.
(Point of Release)

E3.3 Gravity affects the flight paths of objects.
(Gravity)

E3.4 When a ball or other object hits a flat, hard surface, it will leave the surface (rebound) at almost the same angle at which it contacts the surface.
(Angle of Rebound)

E3.5 Spin on an object will effect the angle of rebound.
(Spin)

E3.6 In flight, an object will tend to veer toward the direction of its spin.
(Spin)

Goal E4.
Children need to understand the effects of physical activity on the body.

Objectives:
Children need to know:

E4.1 That physical fitness can only be maintained through a regular and vigorous program of physical activity.
(Maintenance)

E4.2 That physical fitness can be improved by increasing the number of repetitions, the amount of resistance and/or the speed of the activity.
(Improvement)

E4.3 That activities to improve physical fitness should begin at one's present level, and be gradually increased over a reasonable period of time.
(Progression)

Goal E5.

Children need to understand and use knowledges, rules, and strategies basic to a variety of game activities.

Objectives:

Children need to:

E5.1   Recognize, understand and assume responsibility for rules which govern play.
(Rules)

E5.2   Understand the advantages of teamwork.
(Teamwork)

E5.3   Understand the principles of offensive and defensive play.
(Offense-Defense)

E5.4   Be able to position themselves advantageously in relation to the goal, ball, opponents, and teammates.
(Positioning)

Scope and Sequence Charts

Manitoba Department of Education

Overview of Program

The core objectives (fundamental movement skills and concepts) are developed progressively from K-12. The activities are the means of achieving these objectives. Selection will be determined in large measure by the facilities that are available.

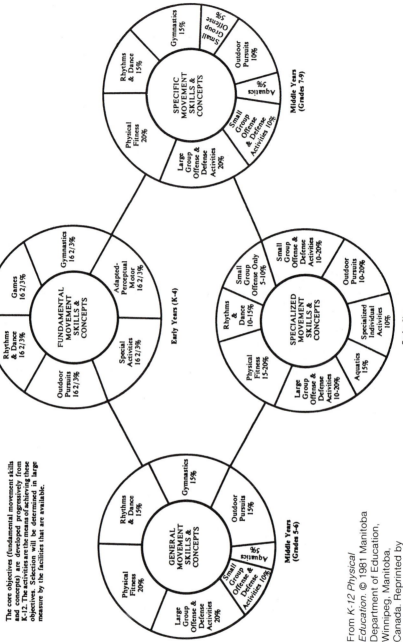

From *K-12 Physical Education.* © 1981 Manitoba Department of Education, Winnipeg, Manitoba, Canada. Reprinted by permission.

ACTIVITY SCOPE AND SEQUENCE: K-12 PHYSICAL EDUCATION

The following chart has been prepared to help teachers determine the appropriate grade levels for introducing activities. It should be noted that where specific activities are identified, they are regarded as an optional means to achieving the objectives identified in the guide.

ACTIVITY	K	1	2	3	4	5	6	7	8	9	SH
1.0 Motor Skills											
1.1 Development of basic motor skills				↑							
1.2 Use in activities											↑
1.3 Adapting for specific activities											↑
1.4 Refining activity skills											↑
2.0 Physical Fitness											
2.1 Development and maintenance											↑
2.2 Self-testing											↑
2.3 Fitness testing											↑
2.4 Specific training methods											↑
2.5 Theory											
2.5.1 Components of fitness											↑
2.5.2 Nutrition											↑
2.5.3 Posture – incidental											↑
– specific											↑
2.5.4 Principles of exercise											↑
2.5.5 Physiology of exercise											↑
2.6 Remedial and corrective programs											↑
3.0 Aquatics											
3.1 Basic strokes											↑
3.2 Dives											↑
3.3 Lifesaving (survival and safety)											↑
3.4 Speed swimming											↑
3.5 Scuba diving											↑
3.6 Synchronized swimming											↑
3.7 Water awareness		↑									
3.8 Water safety											↑

From *K-12 Physical Education*. © 1981 Manitoba Department of Education, Winnipeg, Manitoba, Canada. Reprinted by permission.

ACTIVITY	K	1	2	3	4	5	6	7	8	9	SH
3.9 Water polo – lead ups											▲
– game											▲
4.0 Rhythm and Dance											
4.1 Creative											▲
4.1.1 Modern											▲
4.1.2 Jazz											▲
4.1.3 Modern rhythmic gymnastics											▲
4.1.4 Synchronized swimming											▲
4.2 Folk and square											▲
4.3 Social and popular											▲
5.0 Gymnastics											
5.1 Educational										▲	
5.2 Modern rhythmic											▲
5.3 Olympic											▲
6.0 Low-Organized Games											
7.0 Large-Group Offense/Defense											
7.1 Basketball – lead-ups									▲		
– game											▲
7.2 Broom ball											
7.3 Field hockey – lead-ups									▲		
– game											▲
7.4 Floor hockey – lead-ups						▲					
– game											▲
7.5 Flag/touch football – lead-ups									▲		
– game											▲
7.6 Lacrosse							▲				
7.7 Ringette											▲
7.8 Rugby								▲			
7.9 Speedball and speed-away							▲				
7.10 Soccer – lead-ups								▲			
– game											▲

ACTIVITY	K	1	2	3	4	5	6	7	8	9	SH
7.11 Softball – lead-ups									↑		
– game										↑	
7.12 Team Handball – lead-ups								↑			
– game											↑
7.13 Volleyball – lead-ups								↑			
– game											↑
8.0 Small-Group Offense/Defense											
8.1 Badminton – lead-ups									↑		
– game											↑
8.2 Combatives											↑
8.3 Cross-country run							↑				
8.4 Handball											↑
8.5 Judo											↑
8.6 Karate											↑
8.7 Pursuit relay											↑
8.8 Racquet ball											↑
8.9 Squash											↑
8.10 Shuttle relay										↑	
8.11 Table tennis											↑
8.12 Wrestling											↑
8.13 Tennis – lead-ups									↑		
– game											↑
9.0 Small-Group Offense Only											
9.1 Archery											↑
9.2 5-pin bowling											↑
9.3 10-pin bowling											↑
9.4 Golf											↑
9.5 Smallbore shooting											↑
9.6 Trap shooting											↑
10.0 Outdoor Pursuits											
10.1 Backpacking											↑

Scope and Sequence Chart, cont.

ACTIVITY		K	1	2	3	4	5	6	7	8	9	SH
10.2	Camping											↑
10.3	Climbing											↑
10.4	Cross-country skiing							↑				↑
10.5	Curling – jam-pail											↑
	– game											
10.6	Cycling											↑
10.7	Inuit games							↑				↑
10.8	Hiking											↑
10.9	Horseback riding											↑
10.10	Ice skating											↑
10.11	Orienteering											↑
10.12	Roller skating											↑
10.13	Snowshoeing											↑
10.14	Survival skills and techniques											↑
10.14.1	Cardiopulmonary resuscitation											↑
10.14.2	First aid											↑
10.14.3	Small craft safety											
10.14.4	Shelter building							↑				
10.15	Tobogganing											↑
10.16	Track and field											↑
10.16.1	Discus											↑
10.16.2	High jump											↑
10.16.3	Hurdles											↑
10.16.4	Long jump											↑
10.16.5	Long-distance runs											↑
10.16.6	Middle-distance runs											↑
10.16.7	Sprints											↑
10.16.9	Triple jump											↑
10.16.10	Pole vault											↑
10.16.11	Water skiing											↑

Physical Education

Preschool Through Grade Six

From Marion Sanborn and others, *Elementary School Physical Education.* © 1978 Ohio Department of Education, Columbus, OH. Reprinted by permission.

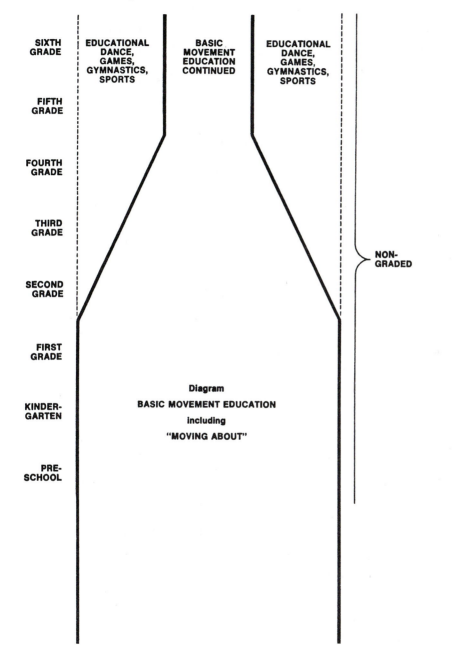

SIXTH GRADE

FIFTH GRADE

FOURTH GRADE

THIRD GRADE

SECOND GRADE

FIRST GRADE

KINDER-GARTEN

PRE-SCHOOL

EDUCATIONAL DANCE, GAMES, GYMNASTICS, SPORTS

BASIC MOVEMENT EDUCATION CONTINUED

EDUCATIONAL DANCE, GAMES, GYMNASTICS, SPORTS

NON-GRADED

Diagram
BASIC MOVEMENT EDUCATION
including
"MOVING ABOUT"

Content Emphasis in Kindergarten Through Grade 6

Included in this section are goals, objectives, and activities which can be used to introduce or review basic goals and skills introduced earlier in the year. Whether you spend a few minutes or weeks on each activity will be determined by the needs of your class. For this reason, the lessons are not organized into daily plans.

Two lists of activities are suggested for each grade level; one with equipment and one without. Although equipment is essential in teaching physical education, not all teachers will have adequate equipment when they begin to use this guide. These model programs will get classes started until equipment is available.

Eleven goals underlie these activities:

Goal A1—Moving about
     B1—Accepting and trusting others
     B2—Contributing to the group
     C1—Space, time, effort, flow
     C2—Awareness of body parts
     C4—Controlling objects
     D1—Movement as a total experience
     D2—Effects of movement

For fifth and sixth graders, in addition to the above—

Goal E1—Stability
     E4—Effects of physical activity
     E5—Knowledges, rules, strategies

Although some of the activities are identical in each grade level, the approach to each group should be different. The amount of time spent on certain activities should also vary with each grade level, as indicated by the diagrams.

Suggested Model Programs for Third Grade

With equipment			Without equipment		
A1.2	a.	apparatus	A1.1	b.	explore room
B1.1	c.	others' safety	D2.1	a.	run-walls
C3.1	a.	hanging	C1.1	a.	self space
A1.3	a.	stations		b.	explore self space
C4.1	h.	throw hard		d.	general space
	j.	beanbags		e.	move to space
E2.1	a.	throw-rhythm		f.	explore self space
E2.4	b.	kick		g.	explore general space

B1.3	b. getting partners	B1.3	b. getting partners
	c. discuss partners		c. discuss partners
B2.1	a. agree		d. partner shapes
	d. share time	C1.2	a. accelerate
C4.1	e. dribble		c. decelerate
	f. other hand	D2.5	a. run, feel
C4.3	h. kick to a partner	E1.1	a. stable
			b. balance
C1.1	a. self space	E1.2	a. balance, arms
	b. explore self space		c. front scale
	c. space bubble, general space	E1.6	d. front scale
	d. general space	E1.3	a. shape, base
	e. move to space	E1.5	a. tension
C1.2	b. increase speed		b. tension
	d. decrease speed	E2.1	b. jump, absorb
	e. shape-roll		
B3.2	a. choices, behavior		
B3.2	c. choices		

Resource Units

Activity sequence chart—Flag Football
Skills

From *Secondary Physical Education Curriculum and Resource Guide.* © 1980 Ministry of Education, Province of British Columbia, Victoria, B.C., Canada. Reprinted by permission.

	Flag football Level			
	I	II	III	IV
A. Basic skills				
1. Stance				
a) lineman				
i) 3 pt.		●		
ii) 4 pt.		●		
b) back				
i) 2 pt.	●			
ii) 3 pt.		●		
B. Individual offensive skills				
1. Centering				
a) T formation	●			
b) shotgun formation		●		
2. Passing				
a) overhand				
i) stationary	●			
ii) drop back	●			
iii) running		●		
iv) jump			●	

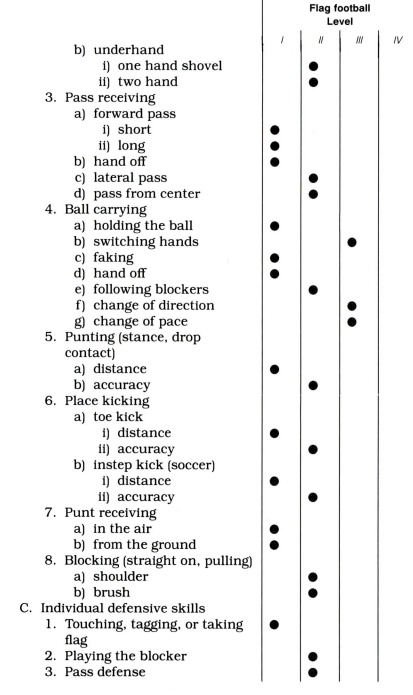

Skills	Flag football Level			
	I	II	III	IV
b) underhand				
i) one hand shovel		●		
ii) two hand		●		
3. Pass receiving				
a) forward pass				
i) short	●			
ii) long	●			
b) hand off	●			
c) lateral pass		●		
d) pass from center		●		
4. Ball carrying				
a) holding the ball	●			
b) switching hands			●	
c) faking	●			
d) hand off	●			
e) following blockers		●		
f) change of direction			●	
g) change of pace			●	
5. Punting (stance, drop contact)				
a) distance	●			
b) accuracy		●		
6. Place kicking				
a) toe kick				
i) distance	●			
ii) accuracy		●		
b) instep kick (soccer)				
i) distance	●			
ii) accuracy		●		
7. Punt receiving				
a) in the air	●			
b) from the ground	●			
8. Blocking (straight on, pulling)				
a) shoulder		●		
b) brush		●		
C. Individual defensive skills				
1. Touching, tagging, or taking flag	●			
2. Playing the blocker		●		
3. Pass defense		●		

Skills

	Flag football Level			
	I	*II*	*III*	*IV*
D. Team play				
1. Offensive team play				
a) shotgun formation		●		
b) T formation		●		
c) variations of T			●	
d) double wing			●	
e) place kick		●		
f) kick off long, short			●	
g) punt long, short			●	
2. Defensive team play				
a) line play	●			
b) containing end play	●			
c) deep backs	●			
d) linebackers		●		
e) block kicks			●	
f) man-to-man coverage		●		
g) zone coverage			●	
3. Strategy				
a) offensive				
i) formations		●		
ii) pass patterns		●		
b) defensive				
i) against pass		●		
ii) against run		●		
iii) standard defensive alignments 5–2,4–4,4–3,6–2				●
E. Rules	●			
F. Officiating			●	

Suggested References
1. Allen, George H. *George Allen's New Handbook of Football Drills.* New Jersey: Prentice-Hall, 1974.
2. Canada. Royal Canadian Air Force. *Flag Football: Playing, Coaching and Officiating.* Ottawa: Queen's Printer, 1960.
3. Marciani, Louis M. *Touch and Flag Football. A Guide for Players and Officials.* South Brunswick: A. S. Barnes, 1976.
4. Moore, Jim and Tyler Micoleau. *Football Techniques Illustrated.* New York: Ronald Press, 1978.

From LeRoy Pellatier, et al., *Calgary Separate Physical Education Project.* © 1977 Calgary Catholic School District, Calgary, Alberta, Canada. Reprinted by permission.

Grade 5, Unit 22. Group Interaction Games—Goal Oriented

1. *Concepts to be developed*

Teamwork	Participation (Partners, One on One,
Competition	Two on One, Two on Two)
Joy of movement	Self-knowledge

2. *Skills to be developed*

   Co-operating with a partner to plan a game
   Challenging a partner in offense or defense
   Sharing ideas
   Recognition of strategies

3. *Generalizations*

   How movement occurs within the spatial area determines how successful a player or team is.
   Fast cutting can create spaces.
   Defensive play depends on the person's ability to anticipate movement and make perceptive judgments quickly.

4. *Performance objectives*

   To demonstrate co-operation and skill development through planning and playing goal-oriented games using a one on one, two on one, or two on two relationship.

   1. To co-operate with a partner to plan a "goal-oriented" game establishing
      a) equipment
      b) rules for play
      c) spatial boundaries and target
   2. To plan and demonstrate offensive strategy to challenge and score.
   3. To plan and demonstrate a defensive strategy to prevent scoring.
   4. To share your game with other students by demonstrating the game for other students and/or changing partners.
   5. To discuss "tactics" involved in offensive and defensive strategy.

5. *Problems for students*

   Suggestions for teachers

   Cue questions. Classroom planning—What information do we need to plan a "goal-oriented game"?

   What do we mean by "goal-oriented"? Can you give an example of some equipment we have that could be used for a goal? (hoops, pylons, chalked wall markers, etc.) Do each of these goals or targets have a space the object can go through or hit?

What object can we use on a one to one situation that we could move through space to score on the goal? (variety of size and shaped balls, pucks, bean bags, etc.)

What limitation can we have for boundary space so we will all have space to participate? (areas, lines, etc.) This can be co-operatively determined by the class.

What rules must we consider when planning our game? Let us list ideas on the board. How do we move the object? What method do we use to score on goal? How do we change from offense to defense? What conditions or restrictions do we have on the offense and defense? How do we settle disputes?

What is a game "strategy"? (game plan) What do we mean by "tactics" (way you can move or manipulate your body or the object to implement your game plan.)

Cue Questions. What are the responsibilities of the offensive and defensive player?

What do we mean by offense? (attempt to maintain possession and to score) What do we mean by defense? (retrieving the object and preventing the opponent from scoring) What do we mean by a strategy for offense or defense? (a plan or method used to achieve the desired results) Strategy can be a plan for the whole team as well as for each person on the team. What tactics can you use to co-operate with your partner to assist in defense? (help out, watch your check and try to watch the object at the same time.)

Cue Questions. What safety procedures must we be concerned about when planning or playing a goal game?

Is the field (environment) safe? Is it free from objects? Is there enough space for the participants? Is the equipment safe? What protective clothing do we need? (feet, body, hands, face.)

Tasks

1. Co-operate with a partner to plan and play a "goal-oriented" game using: (Do any one of the following.)
   a) a ball, a chalk wall target, your foot for projection.
   b) a ball, two sticks, a hoop target.
   c) a bird, two paddle bats, a hoop target.
   Plan - rules for offense, defense, strategy for scoring, taking turns, etc.
   Can you stop on the signal and share and discuss with your partner the strategy (plan) you used for offense and defense? What tactics (movement etc.) helped you in your game plan?

2. Can you change partners as directed; you learn and play your new partner game, you teach your new partner your game? Have you checked the safety procedures? Stop on signal - can you discuss with your partner strategies for offense and defense and the tactics you used to implement the strategy?
3. Volunteer to share your game with the class. Have the students try a variety of "goal-oriented" games.
4. Can you adjust your game so that you and your partner can cooperate as a team and challenge two other students? Decide which of the two games will be played first. Explain to the opposition the rules that will be used. Check to see if the opposition has questions before you begin. Have you checked the safety procedures?
5. Can you discuss with your group and finally with the whole class ideas you have discovered about offensive strategies and defensive strategies and the tactics you used to implement these strategies that seem to be common in all the "goal-oriented" games you played?
6. Can you identify "goal-oriented" games you have watched or played? (hockey, basketball, football, etc.)

6. *Learning Aids - Integration Ideas*
   Religion
   —What are goals we as Christians should strive for?
   —How do we apply goals in our own Christian living?
   —Is listening important when something is told to you? Why or Why not?
   Language Arts
   —Tell your partner who has their back to you how to do an activity.
   —Write the rules of a game and give them orally. Does the group understand? Can they do the game?

A teaching style emphasizing positive reinforcement is necessary - Can you accommodate this request?

Badminton

From *Physical Education and Recreation Guide*, State of Louisiana, 1980. Reprinted by permission.

Activity Content Outline

I. Skill development
   A. Grip
   B. Stroking
      1. Clear
         a. Underhand
         b. Overhead
      2. Drop
         a. Net
         b. Overhead
      3. Serve
         a. High deep
         b. Low short
      4. Smash
      5. Drive
   C. Court positions
      1. Ready position
      2. Movement during singles play
      3. Movement during doubles play
         a. Parallel position
         b. Up and back position
II. Knowledge
   A. Game rules
      1. Singles
      2. Doubles
   B. Scoring
      1. Singles
      2. Doubles
      3. Setting
   C. Playing court
      1. Singles
      2. Doubles
   D. Equipment
      1. Identification
      2. Care
   E. Terminology
   F. Skill execution
   G. Strategy
   H. Safety precautions
   I. Etiquette
   J. History of badminton
   K. Nature of badminton
   L. Values of badminton
   M. Conditioning
   N. Tournament play
III. Attitude
   A. Responsibilities to other court players
   B. Care of equipment
   C. Participation

Topic	Performance objectives	Grade	Corrections and comments

Grip	1. To demonstrate the correct grip in a style characterized by:
	  a. Shaking hands with the racket
	  b. Placing the "V" which is formed by the thumb and index finger on the top side of the handle
	  c. Holding the racket lightly with the thumb and index finger applying most of the pressure
	  d. Holding the racket so that the face is an extension of the palm of the hand
	  e. Placing the index finger around the handle as in a position to "pull a trigger."
	The student will:
	1.1 Demonstrate the correct grip within 3 attempts
	1.2. Use the correct grip during play
		
		5
		8–10	

Underhand Clear	2. To demonstrate a correct underhand clear in a style characterized by:
	  a. Facing the expected point of contact
	  b. Rotating the pelvis, upper arm, and forearm toward the expected point of contact shifting body weight from the rear to the forward foot
	  c. Sending the shuttle high and deep into the opponent's court.
	The student will:
	2.1. Return a shuttle over the net with an underhand forehand clear 5 out of 10 attempts
	2.2. Return the shuttle over the net with an underhand backhand clear 3 out of 10 attempts
	2.3. Return a shuttle with a forehand underhand clear sending it to the back 1/3 of the opponent's court 4 out of 10 attempts
	2.4. Return a shuttle with a backhand underhand clear performed as above 2 out of 10 attempts
	2.5. With an underhand forehand clear return a shuttle from the back 1/3 of the court clearing a rope stretched 9' high parallel to and 9' in from the end line of the opponent's court in 4 out of 10 attempts
	2.6. With a backhand clear perform as above in 3 out of 10 attempts.
		
		5
		
		5
		
		8
		
		8
		
		10
		
		10	

Performance Objectives also identified for:

Overhead clear	Scoring
Net Drop	Court
Overhead Drop	Equipment
High Deep Serve	Skill Execution
Low Short Serve	Strategy
Smash	Tournaments
Court Position	Attitude
Rules	

Topic	Activities
Grip	1. Rest the racket head on its edge on the floor. Grasp the racket with the dominant hand and "shake hands" with it. Upon command change to the backhand grip. Assume the grip commanded by the leader. The leader or a partner checks that the grip is correct.
Underhand	1. Using the grip as above, tap the shuttle or fleece underhand and on the forehand side of the body into the air as high as possible maintaining control for 15 seconds. Count the number of consecutive hits. Repeat on the backhand side. The time might be increased as proficiency increases. A partner should check to determine that the correct grip is maintained throughout the drill.
	2. Self-drop: Drop a shuttle stroking with an underhand pattern and sending the shuttle over the net. Repeat 10 times.
Overhead Clear	1. Rally in rotation: #1 underhand clear to #2 who overhead clears to #3. Continue overhead clearing in numerical order. $$\frac{1 \ \ 3 \ \ 5}{2 \ \ 4 \ \ 6}$$
Net Drop	1. Drill for 8: Using 4 shuttles, A's hit net drop shots to each other or B's hit overhead clears to each other. A's and B's might change positions at a specified time. B B A A A A B B
	2. Little games: This is designed for practice of a particular stroke with one set of partners on a whole court or half court. Low serve and net play—Play between the net and the short service line and the side lines as designated. Points are scored by the server until the designated game point is reached.
Serve	1. Serve "X" number of shuttles or fleece balls from behind the service line into the diagonal service court.
	2. Serve to targets: Serve "X" number of shuttles to a target on the court. Increase difficulty by: decreasing the size of the target; adding a rope at least 6" above the net below which the short low serve should pass; or placing a rope 9' in from the back line over which the long high serve must pass.

Additional activities listed for: (pp. 305–307)

Smash
Conditioning
General stroking
Court position
Knowledge
Attitude

Bibliography
1. Department of Education of Florida, *Project C.O.P.E., Curriculum Objectives for Physical Education,* Tallahassee: Department of Education of Florida, 1975.
2. Johnson, M. L., "Badminton," *Saunders Physical Activities Series,* Philadelphia: W. B. Saunders Company, 1974.

3. East Baton Rouge Parish, *Health and Physical Education Curriculum Guide.* Baton Rouge, East Baton Rouge Parish School Board, 1979.

4. Shanks, Robb L., et al., *Illinois, Michigan, Minnesota, Wisconsin Interstate Project on Psychomotor Skills.* Wisconsin: Department of Public Instruction, 1974.

5. Mississippi State Department of Education, *The Mississippi Catalog of Competencies for Public Elementary and Secondary Physical Education,* Jackson, Mississippi: Mississippi Department of Education, 1976.

6. Ainsworth, Dorothy S., et al., *Individual Sports for Women,* Third Edition, Philadelphia: W. B. Saunders Company, 1949.

7. Butcher, Charles A. and Nolan A. Thaxton, *Physical Education for Children: Movement Foundations and Experiences,* New York: Macmillan Publishing Company, Inc., 1979.

8. Badminton Clinic: *Lifetime Sports Follow-up*—unpublished material through Orleans Parish School Board, New Orleans, Louisiana, no date given.

Grade 7—Fitness

Goals/objectives	Activity suggestions	Notes to teachers

The students should demonstrate an increasing ability to:
 	
1. DEVELOP PHYSICAL WELL-BEING.
 	
    a. Understand that physical fitness and physical activity are necessary to have a healthy body.
 	
        1) Experience and enjoy physical fitness through physical activity.
 	
        2) Know and define the components of fitness and the principles of exercise.
		THE MANITOBA PHYSICAL FITNESS TEST OR THE C.A.H.P.E.R. PERFORMANCE II FITNESS TEST CAN BE USEFUL TEACHING TOOLS.
		
		Integrate when teaching other subject areas; e.g., Health, Math, Science, Home Economics.

—The FITT principle as related to cardiovascular endurance	Define cardiovascular endurance to the students. Have the students perform the Harvard Step Test and take their heart rates at rest, immediately after exercise, and at minute intervals to determine the rate of recovery. Introduce the FITT principle of exercise—frequency, intensity, time, and type of exercise. Use cardiovascular activities; e.g., jogging, rope skipping, rhythm aerobics.	Discuss the FITT principle with the students and explain the principle of exercise: F. Frequency—three to five times a week I. Intensity—working up to a pre-determined heart rate (target heart rate) T. Time—sustained activity for a period of time (15 minutes once the body is accustomed to exercise) T. Type—any endurance exercise
—Flexibility	Have the students: 1. Define flexibility. 2. Measure flexibility; e.g., sit and reach test. 3. Discuss how flexibility can be achieved/maintained. 4. Perform flexibility exercises for various joints.	A slow, sustained stretch is desirable, rather than ballistic (fast) movement.

From *K-12 Physical Education.* © 1981 Manitoba Department of Education, Winnipeg, Manitoba, Canada. Reprinted by permission.

Goals/objectives	Activity suggestions	Notes to teachers
	Hamstring Stretch: The children lie on their backs with knees bent; lift their bent legs, grasping the thighs with their hands; extend their legs and point their toes; slowly pull on their legs and hold.	All exercises should be done *slowly* and *held.* There should be absolutely *no* bouncing, as this can injure tissue. These positions are to be held for 5 seconds.
	Fencer's Stretch: The children lunge forward with the same arm and leg and hold.	Emphasize keeping the back straight.
	Pelvic Tilt: The children lie on their backs with bent knees, press their lower backs to the floor and hold the position for 5 seconds, then repeat the exercise.	
	Achilles Tendon Stretch: The children stand with their feet together, lean forward, placing their hands on the wall, then hold.	
	Quadracep Stretch: The children stand on one leg and grasp the foot of the other leg behind their backs.	
	Cross Lateral Knee to Chest: The children lie on their backs, bring one knee up and across to the opposite shoulder, and hold.	
	Bilateral Knees to Chest (Lower Back Stretch): The children lie on their backs, raise their knees to their chests, and hold them there.	
	Butterfly: The children sit with the soles of their feet together, grasp their ankles or feet, and push down on their legs with their elbows while keeping their backs straight. The exercise should be repeated 3 times.	
	Upper Back Stretch (Upper spine and thorax): Have the children work in pairs. One sits with arms raised overhead. The partner places a knee between the shoulder blades, grasps the other's wrists and gently pulls the arms backward.	
3) Maintain/develop cardiovascular endurance, flexibility, and muscular strength/ endurance.	Review and have the students use the following intermittent types of training: —Circuit training —Fartlek (speed play) —Interval training —Parlauf —Windsprints	Precede training methods with a warm-up. (Include activities for all fitness components.) Be certain to select exercises for abdominals, back, and legs.

Goals/objectives	Activity suggestions	Notes to teachers
	Introduce and have the students use the following training methods: —Aerobic training —Self-testing techniques which measure maximal effort; e.g., ''Burn Out.''	Different fitness components should be identified, and appropriate remedial exercises should be incorporated into the program.
4) Evaluate personal fitness levels.	Administer a physical fitness test. After testing: 1. Convert the raw scores to norms. 2. Examine and discuss with the students the implications of the results. 3. Determine what fitness components need emphasis.	It is suggested that a 12-minute walk/run be used to evaluate cardiovascular endurance. Discuss what percentile means.
b. Understand that body composition, appearance, nutrition, weight control, and exercise are interrelated.		
—Identify the relationship of caloric intake and expenditure as related to weight control.	Discuss physical activity as it relates to caloric expenditure. Have the students: 1. Keep a record of their food intake for a period of time. 2. Work out the caloric intake and expenditure and apply this information to a particular activity. For example, calculate the distance you have to walk or jog to expend the equivalent calories in food; e.g., pizza.	Develop this area in conjunction with fitness. Have students compare caloric expenditure at various times during the day. Remember that caloric expenditure includes basal needs. Coordinate this project with home economics and science teachers. *Resources:* Contact the —Manitoba Milk Marketing Board —Manitoba Home Economics Directorate, Health and Community Services
c. Understand the importance of proper alignment (posture) in relationship to self-image and body function.		
—Identify what comprises desirable posture and why it is necessary.	Do a postural analysis. Review what good posture is and why it is necessary. Discuss and have students try out a variety of corrective exercises. Establish an individualized program for postural problems.	Refer serious problems (KYPHOSIS, SCOLIOSIS) to the appropriate health authorities. Discuss related future health problems; e.g., lower back problems.

Grade 6—Games

Unit focus: Striking a shuttlecock with a racquet while concentrating on the speed, force, directness/indirectness of the hit.

Content: Body:

                                                Space:

                                                Effort: controlling the
                                                        speed, force,
                                                        directness/
                                                        indirectness of the
                                                        hit while working
                                                        with a shuttlecock
                                                        and racquet

                            Relationship:

Appropriate for: Children who have had experiences in
                        working with shuttlecocks and racquets, but
                        need further refinement in the effort aspect.
Equipment: badminton racquet for each child
                1 shuttlecock/two children
                1 net and stands for every four

Unit Objectives:
   Each child should be willing to try to:

1. Strike a shuttlecock to various places in a designated area
   by varying the flight of the shuttlecock.
2. Return a shuttlecock that has been struck to various areas
   on a court.
3. Move quickly to position self to receive the shuttlecock.
4. Show an understanding of how to move an opponent on a
   court by varying the flight and speed of the shuttlecock.
5. Develop a cooperative/competitive type game with a
   partner or group of four which includes the use of varying
   the flight and speed of the shuttlecock.

   The teacher should be able to:

1. Plan various situations for children to practice making the
   shuttlecock take different flight paths both on the serve
   and on the return.
2. Encourage purposeful practice from the students.

3. Give feedback in relation to the flight of the shuttlecock and position of the racquet.
4. Continuously challenge the highly skilled while encouraging the less skilled to improve.

Learning Experiences:

1. See how you can vary the speed of the shuttlecock as you strike it with a partner.
   —in an open space
   —over a low net *or* rope
   —over a higher net *or* rope (5 ft.)
2. See how you can vary the flight of the shuttlecock as you strike it with a partner.
   —in an open space
   —over a low net *or* bench
   —over a high net (5 ft.)
3. Try to vary the speed and flight of the shuttlecock as you strike with a partner.
   —in an open space
   —over a low net/bench
   —over a high net (5 ft.)
4. Practice sending the shuttlecock to various spaces within your own area by varying the speed and flight of the shuttlecock.
   —in an open space
   —over a low net/bench
   —over a high net (5 ft.)
5. Repeat #4 and see how long you can keep it going.
   —try to break your record
6. In groups of four, see how long you can keep the shuttlecock going by:
   —varying the speed in open space
   —varying the speed over a low net
   —varying the speed over a high net
   —varying the flight in open space
   —varying the flight over a low net
   —varying the flight over a high net
   —varying the speed and flight in open space
   —varying the speed and flight over a low net
   —varying the speed and flight over a high net

7. In groups of four, begin to make the opposite two people cover space quickly by consciously varying the:
   —speed of the hit in an open space
   —speed of the hit over a low net
   —speed of the hit over a high net
   —flight of the shuttlecock in an open space
   —flight of the shuttlecock over a low net
   —flight of the shuttlecock over a high net
   —speed and flight of the hit in an open space
   —speed and flight of the hit over a low net
   —speed and flight of the hit over a high net
8. All of the previous tasks can be worked on in relation to:
   —the serve
   —returning service

Yearly Plan

Lyons Township High School, LaGrange, Illinois
Physical Education Department
South Campus Activities Calendar 1981–82

Freshmen

Unit I 9/3--10/2
  A & B--Track--Outside
  C & D--Choice:
      Flag Football--
      Outside
    or LaCrosse

Unit II 10/5--11/6
  A & B--Choice:
      Flag Football--
      Outside
    or LaCrosse
  C & D--Track--Outside

Unit III 11/9--12/14
  A & B
    Gymnastics--West Gym
    Basketball--Middle Gym
  C--Volleyball--East Gym
  D--Fitness--Wrestling
  Wt. Room

Unit IV 12/15--1/28
  A & B
    Gymnastics--West Gym
  C--Fitness--Wrestling
  Wt. Room
  D--Volleyball--East Gym

Unit V 2/1--3/3
  A--Volleyball--East Gym
  B--Fitness--Wrestling
  Wt. Room
  C & D
    Gymnastics--West Gym
    Basketball--Middle Gym

Unit VI 3/4--4/2
  A--Fitness--Wrestling
  Wt. Room
  B--Volleyball--East Gym
  C & D
    Gymnastics--West Gym
    Basketball--Middle Gym

Sophomores

Unit I 9/3--10/2

Unit II 10/5--10/30
  Sections: Y & Z
  Choices: Tennis I & II
         Flag Football I
         & II
         Soccer

Unit III 11/3--12/1
  Sections: Y & Z
  Choices: Badminton
         Volleyball
         Basketball I &
         II

Drivers Education Switch--
12/1

Unit IV 12/2--1/25
  Sections: X & Z
  Choices: Badminton/
         Pickle Ball
         Basketball I &
         II
         Folk & Social
         Dance

Unit V 1/26--3/9
  Sections: X & Z
  Choices: Badminton/
         Pickle Ball
         Volleyball/Team
         Handball

Drivers Education Switch--
3/9

Unit VI 3/10--4/2
  Sections: X & Y
  Choices: Volleyball
         Badminton
         Basketball
         Floor Hockey

Courtesy of Dr. Jo Mancuso, Lyons Twp. High School, LaGrange, Il.

Yearly Plan, cont.

Freshmen	Sophomores
Unit VII 4/5--5/7	Unit VII 4/5--5/7
A--B--C--D	Sections: X & Y
Badminton--Gyms 1 & 2	Choices: Gymnastics
Wrestling--Wr. Room 57	Conditioning,
	Wt. Rm. &
Unit VIII 5/10--Last Day	Jogging
A--B--C--D	Tennis
Softball--Outside	Floor Hockey
Fitness Testing--	
Outside	Unit VIII 5/10--Last Day
	Sections: X & Y
	Choices: Tennis
	Softball
	Track

Lyons Township High School
LaGrange, Illinois
Physical education teacher schedule 1985–86

south campus

Period										
1st			Fresh. C Holtz	Fresh. D Lazier						RB RL DC MM FD CH BK CM/s
2nd	Fresh. A Dryanski		Fresh.C Marasovich	Fresh.D Kopecky	Soph. 1 Burson	Soph. 2 Leiber		Modified Curby Fr.B Facilities		Holtz Hubbard McKee
3rd	Fresh.A Hubbard	Fresh.B Curby	Fresh. C Holtz	Fresh. D Kopecky	Soph. 1 McKee	Soph. 2 Leiber				Dryanski Burson Marasovich
4/5th	Fresh.A Hubbard	Fresh. B Kopecky	Fresh. C Marasovich	Fresh. D Dryanski	Soph. 1 McKee	Soph. 2 Leiber	Soph. 3 Burson			Holtz Curby
7/8th	Fresh.A Hubbard	Fresh. B Curby	Fresh. C Holtz	Fresh. D Dryanski	Soph. 1 McKee	Fall Soph. 2 RL / Spring Soph.2-CM	Soph. 3 Burson		Fall Dance Studies Baldner	Kopecky Leiber
9th	Fresh. A Dryanski	Fresh. B Curby	Fresh. C Holtz	Fresh. D Kopecky	Soph. 1 Leiber	Soph. 2 Marasovich	Soph. 3 Burson	STEP Dopp		Baldner Hubbard McKee
10th	Fresh.A Dryanski		Fresh. C Holtz	Fresh. D Kopecky	Soph.1 Leiber	Soph. 2 Marasovich	Soph. 3 Burson	Modified Curby Fr.B Facilities	Fall Dance Studies Baldner	Hubbard McKee

Lyons Township High School
LaGrange, Illinois
Department of Physical Education—North Campus
1983–1984

Fall Semester
Unit 1--9/6-10/4
Unit 2--10/5-11/4

1st Hour
Jr. Swim/Weber--Volleyball/
    Schneider
Volleyball/Schneider--Jr.
    Swim/Weber
Conditioning Wt. Trng.--
    Foster
Flag Football/Jogging--
    Jackson
Flag Football/Outdoor
    Survival--Snead
Golf/Badminton--Sandusky
Tennis/Soccer--Williams
Dance Studies--Baldner

2nd Hour
Volleyball/Jr. Swim--Snead
Conditioning Wt. Trng.--
    Wojick
Golf/Badminton--Sandusky
Flag Football/Outdoor
    Survival--Ingersoll
Flickerball/Soccer--
    Jackson
Tennis/Soccer--Williams
Dance Studies--Baldner
STEP Swim--Ray

3rd Hour
Volleyball/Baldner--Jr.
    Swim--Weber
Conditioning Wt. Trng.--
    Wojick
Flag Football/Jogging--
    Jackson
Flag Football/Outdoor
    Survival--Snead
Flickerball/Soccer--Foster
Golf/Weber--Badminton--
    Baldner
Tennis/Soccer--Schneider
STEP Swim--Weber & Ray

Unit 3--11/7-12/9
Unit 4--12/12-1/24

1st Hour
Jr. Swim/Weber--Volleyball/
    Sandusky
Sr. Swim/Weber--Volleyball/
    Sandusky
Aerobics/Yoga--Schneider
Conditioning Wt. Trng.--
    Foster
Floor Hockey/Basketball--
    Jackson
Net Games/Cross Country Ski
    (or Western Dance)--
    Williams
Tension Control/Pickle
    Ball--Snead
Dance Studies--Baldner

2nd Hour
Jr. Swim/Ingersoll--
    Volleyball/Snead
Volleyball/Snead--Jr. Swim/
    Ingersoll
Aerobics/Yoga--Williams
Conditioning Wt. Trng.--
    Jackson
Floor Hockey/Basketball--
    Sandusky
Net Games/Cross Country Ski
    (or Western Dance)--Wojick
Dance Studies--Baldner
STEP--Ray

3rd Hour
Jr. Swim/Weber--Volleyball/
    Schneider
Volleyball/Schneider--Jr.
    Swim/Weber
Aerobics/Yoga--Baldner
Conditioning Wt. Trng.--
    Jackson
Floor Hockey/Basketball--
    Foster
Net Games/Cross Country Ski
    (or Western Dance)--Wojick
Tension Control/Pickle
    Ball--Snead
STEP--Ray

Appendix B

Unit 1--9/6-10/4
Unit 2--10/5-11/4

4th Hour
Jr. Swim/Weber--Volleyball/
    Schneider
Volleyball/Schneider--Jr.
    Swim/Weber
Conditioning Wt. Trng.--
    Wojick
Flag Football/Jogging--
    Sandusky
Flag Football/Outdoor
    Survival--Ingersoll
Flickerball/Soccer--Foster
Golf/Badminton--Mancuso
Tennis/Soccer--Williams

5th Hour
Jr. Swim/Weber--Volleyball/
    Foster
Volleyball/Foster--Jr.
    Swim/Weber
Conditioning Wt. Trng.--
    Jackson
Flag Football/Jogging--
    Wojick
Flag Football/Outdoor
    Survival--Ingersoll
Golf/Badminton--Snead
Tennis/Soccer--Williams

6th Hour
Jr. Swim/Weber--Volleyball/
    Williams
Volleyball/Williams--Jr.
    Swim/Weber
Conditioning Wt. Trng.--
    Wojick
Flag Football/Jogging--
    Ingersoll
Golf/Badminton--Sandusky
Tennis/Soccer--Schneider
Modified--Ray

Unit 3--11/7-12/9
Unit 4--12/12-1/24

4th Hour
Jr. Swim/Weber--Volleyball/
    Schneider
Volleyball/Schneider--Jr.
    Swim/Weber
Aerobics/Yoga--Williams
Basketball/Floor Hockey--
    Sandusky
Conditioning Wt. Trng.--
    Wojick
Floor Hockey/Basketball--
    Foster
Net Games/Cross Country Ski
(or Western Dance)--
    Ingersoll
Tension Control/Pickle
    Ball--Mancuso

5th Hour
Jr. Swim/Weber--Volleyball/
    Foster
Volleyball/Foster--Jr.
    Swim/Weber
Aerobics/Yoga--Williams
Conditioning Wt. Trng.--
    Wojick
Floor Hockey/Basketball--
    Jackson
Net Games/Cross Country Ski
(or Western Dance)--
    Ingersoll
Tension Control/Pickle
    Ball--Snead

6th Hour
Sr. Swim/Weber--Volleyball/
    Ingersoll
Volleyball/Ingersoll--Sr.
    Swim/Weber
Aerobics/Yoga--Schneider
Conditioning Wt. Trng.--
    Wojick
Floor Hockey/Basketball--
    Sandusky
Net Games/Cross Country Ski
(or Western Dance)--
    Williams
Modified--Ray

Lyons Township High School, cont.

Fall Semester
Unit 1--9/6-10/4
Unit 2--10/5-11/4

7th Hour
Jr. Swim/Schneider--
    Volleyball/Sandusky
Volleyball/Sandusky--Jr.
    Swim/Schneider
Conditioning Wt. Trng.--Ray
Flag Football/Jogging--
    Jackson
Flag Football/Outdoor
    Survival--Ingersoll
Golf/Badminton--Snead
Tennis/Soccer--Foster

Spring Semester
Unit 5--2/1-2/29
Unit 6--3/1-4/6

1st Hour
Sr. Swim/Weber--Volleyball/
    Foster
Volleyball/Foster--Sr.
    Swim/Weber
Basketball/Floor Hockey--
    Sandusky
Cross Country Ski/Net Games
(or Western Dance)--
    Williams
Conditioning Wt. Trng.--
    Jackson
Figure Fitness/Self
    Defense--Schneider
Pickle Ball/Tension
    Control--Snead
Dance Studies--Baldner

2nd Hour
Sr. Swim/Williams--
    Volleyball/Jackson
Volleyball/Jackson--Sr.
    Swim/Williams

Unit 3--11/7-12/9
Unit 4--12/12-1/24

7th Hour
Jr. Swim/Schneider--
    Volleyball/Sandusky
Volleyball/Sandusky--Jr.
    Swim/Schneider
Aerobics/Yoga--Snead
Conditioning Wt. Trng.--
    Foster
Floor Hockey/Basketball--
    Ray
Net Games/Cross Country
(or Western Dance)--
    Ingersoll
Basketball/Floor Hockey--
    Jackson

Unit 7--4/9-5/4
Unit 8--5/7-6/4

1st Hour
Sr. Swim/Softball--Weber
Badminton/Golf--Sandusky
Jazz Dance/Softball--
    Williams
Jogging/Softball--Jackson
LaCrosse/Softball--Foster
Outdoor Survival/Frisbee
    Games--Snead
Soccer/Tennis--Schneider
Dance Studies--Baldner

2nd Hour
Sr. Swim/Softball--Snead
/STEP Swim--Ray
Badminton/Golf--Sandusky
Jazz Dance/Softball--
    Baldner
LaCrosse/ Softball--Wojick
Soccer/Tennis--Williams
Outdoor Survival/Frisbee
    Games--Ingersoll
Jogging/Softball--Jackson

Lyons Township High School, cont.

<u>Spring Semester</u>
Unit 5--2/1-2/29
Unit 6--3/1-4/6

Basketball/Floor Hockey--
    Sandusky
Cross Country Ski/Net Games
(or Western Dance)--
    Ingersoll
Conditioning Wt. Trng.--
    Wojick
Figure Fitness/Self
    Defense--Snead
STEP--Ray
Dance Studies--Baldner

<u>3rd Hour</u>
Jr. Swim/Weber--Volleyball/
    Baldner
Volleyball/Baldner--Sr.
    Swim/Weber
Basketball/Floor Hockey--
    Jackson
Cross Country Ski/Net Games
(or Western Dance)--Wojick
Conditioning Wt. Trng.--
    Foster
Figure Fitness/Self
    Defense--Schneider
Pickle Ball/Tension
    Control--Snead
STEP--Ray

<u>4th Hour</u>
Sr. Swim/Weber--Volleyball/
    Ingersoll
Volleyball/Ingersoll--Sr.
    Swim/Weber
Aerobics/Yoga--Baldner
Basketball/Floor Hockey--
    Sandusky
Cross Country Ski/Net Games
(or Western Dance)--Wojick
Conditioning Wt. Trng.--
    Foster
Figure Fitness/Self
    Defense--Schneider
Pickle Ball/Tension
    Control--Mancuso

Unit 7--4/9-5/4
Unit 8--5/7-6/4

<u>3rd Hour</u>
Sr. Swim/Weber--Softball/
    Jackson
Volleyball/Jackson--Sr.
    Swim/Weber
Badminton/Golf--Wojick
Jazz Dance/Softball--
    Baldner
LaCrosse/Softball--Foster
Outdoor Survival/Frisbee
    Games--Snead
Soccer/Tennis--Schneider
STEP--Ray

<u>4th Hour</u>
Sr. Swim/Weber--Softball/
    Schneider
Volleyball/Schneider--Sr.
    Swim/Weber
Badminton/Golf--Mancuso
Jazz Dance/Softball--
    Baldner
Jogging/Softball--Sandusky
LaCrosse/Softball--Wojick
Outdoor Survival/Frisbee
    Games--Ingersoll
Soccer/Tennis--Foster

<u>5th Hour</u>
Sr. Swim/Weber--Softball/
    Jackson
Jogging/Jackson--Water
    Games/Weber
Badminton/Golf--Snead
Jazz Dance/Softball--
    Williams
LaCrosse/Softball--Wojick
Outdoor Survival/Frisbee
    Games--Ingersoll
Soccer/Tennis--Foster

<u>6th Hour</u>
Life Saving--Weber
Badminton/Golf--Sandusky
Jazz Dance/Softball--
    Williams
LaCrosse/Softball--
    Ingersoll

Curriculum Planning Documents   377

Lyons Township High School, cont.

Spring Semester
Unit 5--2/1-2/29
Unit 6--3/1-4/6

5th Hour
Sr. Swim/Weber--Volleyball/
    Wojick
Volleyball/Wojick--Sr.
    Swim/Weber
Cross Country Ski/Net
    Games*--Ingersoll
Conditioning Wt. Trng.--
    Jackson
Figure Fitness/Self
    Defense--Williams
Tension Control/Pickle
    Ball--Snead
Basketball/Floor Hockey--
    Foster

6th Hour
Sr. Swim/Weber--Volleyball/
    Schneider
Volleyball/Schneider--Sr.
    Swim/Weber
Basketball/Floor Hockey--
    Sandusky
Cross Country Ski/Net
    Games*--Ingersoll
Conditioning Wt. Trng.--
    Wojick
Figure Fitness/Self
    Defense--Williams
Modified--Ray

7th Hour
Sr. Swim/Ingersoll--
    Volleyball/Foster
Volleyball/Foster--Sr. Swim
    --Ingersoll
Basketball/Floor Hockey--
    Sandusky
Cross Country Ski/Net
    Games*--Williams
Conditioning Wt. Trng.--
    Jackson

Unit 7--4/9-5/4
Unit 8--5/7-6/4

Figure Fitness/Self
    Defense--Schneider
Pickle Ball/Tension
    Control--Snead
*Or Western Dance
Outdoor Survival/Frisbee
    Games--Snead
Soccer/Tennis--Schneider
Modified--Ray

7th Hour
Sr. Swim/Schneider--
    Softball/Sandusky
Badminton/Golf--Ray
Jazz Dance/Softball--
    Williams
Jogging/Softball--Jackson
LaCrosse/Softball--Foster
Outdoor Survival/Frisbee
    Games--Ingersoll
Soccer/Sandusky--Tennis/
    Schneider

Appendix B

Unit Plans

Unit Plan for Group Instruction—Grade 9 Archery

School:	High School for the Health Professions Houston, Texas
Instructor:	Bede Leyendecker (student teacher) Doris Robins (supervising teacher)
Activity:	Archery (9th grade)

I. Objectives
   1. The student will demonstrate a basic level of skill in archery by scoring at least 60 points in a range round tournament (10 ends at 20 meters).
   2. The student will demonstrate a knowledge of archery by scoring at least 70 points on a 100 point written test.
   3. The student will demonstrate a basic skill in archery by achieving at least 70% on a skills test.
   4. The student will demonstrate basic archery skills well enough to feel confident to voluntarily participate in activities outside of class.
   5. The student will demonstrate cooperation by voluntarily taking turns with classmates.
   6. The student will demonstrate a knowledge of archery rules and scoring by correctly performing them daily in class.
   7. The student will play 3 archery novelty games by participating in class.

II. Skills
   1. Stringing the bow
   2. Nocking an arrow
   3. Anchoring
   4. Aiming at a target
   5. Releasing
   6. Follow through
   7. Drawing arrows from target
   8. Addressing the target--7 step method
   9. Addressing the target--4 step method
   10. Unstringing the bow
   11. Self error correction

III. Areas of knowledge
   1. Rules in archery (including safety)
   2. Scoring in archery
   3. Selection and care of archery tackle

Courtesy of Dr. Bede Leyendecker, University of Houston, Houston, Texas.

IV. Equipment/supplies
    4 targets, target faces and stands
    8 cones
    18 bows
    108 arrows
    balloons
    score sheets
    apples
    Handouts (4)--2 Rainy Day Activities
    Straight pins or tacks
    String
    Masking tape
    Whistle
    Posters--class composite scores
 V. Evaluation Procedures
    50% skills tests
    25% correct demonstration of 7 and 4 step address
    25% score total on one end at 20 yards
    25% written test
    25% participation, dress
VI. Miscellaneous Information
    A. The unit will be introduced with a question and
       answer session on the uses of archery--as well as a
       lecture on the history of archery and safety rules
       in archery. Equipment will be selected.
    B. Rainy Day Activities
       1. Archery puzzle
       2. Name the archer's faults
       3. Floor hockey
       4. Circuit drills
    C. The unit will close with the playing of a novelty
       game in archery, as well as announcement of
       interclass winners and intraclass winners.
    D. Students will compete in a range round tournament.
       Competition will occur individually as well as
       among classes. There will also be an award for the
       most bullseyes during competition days.

Calendar

	Monday	Tuesday	Wednesday	Thursday	Friday
Week one	Introduction History Value Safety Selection of equipment Handouts	Distribute equipment Review safety Stringing and unstringing bow 7 step address Practice—no arrows Scoring	Review safety Review 7 step address Dem./expl. 7 step w/ arrows Practice 7 step w/ arrows at 10 yards	Review safety Review 7 step Review scoring Practice 7 step at 15 yards Scores	Review safety Dem./expl. 4 step address w/ arrows Practice 4 step w/ arrows at 10 yards Bursting balloons
Week two	Review safety Review 4 step Practice 4 step at 15 yards Scores	Review 7 & 4 step Practice 7 & 4 step at 20 yards Scores	Skills test— (first half) 7 step address 4 step address 'Wand shooting' at 20 yards	Written test	Practice 4 step at 30 yards Scores Play 'Tic-tac- toe' at 20 yards
Week three	Review Safety Range	round	tournament		
Week four	Skills test— (second half) Shooting accuracy at 20 yards	Play 'William Tell' at 20 yards Distribute individual awards 1st- 5th Announce bullseye contest winners and total class scores			

From Heitmann, H. M. and M. E. Kneer. *Physical Education Instructional Techniques: An Individualized Humanistic Approach.* Prentice-Hall, Inc., 1976, Englewood Cliffs, NJ.

Unit Plan for Individualized Instruction—Grade 5 Track and Field

School: Campanelli Elementary School
         Schaumburg, Illinois
Facilitator: Donna White
Principal: Susan McCann

Objectives:

Global Goal: To be able to participate in a track meet as a
 contestant and as a scorer

Student will be able to:

 Perform one running event (50-yard dash, 75-yard dash,
 440-yard run, 600-yard run, 440-yard relay)

 Perform one throwing event (shot put, softball throw)

 Perform one jumping event (high jump, standing long
 jump, running long jump)

 Score for one running event

 Score for one throwing event

 Score for one jumping event

Equipment:

 High jump: 2 high jump standards, 2 crossbars, 2 landing
 pits

 Running long jump: 1 sand pit, 1 cloth tape, 1 rake

 Standing long jump: 2 mats with starting line and
 measurements taped on

 Softball throw: 9 softballs, 1 cloth tape, 6 cones to mark
 running area set at 10-foot intervals, 1 short rope to use as
 starting line

 Shot put: 3 shots, 1 cloth tape, 1 rope to use as circle to
 help place small stakes to mark the distance of each put

 Dashes: 3 lanes painted on blacktop drive

 Runs and relay: area in grass marked with sawdust, 3
 batons, 1 clock

Media:

 The following equipment will be placed on a wagon to store
 and to move to activity area:

 battery operated slide viewer and slides

 transparency viewer and slides

 books

Block plan:

Monday	Wednesday	Friday
Orientation to unit and method presentation: 1. High jump 2. Running long jump 3. Standing long jump 4. Use of equipment 5. Scoring and recording 6. Media	**Presentation of:** 1. Softball throw 2. Shot 3. Running events 4. Use of equipment 5. Scoring and recording 6. Media	Pick up any of presentation not covered in first two days. Experiment with events to find area of specialization.
Monday Experiment Conferences and agreement cards	**Wednesday** Experiment Conferences and agreement cards	**Friday** Carry out agreements Conferences and guidance
Monday Carry out agreement ———— Conferences and guidance	**Wednesday**	**Friday** ————————→
Monday	**Wednesday** ——————————→ Sign up for events	**Friday** Meet Two hours all fifth graders (with classroom teacher's help)

Management:

Equipment: To be moved and set up with student help.
Record Keeping: Each student will have a daily log to keep track of his or her progress; pencils will be kept in a box near each event area and will be returned after use.

Each student will have an agreement card to be filled out at the time of the first conference (sample below). On this card his goals will be stated, and the card will be kept on file in the library wagon. When a child reaches his or her goals, this will be recorded.

Goal Cards: These cards, describing basic rules for each event, telling where to go for more information, will be kept near each event area. There will be three copies of each. Directions for scoring each event are on the back of each card.

Field Layout:

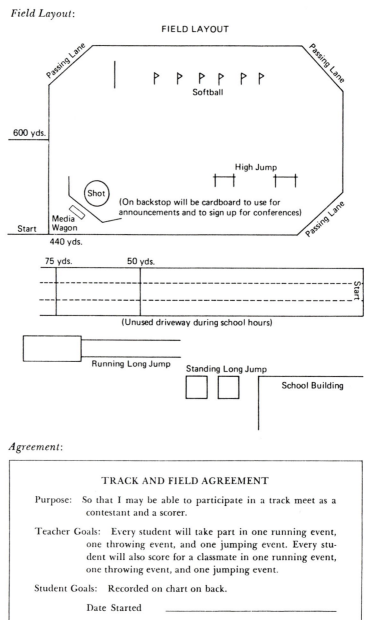

FIELD LAYOUT

Passing Lane

Passing Lane

P P P P P P
Softball

600 yds.

High Jump

Shot

(On backstop will be cardboard to use for
announcements and to sign up for conferences)

Media
Wagon

Passing Lane

Start

440 yds.

75 yds.   50 yds.

Start

(Unused driveway during school hours)

Running Long Jump

Standing Long Jump

School Building

Agreement:

TRACK AND FIELD AGREEMENT

Purpose: So that I may be able to participate in a track meet as a
contestant and a scorer.

Teacher Goals: Every student will take part in one running event,
one throwing event, and one jumping event. Every student will also score for a classmate in one running event,
one throwing event, and one jumping event.

Student Goals: Recorded on chart on back.

Date Started   _____

Conferences   _____

_____

_____

Date Completed _____

_____   _____

Student Signature   Teacher Signature

	Starting score	My goal	I did it!	I scored it!	I scored for:
Running Events					
50-yard dash					
75-yard dash					
220-yard dash					
600-yard run walk					
440-yard relay					
Jumping Events					
High jump					
Standing long jump					
Running long jump					
Throwing Events					
Softball throw					
Shot put					

Bibliography

American Alliance for Health, Physical Education and Recreation. 1967. *Sports skills tests.* Washington, DC: AAHPER.

———. 1972. *This is physical education.* Washington, DC: AAHPER.

———. 1976. *Personalized learning in physical education.* Washington, DC: AAHPER.

———. 1976. *Youth fitness test manual.* Washington, DC: AAHPER.

———. 1977. *Assessment guide for secondary school physical education programs.* Washington, DC: AAHPER.

———. 1980. *Health related physical fitness manual.* Washington, DC: AAHPERD.

———. 1981. *Essentials of a quality elementary school physical education program.* Reston, VA: AAHPERD.

Anderson, W. and G. T. Barrette, eds. 1978. *What's going on in gym: Descriptive studies of physical education classes.* Newtown, CT: Motor Skills: Theory Into Practice.

Arnold, P. J. 1979. *Meaning in movement, sport and physical education.* London: Heinemann.

Association for Supervision and Curriculum Development. 1962. *Perceiving, behaving, becoming.* Washington, DC: The Association.

———. 1979. *Lifelong learning: A human agenda.* Alexandria, VA: The Association.

———. 1983. *Effective schools and classrooms: A research-based perspective.* Alexandria, VA: The Association.

———. 1983. *Fundamental curriculum decisions.* Alexandria, VA: The Association.

Bain, L. L. 1974. Description and analysis of the hidden curriculum in physical education. Doctoral Dissertation, Univ. of Wisconsin, Madison.

Bain, L. L. 1978. Status of curriculum theory in physical education. *Journal of Physical Education and Recreation* 49 (3) (March): 25–26.

Barone, T. 1983. Education as aesthetic experience: "Art in germ." *Educational Leadership* 40 (4): 21–26.

Barrow, H. M., and R. McGee. 1979. *A practical approach to measurement in physical education.* Philadelphia: Lea and Febiger.

Baumgartner, T. A., and A. S. Jackson. 1982. *Measurement for evaluation in physical education.* Dubuque, IA: Wm. C. Brown.

Beauchamp, G. A. 1975. *Curriculum theory.* Wilmette, IL: Kagg Press.

Berman, L. M., and J. A. Roderick. 1977. *Curriculum: Teaching the what, how and why of living.* Columbus, OH: Merrill.

Bernstein, B. 1973. On the classification and framing of educational knowledge. In *Knowledge, education and cultural change,* ed. Richard Brown. London: Tavistock Publications.

Bloom, B. S., ed. 1956. *Taxonomy of educational objectives. Handbook I: The cognitive domain.* New York: David McKay.

Bloom, B. S., J. T. Hastings, and G. F. Madaus. 1971. *Handbook on formative and summative evaluation of student learning.* New York: McGraw-Hill.

Borg, W. R. 1979. Time and school learning. *Newsletter: Beginning Teacher Evaluation Study* (March): 2–7.

Borko, H., R. Cone, N. Atwood-Russo, and R. J. Shavelson. 1979. Teachers' decision-making. In *Research on teaching: Concepts, findings and implications,* ed. P. L. Peterson and H. J. Walberg. Berkeley, CA: McCutchan.

Brandwein, P. F. 1971. *The permanent agenda of man: The humanities.* New York: Harcourt, Brace, Jovanovich.

Bronowski, J. 1977. *A sense of the future.* Cambridge: The MIT Press.

Brophy, J. E. 1977. *Child development and socialization.* Chicago: SRA.

Brophy, J. E., and C. M. Evertson. 1981. *Student characteristics and teaching.* New York: Longman.

Brown, C., and R. Cassidy. 1963. *Theory in physical education: A guide to program change.* Philadelphia: Lea and Febiger.

California Department of Education. 1962. *California physical performance tests.* Sacramento, CA: State Department of Education.

Callois, R. 1961. *Man, play and games.* New York: The Free Press of Glencoe.

Carmack, M. A., and R. Martens. 1979. Measuring commitment to running: A survey of runners' attitudes and mental states. *Journal of Sport Psychology* 1: 25–42.

Cassidy, R. F., and S. F. Caldwell. 1974. *Humanizing physical education.* Dubuque, IA: Wm. C. Brown.

Clark, C. M., and R. J. Yinger. 1979. Teachers' thinking. In *Research on teaching: Concepts, findings and implications,* ed. P. L. Peterson and H. J. Walberg. Berkeley, CA: McCutchan.

Clarke, H. H. 1976. *Application of measurement to health and physical education.* Englewood Cliffs, NJ: Prentice-Hall.

Clein, M. L., and W. J. Stone. 1970. Physical education and the classification of educational objectives: Psychomotor domain. *The Physical Educator* 27 (March): 27–34.

Cooper, K. H. 1977. *The aerobics way.* New York: Bantam.

Corbin, C. B., and R. Lindsey. 1983. *Fitness for life.* Glenview, IL: Scott, Foresman.

Cornish, E. 1980. An agenda for the 1980s. *The Futurist* 14 (1) (February): 5–13.

Cronbach, L. J., and R. E. Snow. 1977. *Aptitudes and instructional methods.* New York: Irvington.

Curriculum Theory in Physical Education Conference Proceedings, Univ. of Georgia, Athens, 1979, 1981, 1983.

Dede, C. 1979. Ten agendas for the future of education. *Futurics* 3 (2) (Spring): 117–26.

Dillon-Peterson, B., ed. 1981. *Staff development/organization development.* Alexandria, VA: Association for Supervision and Curriculum Development.

Doyle, W. 1979. Classroom tasks and student abilities. In *Research on teaching: Concepts, findings and implications,* ed. P. L. Peterson and H. J. Walberg. Berkeley, CA: McCutchan.

Doyle, W., and G. Ponder. 1977. The ethic of practicality: Implications for curriculum development. In *Curriculum Theory.* Washington, DC: Association for Supervision and Curriculum Development.

Dunkin, M. J., and B. J. Biddle. 1974. *The study of teaching.* New York: Holt, Rinehart and Winston.

Eisner, E. W. 1983. The art and craft of teaching. *Educational Leadership* 40 (4): 4–13.

Eisner, E. W., and E. Vallance, eds. 1974. *Conflicting conceptions of curriculum.* Berkeley, CA: McCutchan.

English, F. 1980. Curriculum mapping. *Educational Leadership* 37: 558–59.

Ferguson, M. 1980. *The aquarian conspiracy.* New York: St. Martin's Press.

Gage, N. L. 1978. *The scientific basis of the art of teaching.* New York: Teachers College Press.

Gallahue, D. L., P. H. Werner, and G. C. Luedke. 1975. *A conceptual approach to moving and learning.* New York: John Wiley and Sons.

Giroux, H. A., A. W. Penna, and W. F. Pinar, eds. 1981. *Curriculum and instruction: Alternatives in education.* Berkeley, CA: McCutchan.

Goldberger, M., and S. Moyer. 1982. A schema for classifying educational objectives in the psychomotor domain. *Quest* 34 (2): 134–42.

Goodlad, J. I., and Associates. 1979. *Curriculum inquiry.* New York: McGraw-Hill.

Haag, H. 1978. *Sport pedagogy: Content and methodology.* Baltimore, MD: University Park Press.

Harrow, A. J. 1972. *A taxonomy of the psychomotor domain: A guide for developing behavioral objectives.* New York: David McKay.

Havelock, R. 1973. *The change agent's guide to innovation in education.* Englewood Cliffs, NJ: Educational Technology Publications.

Heitmann, H. M., and M. E. Kneer. 1976. *Physical education/instructional techniques: An individualized humanistic approach.* Englewood Cliffs, NJ: Prentice-Hall.

Hellison, D. 1973. *Humanistic physical education.* Englewood Cliffs, NJ: Prentice-Hall.

Hellison, D. 1978. *Beyond balls and bats.* Washington, DC: American Alliance for Health, Physical Education and Recreation.

Hellison, D. 1982. Philosophy—Back to the drawing board. *Journal of Physical Education, Recreation and Dance* 53: 43–44.

Hendricks, J. H., and C. D. Hendricks. 1981. *Aging in mass society: Myths and realities.* Cambridge, MA: Winthrop.

Hendry, L. B. 1975. Survival in a marginal role: The professional identity of the physical education teacher. *British Journal of Sociology* 26: 456–76.

Henry, F. 1978. The academic discipline of physical education. *Quest* 29: 13–29.

Hoffman, H. A., J. Young, and S. E. Klesius. 1981. *Meaningful movement for children.* Boston: Allyn and Bacon.

Holman, E. L. 1980. The school ecosystem. In *Considered action for curriculum improvement.* Alexandria, VA: Association for Supervision and Curriculum Development.

Howey, K., and R. Bents. 1979. A general framework for induction and continuing teacher education. In *Toward meeting the needs of the beginning teacher,* ed. K. Howey and R. Bents. Minneapolis, MN: Midwest Teacher Corps Network.

Huebner, D. 1966. Curricular language and classroom meanings. In *Language and meaning,* ed. J. B. Macdonald and R. R. Leeper. Washington, DC: Association for Supervision and Curriculum Development.

Huenecke, D. 1982. What is curriculum theorizing? What are its implications for practice? *Educational Leadership* 39 (4) (January): 290–94.

Hunt, D., and E. Sullivan. 1974. *Between psychology and education.* Hinsdale, IL: Dryden Press.

Jewett, A. E. 1977. Relationships in physical education: A curriculum viewpoint. In *The academy papers,* 11. Washington, DC: The American Academy of Physical Education.

Jewett, A. E. 1980. Status of physical education curriculum theory. *Quest* 32 (2): 163–73.

Jewett, A. E. 1980. Tomorrow, tomorrow . . . on the optimistic side of pessimism. *Quest* 32 (2): 130–42.

Jewett, A. E. 1981. Purpose process curriculum framework. In *Proceedings of the second conference on curriculum theory in physical education,* ed. W. M. Harrington. Athens: Univ. of Georgia.

Jewett, A. E. 1982. Program development. In *Physical education and sport: An introduction,* ed. E. F. Zeigler. Philadelphia: Lea and Febiger.

Jewett, A. E. 1982. Curriculum designs for fulfilling human agendas. In *Education in the 80's: Physical education,* ed. C. Ulrich. Washington, DC: National Education Association.

Jewett, A. E., and M. R. Mullan. 1977. *Curriculum design: Purposes and processes in physical education teaching-learning.* Washington, DC: AAHPER.

Johnson, B. L., and J. K. Nelson. 1979. *Practical measurements for evaluation in physical education.* Minneapolis, MN: Burgess.

Johnson, P. B., W. S. Updyke, M. Schaefer, and D. C. Stoldberg. 1975. *Sport, exercise and you.* New York: Holt, Rinehart, and Winston.

Joyce, B. R., and M. Weil. 1972. *Models of teaching.* Englewood Cliffs, NJ: Prentice-Hall.

Joyce, B., and B. Showers. 1982. The coaching of teaching. *Educational Leadership* 40 (1): 4–10.

Kaufman, R. O., and F. W. English. 1979. *Needs assessment: Concept and application.* Englewood Cliffs, NJ: Educational Technology Publishers.

Kennedy, C. E. 1978. *Human development: The adult years and aging.* New York: Macmillan.

Kenyon, G. S. 1968. A conceptual model for characterizing physical activity. *Research Quarterly* 39: 96–105.

Kenyon, G. S. 1968. Six scales for assessing attitude toward physical activity. *Research Quarterly* 39: 566–74.

Keough, J. 1963. Extreme attitudes toward physical education. *Research Quarterly* 34: 27–33.

Kerlinger, F. N. 1979. *Behavioral research: A conceptual approach.* New York: Holt, Rinehart and Winston.

Kliebard, H. M. 1972. Metaphorical roots of curriculum design. *Teachers College Record* 72 (3) (February): 403–44.

Kliebard, H. M. 1975a. Persistent curriculum issues in historical perspective. In *Curriculum theorizing: The reconceptualists,* ed. W. Pinar. Berkeley, CA: McCutchan.

Kliebard, H. M. 1975b. Reappraisal: The Tyler rationale. In *Curriculum theorizing: The reconceptualists,* ed. W. Pinar. Berkeley, CA: McCutchan.

Kliebard, H. M. 1982. Curriculum theory as metaphor. *Theory Into Practice* 21 (1): 11–17.

Kneer, M. E., ed. 1980. *NASPE basic stuff series.* Reston, VA: AAHPERD.

Krathwohl, D. R., B. S. Bloom, and B. B. Masia. 1964. *Taxonomy of educational objectives, handbook II: Affective domain.* New York: David McKay.

Krathwohl, D. R., and D. A. Payne. 1971. Defining and assessing educational objectives. In *Educational Measurement,* ed. R. L. Thorndike. Washington, DC: American Council on Education.

Kuhn, T. 1970. *The structure of scientific revolutions.* Chicago: Univ. of Chicago Press.

Laban, R., and F. Lawrence. 1947. *Effort.* London: Unwin Brothers, Ltd.

Laban, R. 1963. *Modern educational dance,* 2d ed. Revised by L. Ullman. New York: Frederick A. Praeger.

LaPorte, W. R., and J. M. Cooper. 1973. *The physical education curriculum (A national program).* Columbia, MO: Lucas Brothers.

Lawson, H. A., and W. R. Morford. 1979. The cross-disciplinary structure of kinesiology and sport studies: Distinctions, implications and advantages. *Quest* 31: 222–30.

Lawson, H. A., and J. H. Placek. 1981. *Physical education in the secondary schools.* Boston: Allyn and Bacon.

Lawther, J. D. 1977. *The learning and performance of physical skills.* Englewood Cliffs, NJ: Prentice-Hall.

Locke, L. F. 1969. Movement education—A description and critique. In *New perspectives of man in action,* ed. R. C. Brown and B. J. Cratty. Englewood Cliffs, NJ: Prentice-Hall.

Locke, L. R., and J. D. Massengale. 1978. Role conflict in teachers/coaches. *Research Quarterly* 49: 162–74.

Logsdon, B. J., K. R. Barrett, M. Ammons, M. R. Broer, L. E. Halverson, R. McGee, and M. A. Roberton. 1984. *Physical education for children.* Philadelphia: Lea and Febiger.

Loy, J. W., B. D. McPherson, and G. Kenyon. 1978. *Sport and social systems.* Reading: Addison-Wesley Publishing Co.

Macdonald, J. B. 1975. Curriculum theory as intentional activity. Paper presented at The Curriculum Theory Conference, Charlottesville, Virginia.

Macdonald, J. B. 1977. Values, bases and issues for curriculum. In *Curriculum theory*, ed. Alex Molnar and John A. Zahorik. Washington, DC: Association for Supervision and Curriculum Development.

Macdonald, J. B. 1981. Theory-practice and the hermeneutic circle. *The Journal of Curriculum Theorizing* 3 (2) (Spring): 130–38.

Macdonald, J. B., B. J. Wolfson, and E. Zaret. 1973. *Reschooling society: A conceptual model.* Washington, DC: Association for Supervision and Curriculum Development.

Mager, R. F. 1962. *Preparing instructional objectives.* Palo Alto: Fearon Publishers. (Previously published as *Preparing Objectives for Programmed Instruction.*)

Manitoba Department of Education. 1977. *Manitoba Physical Fitness Performance Test Manual and Fitness Objectives.* Manitoba, Canada: Department of Education.

Mann, J. S. 1969. Curriculum criticism. *Teachers College Record* 71: 27–40.

Martens, R. 1977. *Sport competition anxiety test.* Champaign, IL: Human Kinetics.

Mathews, D. K. 1978. *Measurement in physical education.* Philadelphia: W. B. Saunders.

McCutcheon, G., ed. 1982. *Theory into practice* 21 (1) (Winter).

McNeil, J. D. 1977. *Designing curriculum.* Boston: Little, Brown.

Medley, D. A. 1979. The effectiveness of teachers. In *Research on teaching: Concepts, findings, and implications,* ed. P. L. Peterson and H. J. Walberg. Berkeley, CA: McCutchan.

Melograno, V. 1979. *Designing curriculum and learning: A physical coeducation approach.* Dubuque, IA: Kendall/Hunt.

Metheny, E. 1968. *Movement and meaning.* New York: McGraw-Hill.

Mood, D. 1971. Test of physical fitness knowledge: Construction, administration and norms. *Research Quarterly* 42: 423–30.

Morrish, I. 1976. *Aspects of educational change.* London: George Allen and Urwin Ltd.

Mosston, M. 1981. *Teaching physical education,* Columbus, OH: Merrill.

Naisbitt, J. 1982. *Megatrends.* New York: Warner Books.

National Commission on Excellence in Education. 1983. A nation at risk: The imperative for educational reform. *Education Week* 2 (31) (April 27).

National Education Association. 1978. *A teachers' reference guide to PL 94–142.* Washington, DC: NEA.

Nixon, J. E., and A. E. Jewett. 1980. *Introduction to physical education.* Philadelphia: W. B. Saunders.

Nixon, J. E., and L. F. Locke. 1973. Research on teaching physical education. In *Second handbook of research on teaching,* ed. Robert M. Travers. Chicago: Rand McNally.

Orlosky, D. E., and B. O. Smith. 1978. *Curriculum development: Issues and insights.* Chicago: Rand McNally.

Peters, R. S. 1965. Education as initiation. In *Philosophical analysis and education,* ed. R. D. Archambault. New York: Humanities Press.

Peterson, P. L. 1979. Direct instruction reconsidered. In *Research on teaching: Concepts, findings and implications,* eds. P. L. Peterson and H. J. Walberg. Berkeley, CA: McCutchan.

Phenix, P. H. 1964. *Realms of meaning.* New York: McGraw-Hill.

Pinar, W. 1978. The reconceptualiza-tion of curriculum studies. *Journal of Curriculum Theorizing* 10 (3).

Popham, W. J., and E. I. Baker. 1970. *Systematic instruction.* Englewood Cliffs, NJ: Prentice-Hall.

Prigogine, I. 1980. *From being to becoming.* San Francisco: W. H. Freeman.

Reid, W. A. 1978. *Thinking about the curriculum.* London: Routledge and Kegan Paul.

Ridenour, M. V., ed. 1978. *Motor development.* Princeton: Princeton Book Co.

Roark, A. E., and W. E. Davis, Jr. 1981. Staff development and organization development. In *Staff development/organization development,* ed. E. Dillon-Peterson. Alexandria, VA: Association for Supervision and Curriculum Development.

Rosenshine, B. 1979. Content, time and direct instruction. In *Research on teaching: Concepts, findings and implications,* ed. P. L. Peterson and H. J. Walberg. Berkeley, CA: McCutchan.

Safrit, M. J. 1981. *Evaluation in physical education.* Englewood Cliffs: Prentice-Hall.

Schlechty, P. C. 1976. *Teaching and social behavior.* Boston: Allyn and Bacon.

Schwab, J. J. 1969. The practical: A language for curriculum. *School Review* 78: 1–24.

Siedentop, D. 1980. *Physical education: Introductory analysis.* Dubuque, IA: Wm. C. Brown.

Siedentop, D. 1983. *Developing teaching skills in physical education.* Palo Alto, CA: Mayfield.

Simpson, E. J. 1966. The classification of educational objectives: Psychomotor domain. Vocational and Technical Education Grant Contract No. OE–85–104. Washington, DC: U.S. Department HEW.

Singer, R., and W. Dick. 1980. *Teaching physical education: A systems approach.* Boston: Houghton Mifflin.

Smart, M. S., and R. C. Smart. 1977. *Children: Development and relationships.* New York: Macmillan.

Society of State Directors of Health, Physical Education and Recreation. 1972. *School programs in health, physical education and recreation: A statement of basic beliefs.* Kensington, MD: The Society.

Sonstroem, R. J. 1978. Physical estimation and attraction scales: Rationale and research. *Medicine and Science in Sports* 10: 97–102.

Stamm, C. L. 1978. Title IX: Implications for measurement in physical education. In *Proceedings of the Colorado measurement symposium.* Boulder, CO: Univ. of Colorado Conference Center.

Stanley, S. 1969. *Physical education: A movement orientation.* Montreal: McGraw-Hill of Canada.

Texas Governor's Commission on Physical Fitness. 1973. *Physical fitness—Motor ability test.* Austin, TX: The Commission.

Thompson, M. M., and B. A. Mann. 1977. *An holistic approach to physical education curricula: Objectives classification system for elementary schools.* Champaign, IL: Stipes.

Tiburzi, A. 1979. Validation of the construct of physiological fitness. Doctoral Dissertation, Univ. of Georgia, Athens.

Toffler, A., ed. 1974. *Learning for tomorrow.* New York: Random House.

Toffler, A. 1980. *The third wave.* New York: Morrow.

Tyler, R. W. 1950. *Basic principles of curriculum and instruction.* Chicago: Univ. of Chicago Press.

Tyler, R. W. 1981. Curriculum development since 1900. *Educational Leadership* 38 (May): 598–601.

Ulrich, C., ed. 1982. *Education in the 80's: Physical education.* Washington, DC: National Education Association.

Ulrich, C., and J. E. Nixon. 1972. *Tones of theory.* Washington, DC: AAHPER.

U.S. Department of Health, Education and Welfare. 1976. *Title IX and physical education: A compliance overview.* Washington, DC: U.S. Dept. HEW.

Vallance, E. 1982. The practical uses of curriculum theory. *Theory Into Practice* 21 (1) (Winter): 4–10.

Van Dalen, D. B., and B. L. Bennett. 1971. *A world history of physical education: Cultural, philosophical, comparative.* Englewood Cliffs, NJ: Prentice-Hall.

Walker, D. F. 1971. A naturalistic model for curriculum development. *School Review* 80: 51–65.

Walker, D. F. 1973. What curriculum research? *Journal of Curriculum Studies* 5: 58–72.

Walker, D. F. 1975. Curriculum development in an art project. In *Case studies in curriculum change,* ed. W. A. Reid and D. F. Walker. London: Routledge and Kegan Paul.

Walker, D. F. 1982. Curriculum theory is many things to many people. *Theory Into Practice* 21 (1) (Winter): 62–65.

Watson, L. 1979. *Lifetide.* New York: Simon and Schuster.

Weber, J. C. 1968. Physical education: The science of exercise. *Physical Educator* 25 (1): 5–7.

Willie, R., and K. R. Howey. 1980. Reflections on adult development: Implications for inservice teacher education. In *Staff development and educational change,* ed. W. R. Houston and R. Pankratz. Reston, VA: Association of Teacher Educators.

Willis, G., ed. 1978. *Qualitative evaluation: Concepts and cases in curriculum criticism.* Berkeley, CA: McCutchan.

Wilson, S. 1977. The use of ethnographic techniques in educational research. *Review of Educational Research* 47 (1) (Winter): 245–65.

Worthen, B. R., and J. R. Sanders, eds. 1973. *Educational evaluation: Theory and practice.* Worthington: L. A. Jones.

Young, M. F., ed. 1971. *Knowledge and control.* London: Collier-Macmillan.

Zeigler, E. F., ed. 1979. *A history of physical education and sport.* Englewood Cliffs, NJ: Prentice-Hall.

Zeigler, E. F., ed. 1982. *Introduction to physical education and sport.* Philadelphia: Lea and Febiger.

Index